MENC Handbook of Research on Music Learning

Volume 2

MENC HANDBOOK OF RESEARCH ON MUSIC LEARNING
VOLUME 2: APPLICATIONS

Edited by

Richard Colwell
Peter R. Webster

OXFORD
UNIVERSITY PRESS

OXFORD
UNIVERSITY PRESS

Oxford University Press, Inc., publishes works that further
Oxford University's objective of excellence
in research, scholarship, and education.

Oxford   New York
Auckland   Cape Town   Dar es Salaam   Hong Kong   Karachi
Kuala Lumpur   Madrid   Melbourne   Mexico City   Nairobi
New Delhi   Shanghai   Taipei   Toronto

With offices in
Argentina   Austria   Brazil   Chile   Czech Republic   France   Greece
Guatemala   Hungary   Italy   Japan   Poland   Portugal   Singapore
South Korea   Switzerland   Thailand   Turkey   Ukraine   Vietnam

Copyright © 2011 Oxford University Press

Published by Oxford University Press, Inc.
198 Madison Avenue, New York, New York 10016

http://www.oup.com

Oxford is a registered trademark of Oxford University Press.

Library of Congress Cataloging-in-Publication Data
MENC handbook of research on music learning / edited by Richard Colwell and Peter Webster.
    v.   cm.
Includes bibliographical references and index.
Contents: Vol. 2. Applications
ISBN 978-0-19-975439-7 (hardcover)
ISBN 978-0-19-975434-2 (pbk.)
1. Music—Instruction and study.   2. Musical ability.
I. Colwell, Richard.   II. Webster, Peter Richard, 1947-
III. MENC, the National Association for Music Education (U.S.)
MT1.M444 2011
780.71—dc22   2009050097

Printed in the United States of America
on acid-free paper

Preface

The success of the two books *Handbook of Research on Music Teaching and Learning* and the *New Handbook of Research on Music Teaching and Learning* exceeded the expectations of the authors and the publishers. The publisher's supply of the 1992 *Handbook of Research on Music Teaching and Learning* was exhausted in half the projected time, and its value, as judged by a continuing demand, is considerable. The *New Handbook of Research on Music Teaching and Learning* (2002) has become essential for scholars, researchers, and graduate students. The profession of music education seems sufficiently mature to support syntheses of valid research; thus, when Oxford University Press suggested a smaller publication based on the philosophy of the handbooks, we elected to respond. In considering the multiple possibilities of topics, it became obvious to us that what was needed was a focus on "learning" (the title, after all, includes the word *learning*). Handbooks I and II both had chapters directly and indirectly related to learning, but what seemed to be missing was a laserlike focus on what is currently known about learning in music, as much of the material in the first handbook was written nearly 20 years ago.

The profession has become more diverse over the past several decades, changing, focusing, specializing, and divided by local, state, and federal education policies. In some cases, the offerings and purposes of music education have been altered by local priorities and circumstances, requiring a renewed focus on music and what is known about teaching and learning. Members of the profession have long shown concern for the disconnect between research and practice, which at present has become enlarged by a lack of coherence among theory, research, and practice. Our task was to create a publication that would address these changes, at the same time offering suggestions addressing issues of learning for musical competence. Our basic premise was that any material offered in a new publication needed to be based on a reasonably unbiased presentation of present knowledge, knowledge based on valid research and documented successful practices. Thus, present knowledge, drawn selectively from several fields and interpreted by outstanding scholars, became the starting point, along with our goal of structuring the publication so as to place this research knowledge in a teaching-learning context. That context required that learning theories should provide some type of umbrella of ideas and that any treatment of such theories be sufficiently concrete that the reader can see how the ideas apply to the teaching task.

In reviewing the material in the first two handbooks, we were struck by how fresh and relevant many chapters were to the 21st century. An update was needed in some cases; a few chapters were more than adequate. There was a strong temptation to reprint the earlier chapters on a philosophical approach advocated by Bennett Reimer and David Elliot and the quite original chapters by Roger Edwards and Henry Cady; we resisted this temptation and elected to retain and update only two chapters, while identifying authors who could supplement or fill in the gaps that exist in the two basic handbooks. The "publication" soon became two publications, each meeting specific needs in the profession, one focused on planning and the second on applications. The chapters in each publication are, of course, related to each other. There exists a meaningful relationship among all chapters in both volumes; thus, the publications are stand-alone contributions to the profession but can also be viewed as a set, something like volumes 1 and 2 of the *Handbook on Music Learning*. Because of the relationship between the two volumes, we list the chapter titles and authors for volume 1, *The MENC Handbook of Research on Music Learning, Volume 1: Strategies*, at the end of this preface.

If there is one thread that connects all the chapters in this volume, it is the importance of musical context. It is clear that materials must be developmentally appropriate. Our multiple prepublication reviewers provided valuable advice that the aims of teaching music are so varied—almost as varied as are the recipients of our instruction—that the social-culture nature of the teaching situation is often as influential as the teaching competency of the instructor. With limited resources and time allotted for music instruction, our writers found little research to suggest that universal aims and competence standards are at present as feasible as one might like.

This volume consists of a scholarly description of what research and practice inform us about many of the important experiences in the music classroom: listening, music reading, movement, vocal production at both the elementary and secondary school levels, (individual and group) early childhood, self-regulation in the development of musical skills, and issues issues with the student with autism spectrum disorder who is mainstreamed into music classes. In working with the authors of these chapters, we were surprised at how little had been written about these important topics. This realization inspired us to broaden the definition of research and to include the results of single studies, where these studies had been carefully crafted and the results validly interpreted. The reader, like our authors, should adopt a critical approach in applying new information gained from reading these chapters to one's own endeavors in teaching and learning in music.

We were impressed that several authors referred to the importance of instruction of very young children and to the importance for research into studies of the brain. Gruhn emphasized the social environment of the infant and the universality of music learning among infants, and that in the process much differentiation occurs as to whether the learner uses the musical stimuli (both direct and tacit). Research evidence is presented on the importance of focus and nurturing and on how early experiences lead to the infant's perception of groups of musical stimuli.

The update on music reading by Hodges and Nolker indicates that, as important as music reading is, there has not in the past 50 years been a direct focus on researching the process of music reading. We have brain studies, eye movement studies, pattern recognition material, and studies connecting music reading with the ear, but there remain several unknowns related to learning to read a full score, how horizontal reading differs from linear reading, and the relationships of reading to performing from charts and other music, using symbols rather than traditional notation. There should be a relationship between reading text and reading music, but studies of exactly what that relationship is and whether that relationship is learning in the same way have resulted in conflicting evidence.

Music reading is a skill, and the learning of skills is investigated in depth by McPherson and Zimmerman in terms of self-regulated music learning. This chapter spans age levels where a student can self-assess and assume responsibility for his or her own learning. There is much to consider with respect to self-regulation, self-observation, and whether this important strategy remains only one way of learning. The reader will profit from a close reading of this chapter, especially the speculation on how the learning of music differs from (or is similar to) other academic subjects in homework, in the relationship between parent and child (one social aspect), and in the importance of the topic to the student (one type of motivation). Self-assessment is inadequate in the learning of skills: Indeed, one has to learn how to learn coaching and peer criticism, and a demanding teacher remains essential in self-learning.

Dunn addresses the listening component of a complete music education, and Abril synthesizes the role of movement in attaining competency in music. In both chapters, the authors emphasize the importance of the context and the classroom–social situation. Dunn begins his review with aural perception while in the womb and continues his review of the research in listening to an advanced age. His approach is holistic, criticizing most of the extant research and arguing that we have been too little concerned about all of the factors that influence preference, understanding, and meaning in the music experience. Although much of one's ability to move is affected by one's personal tempo, movement can enhance the learning of music, and Abril argues that such enhancing movements can be taught. He identifies a fascinating research topic, which is separating the competence coming from maturation from that attained through systematic teaching. Both of these topics are vital for our understanding of music learning and serve as a strong foundation for continued study.

Sobol calls to our attention the importance of inclusion and the need to consider more than the traditional learning style, using as her example students with autism and the connection between giftedness, talent, and other special populations. Her perspectives are important for an inclusive consideration of the mandate that faces us for understanding comprehensive aspects of music learning.

Phillips and Doneski provide the results of systematic research on singing. This chapter is an update of a chapter that Phillips wrote on this subject for the first (1992) handbook. In the present volume, he and his coauthor have identified a surprising number of valid research studies on teaching and learning in choral music. Vocal teachers have been active in determining what we know about the role of accompaniment, attitude, audiation, the home, grouping, modeling, the literature itself, and more. In addition, the authors address the relation of these multiple factors to the teaching situation, as well as sequencing, vocal problems, song acquisition, and competency in individual and group vocal situations. The critical reader can relate the issues in vocal music to the issues addressed in each of the chapters in both volumes of this set, and we suggest it as an enlightening exercise.

As we concluded our work on these two companion volumes, we were struck by how much work remains to be done on music learning. Our profession typically does not benefit from the results of extensive meta-analyses or well-crafted longitudinal research. Although we see the beginnings of a research initiative that focuses on specified research problems related to music learning, we still suffer from very diverse studies that do not coalesce to form the basis for much detailed conceptual understanding. That said, these two new volumes, along with the many other handbook projects published in the last 20 years, help scholars interested in music learning to understand what we do know and what we need to pursue in the next decades. We feel that it has never been a more exciting time to be engaged in the study of music teaching and learning.

Richard Colwell and Peter R. Webster, Editors

Chapter titles in *The MENC Handbook of Research on Music Learning, Volume 1: Strategies*

Acknowledgments

These two handbooks were made possible by the adept leadership of Suzanne Ryan, Editor-in-Chief, Humanities and Executive Editor, Music at Oxford University Press. She was a constant source of inspiration and guidance and her persistence and insights made this two-volume set of *Research on Music Learning* a possibility. Thanks too to Karen Kwak at Oxford for her expert assistance.

The editors would like to acknowledge the contributions of the many scholars who made the *Handbook* possible. In addition to the authors for chapters, we appreciate the many reviewers who took time to provide feedback to us and to the many drafts of chapters. Several music education doctoral students at Northwestern's Bienen School of Music, including Ken Elpus, Nassim Nikfafs, Linda Aiker, and Richard Webb, assisted with aspects of manuscript preparation. Of this doctoral group, Jon Harnum deserves a special word of thanks for reading the entire manuscript and offering many helpful comments to the editors.

Contents

Contributors

RICHARD COLWELL is professor emeritus at the University of Illinois. He founded the *Bulletin of the Council for Research in Music Education* and the *Quarterly Journal of Music Teaching and Learning* and edited the *Handbook of Research on Music Teaching and Learning*, the *Handbook of Musical Cognition and Development*, the *Handbook of Research Methodologies*, and *Basic Concepts in Music Education, II*, which is also available in Chinese. He coedited *The New Handbook of Research on Music Teaching and Learning*. His *The Teaching of Instrumental Music* is in its fourth edition. His awards include the Horace Porter for Scholarship, a Fulbright, a John Simon Guggenheim fellowship, membership in the MENC Hall of Fame, and special citations from the International Society for Music Education, Warsaw's Chopin Academy, Illinois Music Educators, and the national Federation of Music Clubs. Other faculty appointments include Boston University, the University of Michigan, and most recently the New England Conservatory of Music. Contact: toaster34@charter.net

PETER R. WEBSTER is the John Beattie Professor of Music Education at the Bienen School of Music, Northwestern University in Evanston, Illinois. He has earned degrees in music education from the University of Southern Maine (BS) and the Eastman School of Music at the University of Rochester (MM, PhD) and has been a public school music teacher in Maine, Massachusetts, and New York, followed by 14 years at Case Western Reserve University; he moved to Northwestern in 1988. Administrative positions include terms as Department Chair and Associate Dean. Teaching includes courses in philosophy, graduate research, music technology, assessment, and creative thinking in music. Webster's published work includes more than 70 articles and book chapters on technology, music cognition, and creative thinking in music that have appeared in journals and handbooks in and outside music. Webster is coauthor of *Experiencing Music Technology*, 3rd edition Update (Cengage/Schirmer, 2008), the standard textbook used in introductory college courses in music technology. He is the author of *Measures of Creative Thinking in Music*, an exploratory tool for assessing music thinking by using quasi-improvisational tasks. Contact: pwebster@northwestern.edu

CARLOS ABRIL is Associate Professor and Coordinator of Music Education at the Bienen School of Music of Northwestern University, where he teaches courses in general music, cultural diversity, and philosophy. He received his PhD in music education from The Ohio State University and studied movement through the methods and approaches of Dalcroze Eurhythmics, High Scope Education Through Movement, and Orff Schulwerk. His research focuses on the sociocultural dimensions of music teaching and learning, music perception, and policy. Abril has presented his work at state, national, and international conferences. His work is published in books and journals, including: *Bulletin of the Council for Research in Music Education, International Journal of Music Education, Journal of Research in Music Education, Music Education Research*, and *Music Educators Journal*. Abril serves on the editorial board of the *Journal of Research in Music Education*, as well as other journals in the U.S. and Spain. He is coeditor of the book *Musical Experience in Our Lives: Things We Learn and Meanings We Make* (Rowman and Littlefield, 2009). Contact: c-abril@northwestern.edu

SANDRA M. DONESKI is Associate Professor of Music at Gordon College in Wenham, Massachusetts, and serves as Director of Undergraduate Music Education and Assistant Director of Graduate Programs in Music. Doneski teaches courses in curriculum development, learning and assessment, and elementary and secondary general music education, and she supervises student teachers. Previously, she taught general music and chorus for grades K-12 in the Massachusetts public schools. In 2000, she founded the Gordon College Children's Choir to give children in the community an opportunity to grow as musicians and give music education majors an opportunity to develop as teachers and conductors. Doneski has also served on the faculty of the New England Conservatory (NEC) Preparatory School, where she was Associate Conductor of the Children's Choir Program. Under her guidance, NEC implemented choral programs for early elementary and middle school students that focused on vocal pedagogy and building musicianship. Doneski is a frequent choral festival conductor and clinician in the areas of vocal and general music education. Contact: sandra.doneski@gordon.edu

ROB DUNN is a Professor of Music Education at the Brigham Young University School of Music in Provo, Utah, where he supervises the graduate music education program. Among his teaching responsibilities are graduate courses in theories of music learning and motivation, research, philosophy of music education, and undergraduate secondary general music methods. His areas of interest include lifelong music learning for children and adults, music listening, listening maps, and creative thinking. Dunn received the Outstanding Dissertation in Music Education Award from the Council for Research in Music Education, has many articles published in national and international journals, and presented at many national and international venues. He is the author of educational materials for the Cleveland Orchestra and the Chicago Symphony Orchestra. He has served on several editorial boards, including College Music Symposium and Contributions to Music Education, and currently serves for Music Education Research International. His past appointments include Western Michigan University, and director of music education at Case Western Reserve University. Contact: robdunn@byu.edu

WILFRIED GRUHN is Professor Emeritus of Music Education at the University of Music (Musikhochschule), Freiburg, Germany. He served as Chair of the Music

Education Department and worked as coeditor of several journals for music education. From 1995 to 1997, he was president of RAIME, and from 2000 to 2004, he served on the Board of Directors of the International Society for Music Education (ISME). He founded the Gordon-Institute for Early Childhood Music Learning (GIFM) in Freiburg, Germany, and was its director until 2009. Gruhn has presented at many national and international conferences. His research areas include historical musicology, historical and systematic music pedagogy, and psychology; his many publications cover these areas. He specialized in the neurobiology of music learning and in music perception and cognition. Contact: mail@wgruhn.de

DONALD A. HODGES is Covington Distinguished Professor of Music Education and Director of the Music Research Institute (MRi) at the University of North Carolina at Greensboro. He is coauthor of *Music Psychology for Musicians* (in press) and contributing editor of the *Handbook of Music Psychology* (1980, 2nd ed. 1996) and the accompanying *Multimedia Companion*, and he has published numerous book chapters, articles, and research papers in music education and music psychology. He has made presentations to state, national, and international conferences and has served on the editorial boards of the *Journal of Research in Music Education*, *Music Educators Journal*, and *Update: Applications of Research in Music Education*. At the MRi, he oversees more than 40 active research projects in BioMusic, neuroimaging of musicians, music-related hearing loss, music education, music performance, and ethnomusicology/ecocriticism. Recent research has focused on a series of brain imaging studies of pianists, conductors, and singers. Hodges will be included in the next edition of the *New Grove Dictionary of American Music*. Contact: dahodges@uncg.edu

GARY E. MCPHERSON is Ormond Professor and Director of the Melbourne Conservatorium of Music. He is currently an Associate Editor for *Psychology of Music, Research Studies in Music Education* (which he helped establish in 1993), and the *Journal of Interdisciplinary Music Studies*. He has published well over 100 articles and book chapters in a wide range of journals and books, and many co-edited books including: *The Science and Psychology of Music Performance: Creative Strategies for Teaching and Learning* (OUP) and *The Child as Musician: A Handbook of Musical Development* (OUP). He is currently finishing editorial work on the *Oxford Handbook of Music Education*. McPherson studied music education at the Sydney Conservatorium of Music before completing a master of music education at Indiana University, a doctorate of philosophy at the University of Sydney, and a Licentiate and Fellowship in trumpet performance through Trinity College, London. He served as the Marilyn Pflederer Zimmerman endowed chair in music education at the University of Illinois at Urbana-Champaign before moving back to Australia. His research interests are broad and his approach interdisciplinary. His most important research examines the acquisition and development of musical competence and motivation to engage and participate in music from novice to expert levels. Contact: g.mcpherson@unimelb.edu.au

BRETT NOLKER is Associate Professor of Music Education, University of North Carolina at Greensboro, specializing in choral and secondary-level general music education. He is a founding member of the Music Research Institute at UNCG and is active in music education research, primarily in the areas of music teacher education, music literacy, and developing individual skills in the ensemble and classroom setting. Nolker currently serves as a board member of the North Carolina Music Educators Association and the American Choral Directors Association. Active in MENC: the National Association for Music Education, he has served as facilitator for Policy and Partnerships action group for the Society for Music Teacher Education, chair for the Special Research Interest Group for Sociology in Music Education, and is currently Chair for the Special Research Interest Group for Music Perception and Cognition. Prior to joining the faculty at UNCG, Nolker served as the Director of Music Education and conductor of the Collegiate Chorale and Jenny Lind Women's Ensemble at Augustana College in Rock Island, Illinois. Nolker taught vocal and instrumental music in the public schools of Colorado and Missouri, where his ensembles were frequently invited to appear on convention and festival programs. He appears throughout the nation as a guest conductor, clinician, and festival adjudicator. He holds degrees from Central Methodist College, Fayette, Missouri; The Wichita State University in Wichita, Kansas; and the University of Missouri–Columbia. Contact: dbnolker@uncg.edu

KENNETH H. PHILLIPS, PhD, is Professor Emeritus of The University of Iowa. An award-winning researcher and teacher, Phillips is the author of four books: *Teaching Kids to Sing* (Schirmer Books/Cengage), *Basic Techniques of Conducting* (Oxford University Press), *Directing the Choral Music Program* (OUP), and *Exploring Research in Music Education and Music Therapy* (OUP). He has also written more than 100 chapters, reviews, and journal articles for leading publications of the music education profession. The recipient of three outstanding teaching awards from the University of Iowa, MENC has recognized him as one of the nation's most accomplished music educators. He also was the recipient in 2005 of the Robert M. McCowen Memorial Award for Outstanding Contribution to Choral Music in Iowa, presented by the Iowa Choral Directors Association. Phillips's choral methods book is cited for "raising the bar for choral music textbooks" (*Choral Journal*, May 2004). Phillips has presented vocal workshops throughout the United States and in Australia, Canada, China, and New Zealand. Teachers throughout the world have used his vocal methodology (*Teaching Kids to Sing*) to enhance the singing of young people. Contact: Ken.Phillips@gordon.edu

ELISE S. SOBOL is the New York State School Music Association Chair for Music for Special Learners. She is on the adjunct music education faculty of both New York University and C. W. Post/Long Island University, where she teaches graduate and undergraduate music in special education courses. A full-time music teacher for the Nassau BOCES, Department of Special Education, she currently teaches students with autism and developmental disabilities at the Rosemary Kennedy School. A presenter at county, state, national, and international forums, she is author of *An Attitude and Approach for Teaching Music to Special Learners*, 2nd edition (2008, Rowman & Littlefield, 1ˢᵗ edition (2001, Pentland Press, USA)) and a contributing author to numerous education publications, including the "Special Needs Series" (2010, MENC) *Blueprint for Teaching and Learning in Music, prek*-12 (2008,New York City Board of Education), *Spotlight on Making Music with Special Learners* (2004, MENC), and *Music: A Resource Guide for Standards-Based Instruction* (2002, NYSSMA/State Education Department). Contact es86@nyu.edu%20or%20elise.sobol@liu.edu

BARRY J. ZIMMERMAN is Distinguished Professor of Educational Psychology and Head of Learning, Development, and Instruction at the Graduate School and University Center of the City University of New York. He has written more than 200 research articles, book chapters, and professional conference papers. He has also written or edited 13 books or journal volumes on social cognitive and self-regulatory processes in the learning of children and youth. His most recent books are *Self-Regulated Learning and Academic Achievement: Theoretical Perspectives* (2001), *Educational Psychology: A Century of Contributions* (2002), and *Motivation and Self-Regulated Learning: Theory, Research, and Application* (2007). Zimmerman is an editorial board member for seven journals and has served as editor for several special issues. He served as President of Division 15 of the American Psychological Association (Educational Psychology). He has received the Senior Scientist Award of American Psychological Association Division 16 for sustained and exceptional program of scholarship and the Sylvia Scribner Award of the American Educational Research Association for exemplary research in learning and instruction. He is a Fellow of three divisions of the American Psychological Association, a Fellow of the American Psychological Society, and a Fellow of the American Educational Research Association. Contact: bzimmerman@gc.cuny.edu

MENC Handbook of Research on Music Learning
Volume 2

Contemporary Research on Music Listening

A Holistic View

ROB E. DUNN

Coming to know our own "life music" is a natural part of intuitive human experience. From the womb (Lacanuet, 1996), we develop a meaningful, life-long relationship with the music we encounter within our social and cultural contexts. But our relationship with the music listening experience has been a difficult one to fully probe and understand. As Polanyi (1969) pointed out, all human experience is comprised of intuitive, simultaneous, and complex experiencing that functions beyond the realm of words and explicit rules; there will always be aspects that are beyond our human capacity to adequately share with another person. This experience is especially true of listening to music. When we listen and are captivated by what we hear, we know what we are experiencing and respond in a very real way. But when we are asked to describe our music listening experience, to translate it into words or explicit rules, we quickly find that aspects of the experience are difficult to communicate.

How we learn to listen to music is also difficult to probe and understand. What we "know" about this process is limited by observation, what questions researchers ask, and what they are able to operationalize into research measures. Further complicating the picture are the dimensions of the two components of listening: intuitively learned listening and formally learned listening to music. What is the difference between the two, and can they be measured? And even the process of trying to convert a music listening experience into words or another forum for examination may change the listening experience itself in subtle ways (Reimer, 1997). Nevertheless, although the results may be imperfect, the insights to be gained are worth the effort, and the implications for music education are especially important.

Researchers have approached music listening from a variety of methodologies to better understand this complex human phenomenon. The reader is urged to read Haack's (1992) commendable review of research regarding the acquisition of music listening skills for a sampling of methodologies that have been used. In writing this chapter, I primarily draw from representative studies conducted after 1990. I took a holistic view of music listening, focused on authentic-type listening experiences. I leave the issues of perception, preference, and different cultures to be addressed in depth elsewhere, although they are mentioned in some of the reviewed studies.

The chapter is organized in three main parts. First, I examine what we are learning about how people listen to music when they engage it directly or reflect in some way on having engaged it in the past. Second, I look at what we are learning about facilitating listening to music. Third, I examine the listening process more closely from a holistic view and offer implications and suggestions for the future.

Types of Data

Before we begin, however, it will be useful to note the types of data researchers in music listening typically employ. This review will make reporting studies clearer and help the reader to understand the difficulty and complexity of research in this area.

Observations of Behavior

Observations of behavior generally include two types of data: (1) observations of natural behavioral interactions with music listening (e.g., observing a child listening to a mother's lullaby) and (2) observations of behavioral interactions with music when an intervention/direction is introduced (e.g., instruction: move and/or respond to show what you hear in the music).

Verbal Reports about a Specific Listening Event

Verbal reports are generated from individuals about a specific listening experience. These reports are generally of two types: (1) concurrent verbal reports, in which one speaks her thoughts as she listens to the music and (2) retrospective verbal reports, in which one speaks her thoughts after listening to the music. Most often, retrospective verbal reports are given immediately or soon after listening, but it is possible that considerable time may have passed. Verbal reports are transcribed into written language for analysis. Sometimes, concurrent and retrospective verbal reports are collected as written thoughts rather than spoken data, but they are still considered verbal reports as they are expressed in language.

Self-Report Data

Self-report data are collected from people thinking back and reporting on their own life experiences and opinions. These generally include two types of data: (1) surveys and (2) interviews.

Performance on a Measure

Performance data on a standardized test or on a measure created by researchers are generally used in three ways: (1) to see if one method is more effective (e.g., listening with video or without); (2) to measure the effectiveness of something such as a teaching method (e.g., giving a pretest, teaching children a listening skill, then using the same measure as a posttest to see if the treatment was effective in helping children listen more effectively to a certain aspect of music); or (3) to measure choice or degree (e.g., provide an answer, or turn the a dial to show how much).

Performance on a Problem-Solving Task

Researchers sometimes devise problem-solving tasks for subjects as they engage in a listening task. Generally, these fall into two categories: (1) tasks that ask subjects to conceptually represent the music in the abstract by using words (e.g., a cooperative listening group listens and discusses to categorize selections into styles, forms, etc.) and (2) tasks that ask subjects to represent the music in some way as it unfolds (e.g., movement, drawings, invented notation-or musical maps).

While a researcher may use only one type of data, it is not uncommon for researchers in music listening to use multiple kinds of data in one study in an effort to provide a richer picture. With this as background, let us proceed.

Section I: What We Know about How People Listen to Music

What have we learned about music listening at different ages? What do we know about how people listen to music as it unfolds? What do we know about how people listen to music in their everyday lives? In this section, I review representative studies that examined music listening as it occurs "naturally"—that is, without a researcher getting in the middle of the listening process (i.e., "what is happening as they listen?" rather than "what happens if I change this?"). In the first part of this section, I present studies ordered as closely as I can by the age of the subjects from infancy through secondary school. After that, specialized topics are presented without regard to age.

Infants

Barring a physical handicap such as deafness, listening to music is a natural, intuitive process. Trehub and Nakata's observational study (2001/2002) examined an infant's initiation into a musical world through a mother's inter-actions. Seemingly from the moment of birth, mothers instinctively begin singing or speaking in a singsong manner to their children, a pattern that continues and is shaped in part by the baby's responses. The mother's mes-sages are "primarily affective, delivered in rich emotional tones" (p. 52). Through repeated associations delivered via listening, the infant comes to recognize the mother's voice, engages in receptive learning (e.g., recognizing a song), and makes extramusical associations (e.g., a bath time song). For the infant, listening to mother's music may help create a personal identity (Trehub and Nakata link this with what music listening does for adolescents; see North, Hargreaves, and O'Neill, 2000), and its importance may come from being embedded in a social context, its familiarity, and its affective quality. From the beginning, then, learning to listen to this music is much more than perception; already it affects who one is, how one feels, whom one associates with, and perhaps much more beyond our capacity to perceive at this time.

Preschool

A preschool child's listening life might seem simple to adults. However, Sims has accumulated an impressive body of research showing preschool children's listening lives are more complex than one would suppose (Sims, 1985, 1988, 1995, 2001, 2004). In her 2001 observational study, she used an intact pre-school class with a music listening center where children could choose whether and when to listen during free-choice time. The results confirmed earlier findings: listening times varied substantially between children (e.g., one child's mean for the four pieces was 11.75 seconds; another's was the full 3 minutes) but were individually consistent across pieces. In looking back at her body of research, Sims (2004) noted that children differ greatly in their individual listening responses and concluded that listening time is not a function of preference for young children. Rather, it is based on individual characteristics of the child related to listening style, attention span (or what she calls listening span), ability, or some internally regulated propensity to sit and listen for a given period of time. Sims and Nolker (2002) found that kindergarten teachers' ratings of individual children's attention spans dur-ing large group or center-based listening activities had no correlation with students' actual listening times. Furthermore, the teachers rated the boys with shorter attention spans than the girls, but the actual listening span results showed no gender differences.

Sims (2004) describes a typical preschool or kindergarten music program with a "drop in" teacher who comes once or twice a week and does not have the chance to get to know the children on an individual basis.

So we perpetuate what I would now claim is a myth, that "young children have short attention spans for listening to music." I wouldn't say that listening for 12 to 30 minutes is short at all. The problem comes when several children who listen for longer periods are members of a group in which some children are likely to be 30-second listeners and others 3-minute listeners. As children start to lose interest, their behavior affects the whole group. (p. 9)

She suggests shorter listening examples for groups while trying to extend group listening spans, at the same time providing listening centers or home listening opportunities for children who will want to listen longer.

These results underscore how adults may underestimate young children's individual ability to listen attentively to music. Among Sims's (2001) conclusions was this important point: the more we know about young children, the more we realize that they are complex individuals, and this must include the complexity of their music listening lives. She counseled that any generalization about children's responses to music listening should be made with caution.

Kindergarten through Elementary

We move now to the elementary-age child. Rodriguez and Webster (1997) considered the development of 33 K-5 children's retrospective verbal reports in music listening. The children heard a 48-second excerpt from Hindemith's *Mathis Der Maler* multiple times and were asked questions that encouraged interpretive responses. Three judges examined their responses, devised categories, and then categorized the responses. Data were analyzed for content and developmental patterns. The process was: Listen, then Question 1 (*What were you thinking when you listened to this music?*); Listen, then Question 2 (*If you were going to make music like this, how would you start?*), Listen, then Questions 3 and 4 (*How does this music make you feel? What in the music makes you feel that way?*). Increasing age showed a tendency for more global responses, more emotional sensitivity, and more understanding of what is involved in creating music. Single-emotion responses to Question 3 were most prevalent, but multiple-emotion responses were most common in the upper grades and tended to be less concrete. A gradual shift in emotion from happy to sad was noted moving from the younger to older subjects. While no differences in age were found, more than half of the subjects were able to give musical reasons for the emotions they identified. The pattern toward complexity seen in the preschool child appeared to continue here, manifested with a move toward an increase in emotion, less specific emotion, and less simplistic emotion (i.e., no longer only happy).

The question of whether blindness has an impact on one's listening ability is sometimes a point of speculation. Flowers and Wang (2002) chose to compare the retrospective verbal reports of 41 sighted and 17 blind children (K-5) after the children listened to music excerpts. In a very interesting next step, the verbal responses were transcribed and put in random order for a panel of 10 music teachers to review. The teachers' task was to match the verbal descriptions with the intended musical excerpt. The task became easier for the teachers when the author was older, whether sighted or blind. Blind children used substantially more descriptions of musical elements at higher grade levels; sighted children remained consistent across grades. Emotional descriptors and metaphors were used more by the sighted children, significant at the .001 level. Temporal language increased with age, but most notably among the blind students. Making about twice as many temporal statements as the sighted fifth graders, the upper elementary blind students were more on a par with adult musicians, according to the researchers. It appears that for this sample, age increased one's ability to describe music well enough so another can identify it. The fact that sighted children did not improve in the number of descriptions of musical elements, yet used significantly more emotional descriptors and metaphors is interesting, perhaps a function of a difference in attention as compared with the blind children, who increased in their descriptions of musical elements with age.

This study was part of a series of studies Flowers undertook to examine the use of language to describe six musical excerpts in a way that someone who had never heard the pieces might know what they sounded like (Flowers, 1996, 2000, 2002; Flowers and Wang, 2002). The basic procedure was the same, randomly providing the descriptions to experts (music teachers) and giving them the task of matching the descriptions with the correct pieces. The 1996 study compared children and undergraduate students. Overall, Flowers found that the trend continued: age made the matching task easier. Around 30 percent of the primary children's descriptions were correctly matched, approximately 40–50 percent of the upper elementary children's descriptions were correctly matched, and 92 percent of the college music majors' statements were matched to the correct excerpt. Flowers (2002) believes engaging in verbal description of music listening may be a way to bring deeper meaning to the listening experience. She suggested that teachers should encourage meaningful music descriptions by (1) encouraging children to use extramusical analogies or images to describe their ideas about music, (2) introducing musical vocabulary to children in music lessons as a way to focus their attention, and (3) using encouraging comments and questions to help children construct more complete descriptions (e.g., "Yes, the music was fast...and what else did you hear?") (Flowers, 1990, p. 23).

Tait and Haack (1984) suggested that three kinds of learnings, or modes, were essential in musical learning, and should be included in our teaching as appropriate to our goals: the thinking mode, the feeling mode, and the sharing mode. Inspired by Tait and Haack, Theiss (1990) used a case study format to document these modes via the written retrospective reports of a fourth-grade class in the form of listening journals in response to instrumental music listening examples. This intact public school class included 26 students of varying abilities and cultural backgrounds. Written imagery responses often included brief references to musical styles, musical functions, movies, and television. Multiple hearings are often thought desirable, both in instruction and research. Theiss used multiple hearings, but in her case, hearing a piece multiple times did not increase imagery or metaphor vocabulary in the written responses. For all ability levels and ethnic groups, verbal explanations and expansions provided evidence of imagery, metaphor vocabulary, and implied analogue for the experience of music, all an expected part of Tait and Haack's experiential verbal behaviors for music listening, although at a basic level. Thiess reported: "Despite the lack of mature metaphor, life analog, or precise musical vocabulary to describe tonal events and their experiencing of them, the children exhibited frequent instances of what Bamberger (1978) called 'intuitive musical knowing' as opposed to formal musical knowing" (p. 195). This intuitive musical knowing is important to acknowledge. Children do not walk into our classroom as an empty slate; they have some inner musical knowledge of how music works, how it makes sense to them, gained from a lifetime of experience. Rather than something to be fixed, perhaps this should be viewed as something to be developed. More will be said of this in the third section of this chapter.

Wondering about children's inner perceptions, Johnson (2003) was interested in what eight fifth-grade instrumentalists would focus on as they listened to unfamiliar music. Each child had at least one year of experience playing a musical instrument and played in the school band or orchestra. Individually, each child listened to 15 excerpts by clicking on a link on a computer in any order, after an initial demonstration session with the researcher. As he listened, the child was asked to write or draw something on a card to help him remember an excerpt, until he had 15 cards for 15 excerpts. To answer Johnson's first research question ("How do elementary instrumentalists categorize unfamiliar music?" p. 85), the child was asked to sort the cards into groups as the researcher watched. To answer the second research question ("How much attention do students give discrete musical elements as compared to global musical characteristics when describing music?" p. 85), he asked the child about her groupings and what she remembered about the excerpts. He found that the descriptors fell into four themes of groupings, in order of number of occurrence: musical descriptors (e.g., standard musical vocabulary terms), extramusical descriptors (e.g., references based in a subject's particular life experience), affective descriptors (e.g., happy or scary), and other descriptors (e.g., comparisons such as same/different). Johnson stated that he found "evidence suggesting that the extra musical associations the participants used were highly specific and frequently based on their past experiences.... From a constructivist frame of reference, the participants understood the music in terms they could articulate and remember" (p. 92). One of the implications he draws from his study is that music listening experiences in the classroom should encourage both affective and associative responses in conjunction with elemental musical responses.

Later, Johnson (2006) designed a study to see whether the inclusion of opportunities to use affective and associative terms in listening lessons could address this issue. He asked 40 fifth-graders to listen to two pairs of instrumental music examples and respond to a researcher-devised "Listening and Thinking" measure modeled after the *1997 NAEP Arts Report Card* (Persky, Sandene, and

Askew, 1998). The first questions asked about the initial piece, and the next questions asked them to compare the two pieces. Subjects were asked to give either verbal or written responses, later coded as one of two categories: (1) musical terms or (2) affective or associative. The form of response significantly affected the content: verbal responses had more musical terms, and written responses had more affective and associative responses, both at the .001 level of significance. The fact that the responses were affected by what was required of the listener (although closely related) leads me to question whether the listening experience itself was changed in a subtle way by the difference in the task, as was mentioned in the introduction. That the listening experience can be changed by how we present it is a theme that we will see return in this chapter.

Ferguson (2004) studied her fourth- and fifth-grade students as they moved expressively while listening to music in music classes. Her data included video of students in music classes ($N = 95$), researcher logs, video of student interviews ($N = 18$), and audio recordings of teacher interviews. Student movements were considered external evidence of internal thought processes manifested within differing social environments. Her qualitative teacher-researcher approach allowed her to develop a taxonomy for understanding movements in the classroom environment, including (1) peer influence, ranging from movements completely independent to completely dependent on social interaction; (2) movement generation, ranging from movements completely teacher controlled to completely student controlled, and, of note here, (3) musical understanding, demonstrated through filler movements, referential movements, synchronicity, anticipation, expressive match, movement evolution, and rightness. She found various levels of interdependence between social context and movement, with some students being stable in their movements between contexts (e.g., in the classroom or with the researcher), while others were very unstable. Students with a high need for peer approval tended to be less stable. Referring to Maslow's hierarchy of needs, Ferguson noted that a student with esteem needs was less able to focus on knowing/aesthetic needs (pp. 269–270). This example highlights the social aspect of music experience as well: for some students, the social will overwhelm the music for positive or negative reasons; for others, the musical experience will capture their attention. Teachers must be aware of the social aspect and work to make their classrooms a safe and nurturing place for musical experiencing to take place.

Elementary and Secondary

Bundra (1994) examined concurrent verbal reports of seventeen randomly selected second-, fifth-, eighth-, and eleventh-graders, divided equally into grades and those with and without musical training. The children listened to six extended musical examples and spoke aloud about what they were hearing. Afterward, they reflected on their music listening processes. Their verbal reports were transcribed and analyzed. Seventeen categories of response emerged from the data: perceptual descriptions, intramusical classifications, music-making behaviors, music production descriptions, predictions of musical events, comparisons of musical events, affective reactions and associations, programmatic associations, associations with musical settings, associative classifications, kinesthetic classifications, associations with other arts/works of art, evaluations, preferences, reflections on the tasks/processes, recognition of the musical examples, and transitions/concluding statements. These were eventually combined into six clusters of responses: descriptions of music events, feelingful responses to music, responses associated with music events, judgmental/critical responses, other responses related to the listening task, and miscellaneous responses. Perceptual descriptions of music were most prevalent with all children, followed by associative and affective comments. There was an increase in number and depth of comments with age, although she found a wide range of developmental differences. Musical study increased accuracy, analysis, and level of attention. Those without musical training gave more programmatic associations or affective reactions. All children were able to talk about their listening processes, leading Bundra to conclude "words are one way to access, understand, and, ultimately, refine the musical experience of listening" (p. 388). In her study, she found a general developmental pattern for music listening that progressed (moving from second to eleventh grade) from "the personal to convention to sophistication" (p. 380), but as has been suggested before, individual variance precludes the suggestion of any specific developmental pattern.

Kerchner (2000) used a novel, multidimensional approach with young listeners to compare their cognitive processes from several angles and to see if they preferred describing what they heard through one mode more than another. She asked six second- and six fifth-grade students to listen to the same piece repeatedly during two sessions where they listened to the piece, provided a concurrent verbal protocol, moved to indicate what they heard, drew a map (with no specific indications of what a "map" was to be), and verbally described their map as the music played, pointing out details as they went. This process was repeated in the second session. Comparing the second- and fifth-graders, the fifth-graders used more sophisticated thinking, provided more affective responses linked to musical events in the music, were more differentiated in their visual responses, drew more musical events, and appeared to be more kinesthetic learners. Second-graders gave more programmatic responses and drew more pictures. Changing the style of response mode changed the style of thinking for the children (i.e., movement enlisted a linear style of thinking; verbal mode enlisted a more detailed, linear thinking; mapping enlisted both linear and nonlinear thinking). Kerchner found that the children were willing, active participants when asked to respond in the different modes and recommended that teachers employ these different means to help children access their perceptions during music listening.

Kerchner (2005) replicated her previous research with second-, fifth-, eighth-, and eleventh-graders (N = 23). She found that the second-, fifth-, and eighth-grade students preferred to describe the listening experience through the visual mode; fifth- and eighth-graders also found the visual mode (drawing/mapping) to be the easiest response mode; representations and symbols become increasingly detailed with age; and movement was the least favorite response mode of the eighth- and eleventh-grade students. An important conclusion was that the quality of student responses in each mode was directly related to the quality of the teacher-researcher's questions.

Composers Growing Up Listening to Music

Listening to music at home while growing up can have a profound effect on a child. In a modified operational replication of Bloom's (1985) study of the development of talent in young people, Dunn and Casey (1995) studied the lives of 22 successful American composers between the ages of 28 and 50 who had been awarded Composer Fellowship Grants from the National Endowment for the Arts. Interviews were conducted with the composers and, where possible, a parent. Only in a few cases were one or both parents musicians themselves. Listening to music in their homes was a natural part of childhood for each of these composers through a variety of sources: recordings, radio, television, and, less often, live performance. Growing up, these children were often allowed to request pieces to be heard and usually learned to operate the audio equipment on their own so they could play music when they wished. The type of music varied, from country-western to rock, from folk to easy listening; usually classical music formed at least a small part of their musical fare. At some point in each of the composers' lives, they aggressively pursued opportunities to listen to a wide variety of music—it was as if they had developed an insatiable thirst for listening to music. This proved to be a turning point for most, an indicator of wanting to hear and understand more and more about the music. For some, this occurred in junior high or high school; for some, it did not occur until college. Music teachers, ensemble instructors, parents, friends, concerts, or courses served as inspiration and resources for being exposed to new artists and recordings.

National Assessment of Educational Progress

The National Assessment of Educational Progress (NAEP) was first administered in 1971–1972 with the intent to assess "what America's students know and can do" (Persky, Sandene, and Askew, 1998, introduction) in different subject areas, including music, at four age levels (9, 13, 17, and young adult). The music assessment asked children to sing alone and with others, perform on instruments, improvise, sing and play at sight, and perform a prepared solo piece. A second administration of the NAEP took place in 1978. Music was still included, but the performance assessment was not.

Music was not included in the NAEP again until the 1997 assessment, when it was revised and influenced by the National Standards. Only eighth-grade students were included in the results. Music listening was included in sections called responding. Other sections were creating and performing. This version of the NAEP has been critiqued for its limitations and strengths (e.g., Colwell, 1999; Sims, 2000).

In the responding tasks, students were asked to do a number of types of listening tasks. Among them, they were asked to identify phrases as same or different when presented phrase by phrase for "Michael, Row the Boat Ashore." Then they looked at the same piece in their test booklets while they listened to a vocal performance of the first two verses. On the third verse, several mistakes were made after measure 17. They were to indicate where the mistakes were made and tell what the mistake was. Another task was to listen to a Sousa march and indicate which of four places the music would most likely be heard (funeral, wedding, rock concert, parade). A final task example was after listening to "Wade in the Water," they were asked to indicate the time signature, give one specific feature that would help identify it as a spiritual, and give one specific reason why spirituals were important in daily life for people who originally sang them (Persky et al., 1998).

Acknowledging that there were limitations to the sampling, researchers discovered that most eighth-graders in the sample were able to tell if phrases were same or different, could identify some solo instrument timbres, and could perceive the contour of a short melodic phrase going up or down. Fewer than 50 percent of students could tell where the mistakes occurred in "Michael, Row the Boat Ashore" or give the time signature for "Wade in the Water."

The NAEP is unique in its intended goal to give a national snapshot of student competence in music, especially responding to music through listening. The 1997 tasks were not comparable as far as listening with the earlier NAEP tests. The intended overall goals of the later assessment and the usefulness of the data is still cause for debate (Colwell, 1999). At the time of writing, the 2007 NAEP assessment results were not available.

Expressive Ear versus Analytical Ear

On a holistic level, Kirnarskaya and Winner (1997) explored the listener through the lens of developing an "expressive ear" or "analytical ear" for music. According to these researchers, a listener with an expressive ear will be sensitive to performed qualities of sound that "are not captured by notation" (p. 3), what they term the *nonnotational* aspects. These qualities include phrasing, accentuation, articulation, intensity, register, and timbre. "An individual with a heightened *expressive* ear for music may not be able to follow the details of musical structure, but can hear and respond to the emotional message of the music" (p. 3). A listener with an analytical ear will be sensitive to what is easily captured in notation, what they term the *notational* aspects of music: rhythm, pitch, and duration of pitch. A listener with an analytical ear "focuses on structural relationships in the music; that is, recognition of musical elements and themes, hierarchical structure, development of structural themes, transformation of themes, etc." (p. 12). In this study, the researchers provided subjects with six excerpts chosen through their past research and verified by three expert musicians with 100 percent agreement. Based on the way the subjects (N = 397) paired the excerpts, they were scored as expressive, formal, or random pairings. Eight groups participated, including musically trained and untrained children and preteen/teenagers, untrained adults, untrained adults who were classical music lovers, adult music educators, and trained concert performers. As measured by this task, the only two groups with a significantly strong tendency to group the excerpts expressively were the untrained classical music lovers (93 percent) and the concert performers (77 percent). In comparison, only 20 percent of the music educators' responses were expressive. The main response for all other groups was formal. Kirnarskaya and Winner found it "particularly remarkable" that the music educators trained in a conservatory were "no more likely to group expressively than were adults with no music training" (p. 11), supporting their hypothesis that current musical training ignores the expressive ear in favor of the analytical ear. A movement from expressive to formal, or from intuitive to formal, is discussed in the third section of this chapter.

Emotional Responses and Listening

Emotional response is central to the experience of music, yet it is possibly the most problematical part of the human experience to probe. It is difficult to examine it separately from other aspects of listening, and it has already been seen as one facet of previously mentioned studies (e.g., Bundra, 1994; Flowers and Wang, 2002; Johnson, 2006; Rodriguez and Webster, 1997; Theiss, 1990). I present a few studies that represent various aspects of how researchers are approaching this interesting area of music listening.

In a developmental study, Kratus (1993) asked 658 children, ages 6 to 12, to circle one of two icons to indicate the emotion they perceived in each musical excerpt they heard. Depending on the group to which they were assigned, they were asked to respond either happy/sad or excited/calm to the same excerpts. Different from some other studies, no "right" answer was assigned by the researcher; rather, agreement between subjects was the focus. Analysis showed that all age groups were very consistent in agreeing on the emotion for a given piece. There was more consistency for happy/sad than for excited/calm, perhaps due to the more nebulous meanings of the latter words for children. Further analysis showed that children chose the emotional designations for largely musical reasons: happy/sad were related to rhythmic activity and articulation, and excited/calm were related to rhythmic activity and meter. This study used short excerpts and reduced emotion to a very simplistic, categorized-type response. Most emotional responses in life and to music are more holistic and complex. Studies such as this one show how difficult it is to take a complex phenomenon and find a way to actually measure it.

On a more sophisticated level, a large body of literature has been developed employing the Continuous Response Digital Interface (CRDI), where subjects are asked to manipulate a dial to indicate their level of response as they listen to music. The CRDI provides a lens for possibly more complex examination of music listening, as in the case of aesthetic response. Using the CRDI dial, Madsen, Brittin, and Capperella-Sheldon (1993) asked 30 sophisticated musicians to indicate their level of aesthetic response as they listened to the final 20 minutes of Act I of Puccini's *La Boheme*. Responding to a questionnaire after listening, the musicians indicated they had experienced an aesthetic response to the music and that their manipulations of the CRDI dial paralleled this response. The authors purposely left the definition of aesthetic response to the listeners. Lychner (1998) found that defining "aesthetic response" did not result in appreciable differences in CRDI response data when compared with studies where it was not defined.

In a focus of attention study using the same Puccini excerpt, Madsen (1997) sought insight into which musical elements were most tied to aesthetic response: rhythm, melody, timbre, dynamics, or everything. Fifty subjects had each of these elements on their CRDI dial and were asked to turn the dial to indicate what element they were attending at a given point. Fifty other subjects (10 for each element) were asked to indicate their degree of attention to that specific element. A subsequent questionnaire asked respondents to provide more specific information about their aesthetic responses in the music and their CRDI dial responses. The main result was that melody seemed to be the main factor related to aesthetic response in this piece. Musicians' and nonmusicians' results were very similar. It was speculated that perhaps it was the task of manipulating the CRDI dial itself in response to aesthetic experience that had an important impact on the results and should be studied further.

To follow this up, Madsen and Coggiola (2001) used the same Puccini excerpt with nonmusicians and musicians. The purpose was to see if the use of the CRDI dial resulted in a difference in focus of attention and aesthetic response while listening. The 60 nonmusicians were divided into two equal groups: one manipulated a CRDI dial, and one did not. The CRDI dial was not activated and did not collect data. The 30 musicians did not manipulate a CRDI dial, as it was felt their data could be compared with previous studies where they had manipulated a dial on the same piece. Results of the questionnaire showed that 93 percent of the musicians and 90 percent of the nonmusician/CRDI group indicated they had at least one aesthetic experience while they listened; only 63 percent of the nonmusician/non-CRDI group so indicated. Ninety percent of the nonmusician/CRDI group felt their CRDI manipulations paralleled their aesthetic experiences. In addition, the responses to "How long did this experience last?" for musicians and the nonmusician/CRDI were quite high, compared with the nonmusician/non-CRDI group. Most important, a significant difference ($p < .05$) was found between the nonmusician/non-CRDI group and the other two groups, with the latter two giving themselves a higher rating for the magnitude of their aesthetic experience(s). It appeared that the task of manipulating the CRDI not only provided focus of attention but also provided deeper and more opportunities for aesthetic experiences, not defined for them in this study. Given this conclusion, this study would also fit in the facilitating listening section of this chapter.

These three studies employing the CRDI hold potentially valuable implications for learning to listen. Technology can be useful in investigating the complexities of music listening and may help listeners retain focus on the music for longer periods of time, particularly extending listening spans for nonmusicians. Also, although aesthetic experience is a complex concept, the listeners in these studies were able to understand and respond regarding aesthetic experience, without it being defined for them in words, and meaningful results were obtained. In meaningful music listening, not everything must be reduced to words for learning or meaningful experience to occur.

In another type of study examining emotional response to music, Woody and Burns (2001) studied whether past emotional response to music can predict current music appreciation. They surveyed 533 college students in 17 sections of music appreciation courses regarding their musical backgrounds, beliefs, and preferences and then had them respond after listening to four classical music excerpts. The subjects liked music, with rock the most popular and classical the least popular styles. When asked to indicate to which styles of music they had experienced emotional responses, rock was indicated by 87 percent; the 60 percent level included country, rap/R&B, and classical; the 50 percent level included gospel/contemporary Christian and jazz. Although classical music was the favorite style of only 1 percent of the students, it is interesting to note that 63 percent of the sample indicated past emotional response to classical music. Subjects reporting more past experience and past emotional responses with classical music were more likely to respond positively to the emotionality/expression of the classical pieces in the study and were more willing to listen to them at home. Therefore, having positive past emotional responses with classical music was a positive predictor of current positive response to classical music; the lack of past positive response increased negative response. For those with positive past emotional response, it was not clear what the context was, that is, whether exposure happened in the home, school, or another venue. The implication regarding classical music is that positive exposure and interaction at earlier ages is important for positive attitudes and willingness to be open to continued exposure at later ages.

Listening in Everyday Life

So far in this section, we have examined studies touching on the developmental and emotional aspects of the human music-listening experience. I now turn to what we can learn from asking this question: what do we know about how people listen to music in their everyday lives?

According to North, Hargreaves, and Hargreaves (2004), "the value of music in people's everyday lives depends on the uses they make of it and the degree to which they engage with it, which are in turn dependent on the contexts in which they hear it" (p. 41). Various researchers have examined music listening in everyday life in different ways and at different ages in an effort to tease out and better understand the complexities of people's music listening patterns.

Boal-Palheiros and Hargreaves (2001, 2004) engaged in two studies examining the differences between music listening at home and at school. In both studies, they compared Portuguese and British children ages 9–10 and 13–14 years. In the first study (N = 60), children in both groups clearly preferred listening to music at home, for several reasons: listening was done in private, they were able to exercise choice in listening, and home offered shared enjoyment in significant social interactions. The second study (N = 120) confirmed that home listening was preferred. Children appeared to have various levels of emotional involvement and attention with music, depending on the context. Home listening was less structured, often accompanied doing something else, and appeared to serve primarily emotional functions.

Students' musical attitudes and activities were studied by Lamont, Hargreaves, Marshall, and Tarrant (2003). Their sample (N = 1,479) included a cross-section of students age 8 to 14 (years 4, 6, 7, and 9 in English schools, U.S. grades 3, 5, 6, and 8). Music listening was an important part of the students' lives, but more so outside school. Listening to music outside school increased with age, with year 9 students averaging 13 hours per week. The reasons the students gave for listening to music included allowing them to explore their emotions or to change them.

North, Hargreaves, and O'Neill (2000) asked 2,465 13- and 14-year-olds to fill out a questionnaire assessing the relative importance of music listening to a list of activities (e.g., going shopping), asked whether playing an instrument took away from or added to music listening, and asked them to rate reasons that they or others might listen to twelve styles of music, from pop to classical. The average listening time was 2.45 hours a day; that increased to 2.65 hours a day for those who played an instrument. Sixty percent reported listening alone, 25 percent with friends, 5.7 percent with family, and 5.7 percent, other. Adolescents felt that one listened to popular music "in order to enjoy the music; to be creative/use their imagination; to relieve boredom; to help get through difficult times; to be trendy/cool; to relieve tension/stress; to create an image for him/herself; to please friends; and to reduce loneliness" (p. 263). On the other hand, they felt that one would choose to listen to classical music rather than popular music "in order to please parents and to please teachers" (p. 263). More females reported use of music as a means of mood regulation; more males reported use of music as a means of creating an impression with others.

Looking at an older population, Sloboda, O'Neill, and Ivaldi (2001) wanted to move beyond retrospective reports by testing an experience sampling method (ESM) to investigate music listening in real-life episodes. Eight nonmusicians, age 18 to 40, were given pagers for a week and asked to complete self-report forms with scaled and open-ended questions each time the pager was activated. Music was present in 44 percent of the episodes, but few involved listening as the primary focus. When music was involved, participants were more positive, alert, and focused on the situation, more so if they had choice over the music. In nearly every case, music was an accompaniment to doing something else, corroborating Danora's (1999) findings. A major result of the study was that moderation of mood was greater when persons had power over the listening choices. Sloboda et al. (2001) further noted:

only those few respondents who were over the age of 70 and those who were trained musicians tended to consider it antithetical to conceive of music as "background" to anything....This has major theoretical implications for how we conceptualize music use. The focused attentive and "respectful" listening of the "music lover" figures hardly at all in our present sample of non-musicians. (pp. 22–23)

An exploratory study with a naturalistic approach to music listening in everyday life was undertaken by North, Hargreaves, and Hargreaves (2004). For 14 days, 346 cell phone owners (age 13–78, $M = 25.96$) received one text message each day, which prompted them to fill out a questionnaire about what they were hearing at the moment (or had heard), where they were, with whom, why, and their emotional responses at the moment. Results included a high incidence of experiencing music. Contrary to similar previous studies, the majority of listening episodes took place in the presence of other people rather than alone. The latter result may be due to increases in ease of access to music due to technological changes. When listeners were able to choose what they heard, they chose different styles for different reasons (e.g., *It helped me to concentrate. It helped me to create the right atmosphere. I enjoyed it.*). Only 11.9 percent of responses involved what might be thought of as focused listening (*At home deliberately listening to music, Concert*). When asked if listening to music was the main task they were engaged in (no matter what category they had selected), 26.4 percent said yes. When asked to rate their level of attention to the music at the moment (0 = no attention, 10 = complete attention), the mean was 4.87 ($SD = 2.74$), indicating that music was not the central focus. The most common reasons for listening were *enjoyment, pass the time, habit,* and *create the right atmosphere,* indicating that when respondents could choose, they seemed to do so "with little thought, and seemed to opt deliberately to be subjected to a form of 'sonic wallpaper'" (p. 72). Overall, the results indicated that these subjects consciously and actively employed music listening in their lives in different social and interpersonal contexts, engaging at different levels and psychological states.

Juslin and Laukka (2004) provide a useful review and critique of theories and research about emotional responses in music, perception, and the social contexts of music, before presenting findings of their own exploratory questionnaire study involving 141 "ordinary" listeners (as opposed to "musician" listeners) between the ages of 17 and 74. The questionnaire included seven areas: listening context, musical expressivity, musical communication, emotion perception, emotion induction, relationship between perception and induction, and basic motives for listening to music (p. 226). The results of the study confirmed their hypothesis that emotion is strongly related to the main reasons people listen to music. In their discussion, they presented this summary:

From these findings emerges a picture of the ordinary music listener as someone who listens to music many times a day, often in mundane everyday contexts where music listening is not the primary activity. It's a listener who chooses to listen to music to a large extent because of the valued emotional experiences it offers. Music is used to enhance or change emotions (to relax, to arouse, to comfort) or to evoke emotional memories. The strongest emotional experiences often occur while listening alone (while listening attentively to the music), but it may also occur in social and emotionally charged situations. Positive emotions dominate in people's responses to music, with some of the most common emotions appearing to be feeling happy, relaxed, calm, moved, nostalgic, pleasurable, loving, sad, longing, or tender. (p. 232)

These studies indicate that many humans seek musical experiences on a daily basis. Behne (1997) investigated the development of *Musikerleben*, a German term without a simple English translation. He defined it as "the sum of psychic processes which accompany the experience of music in situations when music is in the focus of interest: When a person is not only hearing, but listening to and appreciating music" (p. 143). Behne cautions that this is not to be confused with music appreciation, a term often associated with more cognitive noticing. *Musikerleben* is involved with aesthetic experiencing but does not need to be an intense, subjective experience, as the term is sometimes used. It must be thought of as having many varying degrees of intensity and attention.

To investigate *Musikerleben*, Behne developed a questionnaire that asked subjects to rate a series of statements on a 5-point scale. Each statement began "When I listen to music," followed by a statement such as "it changes my mood" or "I like to hum and sing." A variable cluster analysis of data from several studies grouped test items into a list of nine listening styles that are worthy of note:

- Compensating (e.g., it changes my mood; it really calms me down if I was excited before)
- Concentrated (e.g., I like to close my eyes, I like to follow the various themes)
- Emotional (e.g., I pay attention to what types of feelings are expressed through the music)
- Distancing (e.g., I like to identify the music style; I try to understand the words of the vocal part)
- Vegetative (e.g., it really gets under my skin; I sometimes feel my heart beat faster)
- Sentimental (e.g., I like to dream, I remember things of the past)
- Associative (e.g., I invent a story)
- Stimulative (e.g., I like to play it very loud; it makes me feel very aggressive)
- Diffuse (e.g., my attention is divided; I like to do other things besides just listening)

(Behne, 1997, p. 147)

Compensating listening style corresponds with allusions to mood regulation we have seen in other studies. Diffuse listening style corresponds with listening while doing something else.

Desiring to examine the development of *Musikerleben*, Behne (1997) conducted a longitudinal study with 155 children in Hannover, Germany. The children were surveyed at ages 11, 12, and 13. To further investigate possible associations of music with their emotional lives, the children were also surveyed regarding problems adolescents may experience. At age 11, Compensating was the most important listening style (listening to change one's mood); the other styles were differentiated but weakly developed. There was a general tendency of styles with initially higher scores to slightly decrease over time and for initially lower scores to increase. Diffuse listening (listening while doing something else) showed the greatest increase. Children indicated that they encountered problems with boredom, depression, family, fear, friends, health, loneliness, outward appearance, school, and worries about the future. Children indicating they had many problems in their lives appeared to choose Compensating listening style slightly more and chose Sentimental listening as a coping style significantly more ($p < .01$). Depression was the dominant problem influencing six of the nine styles. The data indicated that children with different problems chose different coping strategies for listening to music.

That human beings may experience an emotional response to music would appear to be undeniable, probably from our own personal experiences, as well as from the results of research. It is not surprising that a common manifestation of emotional response to music would be selecting music for the purposes of mood regulation, perhaps to lift, calm, excite, or match one's mood; to help one cope with profound feelings of loss; or even to make the time pass more quickly. We have just seen researchers document some ways people use music in this way: to explore emotions or change them (Lamont et al., 2003; Juslin and Laukka, 2004); to match their emotions (Woody and Burns, 2001); to relieve boredom, to help get through difficult times, to relieve tension/stress, to relieve loneliness (North, Hargreaves, and O'Neill, 2000); to evoke emotional memories (Juslin and Laukka, 2004); and to create the right atmosphere or to help concentration (North et al., 2004).

Sometimes musicians or music educators may devalue the use of music to regulate our moods. Behne strongly disagrees with this view. For example, he says:

> Musical experts tend to think of a "compensating" listening style as an inappropriate behavior towards a piece of music as a work of art. As members of a cultural upper class they think of such a plebeian way of using music as a misuse which should be restricted to trivial music, to pop-songs, "Schlager," musical "Kitsch" and to products of low culture in general. But there is no empirical support for this attitude. In a study of concert audiences in Germany, Dollase, Rüsenberg, and Stollenwerk (1986) found that visitors of so-called High-culture concerts (classics by Beethoven or serious entertainment) reported having more problems in their everyday lives than those who attended more popular events. The first rated themselves higher than the latter for using music as a means of consolation. Our own results support this view: having problems seems to enhance the intensity of *Musikerleben*. Adolescents use *Musikerleben* to help them cope with their problems and this, perhaps, is why

for very many adolescents music is one of the most important things in the world. (Behne, 1997, p. 157)

The foregoing studies of everyday listening are necessarily based on self-reported data. Juslin and Laukka (2004) rightly remind us to be cautious about such data, especially in the difficult area of processes involved in emotional responses to music; however, they believe ordinary listeners seem more qualified than musicologists or philosophers to resolve issues such as the experience and uses of music in everyday life and are capable of giving us reasonably valid data. Furthermore:

> The neglect of the social context of music listening (e.g., the way that listeners actually use music and experience it in real-life) might easily lead to a musicological view that emphasizes sublime, "aesthetic" emotions to "works of art." While this view may be popular with musicians, no doubt, it has limited validity in terms of fully accounting for how most *listeners* actually relate to music. The consequence might be theories of musical emotion that overly emphasize musical structures, and sources of emotion related to structure (e.g., expectancy, iconic sources) at the expense of the rich personal associations listeners have to music, and that may involve a wider variety of human emotions. Hence, we argue that a move to extend research on music and emotion to everyday life contexts represents one of the most promising avenues towards a more accurate understanding of how human beings experience emotions in connection with music. (p. 233, emphasis in original)

While there may be extant musicological views that fit Juslin and Laukka's viewpoint, I would argue that views of philosophy of music education have moved in a direction seeking to more fully account for all aspects of a listener's experience. However, the importance of seeking to understand the music-listening experience from the "ordinary listener's" viewpoint is an important one. Bridging the gap between school music and "life music" is an important topic.

Dissonance between School Music and "Life Music" Listening

One result of research into music in everyday life is evidence of a dissonance between school music and "life music". In their comparison of home and school music, Boal-Palheiros and Hargreaves (2001, 2004) found that home listening was preferred. Their 9- to 10-year-old and 13- to 14-year-old subjects generally felt that school listening offered few choices, was structured, was associated with formal learning activities, and did not offer shared enjoyment in shared social interactions. The authors stated that "enjoyment and emotion are neglected in school music listening, yet they are among the most important functions of music for children and therefore deserve more attention at school. The cultural dissonance between school and home listening deserves greater attention" (2001, p. 116).

After questioning nearly 2,500 thirteen- and fourteen-year-olds, North et al. (2000) concluded that there is little doubt that music is a vital part of life for most teenagers outside school. But they found a "disjunction" between music, including listening, at home and school that appears to widen in early adolescence and that needs to be addressed (p. 256).

It may be possible that the traditional courses and formats for teaching are not the most effective for reaching into real-world music listening. In the United States, most school systems provide elementary music experiences for all students and require some music or art requirement in middle or junior high school. From that point, the majority of available music courses are elective ensembles or advanced placement theory courses. This sequence of courses does not fit every student, evidenced by the falling numbers of enrollment in higher grades. For those who stay in the sequence, one wonders how it lends itself to everyday listening as students pass through schooling years and how it prepares them for lifelong listening as they leave.

Woody (2004) stated: "Since the primary purpose of music—and the arts in general—is the communication of expression and emotion, teaching to improve sensitivities in students' listening skills can provide lifelong benefits to students" (p. 32). He describes what is sometimes called the traditional music appreciation model of music listening, combining a study of musical recordings (most often of classical music), historical and cultural facts, and musical elements. "The problem with this approach may be that it requires people to listen to music in a way that is very different from how they normally do it outside of a formal education setting" (p. 32). I think many educators recognize this disjunction as a rift between what might be called "school music" and "real-life music"—or simply, "life music". I choose the term "life music" because I feel it encompasses all the unique, dynamic, and complex facets of an individual's lived musical experience outside school, including the many ways to meaningfully interact with music, as well as social, emotional, psychological, and creative aspects.

The dissonance between school music and life music is illustrated by a study by Williamson (2005). Williamson worked with 21 seventh- and eighth-graders in a study of the music-listening and music-making experiences of students not enrolled in music ensembles. She designed and taught an informal class called "My Music" as a substitute for their "Study Skills" course. Using a variety of data collection procedures such as personal semi-structured interviews and group think-alouds, data were coded and analyzed for emergent themes, and within-case and cross-case analyses were used. Six of the 21 students were involved in informal music making outside school. All students listened to music—all but two on a daily basis. Listening alone, listening in a social situation, and listening while doing something else were documented. School music experiences were associated with conceptual learning (perhaps, one might say, not relating to life music) and were cited as the main reason for not continuing to be in an ensemble. She begins the study with a telling personal example from one of the students:

Victorio walked into my classroom on the first day of middle school general music class and announced, "I just want you to know, I hate music."... As an experienced teacher, I replied, "thank you for being honest. Now, I have a question for you. Do you hate music, or do you hate music class?"

I learned some of the answers to my question as the semester advanced. Victorio did not *hate* music at all and was an avid fan of several local and nationally known rock bands. He was an active music listener and spent hours in his room memorizing song words and polishing fantastic air guitar licks. On listening days, he enthusiastically brought in Nirvana recordings and provided insightful information concerning his musical choices to his peers. He also exhibited a strong sense of musical identity; while he was not currently performing... he saw himself as a very musical person. His peers viewed him as a musical guru, whose knowledge and opinions were frequently consulted and infrequently challenged. He did, however, hate school music, due to his conflict with his previous elementary general music teacher and the exclusion of his favorite genres in the music curriculum. (Williamson, 2005, pp. 1–2, emphasis in the original)

In the conclusion of their cross-sectional study of 8- to 14-year-olds, Lamont et al. (2003) challenged school music programs to find ways to enhance the musical experience of all students, not just the musically gifted, and "to help all those who show an additional interest in music beyond the classroom to develop that, recognizing the value of their own contributions, developing their individual skills through valuable social, cultural, and primarily *musical* experiences and activities, and providing the confidence to partake in musical activities in whatever personal or social context they choose" (pp. 22–23, emphasis in the original). This is a challenge that we need to take seriously as a profession.

It may be that there are effective music-listening teaching and learning experiences taking place in educational settings that address this issue that are not documented. Studies of effective approaches that bridge the cultural dissonance between everyday life and school music listening are needed.

Summary

These studies provide evidence to support a lifelong human involvement in music listening. From birth, listening to music is linked with affective expression, embedded in a social context, and may provide the beginnings of self-identity, trends that appear to continue through life. A child entering preschool or kindergarten already has a relationship with his or her own life music and, more than we perhaps have understood, has already begun filling a personal mental library of intuitive musical knowing and is ready for more. As children age, their affective sensitivity appears to increase, while their responses become more global and less simplistic. There appear to be wide differences in individual listening patterns and responses to music listening that begin early and continue through later life.

Listening to music, any type of music, early in life may have a profound impact on children's lives. Early positive interactions with a given style of music listening may increase the likelihood a person will have positive reactions to it in later life.

Studies of music in everyday life focus the importance of music on (1) how it is used in real-life situations, (2) the reasons it is used, and (3) the contexts where it is employed. Listening to music at home or out of school is associated primarily with emotional or enjoyment functions. A dissonance was noted between what might be called "school music" and "life music" listening, where school seems dissociated from the ways people use music in their everyday lives. Several researchers suggested that schools need to find ways to make school music experiences more relevant to everyday life music.

Musikerleben was addressed, which involves a personal connection with listening to music at some level, not just hearing it. Different types of responses to listening to music beyond what has been considered typically valued in the classroom and university were discussed, including regulation of mood, as valid ways to interact with music. It appears that human connections to music through listening are more varied, widespread, and natural than was accounted for in some prior philosophical or musicological views of how humans responded to music. The way we teach music listening should reflect this more intuitive view as well.

The social impact of listening to music in groups is important to take into account. In a classroom situation, a student concerned with social interactions, positive or negative, is likely to be unable to focus on a listening lesson. Teachers must be aware of the social needs of students and work to make their classrooms a safe and nurturing place for learning to take place.

Finally, it is likely that researchers and practitioners desire a clear developmental description of music listening. While some general tendencies of progression have been identified, the wide range of individual differences found at different stages of development appears to make this an impractical task. Most, if not all, children are exposed to music listening throughout their lives in their different environments—some to a great deal of it. Is it the amount of exposure that makes a difference? Is it a matter of home environment, schooling, social factors, individual characteristics such as aural skills, a combination of these, or some other aspect that accounts for it? We are unable to answer these questions definitively at this time. These are interesting areas for further research.

Section II: What We Know about Facilitating Listening to Music

We have just examined some of what we know about how children and adults listen to music. How does inserting instruction change the listening experience for children? Do visuals or movements make listening experiences more effective? How effective are teacher-directed music listening experiences? Is it possible to present specific self-constructed listening experiences to build listening skills? In this section, I review representative studies dealing with facilitating the music listening experience from widely differing aspects. Much of the concern about facilitating listening to music is centered on focus, usually concentrating on particular elements within a given listening experience. Sometimes the concern is simply maintaining focus on the music, rather than allowing the mind to wander to something else. First, I present teacher-directed efforts at enhancing the listening experience. Then I address self-constructed listening experiences presented through problem-solving opportunities set up for the listener by the teacher or researcher. Finally, I mention a review of the effect performance has on music listening.

Teacher-Directed Instruction

Decentration   Given that research seems to verify the Piagetian idea that young children seem to focus their attention on one aspect of a musical stimulus at a time, *centration* in Piagetian terms, Sims (1991) decided to test whether 4- and 5-year-olds could *decentrate* by concentrating on two elements at once. Her study involved more than listening, but listening was involved in the instruction, and she employed a listening test for the assessment. In the first part of this study, the 30 children were given four small-group instruction sessions using speech, singing, movement, and listening activities where they experienced single and paired elements: fast, slow, smooth, choppy, fast and slow, and smooth and choppy. The group was compared with a control group who received no instruction. Although the experimental group performed dramatically better on the listening test when only one element was involved (centration), they performed about the same as the control group when asked to perceive two at one time (decentration). Among implications for teaching, Sims noted that preschool teachers need to be aware that children this age are likely to favor attending to one element in music listening, possibly ignoring others. Therefore, in designing a listening lesson, for example, particular attention would need to be paid to making sure that a movement was directly related to the desired musical element or contrast that was to be highlighted. She also found that once children were able to make these single discriminations, they were able to learn and apply musical terms to what they heard, making preschool "an ideal time to begin building children's music vocabulary and discrimination skills" (p. 308).

Incidental Exposure to Prototypes   Hearing music in the background is a normal part of our Western culture. Lineburgh (1994) wanted to know if there could be any effect from incidental exposure to music on discrimination of style in kindergarten (*n* = 245) and second grade (*n* = 235). Further, she explored whether repeated listening to a few examples would have a different effect than listening to many nonrepeated examples from each composer.

She used three musical prototypes as the basis for her study: Mozart, Debussy, and Joplin. The treatment students were shown the pictures of the composers and taught to line up in a certain way by the music teacher when they heard the music of one of the three composers: Mozart = single file, Joplin = line up with a partner, Debussy = line up in a boy line and a girl line. Audiotapes were prepared for their regular classrooms (depending on treatment, with either repeated examples or nonrepeated examples). These tapes were played at different times of the day in their regular classes as part of their routines, and the students were asked to line up accordingly. The children in the experimental groups scored better than the control groups, significant at the .05 level, with the groups hearing the nonrepeated examples scoring slightly better; second-grade students' scores were higher than the scores of kindergartners, significant at the .05 level; and all groups improved their scores. Lineburgh concluded that incidental exposure to music was effective and appropriate for children to learn style discrimination as early as kindergarten in this manner. This means that, with a little planning and instruction, a teacher can use background music as a tool for student learning; also, a variety of examples of the same prototype may be more valuable than the same example played repeatedly for conceptual learning.

Presentation Mode and Perceptual Strengths   Some learners appear to vary in their ability to perceive and process information gleaned through the environment through the visual, auditory, and kinesthetic modes. A person who learns best through one perceptual mode may be said to have a perceptual strength in that mode; for example, a visual learner has a visual perceptual strength. A person who exhibits perceptual strengths in two or all three modes is termed a mixed modality learner (Cassidy, 2004). To see whether individual perceptual strengths made a difference in an individual listening experience, I presented 16 third-grade students with repeated-listening experiences in three presentation modes: listening only, listening with visual reinforcement, and listening with movement reinforcement (Dunn, 2008). To strengthen the data, students went through a second round of the presentation modes, for a total of six sessions. Students experienced one presentation mode in each individual session and heard the same musical excerpt three times in a session, six different classical pieces overall. The order of the presentation modes and the selections was assigned through randomization. After each listening, the student was asked, "Tell me as much as you can about what went on in the music" to collect retrospective verbal reports. Additional data were collected from the subject from five other sources: video recordings of each session, researcher field notes, a subject's response to metacognitive-type questions at the end of each session, and a subject's responses to introductory and exit interviews. The retrospective verbal reports were analyzed and categorized into 14 categories of statements: affective response, classification, comparison, concluding statement, evaluation, kinesthetic association, musical perception, null statement, preference, programmatic association, recognition, strategy for listening, testing conditions, and visual association—many categories similar to Bundra's (1994) work. When asked about their preferred presentation mode, 7 preferred the listen/visual, 5 multiple modes, 3 listen/movement, and 1 listen only. When asked about their least favored presentation mode, 7 chose listening only, and the rest did not have a least favored mode. If the results had been analyzed by group statistics, as most perceptual studies in music education have been in the past, the results would have been insignificant. However, when examined on an individual basis, it was clear that six of the students (37 percent) appeared to perceive, process, and recall musical events more effectively through only one presentation mode. Depending on the child, adding visual stimuli or movement aided, had no effect on, or in some cases hindered musical perception. While multisensory teaching is often advised, one implication is that adding additional stimuli for some students may become sensory overload; for example, having to concentrate on the movement causes the student to lose track of perception of the music. In a possible link with Kercher's (2000) research, changing the presentation mode by adding visual stimuli or movement qualitatively changed the listening experience for some students. Finally, the connection between added visual stimuli/movement and the music for children cannot be assumed. In some cases, the children could describe/demonstrate the movements or visual stimuli, but there was no evidence that they were able to link them to musical events. In other cases, the link between them was very clear. Teachers may need to find ways to help the connection become explicit in the minds of the learners.

Picture Books   Picture books are often used with pre-K children as teaching aids, often helping with focus and learning. Mack (1995) examined the use of picture books and instrument pictures during music listening with pre-K children. She was specifically interested in their effects on memory for melodic themes, instrument identification, attitude, and attentiveness during two small-group lessons based on *Peter and the Wolf*. Attention data were gathered from videotape; all other data were gathered from posttreatment individual sessions. The results showed no significant effect of picture book or instrument pictures on any variables, although the students who saw the pictures of the instruments scored somewhat higher on instrument identification. As the attention of many of the children began to decline after 2.5 minutes, Mack recommended using short musical examples for pre-K children, perhaps 1.5 to 2 minutes in length, and suggested that extending listening time may be accomplished through introducing an interesting activity, as demonstrated by children's attention being recaptured when a new character was introduced to the story. Although the results of this study did not reach significance, it underscores the differences in preschoolers' listening spans as found by Sims (2001). Not all the children began to lose interest; some may have sat and listened with or without the book or pictures intermittently recapturing their attention.

Call Charts   Creating aids for directed listening is a continuing quest. Call charts, commonly found in many music texts for the general student today, from elementary school to college level, can be traced to early work by Reimer (1967). Through the U.S. Department of Health, Education, and Welfare (USHEW), under Reimer's direction, a 2-year trial curriculum in general music was developed and tested at the junior and senior high school levels. Three schools of disparate socioeconomic levels were chosen at each level, one class at each school (seventh grade, N = 80; high school, N = 74). Reimer's call charts provided a central part of the listening activities in the curriculum. The need for such a device was given in Reimer's 1967 USHEW report:

> One of the central problems of any music course which attempts to foster active listening responses is to provide a means whereby the student is clear about what should be heard. Unlike paintings or poems or sculptures or novels or buildings, music does not exist all at once in a tangible form which can be analyzed without disturbing the whole art work. The fluid and intangible nature of sound moving in time makes isolation of elements troublesome and focusing of attention on particulars, in the context of the whole, extremely difficult. (p. A-8)

The call chart was named and devised to overcome this difficulty and "to insure that music's expressiveness could be pointed out in actual musical experience" (p. A-8). These first charts divided a piece into numbered sections, with the score measure number provided for the teacher, and an analysis of the music following each call number describing the particular expressive content in the music that was being highlighted for study. Teachers implementing the materials followed along with the score and called out the call chart number at the appropriate moment; students were able to view the corresponding description of the expressive content on their own copied sheets. The goal was to "develop keener musical perception in a context which encourages deeper musical reaction" (p. 36). In implementation, it was found that junior high students were not able to maintain concentrated intensive listening for as long as the high school students. However, the call charts were found to be "extremely effective" (p. A-6) overall in promoting listening concentration and in extending listening time span at both levels.

Reimer and Evans (1972) employed call charts in their college appreciation text, the first text to require recordings for its use rather than as supplemental materials. Call charts were also introduced in the 1970s Silver Burdett Music series (cf Reimer, Hoffman, and McNeil, 1976). For this series, the LP recordings were recorded in two tracks with a voice calling the numbers on one track and the music on the other. This way, the teacher could turn down one track and allow the class to listen again to the music without the interruption of the numbers for a more authentic listening experience.

As mentioned, some form of call charts is common practice in classrooms and textbooks today. However, there is little or no systematic research into their effectiveness for facilitating listening. This is an area that merits further study.

Using Commercially Developed Listening Maps   The next three studies used commercially developed listening maps, sometimes called "musical maps" or simply "maps," that are used in elementary music teaching materials. Richards (1973) appears to have been the first to develop listening maps for use in classroom experiences. Initially, she called this type of map a "lead map" because a leader would lead the children through it until the children were able to follow it for themselves. Some maps are more intuitive for listeners to follow than others, for example, requiring only one time through with a leader before they are able to do it on their own. Today, there is a wide variation of what is called a map in these materials, ranging from figural drawings, icons, or symbolic notation with animal faces as noteheads, to symbols or pictures representing instruments and musicians. The level of representation of musical events varies from map to map and may even vary within a map, from representing each note or phrase as it unfolds, to representing whole sections of a piece with a single symbol or figure. The variety makes it difficult to compare results of research using maps.

The following researchers are diligent about giving details so readers can find what maps were used to better understand results. Desiring to compare children's ability to perceive form in patterned art music, Gromko and Poorman (1998) divided 29 upper elementary children into two groups, *passive* and *active*. The passive group[1] listened to the music with an individual copy of a musical map in front of them. They were instructed to use a finger to follow the map along with the music, and the researcher told them when to move to the next line. The researcher did not trace the map for these students as the music was played several times. Looking at the map afterward, students were asked to identify the first two lines that were the same, and identify them both as A, and so on, as the letter form of the excerpt was worked out. The active group mirrored the teacher's movements as they listened several times to the music and then were given the same map cut up into 12 strips. They assembled the map after determining with a partner which sections of the map matched the movements as the teacher demonstrated them again. To test their perception of pattern, all students were given a paper with numbered boxes and colored stickers. As they listened to the piece again, they were instructed to indicate same/similar sections with the same color stickers in the corresponding boxes. The results showed the active movement group performed significantly better in perception of patterned form ($p < .05$). The authors suggest that perhaps icons, such as maps, may not be enough for some children to form needed mental imagery; some may need the embodiment that perceptual-motor involvement can provide.

It appears that the movement group had the added learning experience of linking movement to the visual map with the help of the instructor and a partner, making the experiences of the two groups less comparable. Maps are traditionally introduced with a leader tracing the map, linking the icons to the music in real time for the children, and as the leader in this study modeled movements, linking them to the music as it played. This study has been cited for support that musical maps may not be effective tools for elementary children (Woody, 2004). As the map was not presented to the children in a traditional way, more research is needed.

A study by Gromko and Russell (2002) underscores the variation in what can be called a listening map for research purposes. Initially, they selected three "graphic maps" commercially available from a music series text to use in the study, one each from the books for grades 1, 3, and 4. Researchers decided to delete the grade 4 map due to its level of difficulty, noting "it consisted of metrically accurate beamed stars that were very nearly standard notation, including beamed eighth notes, a dotted quarter note followed by an eighth note, and dotted half notes. Following the map required that the reader understand conventional notation" (p. 337). Forty-one children were divided into three groups: passive (listen once, then trace the map as they listen; no model provided); unstructured active (spontaneously move hands through sand as they listen, then trace the map); and structured active (mirror the arm movements of the teacher, choreographed to reflect the rhythmic motives and contours of the music). The students then were instructed to trace the map. The map was not traced for the students, but they were instructed that the map moved from left to right when the music was playing. According to the researchers, no significant difference in accuracy of following the map was found for any listening condition, but children who had experience playing the piano performed significantly better (p <.01). This result may indicate that without the experience of a leader helping students make the intuitive connections between the music and the iconic representations on a map, the symbols could have remained abstract representations, much like musical notation. Students with note-reading ability were more successful at decoding the iconic representation, but this seems to defeat the major purpose of using maps, facilitating listening for students with less formal experience.

Cassidy's (2001) study of undergraduate students' ability to interpret various iconic representations used three levels of listening maps: (1) one icon per pitch representing melody/pitch and/or rhythm, either in abstract representation or standard notation; (2) one icon representing each steady beat or measure; and (3) one icon representing each section of the music (p. 16). Seventeen music education majors could follow all the maps. Fifty-one nonmusic elementary education majors experienced more difficulty as the maps moved from level 1 to level 3. Although the music education majors could do all three, both groups overwhelmingly preferred the least abstract musical map. Cassidy also found that while listening maps can enhance students' listening experiences, they must first be clear to the teachers. This may be especially true when no music specialist is available in the regular classroom.

Audio versus Video versus Live   Researchers have tried using different presentation modes, including movement and visual representations of the music while listening. The next studies probe what differences are found when a video is added or when the visual experience of a live performance is added.

Geringer, Cassidy, and Byo (1996) conducted an exploratory study with college nonmusic majors (N = 103) examining the effects of music with video on their cognitive, affective, and verbal responses. Students either listened to a musical example (e.g., an excerpt from Dukas's *Sorcerer's Apprentice*) or listened while watching an accompanying video (the same music with the familiar video from Disney's *Fantasia*; Bach's *Toccata and Fugue in D Minor* from *Fantasia* was also used). No significant differences were found between music-only and music-plus-video for the Bach piece, where the video was more abstract and followed more of the musical elements of the piece. Scores were higher for the music-plus-video group for the Dukas group, although the magnitude of the differences between the scores were "not robust, and differences in cognitive scores were not independent of presentation order" (p. 240). Here again, the presentation mode had an effect on the effects of the musical experience. The music-only group used more analytical descriptions of musical elements, significant at the .05 level, than did the music-plus-video group.

In a similar study, Geringer, Cassidy, and Byo (1997) selected two movements of Beethoven's *Symphony No. 6 in F Major* (*Pastoral*). One music-only group heard an excerpt conducted by Stokowski, while a music-plus-video group viewed the corresponding excerpt from *Fantasia*. The other music-only group heard an excerpt conducted by Bernstein, and a music-plus-video group saw Bernstein conducting a performance with an orchestra. All participants (N = 128) completed the same cognitive, affective, and open-ended assessments. The highest cognitive scores came from the group watching the conductor conducting an orchestra, and the lowest scores came from the animated video from *Fantasia*. The ratings for the first movement were higher than for the fourth movement despite treatment group, possibly indicating discriminations made for musical reasons rather than treatment. The authors report that while the results of both studies showed significant differences, the affective and cognitive differences were neither strong nor clear. The kind of visual information contained in a video may make a difference as far as increasing attentiveness and enhancing learning through providing additional visual information (e.g., allowing the listener to match an instrument with the sound being heard, as in the Bernstein video). As there is so much variability in the quality of and information contained in different videos, much more systematic research needs to be done.

Moving to pre-K children, Cassidy and Geringer (1999) studied the effect of video on music listening for 55 4-, 5-, and 6-year-olds. The children were divided into two groups: 4-year-olds in one and 5- and 6-year-olds in the other. The opening excerpt from Disney's *Lion King* and an excerpt from *Sorcerer's Apprentice* (*Fantasia*) were used in the music-only or music-plus-video format, similar to the previous studies. Each group listened and watched in a session. A child could control how long to listen or watch through a button on a controller (in reality, activated by an observer). According to the researchers, there was a significant difference in listening time, independent of order, with music-plus-video being the longest. Response condition led to significant differences at the .01 level. There were significantly more music-related responses for the music-only condition, and significantly more visually related responses for the music-plus-video condition were found. Overall, younger children provided more visually related responses, while older children provided more music-related responses. Again, more study needs to be done before broader conclusions can be drawn.

A thoughtful, comprehensive review of research examining the presentation of music experiences live, audiovisually, or aurally was conducted by Finnäs (2001). It is a recommended study. His focus was on the differences these presentations might make for listeners. He concluded that although there are studies that indicated that live music has positive effects, not enough systematic research has been done to compare live versus video versus aural. Audio and audio with video have yielded mixed results so far. Finnäs calls for more well-controlled studies based on musicopsychological principles, instead of using more visual artistic principles, as in some past studies.

Effects of Instruction in Music Appreciation   Every year, thousands of college students across the United States enroll in various iterations of a music appreciation course. What is the effect of such a course? How can this be measured in a meaningful way? Ellis (1999) decided to employ concurrent verbal reports with 30 university students enrolled in a music appreciation course to explore these questions. In pretesting before the course, the students heard 16 recorded musical excerpts and were encouraged to think aloud about what they were hearing. During the course, students were encouraged to verbalize their responses to music through various class activities. After the course was completed, the pretest materials served as the posttest, and students again provided concurrent verbal reports. Ellis used Bundra's (1994) categories for analysis of the precourse and postcourse verbal reports and found that before the course, there were more affective, associative, judgmental, and miscellaneous references. After the course, there were more musical observations. Ellis wondered whether this movement toward a more objective response to music, the traditional focus of music appreciation courses, truly moved students toward appreciating music more. We will address this point again in the third section of this chapter.

Self-Constructed Listening Experiences Presented through Problem Solving

The studies presented so far in this section are linked by the teacher-researcher directly guiding and/or shaping the listening experience in some way. Another way to facilitate listening experiences is to set up encounters for students with musical listening problems and allow them to work their way through them on their own, creating self-constructed solutions with the teacher either standing aside or acting in the role of facilitator rather than director. Is a self-constructed musical experience different for a child than a teacher-directed one? Are different aspects of musical experience engaged?

Cooperative Listening Groups   Smialek and Bobourka (2006) examined the effect on critical listening skills of using cooperative listening exercises in college music appreciation classes. Twelve sections of Introduction to Western Music were involved over a 4-year period, and 214 students participated in the study. These authors cast the study in terms of activities rather than problem solving. Classes designated as Group 1 received a traditional lecture experience. Classes designated as Group 2 engaged in cooperative learning sessions, where their problem was to listen to 20- to 30-second excerpts and identify the musical characteristics under study. Classes designated as Group 3 engaged in the same problem as Group 2 and then were given an additional problem with more complexity: they participated in five additional class periods where they cooperatively listened to and analyzed whole pieces for style (in the other classes, this information was presented via lecture). The exam for all groups consisted of 45- to 90-second excerpts, heard twice. The subjects were asked to identify musical characteristics and determine musical style. Group 3 scored significantly higher than the other two groups ($p <.01$). The authors concluded the difference was that Group 3 experienced cooperative learning on a more regular basis. It seems possible that the initial group problem involving short excerpts was mostly identification of musical elements, whereas the longer (40-minute) additional meetings for Group 3 related with style involved a more meaningful problem-solving opportunity. As a group, they listened, discussed, and made meaningful connections between the music and the concepts they were studying. Setting up a problem-solving situation with a higher potential for meaningful self-constructed learning was probably the difference in the significantly higher scores, not simply more group work on a regular basis.

Invented Notations and Mapping   Another type of self-constructed problem-solving music listening task is invented notations. Investigators have suggested that children's invented notations provide a concrete, visual means to investigate their musical thinking, that is, their inner musical representations, including aspects of rhythm, melody, and composition (e.g., Bamberger, 1982, 1991, 1994; Barrett, 1997, 2001, 2002, 2004; Davidson and Scripp, 1988). Research into music listening has employed invented notations as well, often using the term "musical maps" or "listening maps" to apply to subjects' creations. There are differences in what the terms mean here, too. With Kerchner (2000), for example, her maps included drawings, markings, words, graphs, and pictures; Blair's (2007) musical maps were more figural or iconic representations of what the children heard. It is helpful when publications allow researchers to publish samples of the invented notations or maps to clarify their studies.

Fung and Gromko (2001) combined invented notation and pieces from an unfamiliar culture in a problem-solving situation for 35 American children age 7 to 12. The children were divided into two groups, passive and active listeners. Both groups listened to the same two Korean pieces. The passive listeners sat quietly for the two listenings. The active listeners spontaneously moved with props for the first listening and, for the second, moved their hands through sand. Afterward, both groups were asked to draw "the way the music goes" (p. 128), resulting in invented notations. The maps were rated for evidence of four of five musical parameters: pitch, rhythm or beat, loudness, timbre, and grouping of notes or phrasing. There was a significant difference between groups at the .05 level: the active listening group referred to more of the music's rhythms, groupings, and beats and preferred the more rhythmically active Korean piece by nearly twice as much as the other group. The researchers inferred that this gives weight to the idea that the body is the source of a child's perception of music's patterns, movement, and nuance and that movement may be helpful in listening lessons for both attention and perception. In other words, the body may be helpful for children in self-constructing musical listening experiences, at least as far as the parameters the authors measured.

Blair (2008) documents the creation of musical maps by small groups of three to five fifth-grade students for Mussorgsky's "Ballet of the Unhatched Chicks" from *Pictures at an Exhibition.* She began by asking students to solve a music-listening problem using iconic puzzle cards with a map of the melodic contour for Kabalevsky's "March" from *The Comedians.* Next she provided students with movement experiences and following a musical map to have an idea of what they were to create. She then presented students their own problem to solve: create a musical map for "Ballet of the Unhatched Chicks." First, however, she prepared them with experiences to help them internalize the piece through singing and gesture, hoping to support the formation of their own musical ideas that would eventually become their visual maps. Through the use of videotape, microphones recording certain individual interactions, and written logs, Blair was able to follow the students' processes and interactions from the beginning, through several versions, to final copy and "performance" of their maps for others.

In reflecting on this mapping study, Blair (2008) refers to Bamberger's term *felt paths* (Bamberger, 1991, p. 10), internalized sequences of actions, such as when one performs a well-learned piece on an instrument. She extends this term to *felt pathways* in the case of music listening, saying she believes "that through tools like musical maps, students can form pathways of knowing and feeling while *listening* to music, in addition to paths that Bamberger describes that are formed when performing music" (p. 10). These are internally created pathways, the result of imaginative response of mind and body as one listens. The maps provide a concrete visual frame for reliving the listening experience, for further exploration of the experience, and for sharing the listening experience with others. Since the students all worked with the same piece, they were given an opportunity to view others' similar yet unique felt pathways when they shared their musical maps in the "performances."

Blair (2007) further reflected on the creation of musical maps as a form of narrative inquiry. She observed parallels between the process of narrative inquiry and the small-group musical-mapping assignment she gave these same fifth-grade students:

> Their conversation with the materials of music and map, with each other as collaborators, and later with the class as audience parallels the process of narrative inquiry as the students experienced the music, constructed their story, and shared their story of the musical experience. Like narrative, the process of creating a musical map serves as a form of inquiry, enabling understanding of an experience, and affecting change in self through the living and constructing of the story and affecting change in other[s] through the sharing and telling of the story. (p. 1)

It is understandable that Blair provided support activities for the mapping activity at this age. It would be interesting to see if students needed the same kind of preexploratory activities for the next piece. Also, group dynamics are very different from individual musical experience. Allowing choice in a future mapping opportunity, whether to work alone or in a group, might also provide interesting insights. It is obvious, however, that these children, when given the opportunity, were very capable of creating a meaningful self-constructed music-listening experience. Whether a teacher-directed listening experience (which would have taken much less class time) with the same piece would have the same effect on facilitating listening would be an interesting study.

Kerchner (2009) used an intrinsic case study (Stake, 1995) to follow her experience as she introduced mapping as a part of teaching an intact middle school general music class (grades 6–8) made up of 45 mostly at-risk and a few gifted students not interested in participating in music ensembles. She documented the process of the students' first experience following another's map, being drawn into reworking parts of that map to make it look right, and eventually buying into a project of taking on a piece and finding a way to map it on their own or in small groups. The presentation day became a big event in their lives, both musically and socially. Kerchner states: "I wondered how many times in their schooling these adolescents would encounter situations that invited creative problem-solving, in which their unique solutions would be accepted and celebrated because they were meaningful to *them*, instead of fitting a construct imposed by a teacher" (p. 195, emphasis in the original). She makes the connection with Vygotsky (1978) that learning is internalized through a contextualized process involving past and present experiences, cultural artifacts, and interaction with peers and adults. This study makes a strong case for self-constructed listening experiences in the school and for using problem-solving tasks such as mapping to give students control over the outcome of a music-listening learning task. Particularly compelling is the success she finds with the type of student who does not typically respond to the traditional model of general music or ensemble curriculum.

Working with students in a college music-listening course, I asked 29 non-music majors to create their own individual listening maps (Dunn, 1997). Students were introduced to a listening map (Mozart's *Symphony No. 41*,

Mvt. 3) and then asked to map the opening notes of Mozart's *Eine Kleine Nachmusik*, Mvt. 2, and share the results with the group. Finally, they were given access to a recording of the first minute and 40 seconds of Delibe's "Waltz" from *Coppelia*, a piece unfamiliar to them. They took it home over a weekend and brought their maps back to share with the class the following week. They reflected, in writing, on creating their maps, traced their maps for the group as the music played, then reflected on watching others' maps. Finally, they were asked to trace several maps of peers while the music played and to reflect a final time. Their maps and verbal reports were analyzed for evidence of a creative listening process (addressed in the third section of this chapter). The maps appeared to be a successful vehicle for making an abstract listening experience concrete. Said one student, "It wasn't very hard to see that what I had on paper looked like what I was hearing" (p. 53). Several comments indicated students were thinking in sound as they worked to transform their listening experience into a visual representation.

In a follow-up study (Dunn, 2004), a student in the class who was a musician with years of training, responded to the assignment with this comment:

> As a musician, this was a very different experience for me as I am used to things mostly in technical or Italian terms. This forced me to think about the piece aside from its meter, instrumentation, etc. At first, it was hard to express what I heard in lines and squiggles which weren't notes and rests, but it became easier the more I worked on it and I am pleased with the end product. (student transcript)

This brings to mind Kirnarskaya and Winner's (1997) work with the expressive versus the analytic ear and the effect that music training may have on music listening. Mapping might be one problem-solving approach that can facilitate development of the expressive ear.

Problem Solving with Movement   When Cohen (1997) was faced with a class of "exceptionally energetic (i.e., 'wild') fourth graders" (p. 1) and a teacher who would not allow her to have the children move around the room, she devised what she called "musical mirrors" to explore inner representations of musical schemas. She used choreographed hand gestures as kinesthetic analogues of what one perceives in the music. She began having students mirror her movements as they listened to a piece of music, a sort of moving listening map, teaching them a movement vocabulary that they would use in creating their own mirrors later on. As with visual maps, Cohen found children's original mirrors offer insight into their cognition. She notes that "no 'correct' gesture is ever forgotten. The only movement gestures forgotten were ones about which they were unsure or were convinced that 'that is not it' but could not find a better alternative" (p. 3). In reading the description of suggested possible movements for a Haydn sonata, the level of creativeness desirable in the forming of a musical mirror is not clear; it appears that solutions are described in terms of "satisfying" or "less successful," dependent on the degree to which they match more specific cognitive aspects of the piece.

Creating Soundtracks for Film Clips   In an interesting study, Greher (2002) undertook the task of developing technology for the classroom and conducting a case study of its creation, implementation, and evaluation. Her purpose for the technology was to involve students in music listening through the gateway of a multimedia program she created that allowed students to interactively become involved in a number of problem-solving listening exercises, reacting to and creating soundtracks for film clips. While the program development itself was a major factor, also of importance was the exploration of the interactions of the students from three inner-city sixth- to eighth-grade classes (N = 16, 24, and 22) as they worked with the software. Putting music to film clips was seen as a real-world activity to which students could relate. "Having students experiment with putting music and sound effects against film to see how different moods, rhythms, and melodies affect the pacing and feel of a film, puts them at the center of their learning. Instead of telling them a list of facts, this program will be giving them a series of problems to solve that will allow them to uncover these facts through their own exploration" (p. 21). Despite working through a number of challenges, the results are compelling, as students moved from skepticism to being willing participants, engrossed in the project and passionate about what they were creating. Students became active listeners, engaged a variety of genres they may not have willingly listened to before, and did so in a supportive social environment. The technology was an important launching point, and this real-world, problem-solving group approach to music listening is worthy of emulation.

As seen in these studies, learners appear to respond well to music-listening problem-solving opportunities. Younger children may need appropriate support activities, but perhaps less teacher direction is needed than we suppose—there is great potential for further study. The quality of the problems we set for the students, of course, is paramount. Is there a sequence of such problems that would be most beneficial in the development of listening skills? Is there an optimal combination of teacher-directed and self-constructed learning experiences? Are there different types of learning that result from the two? These and many more questions remain to be answered.

The Effect of Performance Experience

Finally in this section, there is the question of whether performance experience facilitates music listening. There is only one large-scale review on this subject at this time. Kjelland and Kerchner (1998) reported a comprehensive review of the literature on the effects of music performance participation on the music-listening experience. This review represents a unique contribution, as it was undertaken as a group research project by faculty and doctoral students of the Center for the Study of Education and the Musical Experience (CSEME) at Northwestern University over a number of years. Sixty-six studies were identified for review. The studies were grouped into four categories by the effect of music performance on: physical being (e.g., the brain's hemispheric processing of music stimuli), disposition (e.g., taste, preference, attitude, or motivation), perception (discrimination, conservation, and focus of attention), and responses (affect, cognitive response, and critical thinking). Most of the studies fell into the perception category, especially into a discrimination subcategory. The following conclusions are pertinent. Having participated in school music ensembles may motivate graduates to seek out further musical experiences, including music listening. Musically trained students (MTS) performed better on most discrimination, identification, and recognition tasks; however, the ability to identify intervals did not transfer to recognition of contour for the musically trained student, suggesting "the latter involves a more holistic mode of processing" (p. 20). According to this review, MTS appeared to have superior tonal memory, developed different listening strategies, and seemed to have multiple means of retaining and processing music when compared with musically untrained subjects. It appears that the development of children's listening skills and sensitivity is benefited by early performance training; that performance training has a positive effect on listening experiences regardless of gender, age, or socioeconomic status; and that performance experience aids in forming mental representations of sound—the product of the music-listening experience. The report concluded with reservations about making strong, direct connections about the effects of performance on music listening. It also provided recommendations for future research to clarify the issues identified.

Music Teachers and Music Listening

To bring this section to a close, it is fitting to examine evidence of music teachers' attitudes toward music listening in their classrooms. Music listening, at least in our present Western culture, is the primary way most people interact with music in their daily lives. It would follow that enhancing children's ability to listen to music would be a major part of school music programs. While this may be so in a given program, I was unable to find supporting research for this. As a part of her study of elementary music teachers' beliefs and practices in teaching music listening, Cusano (2005) reviewed studies from 1979 to 2002 to compare the percentage of time devoted to music listening in lessons. The time ranged from 1 to 14 percent. In her own nationwide sample of 110 elementary music teachers, she found teachers devoted an average of 5 to 10 minutes of listening in two lessons each month, with shorter listening lessons in the younger grades and longer lessons in grades three to six. These teachers believed strongly that listening to music developed aesthetic sensitivity, but their reasons for selecting pieces for study in teaching were not based on the aesthetic aspects of pieces; instead, they were chosen based on whether they illustrated concepts to be learned in the curriculum. They preferred using classical or jazz music, felt least confident about using non-Western music, yet felt strongly about the value of broadening cultural awareness.

Although we are concerned about facilitating music listening for our students, it appears that little time is given in the classroom for activities that directly address music listening. This may be due to a philosophical stance that learning through doing will result in better listening skills. However, it is not clear that we can move children through our curriculum, confident that such connections have been made.

Summary

Children of all ages appear able to engage in musical-listening tasks. Preschool is not too early to begin building discrimination skills and music vocabulary. However, take care to be sure that the learning tasks are developmentally appropriate, although much more work needs to be done in this area. Individual differences in learning make this a difficult task, as not all children learn at the same rate or in the same way. For example, presenting listening experiences through multisensory lessons is a valuable teaching tool, but it is not equally valuable to every child; in fact, a given presentation mode may be a hindrance for a particular child rather than an aid to learning. As most children appear to learn equally well in most presentation modes, perhaps priority should be given to identifying children who struggle in a given mode (e.g., when movement is added). The teacher can observe whether they learn better in another mode and be sure they also receive instruction in that mode for new learning. Such individual differences may be discovered only through examination of data at the individual level. Researchers should be encouraged to examine data from individual as well as group levels to be certain that every child is represented and served by what we learn.

Music in the background may build a person's mental musical library more than we suppose. It was found that, with a little planning and instruction, incidental music could facilitate children's ability to learn style discrimination as early as kindergarten (Lineburgh, 1994). In the same study, it was found that playing a variety of pieces of the same style, again heard in the background, was more effective than playing the same representative piece repeatedly for conceptual learning. There were times that the music required a greater level of focus in the study (e.g., in the lining-up activity), but this research showed important implications regarding the impact of incidental music on casual listeners.

Other ways to facilitate listening experiences were found to increase perception of and response to music. For example, the body was used as a means to respond to and make sense of musical sound, such as moving one's hands through sand to music or creating musical mirrors of music in one's hands. Verbal and written responses to music were used to explore different kinds of perceptions and reactions to musical experiences. Individual efforts and cooperative groups were employed. Comparisons of music with video, live performances, and audio-only were made, with mixed results. Invented notations and maps were used with interesting results. Problem-solving approaches were employed, using varying levels of higher order thinking. Problems with more intrinsic interest or relevance appear to capture students' efforts and imaginations more effectively and perhaps have a longer lasting effect.

These studies have shown that it is possible to facilitate the listening process, either through teacher-directed or self-constructed problem-solving opportunities set up by the teacher. Performing opportunities apparently may have an effect as well. When taken with what we have learned from the studies about how individuals listen to music when teachers are not involved, do we have enough to fully understand the process? We are making progress, but in my opinion, we do not yet have enough data or enough studies to make definitive conclusions. In many ways, we have opened up interesting questions ripe for further research and corroboration.

Section III: The Listening Process

We have summarized some of the more recent research shedding light on how people interact with music as they listen and how they engage with music in everyday life. We have seen ways researchers have investigated to facilitate music listening from widely varying approaches. It seems appropriate to look more closely at the listening process itself for further possible insights. This section is more speculative in nature. I present ideas regarding the listening process, implications from this review, and some questions for the future. We begin by examining the role of creativity in this process.

Is Listening to Music a Creative Act?

If music teachers were asked what kinds of musical activities are creative, most would probably respond that composing and improvisation are creative activities. Some might include performance. Few, perhaps, would think of listening to music as a creative act. Yet there are those who have been proponents of this view for some time. Blacking (1973) stated that "the importance of creative listening is too often ignored in discussions of musical ability, and yet it is as fundamental to music as it is to language" (p. 10). Mursell (1943) said: "Listening should by no means be considered mere passive reception—not even when the main consideration is the evocation of a mood. The successful listener enters into the music, possesses it, is possessed by it, and so is inspired and enabled to make it for himself" (p. 170). Reimer (1989) suggested that learning to be a creative listener was fundamental in a music education program: "Since the major interaction most people have with music is as listeners, the task of helping them become creative in this most fundamental of musical behaviors is perhaps the most important of all education" (Reimer, 1989, pp. 70–71).

Webster (1987) included music listening in his model of creative thinking, placing it under the category of analysis. Webster argued that there must be a product from any truly creative act. In the case of creative listening, the product is a new "mental form" (p. 162), a unique mental representation of the musical listening experience created by the listener. This creative mental process is described by Bamberger (1991) in this way:

> a hearing is a performance; that is, what the hearer seems simply to find in the music is actually a process of perceptual problem solving—an active process of sense making...[it is] both creative and responsive—a conversation back and forth between the music, as material, and the hearer as he or she shapes its meaning and form in some particular way. (pp. 8–9)

Peterson (2002, 2006) examined the creative dimension of the music-listening experience in depth by studying three bodies of literature: cognition (perception as a form of making), music philosophy (identifying the product of that perception/making as music), and creativity (criteria for judging its creativeness). Her theory of creative listening sees it as music making in its own right, drawing a parallel with the creative processes involved in composition:

> The *thinking in* and *with* sound is the music making carried out by listeners, just as the *thinking in* and *with* sound that generates a composition is the music making carried out by composers....The product of listening is also potentially novel and valuable to the listener and may have varying degrees of impact on the listener's subsequent musical thinking. (Peterson, 2006, p. 18, emphasis added)

Peterson uses an analogy to illustrate her point. A traveler on a journey with a tour guide can be compared with the listener on a journey led by a composer. The tourist-listener's contribution is creating his own experience of that journey, how and where attention is paid, noticing broad vistas or minute details, pausing to ponder, and looking ahead or behind.

There has been little empirical research into creative thinking and music listening (Hickey, 2002; Webster, 1992). Two early studies addressed the topic in different ways. Pfeil (1972) combined creative activities involving improvisation, composition, and imagination with music listening in a college music appreciation course. One activity encouraged "thinking in sound" by imagining how a graphic score would sound with specific instruments playing each of the three lines, listing as many things as they could that they did not like about it based on their imagined listening, and then writing a new piece working around those weaknesses. Feinberg (1973) used music listening as a springboard for creative-thinking activities (e.g., make up as many questions as you can about what you heard after listening to this piece) or for critical-thinking tasks (e.g., checking off musical elements perceived while listening). While the former study encourages thinking in sound, the latter seems further removed from the active link between music listening and creating a new mental form through creative thinking.

My desire to explore the notion of creative listening through making mental forms visible first led me to have students create visual listening maps to represent their music-listening experiences (Dunn, 1997; see the second section of this chapter). Students (1) reflected in writing about creating their maps, (2) traced their maps for the group as the music played, (3) reflected about watching others' maps, (4) traced several peers' maps while the music played, and (5) reflected about tracing their peers' maps. Their maps and verbal reports were analyzed for evidence of a creative listening process. The verbal reports confirmed that the figural maps were the result of active, cognitive interactions with the music. While there were occasional commonalities in the maps, each was unique, and the differences were numerous, indicating the impact an individual had on a music-listening experience and how the music was represented mentally and visually (e.g., "It's amazing how many different things people can hear in the same song...they were not any better or worse than mine—they just heard things different"; "In my head I was saying 'why didn't I think of that before' or 'that doesn't go at all' "). Several comments indicated students were thinking in sound as they worked to transform their listening experience into a visual representation. To some degree, it appeared that the figural maps successfully captured aspects of the holistic mental representations formed in the minds of the listeners.

Is listening to music a creative act? I would argue that there is certainly a strong aspect of individual creativity that is involved. As my own thinking evolved, I subsumed the creative aspects of music listening in what I now view as the intuitive listening process (see Dunn, 2006).

Intuitive Music Listening

Juslin and Laukka (2004) stressed the importance of coming to understand the "ordinary listener." It may be that the ordinary listener is an intuitive listener. As we have seen, a child's music-listening life begins before birth (Lacanuet, 1996), blossoms in a mother's arms (Trehub and Nakata, 2001–2002), and branches out from there. The studies of music in everyday life (e.g., Behne, 1997; North et al., 2000) show us that people engage with music without the aid of formal musical training nearly every day of their lives in some way that is meaningful to them within their own social and cultural context that is a part of natural, intuitive, human experience. Intuitive musical knowing (Bamberger, 1978; Theiss, 1990) is a result of intuitive music listening and experiencing.

What is intuitive music listening? I define it as an active, innate, human process by which we meaningfully engage music through listening that enables us to create mental representations of the music, the creative "product" of intuitive listening. Such representations create a holistic framework that becomes our vehicle for remembering, making sense of, and finding meaning in a given listening experience. In repeated listenings, this mental representation allows us to recognize the piece; to recall objective, subjective, imaginative, and emotional information about it; and to make adjustments and additions to the framework with each new encounter. It involves an individual's unique cognitive and affective responses to music that extend beyond the listener's technical understanding of the music. It is intuitive because no formal instruction is necessary for this to occur as far as we know, at least in healthy individuals. As with Behne's (1997) *Musikerleben,* focus of attention to some degree in some aspect must be present for the intuitive listening process to occur.

What might the intuitive music-listening process look like? Let me suggest a model for discussion that may provide insight into how this may occur (see figure 1.1).

In the Model of the Intuitive Listening Process, the listening experience begins with the *listener* and is filtered through *past experiences,* including

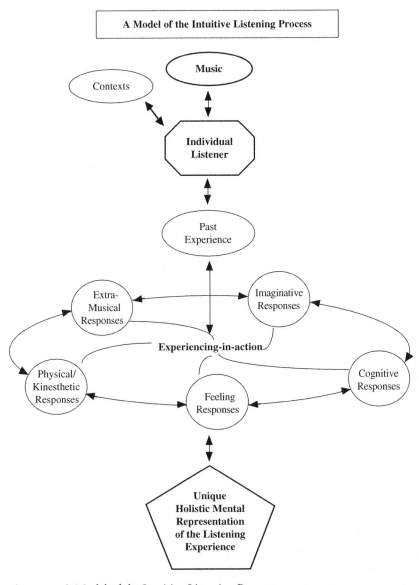

Figure 1.1 A Model of the Intuitive Listening Process.

beliefs and attitudes (cf. Woody and Burns, 2001). The listener's well-being and mood state has a primary impact, especially on focus. Two external factors precede the intuitive listening experience. First, the specific *context* of the listening experience may have a small or profound effect (e.g., social factors, cultural factors, physical surroundings, time of day, events preceding or following) and may include motivational factors (e.g., listening for an assignment, listening to figure out a lead guitar part for a garage band, or listening for mood regulation). Second, the *music* itself is an external factor, the result of the interaction between the specific musicians and the music (the musicians' particular take on the music, their skill level, incidental things that may happen during that performance such as a particularly great musical moment or an unanticipated misstep). The contexts, music, and past experiences combine with the following five types of responses: *extramusical responses* (associations that are not music related can attach themselves to the music, e.g., "they're playing our song"); *imaginative responses* (more than passively experiencing the music, the person cocreates the experience along with the performers, making it come to life for herself or himself); *cognitive responses* (formal or factual noticing and responding to specific or overall aspects of or about the music); *feeling responses* (affect or feeling is aroused, created, remembered); and *physical/kinesthetic responses* (the body responds to the music through outward motion, internal physiological response, or imagined or remembered kinesthetic motion). These different types of responses were documented in verbal reports of students of different ages in several studies (e.g., Bundra, 1994; Dunn, 2008; Ellis, 1999; Rodriguez and Webster, 1997).

All of these factors come together in the listening experience through *experiencing-in-action*, a constant flux of experiencing during the event where we also interact with expectations of what may come and with what does come and does not come as the music unfolds over time. The model in figure 1.1 shows the interrelatedness of this holistic experience, with arrows going in all directions for all the factors. The unlimited possibilities for interaction of the different factors suggest a possible explanation for the uniqueness of every listening experience, even for a piece one has heard multiple times from the same recording. The resulting *inner mental representation* is embodied with meaning, as known by the listener, and forms the basis for reflection, remembering, and differentiating listening experiences. As one ages and encounters new experiences, it is assumed that developmental growth occurs in all aspects of the model, although this remains to be demonstrated.

The question of musical meaning is too complex to be treated in this chapter (cf. Almén and Pearsall, 2006), but one possible view is that for musical meaning to occur, there must be enough focus of attention for the mental representation to gain some clarity and definition. Contrary to formal listening, however, the focus of attention may be minimal, as when music is playing in the background while a person is doing something else. If the listener is still engaged with the music in a way that a mental representation is being created, if their mental musical library is being expanded, the intuitive listening process is still engaged, even though it may be at a minimal level (Lineburgh, 1994). If a person is listening to the music but responding mostly by reminiscing about the last time she heard "our song," the process is still engaged. The same would be true of someone working in the yard while listening and taking two sticks and beating rhythms on trash cans to the music. Putting on music to evoke a mood for a relaxing evening after a tense day is engaging in the process. In a car full of teens talking over the blaring radio, someone may say, "Turn it up, this is my favorite part!" even though it seemed no one was paying attention. If asked, it's possible that none of these people could tell you anything about the instrumentation or meter or form, yet they are still engaged in ways that are personally meaningful that allow them to recognize the music when they hear it again, and they are quite possibly adding response information to their holistic mental representations. It is likely that there are moments when they are not noticing the music at all; in such a case, it is possible the process is mute.

It is how we interact with all these aspects of the musical experience that makes it special to us. It is more than just notes on a page. It is more than just sounds in the air. It is context, musicians, the listener, past experience, and experiencing-in-action that have made it a part of every human culture in recorded history and personally important to us today.

When we teach formalized listening, the listener is no longer in charge of making all the decisions, or at least as many, so the possible responses become somewhat limited as well. As we saw earlier, children preferred listening to music at home over school because they were able to exercise choice (Boal-Palheiros and Hargreaves, 2001). When adults were able to make choices over the music they heard, they were more alert, positive, and focused (Sloboda et al., 2001). Formalized listening takes the listener out of the central role and puts someone else in charge—listening becomes teacher directed.

In thinking about the typical kinds of teacher-directed listening experiences in schools and colleges, for both general and music students, when contrasted with the intuitive listening model, what changes? For discussion, and in very simplistic terms, it appears that the focus of such formal listening would fall under cognitive responses: spending most of the listening time and energy in having students looking for, identifying, and responding to things about the elemental, formal, and factual aspects of the music (see figure 1.2). The cognitive responses are experienced through teacher-directed activities and experiences. The focus is solely on the analytic, factual responses to the music. In so doing, what may often occur is a separation of the other aspects of the intuitive listening experience, perhaps a consideration of the "parts," or of one "part," to the extent that one never really gets back to the "whole" of musical experience while in the classroom. Inherent, too, may be a devaluing of these other responses involved in the intuitive music listening experience. Perhaps it is here that school music and life music begin to diverge. If school music becomes this one-dimensional, it is not only about formal learning; it is also about loss—of the aspect of choice, of music one can relate to, of the musical experience as one knows how to relate with it and loves it.

Certainly, teacher-directed learning has been the model for music teaching for hundreds of years and has been fundamental to music education in the schools. Much effective teaching and learning can and does take place in the teacher-directed model. However, it is incumbent on educators to be reflective about practice and to focus on the most important outcome: what is best

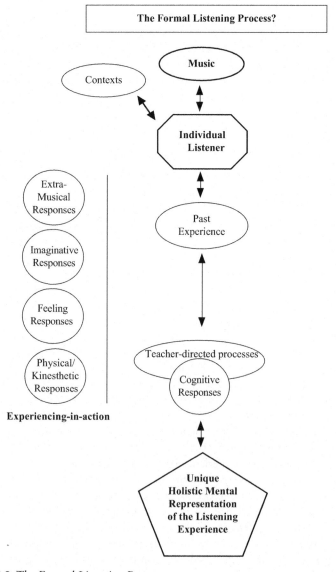

Figure 1.2 The Formal Listening Process.

for enhancing our students' lifelong ability to meaningfully engage with music independently, in this case, with music listening? Teacher-directed learning is an important component, but should only teacher-directed learning be involved? Probably not.

In our quest to promote formalized learning in school, we may cause children to lose touch with their intuitive musical sense. Bamberger (1982) observed that as students gained in their ability to read and write music, they lost their intuitive figural sense of rhythm, what she termed the "wipe-out" phenomenon. Perhaps many of us have experienced this with lessons on instruments or voice study, where striving for better technique or tone leads to a loss of sense of musicality, hopefully only temporarily. In listening to music, perhaps this wipe-out phenomenon is a factor as well. In a music theory course, this could easily happen. After a year-long course, being taught and tested for perceptual and analytical listening could cause one to miss the "music" outside class as well, for example.

It was after I had just taught a formal listening, teacher-directed lesson in middle school general music that I heard a boy remark as he left my room: "I thought I was good at listening to music. I guess I'm not." Contrary to my perception that I had done a great job of inspiring him to greater listening heights, I instead had presented the listening experience in such a way as to undermine his confidence in his ability to interact with his own life music. This experience propelled me into a lifelong interest in music listening (Dunn, 2006). As Woody (2004) has said, expression and emotion are a vital part of the experience of music. Our teaching in school should enhance students' lifelong abilities to respond to the full range of intuitive music-listening experience, not ignore important parts of it.

Two Types of Listening

To sum up this part on the listening process, perhaps we can contrast two types of listening, intuitive and formal, by placing them on a continuum (see figure 1.3). The listening life of the intuitive listener, as we have seen, begins certainly from birth (Trehub and Nakata, 2001–2002), and probably before (Lacanuet, 1996). They are immediately beginning listeners, with the intuitive musical listening process engaged as they come to know their life music. By the time they enter preschool or kindergarten, might they be called experienced listeners? Not fully developed, no, but they are experienced in certain aspects of their musical lives, and they are fully engaged in a lifelong development of intuitive musical knowing (Bamberger, 1978). We need to acknowledge that children have musical lives outside school (hopefully rich ones) and that some teens may be experienced listeners, sometimes even highly experienced listeners who may have more sophisticated ears than some adults with formal training. As not all may become highly experienced listeners (something that would require real focus and energy), I have placed that term in brackets. Victorio (Williamson, 2005), the young man in middle

Figure 1.3 Intuitive Listening Continuum.

school cited earlier with such a vast knowledge of Nirvana and an ability to perform complex guitar licks, would be an example of a highly experienced listener. For intuitive listening, this can happen without formal training. Beyond the early years of childhood, the presence of a boundary for when one can become an experienced listener is not clear.

A major factor in becoming an experienced listener, especially in becoming a highly experienced listener, is focus. For a mental representation of the music listening experience to be created, a degree of focus must be present. It seems logical that with a greater degree of focus on the listening experience, there will be more clarity and depth to the experience, giving more clarity and definition to the mental representation of the experience and making possible more connections with other such experiences.

This brings up the question of the difference between hearing and listening. There is evidence all around us of children and adults who are seldom without an iPod playing in their ears, music playing on their computers, or some other source of music. As worthy as this appears, does this indicate that the intuitive listening process is engaged? In the examination of music in everyday life, one of the common uses of music was as a background to other activities (e.g., North et al., 2004; Sloboda et al., 2001). When music is used, for example, to help one concentrate on a task such as studying, it is likely that the person is hearing rather than listening, using music more as sonic wallpaper (North et al., 2004). The same would be true of any activity where the mind is focused on things other than the music and responding to it. Perhaps there may be moments when one's attention is focused on the music for a time, but when the attention is no longer connected to the music, the intuitive listening process is probably interrupted. However, it may be possible that perception of the music continues at some background level, there is still some kind of intuitive response taking place, and the inner representation may continue to gather some information (Lineburgh, 1994). Behne's (1997) *Musikerleben* was described as operating with varying degrees of attention and intensity. Is it a line that is crossed (hearing or listening) or a matter of degree like a continuum? More opportunities for study lie here.

On the continuum for formal listening, unless one is a gifted prodigy, it is unlikely that a child would become a beginning listener in a formal way until formal instruction begins. Because of the length of time that it takes to begin to perceive specific individual elements (beat, rhythm, melody, pitch, meter, dynamics, form, etc.), it may take quite some time to be able to hear elements combining (e.g., Sims's 1991 study of decentration) or hear them from a large-scale viewpoint. Cutietta (1985, 1993) and Taetle and Cutietta's (2002) work suggests that the traditional musical element approach, common to many music curricula, is counter to the way the mind intuitively engages music. According to Cutietta, a sounder approach would be nonelemental, beginning in helping children make holistic categorizations based in musical moods or styles. The traditional focus on the perceptual and analytical aspects of music listening perhaps may lead to the wipe-out phenomenon, as the intuitive experiencing of the music is lost to seeking formal understanding, hopefully only for a short time. In formal listening, veryone is a beginning listener at some point. The brackets in figure 1.3 indicate that unless some training occurs, a person is unlikely to move toward becoming a capable formal listener. When one thinks about it, few become experienced listeners in formal listening, and even fewer become highly experienced in this kind of listening. This is cause to wonder why this is the case and whether something can be done to change it.

Is it necessary that the two ways of listening be so different? Is there no way to bridge the gap or build on the intuitive listening process to bring formal understanding? In addition to teacher-directed activities, is part of the solution to give students some choice? Or finding ways to address the other areas in the model, as well as the cognitive responses? These are areas worth discussing and worthy of systematic study.

From studies in this chapter, it would appear that providing aspects of self-constructed learning experiences presented through problem-solving opportunities designed by the teacher are valuable. Smialek and Bobourka's (2006) cooperative learning Group 3 simply spent a few additional class periods listening to whole pieces, working together to figure out stylistic aspects for themselves rather than participating in traditional lectures to learn the material—and performed better on the assessment than the other groups. On a more holistic level, various researchers (Blair 2008; Dunn, 1997; Fung and Gromko, 2001; Kerchner, 2009) asked students to listen to the music and create visual maps of how the music sounded to them, sometimes requiring hours of self-guided and self-imposed direct engagement with the music to make the map look just right. Greher's (2002) middle school students may have been reluctant to participate in a traditional music class, but they eventually became fully invested participants in creating sound tracks to movie clips, a real-world task to which they could relate.

These are certainly only scratching the surface of the possibilities of what may be happening in schools or what we might imagine. In addition, there are many ways we can improve traditional teacher-directed learning experiences as well, perhaps incorporating more aspects of problem-solving and/or self-constructed learning. Two other ideas merit further thought: listening literacy and the role of roles.

Listening Literacy

An idea that may help us bridge the gap between life music and school music is an expanded idea of music literacy. Borrowing from the world of literacy, Broomhead (2008) has applied the concept of multiliteracies (Cope and Kalantzis, 2000) to music education. In the expanded view of multiliteracies, literacy is no longer limited to drawing meaning from written texts. Texts are understood to be multimodal representations of meaning, such as visual, aural, gestural/kinesthetic, tactile, oral, and spatial sources. For example, to understand an event in history, texts might include a personal history, photographs, memorabilia, visiting where it took place, films, a visit from a participant, and writing about the experience.

Using this approach, Broomhead similarly expands the notion of music literacy beyond the ability to decode notes and rhythms from a traditional music notation text. He defines music literacy as the ability to act appropriately with and make meaning from a variety of musical texts. In this view, a musical text can be anything that a creator has intentionally embodied with meaning, including, but not limited to, musical scores, a conductor's movements, an instrument, a performance, and even listening to a recording. He proposes four types of music literacies: performing, thinking about, creating, and listening.

Music istening literacy, according to Broomhead, is "the ability to negotiate listening-oriented texts such as live performances, recordings on CD, radio and other media, and fellow ensemble members" (p. 1). Some of the listening literacies that can be taught include those we would expect: the ability to match sounds with symbols, recognizing form and patterns, and recognizing instruments. Some are more unexpected: being open to new sounds, connecting music with our inner life, connecting our personal experience to those of others through music, and feeling comfort through music. He believes that a comprehensive list is probably not possible; once a text is chosen, the literacies within that text may be identified and explored.

The idea of music literacy in this expanded view of interpreting texts has some interesting implications. Exploring the topic of being open to new sounds, connecting music to our inner life as a literacy to be explored in the classroom, for example, might be an avenue worth exploring as one way to address more aspects of the intuitive listening model as well as a way to connect with students' life music experiences.

The Role of Roles

One aspect addressed earlier was the effect of performance on the listening experience. Let's change the question a little: what is the effect on the listener if you are a performer? Reimer (2003) proposed that different roles in music required interrelated and varied aspects of intelligence: composing, performing, improvising, listening, music theory, musicology, and music teaching.

It seems useful to apply the idea of roles to the listener and wonder if there is any effect on the listening experience when the role is changed. In the intuitive music listening model in Figure 1.1, what if the listener were a performer? We have seen some of the effects in Kjelland and Kerchner (1998). Does one listen differently as an ensemble conductor? Does that have an effect on your listening experience? Would that be something worthwhile to develop in our students? How would one do that?

Bauer (2008) used an ensemble critique form modeled on one developed by the *Arts Propel* project (Winner, Davidson, and Scripp, 1992) to put students in the role of thinking and listening as an ensemble director. The main focus of the study was the effect of the use of the critique form and associated teaching process might have on students' metacognitive skills. Over a 6-week period, 106 middle school band students participated in the study. The first week, the students were introduced to the form by the regular classroom teacher, and the musical vocabulary students were to use on the form was discussed, including rhythm, intonation, phrasing, and dynamics. These latter elements are a few of the things a conductor might reasonably listen for. That day, and once for each of the next five weeks, one of the group's pieces would be recorded in an in-class performance for 1 to 2 minutes. Students used the ensemble critique form as they listened to the performance and indicated their specific perceptions of their own and their section's performance. The form also asked for recommendations for practice to improve performance in the specific spots identified. Then they listened again, focusing on the entire ensemble's performance, and filled in the sheet for the group. A group discussion followed, led by the students, where they shared their observations and suggested strategies for improvement. Among the results of the study, Bauer reported that there appeared to be a significant improvement in students' ability to diagnose performance problems and recommend strategies to solve them, student practice time increased significantly, and there were significant differences in posttest items showing increased knowledge about what and how to practice. This is an example of involving students in self-constructed learning through problem-solving opportunities that have potential for meaningful long-term learning. Putting students into the role normally held by the teacher may have a long-term impact.

Obviously, a high-level conductor does much more than find and correct simple errors; this is a possible starting point, a way to begin a dialogue and future experiences that address what a truly fine conductor does as she listens and shapes a wonderful musical performance. Another approach might be to buy two scores for each piece, and each day, have one student sit by the director in an ensemble and simply follow along with the extra score. Would that make a long-term difference? Would a percussionist's listening experience be different than what she has heard since sixth-grade band? Would that be important? Of course, one hopes the director is providing a model worth listening to and watching.

What other roles to be explored might be important? Using Reimer's list, a composer, an improviser, a music theorist, a musicologist (perhaps an ethnomusicologist?), even a music teacher? Perhaps a record producer, an *American Idol* judge, a music critic? It seems likely that there is potential for exploration and study here as well.

Final Thoughts

Engaging in music in a way that is personally meaningful is a part of being human. A student comes into our classes with a complex musical listening life and may be considered an experienced listener, possibly a highly experienced listener, who is very musical. Is it necessary to be "musically trained"? This is a question we must ask ourselves. If so, what does that mean in a day when most students stop taking music classes after middle school and the ones who stay involved are in ensembles? Yet the studies reviewed here show that people are very engaged in their own life music outside school. How do we have an impact?

As children learn about music, they often learn to label it as well. When asked to choose between rock and classical as a teenager, the choice is obvious. But when asked to respond about a specific piece not given a label, that same teenager may respond positively to a given piece of classical music (cf, Gembris, 2002, p. 497). Children grow up hearing classical music in cartoons and continue to hear a diverse range of music in movie sound tracks that they like and listen to, including pieces that might be labeled classical. There are several classical pieces that have been in movies, commercials, and pop songs that are very popular (Howard, 2008). Perhaps labels are dated, and individual pieces should be emphasized more in teaching. Hargreaves, Marshall, and North (2003) note that in this time of globalization and the Internet, people have nearly instant access to and unlimited choice of any kind of music in many different venues, and they make up their own minds; determining what is "serious" music and what is "popular" music is less important or meaningful.

In view of the apparently small numbers of people who listen to classical music, one might expect to see a large proportion of other types of music used in listening studies. However, the majority of music continues to be classical instrumental music. Much more research needs to be done using a variety of non-classical music. Vocal music is often avoided because it distracts the attention of the listener "from the music." Yet much of what students listen to is vocal music; there must be ways to effectively teach and research music with lyrics as a part of a school curriculum that is more relevant to daily life.

Different approaches to secondary general music or college appreciation courses are a prime area for innovation, one where we may have a significant impact in bridging the cultural dissonance spoken of earlier, in addition to using music other than classical. How effective are teacher-directed listening courses? What are the most effective strategies for such a course? Or how might classical music be used in novel ways? For example, different listening strategies might be first experienced in class with a classical or jazz piece; then students might be asked to employ the same strategy on a piece from their own music libraries, no matter what style, and then share the results with the class; such an approach might be one step toward bridging the gulf between school music and life music. Courses for highly experienced listeners—or to help develop skills to become highly developed listeners— that are not based on the typical music training model could be developed and researched. Bringing students into direct contact with music-listening problem-solving activities rather than solely teacher-directed learning is an area where progress is being made, but more study and documentation need to be done and disseminated. What might a listening course focused on self-constructed learning look like? And we have yet to explore all the teaching and research possibilities technology has to offer in this arena as well.

Since the result of music listening is an inner mental representation of the music embodied with all its aspects, researchers are encouraged to continue to explore any avenue to provide further understanding. Particularly helpful are data that make these responses concrete. Verbal responses, invented notations and listening maps, and invented movement provide important, if imperfect, insights into the intuitive processes of music listening. Asking someone to represent their inner representation of what they hear in the music, in any form, is likely to have some effect on their listening experience. However, the possible insights to be gained are worth continued efforts.

There were two notable surprises that arose from this review of listening literature. It was surprising that there appears to be an absence of studies directly addressing how to "improve" listening or investigating how to help listeners reach specific listening goals. There do not appear to be systematic efforts to research how to move students toward becoming expert listeners. The research reviewed here centers more on what people do as they listen to music and how we can facilitate what they do as they listen. Should there be specific listening goals and benchmarks in formal listening as one moves from a beginning listener to a capable listener? What level is reasonable to expect for most people? A capable listener? An experienced listener? What does that mean? If broadening and deepening the intuitive listening experience is sought as a goal, how do we know one is a highly experienced listener, and how do we help others reach that level? It was also surprising that there are not more investigations about the nature of and how to nurture aesthetic and feelingful responses to music, surely one of the more important ways humans find personal meaning in music.

As can be seen from the studies reviewed here and from previous reviews (Gembris, 2002; Haack, 1992), the picture of what we know about the music-listening experience from birth to old age is far from complete. Many studies remain one-time events, but there are more researchers doing multiple studies in an area, and some researchers are doing studies that have close foundational ties that will allow more and more connections to be made from their data. The aspects we have been able to uncover have given depth to our appreciation of the complexity and individuality of the human music-listening experience and encouraged us to find more effective ways to enhance students' lifelong ability to engage in music listening in and out of the classroom.

NOTE

1. It should be noted that the word *passive* is used by some researchers to designate a certain kind of treatment condition in the listening research but may not be indicative of inactive or unengaged behavior by the subjects.

REFERENCES

Almén, B., & Pearsall, E. (Eds.). (2006). *Approaches to meaning in music.* Bloomington: Indiana University Press.

Bamberger, J. (1978). Intuitive and formal musical knowing: Parables of cognitive dissonance. In S. S. Madeja (Ed.), *The arts, cognition and basic skills* (pp. 173–209). St. Louis, MO: CEMREL.

Bamberger, J. (1982). Revisiting children's descriptions of simple rhythms: A function for reflection-in-action. In S. Strauss (Ed.), *U-shaped behavioural growth* (pp. 191–226). New York: Academic Press.

Bamberger, J. (1991). *The mind behind the musical ear: How children develop musical intelligence.* Cambridge, MA: Harvard University Press.

Bamberger, J. (1994). Coming to hear in a new way. In R. Aiello & J. Sloboda (Eds.), *Musical perceptions* (pp. 131–151). New York: Oxford University Press.

Barrett, M. S. (1997). Invented notations: A view of young children's musical thinking. *Research Studies in Music Education, 8*(1), 1–10.

Barrett, M. S. (2001). Constructing a view of children's meaning-making as notators: A case-study of a five-year-old's descriptions and explanations of invented notations. *Research Studies in Music Education, 16*(1), 33–45.

Barrett, M. S. (2002). Invented notations and mediated memory: A case study of two children's use of invented notations. *Bulletin for the Council for Research in Music Education, 153/154,* 55–62.

Barrett, M. S. (2004). Thinking about the representation of music: A case study of invented notation. *Bulletin of the Council for Research in Music Education, 161/162,* 19–28.

Bauer, W. I. (2008). Metacognition and middle school band students. *Journal of Band Research, 43,* 50–63.

Behne, K. (1997). The development of *"Musikerleben"* in adolescence: How and why young people listen to music. In I. Deliège & J. Sloboda (Eds.), *Perception and cognition of music* (pp. 143–159). Hove, UK: Psychology Press.

Blacking, J. (1973). *How musical is man?* Seattle: University of Washington Press.

Blair, D. V. (2007, October 8). Musical maps as narrative inquiry. *International Journal of Education & the Arts, 8*(15), 1–19. Retrieved May 18, 2011 from www.ijea.org/v8n15/.

Blair, D. V. (2008). Do you hear what I hear? Musical maps and felt pathways of musical understanding. *Visions of Research in Music Education, 11,* 1–23. Retrieved May 18, 2011, from www-usr.rider.edu/~vrme/v11n1/index.

Bloom, B. S. (Ed.). (1985). *Developing talent in young people.* New York: Ballantine.

Boal-Palheiros, G. M., & D. J. Hargreaves. (2001). Listening to music at home and at school. *British Journal of Music Education, 18*(2), 103–118.

Boal-Palheiros, G. M., & D. J. Hargreaves. (2004). Children's modes of listening to music at home and at school (in England and Portugal). *Bulletin of the Council for Research in Music Education 161/162,* 39–46.

Broomhead, P. (2008, February). *Literacy in the content area: It means teach music.* Paper presented at the meeting of the Utah Music Education Association, St. George, UT.

Bundra, J. I. (1994). *A study of music listening processes through the verbal reports of school-aged children.* Unpublished doctoral dissertation, Northwestern University, Evanston, IL.

Cassidy, J. W. (2001). Listening maps: Undergraduate students' ability to interpret various iconic representations. *Update: Applications of Research in Music Education, 19*(2), 15–19.

Cassidy, J. W., & Geringer, J. M. (1999). Effects of animated videos on preschool children's music preferences. *Update: Applications of Research in Music Education, 17*(2), 3–7.

Cassidy, S. (2004). Learning styles: An overview of theories, models, and measures. *Educational Psychology, 24*(4), 419–444.

Cohen, V. W. (1997). Explorations of kinesthetic analogues for musical schemes. *Bulletin of the Council for Research in Music Education, 131,* 1–13.

Colwell, R. (1999). The 1997 assessment in music: Red flags in the sunset. *Arts Education Policy Review, 100*(6), 33–39.

Cope, B., & Kalantzis, M. (Eds.). (2000). *Multiliteracies: Literacy learning and the design of social futures.* New York: Routledge.

Cusano, J. M. (2005). *Music specialists' beliefs and practices in teaching music listening.* Unpublished doctoral dissertation, Indiana University, Bloomington, IN.

Cutietta, R. A. (1985). An analysis of musical hypotheses created by the 11–16 year-old recall of familiar learner. *Bulletin of the Council for Research in Music Education, 84,* 1–13.

Cutietta, R. A. (1993). The musical elements: Who said they are right? *Music Educators Journal, 79*(9), 48–53.

Davidson, L., & Scripp, L. (1988). Young children's musical representations: Windows on cognition. In J. A. Sloboda (Ed.), *Generative processes in music: The psychology of performance, improvisation, and composition* (pp. 195–230). Oxford: Clarendon.

Denora, T. (1999). Music as a technology of the self. *Poetics, 27*(1), 31–56.

Dollase, R., Rüsenberg, M., & Stollenwerk, H. (1986). *Demoskopie im Konzertsaal.* Mainz, Germany: Schott.

Dunn, R. E. (1997). Creative thinking and music listening. *Research Studies in Music Education, 8*(1), 42–55.

Dunn, R. E. (2004). Lifelong listening: Enhancing the intuitive ways we listen to music. *International Journal of Community Music, 1.* Retrieved January 10, 2008, from www.intljcm.com/archive.html.

Dunn, R. E. (2006). Teaching for lifelong, intuitive listening. *Arts Education Policy Review, 107*(3), 33–38.

Dunn, R. E. (2008). The effect of auditory, visual or kinesthetic perceptual strengths on music listening. *Contributions to Music Education, 35*, 47–78.

Dunn, R. E., & Casey, D. E. (1995, November). *Developing a talent for composition in young people.* Paper presented at the National Convention of the College Music Society, Portland, OR.

Ellis, M. C. (1999). Spoken responses about music excerpts before and after a course in music appreciation. *Contributions to Music Education, 26*, 7–32.

Feinberg, S. (1973). *A creative problem-solving approach to the development of perceptive music listening in the secondary school music literature class.* Unpublished doctoral dissertation, Temple University, Philadelphia.

Ferguson, L. S. (2004). *I see them listening: A teacher's understanding of children's expressive movements to music in the classroom.* Unpublished doctoral dissertation, University of Illinois, Urbana-Champaign, IL.

Finnäs, L. (2001). Presenting music live, audio-visually, or aurally—does it affect listeners' experiences differently? *British Journal of Music Education 18*(1), 55–78.

Flowers, P. J. (1990). Listening: The key to describing music. *Music Educators Journal, 77*(4), 21–23.

Flowers, P. J. (1996, August). Uniqueness and redundancy in written descriptions of music excerpts by children and undergraduates. Paper presented at the 4th International Conference on Music Perception and Cognition, McGill University, Montreal, Canada.

Flowers, P. J. (2000). The match between music excerpts and written descriptions by fifth and sixth graders. *Journal of Research in Music Education, 48*(3), 262–277.

Flowers, P. J. (2002). What was that? Talking about what we hear in music. *Update, 21*(2), 45–51.

Flowers, P. J., & Wang, C. (2002). Matching verbal description to music excerpt: The use of language by blind and sighted children. *Journal of Research in Music Education, 50*(3), 202–214.

Fung, C. V., & Gromko, J. E. (2001). Effects of active versus passive listening on the quality of children's invented notations and preferences for two pieces from an unfamiliar culture. *Psychology of Music, (29)*2, 128–138.

Gembris, H. (2002). The development of musical abilities. In R. Colwell & C. Richardson (Eds.), *The new handbook of research on music teaching and learning* (pp. 487–508). New York: Oxford University Press.

Geringer, J. M., Cassidy, J. W., & Byo, J. L. (1996). Effects of music with video on responses of nonmusic majors: An exploratory study. *Journal of Research in Music Education, 44*(3), 240–251.

Geringer, J. M., Cassidy, J. W., & Byo, J. L. (1997). Nonmusic majors' cognitive and affective responses to performance and programmatic music videos. *Journal of Research in Music Education, 45*(2), 221–233.

Greher, G. R. (2002). *"Picture This!" (c)1997: An interactive listening environment for middle school general music.* Unpublished doctoral dissertation, Columbia University Teachers College, New York.

Gromko, J. E., & Poorman, A. S. (1998). Developmental trends and relationships in children's aural perception and symbol use. *Journal of Research in Music Education, 46*(1), 16–23.

Gromko, J. E., & Russell, C. (2002). Relationships among young children's aural perception, listening condition, and accurate reading of graphic listening maps. *Journal of Research in Music Education, 50*(4), 333–342.

Haack, P. (1992). The acquisition of music listening skills. In R. Colwell (Ed.), *Handbook of research on music teaching and learning* (pp. 451–465). New York: Schirmer.

Hargreaves, D. J., Marshall, N. A., & North, A. C. (2003). Music education in the twenty-first century: A psychological perspective. *British Journal of Music Education, 20*(2), 147–163.

Hickey, M. (2002). Creativity research in music, visual art, theater, and dance. In R. Colwell & C. Richardson (Eds.), *The new handbook of research on music teaching and learning* (pp. 398–415). New York: Oxford University Press.

Howard, L. (2008, November). How classical music becomes "popular." Paper presented at Brigham Young University, School of Music, Provo, UT.

Johnson, D. C. (2003). Fifth-grade instrumentalists' descriptions of music. *Bulletin of the Council for Research in Music Education, 158*, 81–95.

Johnson, D. C. (2006). Listening and thinking. *Visions of Research in Music Education.* Retrieved January 7, 2008 from www-usr.rider.edu/~vrme/v7n1/index.htm

Juslin, P. N., & Laukka, P. (2004). Expression, perception, and induction of musical emotions: A review and a questionnaire study of everyday listening. *Journal of New Music Research, 33*(3), 217–238.

Kerchner, J. L. (2000). Children's verbal, visual, and kinesthetic responses: Insight into their music listening experience. *Bulletin of the Council for Research in Music Education, 146*, 31–50.

Kerchner, J. L. (2005). A world to know and feel: Exploring children's verbal, visual, and kinesthetic responses to music. In M. Mans & B. Leung (Eds.), *Music in schools for all children: From research to effective practice. Proceedings of the 14th International Seminar of the Music in the Schools and Teacher Education Commission.* Granada, Spain: Campus Universitario de Cartujo-Editorial Universidad de Granada.

Kerchner, J. L. (2009). Drawing middle-schoolers' attention to music. In J. Kerchner & C. Abril (Eds.), *Music experience throughout our lives* (pp. 183–198). Lanham, MD: Rowman & Littlefield.

Kirnarskaya, D., & Winner, E. (1997). Musical ability in a new key: Exploring the expressive ear for music. *Psychomusicology, 16*, 2–16.

Kjelland, J. M., & Kerchner, J. K. (Eds.). (1998). The effects of music performance participation on the music listening experience: A review of literature. *Bulletin of the Council for Research in Music Education, 136*, 1–55.

Kratus, J. (1993). A developmental study of children's interpretation of emotion in music. *Psychology of Music, 21*, 3–19.

Lacanuet, J. (1996). Prenatal auditory experience. In L. Deliege & J. Sloboda (Eds.), *Musical beginnings: Origins and development of musical competence* (pp. 3–34). Oxford: Oxford University Press.

Lamont, A., Hargreaves, D. J., Marshall, N. A., & Tarrant, M. (2003). Young people's music in and out of school. *British Journal of Music Education, 20*(3), 229–241.

Lineburgh, N. E. (1994). *The effects of exposure to musical prototypes on the stylistic discrimination ability of kindergarten and second-grade children.* Unpublished doctoral dissertation, Kent State University, Kent, OH.

Lychner, J. A. (1998). An empirical study concerning terminology relating to aesthetic response to music. *Journal of Research in Music Education, 46*(2), 303–319.

Mack, C. D. (1995). *The effects of picture book and instrument pictures during music listening on the attentiveness, attitude, instrument identification ability, and memory for classical themes of prekindergarten children.* Unpublished doctoral dissertation, University of Missouri-Columbia, Columbia, MO.

Madsen, C. K. (1997). Focus of attention and aesthetic response. *Journal of Research in Music Education, (45)*1, 80–89.

Madsen, C. K., Brittin, R. V., & Capperella-Sheldon, D. A. (1993). An empirical investigation of the aesthetic response to music. *Journal of Research in Music Education, 41*(1), 57–69.

Madsen, C. K., & Coggiola, J. C. (2001). The effect of manipulating a CRDI dial on the focus of attention of musicians/nonmusicians and perceived aesthetic response. *Bulletin of the Council for Research in Music Education 149*, 13–22.

Mursell, J. (1943). *Music in American schools.* New York: Silver Burdett.

North, A. C., Hargreaves, D. J., & Hargreaves, J. J. (2004). Uses of music in everyday life. *Music Perception 22*(1), 41–77.

North, A. C., Hargreaves, D. J., & O'Neill, S. A. (2000). The importance of music to adolescents. *British Journal of Educational Psychology 70*(2), 255–272.

Persky, H. R., Sandene, B. A., & Askew, J. M. (1998). *The NAEP 1997 Arts Report Card.* Washington, D.C.: Office of Educational Research and Improvement, National Center for Education Statistics.

Peterson, E. M. (2002). *The creative dimension of the music listening experience.* Unpublished doctoral dissertation, Northwestern University, Evanston, IL.

Peterson, E. M. (2006). Creativity in music listening. *Arts Education Policy Review, 107*(3), 15–21.

Pfeil, C. (1972). Creativity as an instructional mode for introducing music to non-music majors at the college level. Unpublished doctoral dissertation, Michigan State University, East Lansing, MI.

Polanyi, M. (1969). *The tacit dimension.* Chicago: University of Chicago Press.

Reimer, B. (1967). *The development and trial in a junior and senior high school of a two-year curriculum in general music* (Report Number H-116). Cleveland, OH: U.S. Department of Health, Education and Welfare. (ERIC Document Reproduction Service No. ED 017 526).

Reimer, B. (1989). *A philosophy of music education.* Englewood Cliffs, NJ: Prentice Hall.

Reimer, B. (1997). Episteme, phronesis, and the role of verbal language in "knowing within" music. *Philosophy of Music Education Review, 5*(2), 101–107.

Reimer, B. (2003). *A philosophy of music education: Advancing the vision.* Upper Saddle River, NJ: Prentice Hall.

Reimer, B., & Evans, E. G. (1972). *The experience of music.* Englewood Cliffs, NJ: Prentice-Hall.

Reimer, B., Hoffman, M., & McNeil, A. (1976). *Silver Burdett music: Core book 8.* Morristown, NJ: Silver Burdett.

Richards, M. H. (1973). *The music language.* Portola Valley, CA: Richards Institute of Music Education and Research.

Rodriguez, C. X., & Webster, P. R. (1997). Development of children's verbal interpretative responses to music listening. *Bulletin of the Council for Research in Music Education, 134*, 9–30.

Sims, W. L. (1985). Young children's creative movement to music: Categories of movement, rhythmic characteristics, and reactions to changes. *Contributions to Music Education, 12*, 42–50.

Sims, W. L. (1988). Movement responses of preschool children, primary grade children, and preservice classroom teachers to characteristics of musical phrases. *Psychology of Music, 16*(2), 110–127.

Sims, W. L. (1991). Effects of instruction and task format on preschool children's ability to demonstrate single and combined music concept discrimination. *Journal of Research in Music Education, 39*(4), 298–310.

Sims, W. L. (1995). Children's ability to demonstrate music concept discriminations in listening and singing. *Journal of Research in Music Education, 43*(3), 204–221.

Sims, W. L. (2000). Why should music educators care about NAEP? *Teaching Music, 7*(4), 40–45.

Sims, W. L. (2001). Characteristics of preschool children's individual music listening during free choice time. *Bulletin of the Council for Research in Music Education, 149*, 53–63.

Sims, W. L. (2004). What I've learned about research from young children. *Update: Applications of Research in Music Education, 23*(1), 4–13.

Sims, W. L., & Nolker, D. B. (2002). Individual differences in music listening responses of kindergarten children. *Journal of Research in Music Education 50*(4), 292–300.

Sloboda, J. A., O'Neill, S. A., and Ivaldi, A. (2001). Functions of music in everyday life: An exploratory study using the Experience Sampling Method. *Musicae Scientiae, 5*(1), 9–32.

Smialek, T. W., & Bobourka, R. R. (2006). The effect of cooperative listening exercises on the critical listening skills of college music appreciation students. *Journal of Research in Music Education, 54*(1), 57–72.

Stake, R. E. (1995). *The art of case study research*. Thousand Oaks, CA: Sage.

Taetle, L., & Cutietta, R. A. (2002). Learning theories as roots of current musical practice. In R. Colwell & C. Richardson (Eds.), *The new handbook of research on music teaching and learning* (pp. 279–298). New York: Oxford University Press.

Tait, M., & Haack, P. (1984). *Principles and processes of music education: New dimensions*. New York: Teachers College Press.

Theiss, J. A. (1990). *The relationship of tonal and human phenomena in the musical experience of fourth-grade children*. Unpublished doctoral dissertation, University of Maryland, College Park, MD.

Trehub, S. E., & Nakata, T. (2001/2002). Emotion and music in infancy. *Musicae Scientiae, Special issue*, 37–61.

Vygotsky, L. (1978). *Mind in society: The development of higher psychological processes*. Cambridge, MA: Harvard University Press.

Webster, P. R. (1987). Conceptual bases for creative thinking in music. In C. Peery, I. Peery, & T. Draper (Eds.), *Music and child development* (pp. 158–176). New York: Springer-Verlag.

Webster, P. R. (1992). Research on creative thinking in music: The assessment literature. In R. Colwell (Ed.), *Handbook of research on music teaching and learning* (pp. 266–280). New York: Schirmer.

Williamson, S. J. (2005). *"My music": The music making and listening experiences of seventh and eighth graders not enrolled in school music ensembles.* Unpublished doctoral dissertation, University of Washington, Seattle.

Winner, E., Davidson, L., & Scripp, L. (Eds.). (1992). *Arts Propel: A handbook for music.* Princeton, NJ: Educational Testing Service.

Woody, R. H. (2004). Reality-based music listening in the classroom: Considering students' natural responses to music. *General Music Today, 17*(2), 32–39.

Woody, R. H., and Burns, K. J. (2001). Predicting music appreciation with past emotional responses to music. *Journal of Research in Music Education, 49*(1), 57–70.

The Acquisition of Music Reading Skills

2

DONALD A. HODGES

D. BRETT NOLKER

Music reading is a key component of a richly fulfilling musical life. Although there are many oral musical traditions and practices, music reading holds a special place in contemporary music education curricula. Its importance is exemplified in its status as one of the National Standards for Music Education (Consortium of National Arts Education Associations, 1994). Nearly all the pedagogical approaches (e.g., Orff, Kodály, Gordon) have something to say about music reading. Virtually all beginning instrumental method books and private instructional books (for piano, guitar, band and orchestra instruments, etc.) have sections on music reading, as do general music basal series. Unfortunately, most of the strategies and approaches presented in these pedagogical materials have not been corroborated through independent research.

At its most basic level, music reading is a process of converting special visual symbols—music notation—into sounds. These sounds may be silent, conceived internally, or they may be produced externally through the voice or musical instruments. From this rather simplistic definition, there arise a number of more complex issues to be explored. It is the purpose of this chapter to review and synthesize research on the acquisition of music reading skills and to comment on the extant research base. In doing so, the intent is to extend and deepen our understanding of music reading from an earlier version of this topic that appeared as a chapter in the first *Handbook of Research in Music Teaching and Learning* (Hodges, 1992). The focus is on how people learn to read music. The remainder of this chapter is organized into the following sections: a brief historical overview, basic research, applied research, research on score reading among trained musicians, and a commentary that includes recommendations for practitioners.

Brief Historical Overview of Music Reading

It is beyond the scope of this chapter to provide a comprehensive overview of music reading. However, a few comments may help place the subsequent research sections in context. The earliest means of indicating changes in musical sound patterns was most likely the use of hand signs in the music of pharaonic Egypt, in Indian Vedic chants, in Jewish music, and in Byzantine and Roman chants (Sadie, 1988). Early notational systems included Greek alphabetical systems (from 500 B.C.E.), Chinese writing (400 B.C.E.), and Jewish, Syrian, Armenian, and other Eastern churches' use of ekphonetic notation, which are symbols added to text as an aid to chanting or singing. One of the earliest examples of musical notation is cuneiform signs found on tablet fragments discovered in the royal residence at Ugarit (Syria) and dated at 1250–1200 B.C.E. (West, 1994).

In Western music, notation began with neumatic notation for plainchant in the 9th century (Bent et al., 2008). Innovations associated with Guido of Arezzo in the 11th century include the staff, the Guidonian hand, and solmization syllables. With the advent of notation came the need for musicians to learn to read music. Musical training in monastic and cathedral schools eventually led to university training, and a chair of music was established at Salamanca University as early as 1254 (Anderson, 1994). Jumping ahead to the American colonial period, singing schools were established in the early 1700s for the purpose of improving congregational hymn singing, and music reading was a significant part of that instruction (Birge, 1928). Almost immediately, instruction books were written, beginning with Tufts's *A Very Plain and Easy Introduction to the Singing of Psalm Tunes* in 1714 (Chase, 1955). From there, a veritable cottage industry sprang up, and Perrin (1970) noted that:

> Of the 347 American tune books with theoretical introductions between 1801 and 1860, 230 employed an orthodox European notation (124 recommended singing with four syllables, 99 with seven syllables, 3 with a fixed-do concept, and 4 with no syllable concept at all); 70 employed four-character notation; 19 used seven-character notation; 11 used numeral notation; and 2 utilized a letter notation. (p. 257)

As will be evident from the research reviews that follow, we are still striving to find efficient ways to help students learn to read music.

Basic Research on Music Reading

Some researchers have been interested in basic research on music reading with a primary intent to uncover underlying processes. Once these are better understood, it is more likely that a theory of music reading could be developed, leading to more effective applied research studies. Major topics in basic research on music reading include the brain and music reading, eye movements, pattern recognition, motoric activity, and the relationship of music reading to other music variables, such as playing by ear or improvising.

The Brain and Music Reading

Music and language involve shared, parallel, and distinctive brain regions (Brown, Martinez, and Parsons, 2006), and music reading, specifically, is supported, at least in part, by neural networks distinct from reading words or numerals (Peretz and Zatorre, 2005). Early work by Sergent and colleagues (Sergent, 1993a, 1993b; Sergent, Zuck, Terriah, and MacDonald, 1992) led to the conclusion that music is represented in the brain by widely distributed but locally specialized neural networks. This notion has been confirmed by others who have shown that melody, harmony, and rhythm are processed independently (Bengtsson and Ullén, 2006; Parsons, 2001; Schön, Anton, Roth, and Besson, 2002; Schön and Besson, 2002), though there is also support for an interactive model of pitch and rhythm processing (Waters and Underwood, 1999). The superior parietal cortex and fusiform gyrus have been specifically implicated in music reading (Nakada, Fujii, Suzuki, and Kwee, 1998; Stewart, 2005a; Stewart, Henson, Kampe, Walsh, Turner, and Frith, 2003). For three months, musically untrained adults were taught to read musical notation at the piano (Stewart, 2005b). Music reading involves vertical to horizontal mappings, and the results of brain scans indicated learning-specific changes in superior parietal cortex and supramarginal gyrus; these are areas of the brain known to be involved in spatial sensorimotor transformations (i.e., transforming musical notation into the motor actions of performance) and preparation of learned actions.

Studies of brain-damaged musicians provide confirming evidence of dissociated networks (Stanzione, Grossi, and Roberto, 1990). For example, a right-handed piano teacher with left hemisphere damage preserved pitch reading while showing a deficit in rhythm reading (Midorikawa, Kawamura, and Kezuka, 2003); another professional musician retained rhythm reading skills while losing pitch reading after suffering brain damage in the left posterior temporal lobe and right parieto-occipital region (Cappelletti, Waley-Cohen, Butterworth, and Kopelman, 2000). For a more extensive review of music reading deficits and the brain, see Hébert and Cuddy, 2006.

While it is too simplistic to say that pitch reading occurs in one area of the brain and rhythm reading occurs in another, they can be dissociated (Fasanaro, Spitaleri, Valiani, and Grossi, 1990). In general, the angular gyrus in the left hemisphere is strongly involved in both musical alexia (reading deficits) and agraphia (writing deficits) (Kawamura, Midorikawa, and Kezuka, 2000). Behavioral and neurofunctional evidence indicates that extensive experience in music reading alters brain function and that concomitant changes in brain organization confer benefits to nonmusical visuospatial cognition (Sluming, Brooks, Howard, Downes, and Roberts, 2007). Finally, there is a strong interaction between representations built from the visual score and the auditory perceptions of musical sequences (Schön and Besson, 2003). Reading music with diatonic violations elicits different brain activation patterns than hearing music with similar violations (Gunter, Schmidt, and Besson, 2003).

Eye Movements

The sensation most of us experience in reading is one of fluid eye movements scanning a line of printed music. However, the actual mechanics of music reading involve a rapid series of stops (fixations) and starts as the eye focuses on pertinent information and then sweeps (a saccade) to the next focal point (Rayner, 1998). Progressive saccades are left-to-right movements as readers look ahead in the music. Regressive saccades are right-to-left movements, as readers return to a previous place in the music. Information is brought into the visual system at a fixation, when the eye is not moving and is focusing on a circular area about one inch in diameter. Fixations can last from less than 100 ms to 500 ms (half a second) (Goolsby, 1989).

Several studies have been conducted on the saccadic or eye movement patterns during music reading. Evidence suggests that an individual's level of musical experience significantly influences eye movements (Kinsler and Carpenter, 1995; Polanka, 1995; Waters and Underwood, 1998; Waters, Underwood, and Findlay, 1997). For example, Kopiez and Galley (2002) used an electro-oculogram to compare the saccades of eight professional pianists to those of 254 psychology students on a nonmusical visual processing task. Results indicated that the musicians employed much more efficient strategies, reducing the frequency of misses and having shorter reaction times, increased anticipatory saccades, and faster saccadic movements.

Goolsby (1994a) monitored eye movements in 24 graduate music students who had the 12 highest and 12 lowest music reading achievement tests scores of 72 subjects. Participants vocalized each of four melodies of differing notational complexity three times. They were given 4 minutes of study time between the second and third performance. Horizontal and vertical eye movements were recorded every millisecond with a very high degree of accuracy, such that eye fixation positions were located within the size of two-thirds the area of the head of a quarter note used in the musical notation.

No significant differences were found in the number of progressive or regressive fixations, the length of progressive or regressive saccades, regressive fixation durations, or performance time. Significant differences were found in the duration of progressive fixations. The skilled readers looked ahead more frequently, which necessitated more regressions (returns to the point of performance). Eye movement did vary with notational complexity, but in a counterintuitive way. That is, fewer eye movements were utilized with the most notationally complex music. Also, repeated performances resulted in fewer but longer fixations after practicing the melodies.

Goolsby (1994b) extended the analysis by comparing eye movements of the lowest scoring participant with one of the two who tied with the highest music reading score. The skilled music sight reader used longer progressive saccade lengths (left-to-right eye movements) and slightly more regressions (right-to-left eye movements) than the poorer sight reader. The less skilled sight reader had more progressive fixations and fewer regressions. This indicates that the better sight reader looked farther ahead and then jumped back to the point of actual performance more frequently. Also, the better sight reader acquired more information (e.g., dynamic and expression markings, articulations, etc.) via peripheral vision. In contrast, the less skilled music reader moved virtually note-by-note through the performance with longer fixations.

Experienced music readers read ahead of the point of performance in units or chunks. The eye-hand span (EHS) is the separation between eye position and hand position and is measured either in terms of the number of notes between eye and hand (note index) or length of time between eye fixation and performance (time index). There is a difference between EHS and perceptual span or the effective visual field (Truitt, Clifton, Pollatsek, and Rayner, 1997). Furneaux and Land (1998, 1999) found that professional pianists had significantly larger note indexes than amateurs while sight-reading but that there was no significant difference in time index. Rayner and Pollatsek (1997) found that the actual fixation point for skilled pianists was only about two beats ahead of the point of performance.

Reading ahead or "previewing" allows the eye to fixate on structurally important features, such as chords or melodic fragments, and to skip over less important details that may be filled in. It appears that saccadic movements alter to suit the music (Polanka, 1995; Van Nuys and Weaver, 1943; Weaver, 1943). While sight-playing piano music of a homophonic nature, the saccadic movements tend to consist of a vertical sweep down from treble to bass, then over to the next chord for another vertical sweep downward, and so on. Contrapuntal music elicits a horizontal sweep along an upper line for a unit, followed by a return for a parallel horizontal sweep along a lower line. It has also been found that better keyboard readers economize on eye movements, keeping their eyes focused on the music, while poorer readers engage in many needless shifts from the music to the hands (Banton, 1995). However, it should be noted that even excellent sight readers need visual feedback from hand positions on the keyboard.

Pattern Recognition

Researchers are beginning to learn more about the units of information that are perceived during fixations. Sloboda (1976b) found that musicians were superior to nonmusicians in the recognition of briefly exposed pitch notation patterns of more than three notes, if the exposure was longer than 150 ms. At exposure times of less than 100 ms, musicians were no better than nonmusicians at identifying specific pitches, but they were superior at retaining the contour of notational patterns (Sloboda, 1978a). For isolated pitches, musical experience would not necessarily be advantageous, since the task would be more related to visual-spatial acuity. However, for longer patterns, musical experience would provide an advantage, since individual notes can be grouped into meaningful patterns (e.g., an arpeggio, scalelike passage). These results suggest that a time interval shorter than 150 ms is too brief for the eye, musically experienced or not, to obtain information. However, Goolsby (1989), using sophisticated equipment that determines eye positions 1,000 times per second, discovered that skilled music readers do have fixations of less than 100 ms. Perhaps the difference in results is due to the fact that Sloboda's subjects viewed patterns flashed on a screen and then transcribed what they saw to paper, while Goolsby's subjects were monitored during the act of vocalizing melodies. The average fixations for music reading are between 350 and 400 ms (Rayner and Pollatsek, 1997).

How long are the units of previewed information? Sloboda (1974, 1977) asked instrumentalists to read a single line of music. At some point in the process, the music was removed, and the musicians continued to play as long as possible from memory. Poorer readers could produce only another three or four correct notes; better readers could produce up to seven additional notes. The actual number of notes was somewhat conditioned by how many notes were left in a phrase unit. It is interesting to note that this number corresponds to the magic number 7±2, which Miller (1956) established as the average memory buffer for bits of information. When the same task was given to keyboard players (Sloboda, 1977), it was found that structural markings (important chords or melodic fragments) increased eye-hand span and tended to extend the memory unit to a phrase boundary. Certain notational devices (e.g., beams) are processed automatically in experienced music readers (Brodsky, Kessler, and Henik, 2006). Also, prior knowledge plays a role in constructing mental representations from novel musical patterns (Kalakoski, 2007). Sloboda's general findings on pattern recognition (1978b, 1984, 1985) have been corroborated for pianists (Salis, 1980), flutists (Thompson, 1987), and singers (Fine, Berry, and Rosner, 2006). These findings are also corroborated by research on proofreader's error, discussed in a subsequent section.

Motoric Activity and Music Sight-Reading

Evidence suggests that subvocalization, engaging the vocal apparatus without audible sound, is critical in music reading (Brodsky, Henik, Rubinstein, and Zorman, 2003). Expert musicians performed worse on notational audiation tasks, recognizing familiar themes by silently reading a score, when required to sing or hum a folk song out loud than when other methods of distraction were used. These findings were confirmed when surface audio/electromyographic monitoring of the vocal folds was used (Brodsky, Henik, Rubinstein,

Ginsborg, and Kessler, 2006). There were significant differences in audio output for score reading while singing aloud versus silent reading, but no significant differences in musculoskeletal vocal activity were found. In a follow-up experiment (Brodsky, Kessler, Rubinstein, Ginsborg, and Henik, 2008), vocal fold activity was considerably more dynamic when participants silently read music notation than when they silently read printed text or mathematical sequences. Furthermore, reading musical notation also elicited manual motor activity. The fact that drummers produced both phonatory and manual motor activity suggests that reading musical notation is facilitated by kinesthetic processing.

Relationships among Music Reading and Other Music Variables

Taking a different approach, a number of researchers have been interested in discovering what relationships exist between music-reading skills and other related variables. Boyle (1970) obtained a correlation coefficient of .81 and Elliott (1982) a coefficient of .90 between total sight-reading scores and sight-reading rhythm patterns. McPherson (1994) found that in the beginning stages, sight-reading skills were not significantly correlated with performances of rehearsed music, but with increasing experience, this relationship strengthened markedly. He also found positive correlations between sight-reading and playing by ear (.67), playing from memory (.69), performing rehearsed music (.75), and improvising (.75) (McPherson, 1995). Gromko (2004) found that reading comprehension, rhythmic audiation, visual field articulation, and spatial orientation accounted for 48 percent of the variance on music sight-reading. The strong role of rhythm in sight-reading was confirmed by McPherson (1994) and Fourie (2004), who found that approximately 80 percent of sight-reading errors were rhythmic in nature.

In an often-cited study, Daniels (1986) used a step-wise regression procedure to determine that 11 of the original 84 variables investigated were the most critical for predicting sight-reading success. These predictors included global descriptors of the school (such as ethnic makeup, large size, rural setting), the personal musical background of the student (piano in the home, instrumental background, participation in all-state chorus), and traits of the teacher (e.g., use of rote instruction, positive attitude toward sight-singing instruction). It should be noted that factors of instructional materials and particular methods used were not found to be significant predictors.

A summary of basic research on music reading indicates that music reading is at least partially dissociated from language reading in widely distributed but locally specialized neural networks. Furthermore, melody, harmony, and rhythm are processed independently, although there is also evidence for interactive processing of pitches and rhythms. Extensive training in music reading alters brain function, and this may enhance nonmusical visuospatial cognition.

Eye movements are influenced by the nature of the music being read and by the reader's musical expertise. Proficient music readers use more efficient strategies, looking farther ahead and jumping back more frequently to the point of performance. More complex notation elicits fewer eye movements. Eye movements tend to be horizontal for contrapuntal music and vertical for homophonic music. Good keyboard readers exhibit an economy of eye shifts between the music and their hands; poorer readers have many more visual shifts back and forth from music to keyboard. Experienced music readers scan up to seven notes ahead of performance and are guided by structural elements in the music. They recognize patterns and tend to group notes in units, such as scales or arpeggios, that are viewed within the context of a musical style.

Subvocalization and manual motor activations appear to be integral in sight-reading. Music reading thus appears to be aided by kinesthetic processing. Strong positive correlations have been reported between music reading and rhythm reading. Other positive relationships have been found between sight-reading and playing by ear, playing from memory, performing rehearsed music, and improvising.

Applied Research on Music Reading

A moderate body of literature can be grouped under the rubric of teaching music reading. Unfortunately, these studies are so scattered as to render overall conclusions exceedingly difficult. In more than 50 studies, there are no replications, and few that use similar strategies. Even where several studies can be grouped together, there is rarely enough consensus to lead to a broader conclusion. Because of the fragmentary nature of these studies and space limitations, descriptions are necessarily terse.

Solmization

Bebeau (1982), Cassidy (1993), Colley (1987), Palmer (1976), and Shehan (1987) concluded that the use of syllables or related mnemonic devices is an effective pedagogical approach for teaching music-reading skills. Cassidy (1993) found that the use of solfège syllables alone and in combination with Curwen hand signs increased the sight-singing accuracy of elementary education majors (N = 91) over those using either staff letter names or a neutral syllable. In a study of junior high sight-singing and error-detection skills, Killian (1991) found no significant difference in sight-singing scores between students reading with standard notation or only solfège syllables. Henry and Demorest (1994), comparing the use of movable *do* and fixed *do* in the preparation of high school choirs, found no difference in individual performance between the two choirs tested. In contrast, Demorest and May (1995) found significantly higher scores for a choir using movable *do* but indicated that the results may be due to other factors, such as consistency of instruction and individual assessment. There remains a lack of continuity among the approaches used and in the results obtained. It is not clear, for example, whether one particular approach has a distinct advantage or whether the use of nearly any kind of syllabic or mnemonic device is sufficient.

Body Movement

The use of body movements in music reading was effective in two experiments with instrumentalists. Boyle (1970) tested two groups of beginning band students that each spent 30 minutes per week for 14 weeks in rhythm training. Experimental group students were instructed to mark the beat with foot tapping and to clap rhythm patterns. Students in the control group were restricted from using such body movements. The experimental group scored significantly higher on a sight-reading test and on the *Watkins-Farnum Performance Scale*. Skornicka (1958), too, compared two groups of beginning band students. The experimental group was taught with a method that emphasized rhythmic instruction beginning with quarter notes and rests, combined with foot tapping. Thus, although it outperformed the control group, it is unclear whether the use of a novel method of instruction, foot tapping, or the combination of the two caused the superior performance.

Salzburg and Wang (1989) did not find that foot tapping was an effective means of improving sight-reading among string students. Neither Klemish (1970) nor Martin (1991) found that hand signs and/or body movements were helpful in teaching music-reading skills to first-grade students. There are a number of reasons to account for the disparity of results. For example, Boyle (N = 191) and Skornicka (N = 149) used considerably larger subject pools than Salzburg and Wang (N = 46, divided into five groups). Klemish's and Martin's first-grade students were considerably younger than the middle school band students used by Boyle and Skornicka. Although there are other "hand-sign effectiveness studies" in the literature, they are not specific to music reading.

Pattern Instruction

As indicated in the "Basic Research" section on pattern recognition, better music readers read music based on structural elements in the music (e.g., phrase endings). The results of five studies corroborate this notion in finding that tonal pattern instruction is an effective technique for improving melodic sight-reading. Grutzmacher (1987) assigned 48 fifth- and sixth-grade beginning band students to two treatment groups. The experimental group received instruction on 10 major and 10 minor key tonal patterns through harmonization and vocalization. The control group received parallel instruction except that the tonal patterns were omitted, along with harmonization and vocalization; instead, they were taught using a single-note identification approach. The experimental group was superior to the control group in melodic sight-reading, however, there were no significant differences in abilities to compare aurally presented tonal patterns to visually presented patterns.

Fourth-grade beginning wind instrument students (N = 90) were placed into two groups (MacKnight, 1975). The experimental group was introduced to notation through a series of tonal patterns, while the control group learned new pitches through letter name, fingering, and sound. Results indicated that tonal pattern instruction was superior to note-identification techniques in both sight-reading skills, as measured by the *Watkins-Farnum Performance Scale*, and auditory-visual discrimination skills, as measured by the Colwell *Music Achievement Test*. In a unique approach to pattern instruction, Azzara (1992) developed a curriculum for elementary instrumental music emphasizing improvisation. He found that adding improvisation to a systematic program based on melodic and rhythmic pattern instruction contributed to higher achievement levels in beginning instrumental experiences.

Richardson (1972) placed second-graders into four groups: experimental group A, experimental group B, and two control groups. Students in experimental group A were taught with a sequential presentation of tonal vocabulary patterns; students in experimental group B used the same patterns but in a random order of presentation. Both experimental groups scored significantly higher than control groups on posttest mean scores; however, there were no significant differences between the two experimental groups on gain scores or on a recall or performance test. Group A did score significantly higher on a notation test.

Henry (2004) randomly assigned high school chorus members to one of two treatment groups to determine whether instruction with specific pitch pattern skills emphasizing scale degree and harmonic function would prove an effective strategy for teaching sight-singing in the choral classroom. Both groups received instruction over a 12-week period on targeted pitch skills, one using unfamiliar melodic material in the form of solfège drills and one using familiar melodic material in the form of well-known songs. The resulting comparison of pretest and posttest scores indicated that participants in both groups achieved a significant increase in their sight-singing ability, but there was no significant difference between the two approaches.

Harmonic Context

Lucas (1994) investigated the effect of harmonic context on individual sight-singing. Middle school students were assigned to one of three training contexts: melody-only, piano-harmony, and vocal-harmony. The use of harmonic context for sight-singing support was found to be less effective in both training and testing situations. This finding is in contrast to an earlier study with university students (Lucas and Boyle, 1990) in which harmonic context was found to improve sight-singing accuracy, especially among less experienced students.

Programmed Instruction and Recorded Aural Models

Several researchers investigated the use of recorded aural models or programmed instruction, individually or in combination. Barnes (1964) designated two classes of elementary education majors (N = 42) as an experimental group and a control group. The experimental group, which used a programmed instruction book, scored significantly higher on a test of music fundamentals that primarily covered musical notation. Heim (1976) compared the effects of a self-instructional programmed course in elementary rhythm reading to a traditional teacher-taught method. He used both high school instrumental and elementary school students. Students at both levels who used the programmed instruction book improved significantly over control groups.

Kanable (1969) developed and tested a self-instructional method for teaching sight-singing to high school students. Her programmed instruction method utilized recorded models. Students who used the programmed materials worked alone; control group students were taught by a conventional teacher-classroom approach. Because there was no significant difference in sight-singing between those who used the programmed instruction and those who did not, Kanable concluded that the self-instructional method was as effective as a conventional approach. Puopolo (1971) assigned 52 fifth-grade beginning trumpet students to an experimental treatment consisting of programmed self-instructional materials that were recorded on tape. Students used the recordings during individual practice sessions. Students in a control group practiced identical materials without the use of the programmed tapes. Students in the programmed practice group performed significantly better on the *Watkins-Farnum Performance Scale* than students in the nonprogrammed practice group.

Owen (1973) assigned one seventh-grade class to an experimental treatment, while three other classes served as control groups. The experimental group worked exclusively with tape recordings of sight-singing and rhythmic response drills. Experimental group posttest scores were significantly higher than the control groups' scores on a written test of music fundamentals. Achieving contrasting results, Hodges (1975) compared seven beginning band classes ($n = 97$), who rehearsed with recorded aural models of lesson material, to seven beginning band classes ($n = 103$), who rehearsed without such models. No significant differences were found on performances of a sight-reading test. Similarly, Anderson (1981) placed 20 sixth-grade clarinet students in an experimental group and 20 in a control group. The experimental group students practiced at home with tape-recorded aural models, while the control group students did not have access to such recordings. There were no significant differences in measurements of sight-reading or performance skills.

Researchers have not continued to pursue the approaches reviewed in this section. While there are newer studies in programmed instruction and aural models, no additional published studies have been identified that concern the acquisition of music-reading skills.

The Tachistoscope and Computer-Aided Instruction

A tachistoscope is a device that allows control of the duration of projected images. For example, images of notation can be projected from slower speeds (e.g., half to a fifth of a second) to very brief flashes at 1/100th of a second. The earliest use of a tachistoscope for music reading was unsuccessful, but the remaining attempts have achieved positive results. Earlier work with this device is summarized here, and suggestions for more modern use of similar technology are noted in the concluding sections of this chapter.

Stokes (1965) conducted a very early study of the tachistoscope in 1944 involving 316 secondary school students. Experimental group students used a drill program consisting of slides of melodic material flashed on a screen for very brief durations. There was no significant difference on a written test of music-reading achievement or on a performance test.

Christ (1966) placed 11 freshman theory students into an experimental group and 18 similar students into a control group. Experimental group students practiced rhythmic notation patterns with a tachistoscope. Results of a rhythmic reading posttest indicated that drilling with the tachistoscope led to significant gains over the control group. Hammer (1963) sought to determine the effects of tachistoscopic training on melodic sight-singing skills with fourth-grade classes. The experimental group (n = 22) practiced singing tonal patterns presented via the tachistoscope, while the control group (n = 23) practiced identical materials using conventional means without the tachistoscope. Analysis of posttest data indicated that the experimental group achieved superior scores on melodic sight-singing. DiFronzo (1969) taught third-graders to read music while playing the flutophone. An experimental group was taught music-reading skills with a tachistoscope, and the control group was taught by conventional means. Training with the tachistoscope led to significantly higher scores on a playing test than conventional instruction.

Given the dates of these experiments, it is clear that the tachistoscope is outdated equipment. Unfortunately, very little research has taken advantage of computer applications to teach music-reading skills. Willett and Netusil (1989) taught bass clef notation to fourth-grade students via computer drill or classroom drill. The computer drill group practiced with a commercially available program called *Clef Notes* that allowed students to place note heads on the correct line or space to match a letter name. Traditional classroom drills were used to teach the control group. The computer group achieved significantly higher posttest scores on note naming.

Notational Variables

Several researchers tested notational variables or the effects of different notational systems, with varying results. For example, Hutton (1953) found the use of flash cards, musical games, and slides of notation symbols contributed to higher sight-reading test scores. Placing song texts higher and lower in conjunction with higher and lower melodic pitches was found to facilitate music reading (Franklin, 1977). Using notation based on a binary system (Bukspan, 1979) or using shape notes (Kyme, 1960) led to improvements in music reading. Notational schemes used by Byo (1988) and Gregory (1972) had no observed effect on music-reading test scores. In a related study, Byo (1992) again found no effect for barlines and pitch on rhythm reading ability, but findings indicated an interaction among these factors and variations of meter under certain conditions. In an investigation of beamed versus beam-less notation, Sheldon (1996) found that high school wind musicians exhibited greater rhythmic accuracy with beamed notation but that the difference in notation had no effect on musicality. Using colored rhythmic notation, Rogers (1996) found a significant positive effect for rhythm reading, but no transfer to traditional notation.

Early Instruction in Music Reading

In a comparison of two learning constructs with three- and four-year-old pre-school children, Tommis and Fazey (1999) found that early music-reading instruction using either a method based on stimulus equivalence or a method based on spatial and contextual information processing led to posttest scores that were significantly higher than a control group. Children in both treatment groups received 20 10-minute teaching sessions over a 10-week period. For both teaching groups, the children were presented with what was called *vertical music*, in which the staff was rotated 90 degrees so the ascending written notes moved to the right, corresponding to the direction of ascending pitches on the keyboard. The teaching methods then offered two alternative strategies to present the relationship of note placement in the written score to the keyboard. The children in both teaching groups learned up to five notes and were able to play simple melodies constructed of these pitches. In addition to the significant gains revealed by the posttest, the treatment groups were retested after 7 weeks. There was no significant difference between posttest and retest scores, indicating retention in the skills learned.

Sight-Singing in the Choral Setting

One of the more consistent strains of inquiry related to music-reading instruction has focused on sight singing in the choral setting. For example, use of a specially designed manual during sight-singing drills in a middle school choral setting was found to be effective (Cutietta, 1979). By measuring pitch and rhythm accuracy of individual members of choirs with consistent records of success in group sight-reading, Henry and Demorest (1994) concluded that group achievement was not a valid indicator of individual success. This was confirmed and expanded by Nolker (2006), who compared individual pitch and rhythm accuracy scores for selected members of six choirs, three with consistent Superior (I) ratings and three with consistent

Excellent (II) ratings in group sight singing. Results indicated no significant differences in average scores for individuals between the two groups.

Demorest (1998a), investigating the effect of individualized testing as an instructional strategy, found that subjects who participated in periodic individual testing scored significantly higher on the posttest than did subjects who received only group instruction. These results suggest that individualized testing may be an effective means of improving individual sight-singing performance. For expanded presentations of research in choral sight singing, see Demorest (1998b, 2001).

In response to the lack of continuity in practices used in music-reading instruction, Killian and Henry (2005) attempted to isolate successful and unsuccessful strategies used by high school chorus students while sight-singing. The more successful readers benefited from a 30-second preparation time, during which they sang out loud, tonicized with hand signs, and used body movement to maintain beat. In a follow-up study, Henry (2008) instructed individual singers to employ successful strategies (tonicize, keep the beat in the body, etc.) and to avoid using unsuccessful strategies (don't stop, don't take eyes off the music, etc.). She found no significant differences in sight-reading scores for high-achieving participants, but scores for low-achieving singers did improve significantly. For further details on choral sight-reading, see chapter 5 (Phillips and Doneski) in this volume.

Miscellaneous Studies

In a study of the development of musicianship and sight-singing skills of students preparing to be elementary teachers, Hargiss (1962) included sight-singing in the classroom activity of an experimental group ($n = 32$) who sang each exercise they played on piano. In addition to increases in piano skills and musicianship, as indicated by two standardized tests, results of comparisons of pretest and posttest scores on a sight-singing test indicated a significant increase in sight-singing success. As a result, the researcher concluded, "The act of singing contributes to sight singing ability, not to nonvocal music reading ability nor to musicality" (p. 75).

Bradley (1974) found that a program of instruction emphasizing creative activities, such as composing, performing, and listening, led to increased test scores on measures of visual recognition and perception of music. In comparisons of new approaches using models of conceptual teaching in contrast to more traditional "part to whole" models of instruction, Hewson (1966) and Noble (1969) both found conceptual teaching models more effective. No significant differences were found among vocal, ukulele, or piano groups in auditory-visual discrimination skills (Colwell and Rundell, 1965). Music-reading films were not effective (Rea, 1954), nor was the use of imaged subdivisions (Drake, 1968) or a maximal speed pacing technique (Trisman, 1964).

Perhaps one can account for the dated nature of this miscellaneous research by recognizing that the music-reading research agenda has become more streamlined over time. That is, over a period of years, research topics have tended to coalesce along particular themes, and thus there are fewer outliers; also approaches that were once studied may have been abandoned along the way and fallen into disuse. In some cases, specific topics have been discarded because the technology has become outmoded, as has happened with the promising research involving the tachistoscope. Other innovative approaches may no longer resonate with current understanding of how children learn to read music.

To summarize, from this brief review of the applied research on music reading, it is apparent that the bulk of these studies are technique- or strategy-driven rather than based on any underlying theory of music reading. With the mixed results obtained and the lack of replications, it is difficult to draw any major conclusions about teaching music reading that are derived from research. However, summarizing applied research on the acquisition of music-reading skills does lead to a number of qualified statements. Solmization is generally effective, though the most successful method has yet to be determined. The use of specific body movements, particularly rhythmic movement such as clapping or foot tapping, has been somewhat effective in improving music reading. Better music readers read music by negotiating structural elements in the music, rather than by proceeding in a note-to-note fashion. Instruction using tonal patterns or awareness of specific structural elements was found to be superior to simple note-identification techniques.

The effect of harmonic context on individual sight-singing success was found to vary with the experience level of the students involved. While harmonic support was of positive assistance for university students, it proved to interfere with individual accuracy of younger singers. The use of individual programmed instructional materials was found to contribute to successful music-reading skills. This is also true when combined with recorded aural models. Studies using only tape-recorded models had mixed results. With the exception of one early study, the outcomes of studies using a tachistoscope and a study using computer-assisted instruction indicated consistently positive contributions to music-reading success. Varying notational schemes have had mixed success in improving music-reading skills; however, none of the innovative notational practices (e.g., colored notation) have entered the mainstream of professional practice. The lone study published on reading instruction with preschool children indicated that unique approaches to visual presentation were effective.

Studies of sight singing in a choral setting have received slightly more attention than most topics. Providing personal attention in the form of periodic individualized testing improved sight-singing scores among choral students. Focusing on successful strategies such as tonicizing with hand signs or keeping the beat in the body and avoiding unsuccessful strategies such as stopping or taking eyes off the music aided weaker singers. Employing creative activities such as composing led to improved music-reading scores.

Research on Score Reading among Trained Musicians

Although the focus of this chapter is the acquisition of music-reading skills, there are some additional studies on closely related topics that have to do with how experienced readers use these skills. Because younger musicians rarely have the opportunity to be involved in score reading, the subjects of these studies are primarily college students or music teachers. These ancillary studies are primarily concerned with sight-reading and pianists, proofreader's error, the improvement of error detection skills, and the relationship of error detection skills to other variables.

Sight Reading and Pianists

Watkins and Hughes (1986) investigated the effect of accompanying a tape-recorded soloist on the ability of class piano students to sight-read piano accompaniments. Results indicated a significant increase in rhythm reading, but not on measures of pitch or expressive elements. Lowder (1973) examined scores on a piano sight-reading test administered to university class piano students. The experimental group was taught using a program that emphasized vertical intervallic relationships through the use of figured bass. Results indicated no significant difference on pitch accuracy between the experimental and control groups.

In two related studies, Lehmann and Ericsson (1993, 1996) investigated the development of advanced sight-reading skills within the particular domain of piano accompanying. Both studies use the development of sight-reading skills among expert pianists as a window onto the broader concept of expertise development. This approach allowed for the isolation of individual differences among experienced pianists by comparing accuracy scores for passages played without rehearsal (sight-reading) to passages played after brief rehearsal (accompanying). In the first study, 16 expert pianists, 8 who specialized in accompanying and 8 who did not, were recorded while sight-reading two accompaniments to a prerecorded flute solo. Analysis of the accuracy scores revealed a significant group by trial interaction. Pianists with an accompanying specialization received higher accuracy scores than those with a performance specialization on the first and last trials, but made smaller overall gains. The researchers posited the existence of specialized sight-reading skills among expert pianists. In the second study, participants were asked to sight-read and also to play an accompaniment. In addition, subjects were interviewed on their training background, accompanying experience, and repertoire, and they performed a series of tasks designed to isolate specific subskills. After controlling for the effects of the subskills, age, professional specialization, and general skill, findings indicated that individual differences in sight-reading among expert pianists are uniquely associated with accrued accompanying experience and the amount of relevant accompanying literature played. These studies suggest that sight-reading skill in expert pianists is a specific domain that is set apart from general executive skills on the instrument.

Proofreader's Error

There is an interesting phenomenon, similar to "proofreader's error" in language reading, that corroborates the evidence that experienced musicians read in units. When reading a book, one reads in context and thus may skip over simple typographical errors. The mind infers the meaning of the sentence by taking in the key words, and the eyes skip over less important details. Pianists were asked to sight-read a piece of music that contained carefully implanted notational errors (Sloboda, 1976a). All subjects "corrected" some of the mistakes; that is, they played notes that would normally have been written rather than the errors that were implanted. On a second performance of the piece, the number of proofreader's errors actually increased slightly, as the subjects made even more "corrections." This indicates that more familiarity with the music allowed for greater reliance on units rather than specific details. Also, notational errors were less likely to be detected in the middle of phrases, indicating that subjects made more inferences about middles of phrases than about beginnings or endings. These inferences were based on structural elements of the music.

Improvement of Error Detection

Reading multiple staves in a band or orchestral score presents difficulties beyond reading single-line or two-stave instrumental and piano scores. Recognizing the importance of score reading and error detection to ensemble conductors, a central question is what techniques might be effective in improving error detection. Several researchers (Behmer, 1988; Costanza, 1971; Ramsey, 1979; Sidnell, 1971) demonstrated that programmed instruction, using written musical scores and aural examples, was an effective technique for improving error-detection skills. Deal (1985) found that a computerized version of Ramsey's programmed instructional materials was equally as effective as the original, but not more so. DeCarbo (1982) found that programmed instructional materials were equal to podium-based conducting experiences on a written error-detection test but not on an actual conducting test that included error detection. Forsythe and Woods (1983) found error detection scores were lower when the subjects were actually conducting than when they were only listening. These last two studies suggest that the use of programmed instructional materials needs to be integrated into conducting experiences.

The Relationship of Error-Detection Skills to Other Variables

Another aspect of error detection involves the correlation of error-detection skills with other presumably relevant variables or the comparison of subjects with different demographic profiles. Killian (1991) compared the sight-singing accuracy of junior high singers to their ability to detect errors on recorded examples. Students (N = 75) taped themselves while singing, using both notation and solfège syllables. The students then listened to the sung examples, looked at the notation, and marked errors heard. Based on their scores, students were classified in high-scoring, medium-scoring, or low-scoring groups. Analyses of correct responses revealed no significant differences between sight-singing scores from notation or syllables. In the comparison of sight-singing to error detection, it was determined that there was no significant difference for high- and medium-scoring groups, but a significant difference was discovered for low-scoring singers, who were more accurate on error-detection tasks than on the sight-singing tasks.

In two related investigations of performance error detection, Byo (1993, 1997) found subjects were more accurate in detecting rhythm error than pitch error, and less discerning of error with increased complexity of timbre, texture, and number of parts. Significant interactions were found among variables in both studies. Several researchers started with the premise that various aspects of studies in music theory would be related to error detection. Sheldon (1998) found significant improvement in error-detection skills for students receiving additional training and practice in contextual sight singing and aural skills. Ear-training grades and dictation and sight-singing scores were highly related to error-detection scores; for example, Larson (1977) obtained a correlation of .80 between error detection and dictation on tonal examples, and Ottman (1956) obtained a coefficient of .73 between melodic sight-singing and error detection. Also, students with two years of theory did better on an error-detection test than students with only one year (Hansen, 1961), and A students did better than students with lower grades in music theory classes (Gonzo, 1971). Conversely, Brand and Burnsed (1981) found almost no relationship between error-detection skills and music theory grades (-.19) or sight singing and ear training and grades (.07).

Music performance and teaching experiences have provided additional variables for study. Keyboard study was related positively to the ability to hear vertical aspects (chords) of the score (Pagan, 1973), and pianists performed better than instrumentalists on a test of error detection (Hansen, 1961). However, a lack of relationship was found between error-detection skills and number of instruments played, ensemble experience, and years of private instruction (Brand and Burnsed, 1981). Also, mixed results were obtained when teachers were compared with students (Gonzo, 1971). Essentially, there were no differences between choral teachers and undergraduate students in their ability to detect pitch errors while reading a choral score. However, choral directors with 6 to 10 years of experience did better than college seniors but not juniors. DeCarbo (1984) found that teachers with 11 years or more of teaching experience scored higher on an error-detection test than did teachers who had less experience. He also found that a subject's principal instrument made no difference in error-detection scores.

In summary, it appears that error-detection skills might be improved through the use of programmed instructional materials. These results have prompted the publication of at least two commercially available sets of programmed instructional materials, one choral (Grunow and Fargo, 1985) and one instrumental (Froseth and Grunow, 1979). However, such programs should be integrated into podium-based conducting experiences. Students who have good keyboard and music theory skills are more likely to perform better on error-detection tests than other students, but the relationship between these skills and music reading is not yet clearly defined. Additional error-detection studies in the literature do not measure music reading as an independent variable.

Commentary on Music Reading Research

Lack of Theory

With regard to the research base in music reading, there is perhaps a natural tendency to make some comparisons with research in language reading. Laying aside for a moment the fundamental differences in the two different reading skills, there are at least two other major differences. One difference is the amount of research. According to Singer (1983), more than 12,000 studies in language reading were conducted between 1879 and 1972, and more than 100,000 studies in language reading have been published since 1966 (National Reading Panel, 2000). There are only several hundred such studies on music reading. Of those studies done on music reading, few can be grouped together to provide a core of research leading toward a solid grasp of a particular issue.

A second major difference concerns the role of theory in reading research. The first major theory in language reading was proposed in 1953, and a significant amount of research has been conducted to examine this theory, along with the others that have since been proposed (Gentile, Kanil, and Blanchard, 1983). More recently, the National Reading Panel (2000) conducted an exhaustive review of reading research and determined that phonemic awareness was a highly effective way to teach children how to read.

In music, there are few theories devoted specifically to an explication of music reading; thus, the bulk of the research appears to be devoid of a theoretical underpinning (Lehmann and McArthur, 2002). Wolf (1976) proposed a cognitive model of musical sight-reading based on interviews with four pianists known to be excellent sight readers. As far as can be determined, this model has not been tested. Music learning theory, proposed by Gordon (2007), includes music reading but does not represent a comprehensive theory of music reading. McPherson (2002) created a theoretical model that he tested empirically. Of four factors, two did not directly influence students' ability to sight-read, while *quality of study* had a weak influence on sight-reading, and *length of study* had a moderate influence on sight-reading. Kopiez and Lee (2006) created a dynamic model of music sight-reading that raises the importance of psychomotor skills as the complexity of the music increases. In a follow-up study, these researchers (Kopiez and Lee, 2008) determined that trilling speed, sight-reading expertise acquired up to the age of 15, speed of information processing, and inner hearing accounted for nearly 60 percent of the variance.

Most of the theoretical work has been done on sight-reading, and in spite of these efforts, there is still a need for explicit theories of music reading that would organize knowledge and research about music reading into a system of assumptions, principles, and procedures. Such theories would be useful in predicting and explaining the phenomenon of music reading. Implicit theories, based on observations of what teachers do, abound. Unfortunately, these are of lesser value in providing the solid grounding that is necessary to guide research.

Other Suggestions

Future research efforts might be guided toward three complementary goals: (1) continued basic research geared toward understanding the underlying processes of music reading, (2) applied research designed to determine the most effective means of training proficient music readers, and (3) greater attention to connections between basic and applied research. An important step toward reaching these goals would be a comprehensive theory of music reading. Although the use of theory in language-reading research was held up as a role model, it should be noted that research in that area lacked a viable theory for 75 years (Singer, 1983).

In looking through the diffuse database, several previously unrelated factors might be brought together as a beginning move toward the construction of a music-reading theory. One important factor is the basic research that indicates that good music readers read ahead in meaningful units and that structural units (e.g., phrases) are important signposts. This notion is bolstered by the applied research in tonal pattern instruction. Also, since rhythmic sight-reading is a strong predictor variable, the focus should be broadened to include rhythm pattern instruction as well. Gordon's taxonomy of tonal and rhythm patterns are potentially important in this regard (Gordon, 1976).

Basic researchers should take advantage of the latest in technological developments. Sophisticated equipment, such as the electrooculogram used by Kopiez and Galley (2002) or brain-imaging technologies, provides enormous research potential. Research on reading music from a computer screen is in its early stages and is inconclusive. For example, Picking (1997) found that while reading music from a static presentation on a computer screen was not as effective as from paper (confirming language-reading studies), subjects expressed a preference for animated presentation of music notation over static computer screen or paper. Continued investigation and improvements, such as new models of presenting music notation on a computer screen, interfacing MIDI equipment, and converting programs to run on more accessible personal computers, will allow data collections that have previously been impossible. Keeping abreast of developments in language-reading research is particularly important for persons interested in doing basic research in music reading.

Similarly, applied researchers can also utilize technological advances to their advantage. A small number of unpublished dissertations have been presented on various aspects of computer-assisted techniques for music-reading instruction, with all but a few indicating no significant effect for the treatment. For a more complete presentation of this literature, see Galyen (2005).

The potential role that technology offers to music-reading instruction remains generally untested. For instance, early research using the tachistoscope could easily be replicated and extended on computers. Since this research yielded primarily positive results and it appears to support the previously identified importance of tonal and rhythm patterns, it is a line of experimentation that should be pursued. Another area of potential interest involves digital recording technology in music instruction. The findings of a number of studies present a positive connection between individual experiences or individual assessment and music-reading success (e.g., Demorest, 1998a; Henry, 2004; Killian and Henry, 2005, Nolker, 2006). These findings indicate a potential role for personal digital recording, calling for further investigation.

Finally, basic and applied researchers should coordinate efforts. There is a need for stronger connections between investigation of instructional practice and the music perception and cognition research that can, and should, support and inform it. While many of the individual studies are well conceived and executed, the overall pattern seems haphazard and indicates a lack of coordination and lack of a theoretical base, both of which are needed for a thorough examination of the subject. In an ideal world, a core group of researchers would gather to map a coherent research agenda.

Recommendations for Practitioners

From one viewpoint, basic and applied research on music reading provides less than compelling evidence about how best to assist students in acquiring music-reading skills. No specific topic (e.g., body movements, pattern recognition) has an extensive cohort of studies that collectively provide overwhelming support for the usefulness of this approach. Furthermore, most of the topics include both supportive and nonsupportive studies. A significant amount of the literature is quite dated. Finally, without the guiding influence of a theory of music reading, much of the literature has a feeling of a scattershot approach, rather than a sustained research agenda that builds from study to study.

From a more positive perspective, there are several points of agreement that lend themselves to suggestions for practitioners. In the absence of contradictory evidence, and until further research provides stronger support for particular teaching strategies, the following points are offered as reasonable suggestions for those who teach music reading.

Pattern Recognition   Both basic and applied research support the important role that pattern recognition plays in successful music reading. Teachers should stress knowledge of musical patterns as opposed to note-by-note recognition.

Rhythm Reading   Strong connections between rhythm reading and music reading have been reported. Teachers may wish to emphasize rhythm reading as a strong foundation for music reading.

Solmization   Use of syllables or other mnemonic devices is an effective teaching strategy. Two issues are still in need of confirmation, however. The first issue is whether a particular solmization system is more effective, or whether any system will work. The second issue is that it is unclear whether the use of hand signs to indicate pitch height is an effective complement.

Body Movements   Foot tapping, hand clapping, and related body movements connected to music reading should be utilized. Based on the previous recommendation concerning rhythm, body movements that mark the beat and/or rhythm patterns are especially important. As indicated previously, the use of hand signs to indicate pitch contours is in need of further study.

Programmed Instruction and Computer-Assisted Instruction   Although the research on programmed instruction indicates that it is an effective technique, the heyday of such materials is past. It is unfortunate that so little research has been done on the use of computer-assisted instruction to teach music-reading skills. For those teachers who have access to both adequate hardware and software, this may be an important strategy to pursue. It also would complement the next suggestion—individualized instruction.

Individualized Instruction   Research with choral students indicates that individualized instruction produces superior results to group instruction. Choral directors should investigate the possibility of offering private instruction, using better readers as mentors for weaker readers, and the previously mentioned computer-assisted instruction.

Recorded Aural Models   Using recorded aural models to improve music reading is another strategy that should be encouraged. This is also an opportunity for commercial products to fill a need.

Creative Musical Activities   Creative activities such as composing, performing, listening, and improvising are effective pedagogical strategies for improving music reading.

Music reading is a powerful tool that allows for many independent musical experiences. Music educators have worked tirelessly to determine the most effective means of helping young musicians acquire music-reading skills. While the music research community has supplied practitioners with some guidance, this is a topic that deserves and needs renewed attention. There is much yet to be learned. With creative theory construction and a coordinated strategy involving basic and applied researchers, exciting progress could be made.

REFERENCES

Anderson, J. (1981). Effects of tape-recorded aural models on sight-reading and performance skills. *Journal of Research in Music Education, 29*(1), 23–30.

Anderson, W. (1994). Education in music (I). In S. Sadie (Ed.), *The New Grove Dictionary of Music and Musicians.* Vol. 6, 1–4.

Azzara, C. (1992). Audition-based improvisation techniques and elementary instrumental students' music achievement. *Journal of Research in Music Education, 41*(4), 328–342.

Banton, L. (1995). The role of visual and auditory feedback during the sight-reading of music. *Psychology of Music, 23*(1), 3–16.

Barnes, R. (1964). Programmed instruction in music fundamentals for future elementary teachers. *Journal of Research in Music Education, 12*(3), 187–198.

Bebeau, M. (1982). Effects of traditional and simplified methods of rhythm-reading instruction. *Journal of Research in Music Education, 30*(2), 107–119.

Behmer, C. (1988). *The effect of a learning program on the ability of undergraduate music students to detect errors in performance.* Unpublished doctoral dissertation. University of Illinois at Urbana-Champaign.

Bengtsson, S., & Ullén, F. (2006). Dissociation between melodic and rhythmic processing during piano performance from musical scores. *NeuroImage, 30,* 272–284.

Bent, I., Hughes, D., Provine, R., Rastall, R., Kilmer, A., Hiley, D., et al. (2008). Notation (I). In Grove Music Online. Oxford Music Online, Retrieved October 13, 2008 from www.oxfordmusiconline.com/subscriber/article/grove/music/20114?q=notation&search=quick&pos=1&_start=1#firsthit.

Birge, E. (1928). *History of public school music in the United States.* Washington, DC: Music Educators National Conference.

Boyle, J. (1970). The effect of prescribed rhythmical movements on the ability to read music at sight. *Journal of Research in Music Education, 18*(4), 307–318.

Bradley, I. (1974). Development of aural and visual perception through creative processes. *Journal of Research in Music Education, 22*(3), 234–240.

Brand, M., & Burnsed, V. (1981). Music abilities and experiences as predictors of error-detection skill. *Journal of Research in Music Education, 29*(2), 91–96.

Brodsky, W., Henik, A., Rubinstein, B., Ginsborg, J., & Kessler, Y. (2006). Notational audiation is the perception of the "mind's voice." In M. Baroni,

A. Addessi, R. Caterina, & M. Costa (Eds.), *Proceedings of the 9th International Conference on Music Perception & Cognition*. Unpublished proceedings.

Brodsky, W., Henik, A., Rubinstein, B., & Zorman, M. (2003). Auditory images from musical notation in expert musicians. *Perception & Psychophysics, 65*(4), 602–612.

Brodsky, W., Kessler, Y., & Henik, A. (2006). The automaticity of music reading. In M. Baroni, A. Addessi, R. Caterina, & M. Costa (Eds.), *Proceedings of the 9th International Conference on Music Perception & Cognition*. Unpublished proceedings.[a]

Brodsky, W., Kessler, Y., Rubinstein, B.-S., Ginsborg, J., & Henik, A. (2008). The mental representation of music notation: Notational audiation. *Journal of Experimental Psychology, 34*(2), 427–445.

Brown, S., Martinez, M., & Parsons, L. (2006). Music and language side by side in the brain: A PET study of the generation of melodies and sentences. *European Journal of Neuroscience, 23*, 2791–2803.

Bukspan, Y. (1979). Introduction of musical literacy to children by means of a binary system of music notation: An experimental study. *Bulletin of the Council for Research in Music Education, 59*, 13–17.

Byo, J. (1988). The effect of barlines in music notation on rhythm reading performance. *Contributions to Music Education, 15*, 7–14.

Byo, J. (1992). Effects of barlines, pitch, and meter on musicians' rhythm reading performance. *Journal of Band Research, 27*(2), 34–44.

Byo, J. (1993). The influence of textural and timbral factors on the ability of music majors to detect performance errors. *Journal of Research in Music Education, 41*(2), 156–167.

Byo, J. (1997). The effects of texture and number of parts on the ability of music majors to detect performance errors. *Journal of Research in Music Education, 45*(1), 51–66.

Cappelletti, M., Waley-Cohen, H., Butterworth, B., & Kopelman, M. (2000). A selective loss of the ability to read and write music. *Neurocase, 6*(4), 321–332.

Cassidy, J. (1993). Effects of various sightsinging strategies on nonmusic majors' pitch accuracy. *Journal of Research in Music Education, 41*(4), 293–302.

Chase, G. (1955). *America's music*. New York: McGraw-Hill.

Christ, W. (1966). *The reading of rhythmic notation approached experimentally according to techniques and principles of word reading*. Unpublished doctoral dissertation, Indiana University, Bloomington.

Colley, B. (1987). A comparison of syllabic methods for improving rhythm literacy. *Journal of Research in Music Education, 35*(4), 221–235.

Colwell, R., & Rundell, G. (1965). An evaluation of achievement in auditory-visual discrimination resulting from specific types of musical experiences among junior high school students. *Journal of Research in Music Education, 13*(4), 239–245.

Consortium of National Arts Education Associations. (1994). *National Standards for Arts education: What every young American should know and be able to do in the arts*. Reston, VA: Music Educators National Conference.

Costanza, A. (1971). Programmed instruction in score reading skills. *Journal of Research in Music Education, 19*(4), 453–459.

Cutietta, R. (1979). The effects of including systemized sight-singing drill in the middle school choral rehearsal. *Contributions to Music Education, 7*, 12–20.

Daniels, R. (1986). Relationships among selected factors and the sight-reading ability of high school mixed choirs. *Journal of Research in Music Education, 34*(4), 279–289.

Deal, J. (1985). Computer-assisted instruction in pitch and rhythm error detection. *Journal of Research in Music Education, 33*(3), 159–167.

DeCarbo, N. (1982). The effects of conducting experience and programmed materials on error-detection scores of college conducting students. *Journal of Research in Music Education, 30*(3), 187–200.

DeCarbo, N. (1984). The effect of years of teaching experience and major performance instrument on error detection scores of instrumental music teachers. *Contributions to Music Education, 11*, 28–32.

Demorest, S. (1998a). Improving sight-singing performance in the choral ensemble: The effect of individual testing. *Journal of Research in Music Education, 46*(2), 182–192.

Demorest, S. (1998b). Sightsinging in the secondary choral ensemble: A review of the research. *Bulletin of the Council for Research in Music Education, 137*, 1–15.

Demorest, S. (2001). *Building choral excellence: Teaching sight-singing in the choral rehearsal.* New York: Oxford University Press.

Demorest, S., & May, W. (1995). Sight-singing instruction in the choral ensemble: Factors related to individual performance. *Journal of Research in Music Education, 43*(2), 156–167.

DiFronzo, R. (1969). *A comparison of tachistoscopic and conventional methods in teaching grade three music sight-playing on a melody wind instrument.* Unpublished doctoral dissertation, University of Connecticut, Storrs.

Drake, A. (1968). An experimental study of selected variables in the performance of musical durational notation. *Journal of Research in Music Education, 16*(4), 329–338.

Elliott, C. (1982). The relationships among instrumental sight-reading ability and seven selected predictor variables. *Journal of Research in Music Education, 30*(1), 5–14.

Fasanaro, A., Spitaleri, D., Valiani, R., & Grossi, D. (1990). Dissociation in musical reading: A musician affected by alexia without agraphia. *Music Perception, 7*(3), 259–272.

Fine, P., Berry, A., & Rosner, B. (2006). The effect of pattern recognition and tonal predictability on sight-singing ability. *Psychology of Music, 34*(4), 431–447.

Forsythe, J., & Woods, J. (1983). The effects of conducting on the error detection ability of undergraduate and graduate instrumental conductors. *Contributions to Music Education, 10*, 27–31.

Fourie, E. (2004). The processing of music notation: Some implications for piano sight-reading. *Journal of the Musical Arts in Africa, 1*, 1–23.

Franklin, E. (1977). An experimental study of text notation. *Bulletin of the Council for Research in Music Education, 50*, 18–20.

Froseth, J., & Grunow, R. (1979). *MLR instrumental score reading program.* Chicago: G.I.A.

Furneaux, S., & Land, M. (1998). Eye movements during music reading: How far ahead do pianists look? *Perception 27 ECVP Abstract Supplement, 49.*

Furneaux, S., & Land, M. (1999). The effects of skill on the eye-hand span during musical sight-reading. *Proceedings of the Royal Society of London, Series B: Biological Sciences, 266*, 2435–2440.

Galyen, S. (2005). Sight-reading ability in wind and percussion students: A review of recent literature. *Update Applications of Research in Music Education*, 24(1), 57–70.

Gentile, L., Kanil, M., & Blanchard, J. (Eds.). (1983). *Reading research revisited*. Columbus, OH: Charles E. Merril.

Gonzo, C. (1971). An analysis of factors related to choral teachers' ability to detect pitch errors while reading the score. *Journal of Research in Music Education*, 19(3), 259–271.

Goolsby, T. (1989). Computer applications to eye movement research in music reading. *Psychomusicology*, 8, 111–126.

Goolsby, T. (1994a). Eye movement in music reading: Effects of reading ability, notational complexity, and encounters. *Music Perception*, 12(1), 77–96.

Goolsby, T. (1994b). Profiles of processing: Eye movements during sightreading. *Music Perception*, 12(1), 97–123.

Gordon, E. (1976). *Tonal and rhythm patterns: An objective analysis*. Albany: State University of New York Press.

Gordon, E. (2007). *Learning sequences in music: Skill, content, and patterns*. Chicago: G.I.A.

Gregory, T. (1972). The effects of rhythmic notation variables on sight-reading errors. *Journal of Research in Music Education*, 20(4), 462–468.

Gromko, J. (2004). Predictors of music sight-reading ability in high school wind players. *Journal of Research in Music Education*, 52(1), 6–15.

Grunow, R., & Fargo, M. (1985). *The choral score reading program*. Chicago: G.I.A.

Grutzmacher, P. (1987). The effects of tonal pattern training on the aural perception, reading recognition, and melodic sight-reading achievement of first-year instrumental music students. *Journal of Research in Music Education*, 35(3), 171–181.

Gunter, T., Schmidt, B.-H., & Besson, M. (2003). Let's face the music: A behavioral and electrophysiological exploration of score reading. *Psychophysiology*, 40(5), 742–751.

Hammer, H. (1963). An experimental study of the use of the tachistoscope in the teaching of melodic sight singing. *Journal of Research in Music Education*, 11(1), 44–54.

Hansen, L. (1961). A study of score reading ability of musicians. *Journal of Research in Music Education*, 9(2), 147–156.

Hargiss, G. (1962). The acquisition of sight singing ability in piano classes for students preparing to be elementary teachers. *Journal of Research in Music Education*, 10(1), 69–75.

Hébert, S., & Cuddy, L. (2006). Music-reading deficiencies and the brain. *Advances in Cognitive Psychology*, 2(2–3), 199–206.

Heim, A. (1976). An experimental study comparing self-instruction with classroom teaching of elementary rhythm reading in music. *Bulletin of the Council of Research in Music Education*, 46, 52–56.

Henry, M. (2004). The use of targeted pitch skills for sight-singing instruction in the choral rehearsal. *Journal of Research in Music Education*, 52(3), 206–217.

Henry, M. (2008). The use of specific practice and performance strategies in sight-singing instruction. *Update: Applications of Research in Music Education*, 26(2), 11–16.

Henry, M., & Demorest, S. (1994). Individual sight-singing achievement in successful choral ensembles: A preliminary study. *Update: Applications of Research in Music Education, 13*(1), 4–8.

Hewson, A. (1966). Music reading in the classroom. *Journal of Research in Music Education, 14*(4), 289–302.

Hodges, D. (1975). The effects of recorded aural models on the performance achievement of students in beginning band classes. *Journal of Band Research, 12*, 30–34.

Hodges, D. (1992). The acquisition of music-reading skills. In R. Colwell (Ed.), *Handbook of research in music teaching and learning* (pp. 466–471). New York: Schirmer.

Hutton, D. (1953). A comparative study of two methods of teaching sight singing in the fourth grade. *Journal of Research in Music Education, 1*(2), 119–126.

Kalakoski, V. (2007). Effect of skill level on recall of visually presented patterns of musical notes. *Scandinavian Journal of Psychology, 48*, 87–96.

Kanable, B. (1969). An experimental study comparing programmed instruction with classroom teaching of sightsinging. *Journal of Research in Music Education, 17*(2), 217–226.

Kawamura, M., Midorikawa, A., & Kezuka, M. (2000). Cerebral localization of the center for reading and writing music. *NeuroReport, 11*, 3299–3303.

Killian, J. (1991). The relationship between sightsinging accuracy and error detection in junior high singers. *Journal of Research in Music Education, 39*(3), 216–224.

Killian, J., & Henry, M. (2005). A comparison of successful and unsuccessful strategies in individual sight-singing preparation and performance. *Journal of Research in Music Education, 53*(1), 51–65.

Kinsler, V., & Carpenter, R. (1995). Saccadic eye movements while reading music. *Vision Research, 35*(10), 1447–1458.

Klemish, J. (1970). A comparative study of two methods of teaching music reading to first-grade children. *Journal of Research in Music Education, 18*(3), 355–364.

Kopiez, R., & Galley, N. (2002). The musician's glance: A pilot study comparing eye movement parameters in musicians and non-musicians. In C. Stevens, D. Burnham, G. McPherson, E. Schubert, & J. Renwick (Eds.), *Proceedings of the 7th International Conference on Music Perception and Cognition*, 683–686. Sydney. Retrieved June 2, 2011 from musicweb.hmt-hannover.de/kopiez/ICMPC7.pdf

Kopiez, R. & Lee, J. (2006). Towards a dynamic model of skills involved in sight reading music. *Music Education Research, 8*(1), 97–120.

Kopiez, R., & Lee, J. (2008). Towards a general model of skills involved in sight reading music. *Music Education Research, 10*(1), 41–62.

Kyme, G. (1960). An experiment in teaching children to read music with shape notes. *Journal of Research in Music Education, 8*(1), 3–8.

Larson, R. (1977). Relationships between melodic error detection, melodic dictation, and melodic sightsinging. *Journal of Research in Music Education, 25*(4), 264–271.

Lehmann, A., & Ericsson, K. (1993). Sight-reading ability of expert pianists in the context of piano accompanying. *Psychomusicology, 12*(2), 182–195.

Lehmann, A., & Ericsson, K. (1996). Structure and acquisition of expert accompanying and sight-reading performance. *Psychomusicology, 15*, 1–29.

Lehmann, A., & McArthur, V. (2002). Sight-reading. In R. Parncutt & G. McPherson (Eds.), *The science and psychology of music performance* (pp. 135–150). Oxford: Oxford University Press.

Lowder, J. (1973). Evaluation of a sight-reading test administered to freshmen piano classes. *Journal of Research in Music Education, 21*(1), 68–73.

Lucas, K. (1994). Contextual condition and sightsinging achievement of middle school choral students. *Journal of Research in Music Education, 42*(3), 203–216.

Lucas, K., & Boyle, J. (1990). The effect of context on sightsinging. *Bulletin of the Council for Research in Music Education, 106,* 1–9.

MacKnight, C. (1975). Music reading ability of beginning wind instrumentalists after melodic instruction. *Journal of Research in Music Education, 23*(1), 23–34.

Martin, B. (1991). Effects of hand signs, syllables, and letters on first graders' acquisition of tonal skills. *Journal of Research in Music Education, 39*(2), 161–170.

McPherson, G. (1994). Factors and abilities influencing sightreading skill in music. *Journal of Research in Music Education, 42*(3), 217–231.

McPherson, G. (1995). The assessment of musical performance: Development and validation of five new measures. *Psychology of Music, 23*(2), 142–161.

McPherson, G. (2002). From sound to sign. In R. Parncutt & G. McPherson (Eds.), *The science and psychology of music performance* (pp. 99–115). Oxford: Oxford University Press.

Midorikawa, A., Kawamura, M., & Kezuka, M. (2003). Musical alexia for rhythm notation: A discrepancy between pitch and rhythm. *Neurocase, 9*(3), 232–238.

Miller, G. (1956). The magic number seven, plus or minus two: Some limits on our capacity for processing information. *Psychological Review, 63*(3), 81–97.

Nakada, T., Fujii, Y., Suzuki, K., & Kwee, I. (1998). "Musical brain" revealed by high-field (3 Tesla) functional MRI. *NeuroReport, 19*(7), 3853–3856.

National Reading Panel. (2000). *Teaching children to read: An evidence-based assessment of the scientific research literature on reading and its implications for reading instruction.* Retrieved June 23, 2008, from www.nationalreading-panel.org/Publications/summary.htm.

Noble, R. (1969). *A study of the effects of a concept teaching curriculum on achievement in performance in elementary school beginning bands.* (ERIC Document Reproduction Service No. ED 028189)

Nolker, D. (2006). The relationship between large ensemble sight-reading rating and the individual's sight-singing success. *Missouri Journal of Research in Music Education, 43,* 3–14.

Ottman, R. (1956). *A statistical investigation of the influence of selected factors on the skills of sight singing.* Unpublished doctoral dissertation, North Texas State College, Denton.

Owen, N. (1973). Teaching music fundamentals to the seventh grade via programmed materials. *Journal of Research in Music Education, 21*(1), 55–60.

Pagan, K. (1973). An experiment in the measurement of certain aspects of score reading ability. Rev. by C. Gonzo in *Bulletin of the Council for Research in Music Education, 31,* 29–35.

Palmer, M. (1976). Relative effectiveness of two approaches to rhythm reading for fourth-grade students. *Journal of Research in Music Education, 24*(3), 110–118.

Parsons, L. (2001). Exploring the functional neuroanatomy of music performance, perception, and comprehension. *Annals of the New York Academy of Sciences, 930*, 211–231.

Peretz, I., & Zatorre, R. (2005). Brain organization for music processing. *Annual Review of Psychology, 56*, 89–114.

Perrin, P. (1970). Systems of scale notation in nineteenth-century American tune books. *Journal of Research in Music Education, 18*(3), 257–264.

Picking, R. (1997). Reading music from screen vs. paper. *Behaviour and Information Technology, 16*(2), 72–78.

Polanka, M. (1995). Research note: Factors affecting eye movements during the reading of short melodies. *Psychology of Music, 23*(2), 177–183.

Puopolo, V. (1971). The development and experimental application of self-instructional practice materials for beginning instrumentalists. *Journal of Research in Music Education, 19*(3), 342–349.

Ramsey, D. (1979). Programmed instruction using band literature to teach pitch and rhythm error detection to music education students. *Journal of Research in Music Education, 27*(3), 149–162.

Rayner, K. (1998). Eye movements in reading and information processing: 20 years of research. *Psychological Bulletin, 124*(3), 372–422.

Rayner, K., & Pollatsek, A. (1997). Eye movements, the eye-hand span, and the perceptual span during sight-reading of music. *Current Directions in Psychological Science, 6*(2), 49–53.

Rea, R. (1954). Music reading films. *Journal of Research in Music Education, 2*(2), 147–155.

Richardson, H. V. (1972). An experimental study utilizing two procedures for teaching music reading to children in second grade. *Bulletin of the Council for Research in Music Education, 30*, 47–50.

Rogers, G. (1996). Effect of colored rhythmic notation on music-reading skills of elementary students. *Journal of Research in Music Education, 44*(1), 15–25.

Sadie, S. (Ed.). (1988). *The Norton/Grove concise encyclopedia of music.* New York: W. W. Norton.

Salis, D. (1980). Laterality effects with visual perception of musical chords and dot patterns. *Perception and Psychophysics, 28*(4), 284–292.

Salzburg, R., & Wang, C. (1989). A comparison of prompts to aid rhythmic sight-reading of string students. *Psychology of Music, 17*, 123–131.

Schön, D., Anton, J., Roth, M., & Besson, M. (2002). An fMRI study of music sight-reading. *NeuroReport, 13*(17), 2285–2289.

Schön, D., & Besson, M. (2002). Processing pitch and duration in music reading: A RT-ERP study. *Neuropsychologia, 40*, 868–878.

Schön, D., & Besson, M. (2003). Audiovisual interactions in music reading: A reaction times and event-related potentials study. *Annals of the New York Academy of Sciences, 999*, 193–198.

Sergent, J. (1993a). Mapping the musical brain. *Human Brain Mapping, 1*(1), 20–38.

Sergent, J. (1993b). Music, the brain, and Ravel. *Trends in Neuroscience, 16*(5), 168–171.

Sergent, J., Zuck, E., Terriah, S., & MacDonald, B. (1992). Distributed neural network underlying musical sight-reading and keyboard performance. *Science, 257*(5066), 106–109.

Shehan, P. (1987). Effects of rote versus note presentations on rhythm learning and retention. *Journal of Research in Music Education, 35*(2), 117–126.

Sheldon, D. (1996). Visual representation of music: Effects of beamed and beamless notation on music performance. *Journal of Band Research, 31*(2), 87–101.

Sheldon, D. (1998). Effects of contextual sight-singing and aural skills training on error-detection abilities. *Journal of Research in Music Education, 46*(3), 384–395.

Sidnell, R. (1971). Self-instructional drill materials for student conductors. *Journal of Research in Music Education, 19*(1), 85–91.

Singer, H. (1983). A critique of Jack Holmes's study: The substrate-factor theory of reading and its history and conceptual relationship to interaction theory. In L. Gentile, M. Kanil, & J. Blanchard (Eds.), *Reading research revisited* (pp. 9–25). Columbus, OH: Charles E. Merill.

Skornicka, J. (1958). *The function of time and rhythm in instrumental music reading.* Unpublished doctoral dissertation, Oregon State University, Corvallis.

Sloboda, J. (1974). The eye-hand span: An approach to the study of sight-reading. *Psychology of Music, 2,* 4–10.

Sloboda, J. (1976a). The effect of item position on the likelihood of identification by inference in prose reading and music reading. *Canadian Journal of Psychology, 30,* 228–237.

Sloboda, J. (1976b). Visual perception of musical notation: Registering pitch symbols in memory. *Quarterly Journal of Experimental Psychology, 28,* 1–16.

Sloboda, J. (1977). Phrase units as determinants of visual processing in music reading. *British Journal of Psychology, 68,* 117–124.

Sloboda, J. (1978a). Perception of contour in music reading. *Perception, 7,* 323–331.

Sloboda, J. (1978b). The psychology of music reading. *Psychology of Music, 6*(2), 3–20.

Sloboda, J. (1984). Experimental studies of music reading: A review. *Music Perception, 2*(2), 222–236.

Sloboda, J. (1985). *The musical mind: The cognitive psychology of music.* Oxford: Clarendon.

Sluming, V., Brooks, J., Howard, M., Downes, J., & Roberts, N. (2007). Broca's area supports enhanced visuospatial cognition in orchestral musicians. *Journal of Neuroscience, 27*(14), 3799–3806.

Stanzione, M., Grossi, D., & Roberto, L. (1990). Note-by-note music reading: A musician with letter-by-letter reading. *Music Perception, 7*(3), 272–284.

Stewart, L. (2005a). A neurocognitive approach to music reading. *Annals of the New York Academic of Sciences, 1060,* 377–386.

Stewart, L. (2005b). Neurocognitive studies of musical literacy acquisition. *Musicae Scientiae, 9*(2), 223–237.

Stewart, L., Henson, R., Kampe, K., Walsh, V., Turner, R., & Frith, U. (2003). Becoming a pianist: An fMRI study of musical literacy acquisition. *Annals of the New York Academy of Sciences, 999,* 204–208.

Stokes, C. (1965). *An experimental study of tachistoscope training in reading music*. Unpublished doctoral dissertation, Teachers College, University of Cincinnati, OH.

Thompson, W. (1987). Music sight-reading skill in flute players. *Journal of General Psychology, 114*(4), 345–352.

Tommis, Y., & Fazey, D. M. A. (1999). The acquisition of the pitch element of music literacy skills by 3–4-year-old preschool children: A comparison of two methods. *Psychology of Music, 27*, 230.

Trisman, D. (1964). *An experimental investigation of maximal speed pacing technique for teaching music reading*. Unpublished doctoral dissertation, Cornell University, Ithaca, NY.

Truitt, F., Clifton, C., Pollatsek, A., & Rayner, K. (1997). The perceptual span and the eye-hand span in sight reading music. *Visual Cognition, 4*(2), 143–161.

Van Nuys, K., & Weaver, H. (1943). Memory span and visual pauses in reading rhythms and melodies. *Psychological Monographs, 55*, 33–50.

Waters, A., & Underwood, G. (1998). Eye movements in a simple music reading task: A study of expert and novice musicians. *Psychology of Music, 26*(1), 46–60.

Waters, A., & Underwood, G. (1999). Processing pitch and temporal structures in music reading: Independent or interactive processing? *European Journal of Cognitive Psychology, 11*(4), 531–553.

Waters, A., Underwood, G., & Findlay, J. (1997). Studying expertise in music reading: Use of a pattern-matching paradigm. *Perception & Psychophysics, 59*(4), 477–488.

Watkins, A., & Hughes, M. (1986). The effect of an accompanying situation on the improvement of students' sight-reading skills. *Psychology of Music, 14*, 97–110.

Weaver, H. (1943). A study of visual processes in reading differently constructed musical selections. *Psychological Monographs, 55*, 1–30.

West, M. (1994). The Babylonian musical notation and the Hurrian melodic texts. *Music and Letters, 75*(2), 161–179.

Willett, B., & Netusil, A. (1989). Music computer drill and learning styles at the fourth-grade level. *Journal of Research in Music Education, 37*(3), 219–229.

Wolf, T. (1976). A cognitive model of musical sight-reading. *Journal of Psycholinguistic Research, 5*(2), 143–171.

Music, Movement, and Learning

3

CARLOS R. ABRIL

Music and movement of the body are two naturally linked phenomena of human proportions. This is evident from the earliest years of life, when infants orient their heads toward a music-generating sound source (e.g., Fassbender, 1996), to later years, when children move their bodies to music with greater control and in culturally stylized ways (e.g., Blacking, 1967; Campbell, 1998; Moog, 1976) or adults move to music for therapeutic purposes (e.g., Frego, 2009). In fact, movement may be among the first human responses to music. Noting children's propensity to move as they produce music, some researchers have claimed the two behaviors might be one and the same (Moorhead and Pond, 1978). Others contend that the inherent properties of music create the real or imagined sense of movement. For example, philosopher Steven Davies claims that "movement is heard in music" and music is "experienced as significantly similar to human behavior" (2003, p. 132).

The connection between movement and music may reside in the human brain, where the motor and auditory systems are neurologically linked (Dura, 1998; Janata and Grafton, 2003; Repp, 2006; Sacks, 2007). Movement, music, and nonverbal processing of spatial information are all thought to be the responsibility of the right region of the brain, and much of that region has been found to become activated when people move their bodies, with or without music (Hanna, 2008). Researchers have found that music practice which includes physical movement "results in enlarged representations of somatosenory [*sic*] and auditory cortex...as well as the motor areas in the brain" (Davidson, 2009, p. 365). Daniel Levitin (2006) suggests that music experiences such as singing and playing instruments were a part of the evolutionary process, helping humans refine their motor skills. Regardless of whether the nature of music invokes movement or there are neural or evolutionary links between the two, clearly, humans are predisposed to respond to the properties of music through bodily movement (Blacking, 1973; Campbell, 1998; Hsu, 1981, Moog, 1976; Moorhead and Pond, 1978; Trehub, 2003). As such, movement is an integral component of musical experience, cutting across time, culture, and geography.

Movement as Ends and Means

Movement as part of any musical experience can be viewed as ends or means. When people spontaneously move to music, they often do so naturally, for sheer pleasure. This is commonly observed when an adult spontaneously taps his foot while listening to music or when a preschooler jumps rhythmically to a song she is singing. In these cases, movement is an end in itself. Another example is the formal practice of creating and/or performing to music, using the body as the primary artistic medium of expression as in ballet or modern dance. Movement is a unique way of expressing emotions that cannot be contained in words or a way of emulating the emotions expressed in music.

Movement as part of the musical experience can also serve as a means to an end. The most obvious example, which relates directly to producing music, is moving to create musical sounds on an instrument or the body. This is accomplished through fine motor movements such as plucking a string on a cello, or gross motor movements such as striking a taiko drum. However, lines between means and end can become blurred when, for example, children march for the simple pleasure of moving to music, as well as for the sound they might produce with their feet.

In educational settings, movement is used for a variety of reasons. It might be used as a means to develop or reinforce conceptual knowledge, skill, or understanding. For example, music teachers who seek to reinforce the concept of steady beat might ask their students to walk to the beat of a song. Movement can also be used as a nonverbal means to make music perception and interpretation visible. It can also be used as a means for accommodating and/or developing the kinesthetic learning style.

Movement as Knowing

Although verbal and mathematical ways of knowing are most highly prized in Western societies, other forms of knowing are important because they offer the potential for communication, understanding, and expression. In fact, Gardner (1983) proposed that kinesthetic intelligence is one of many human intelligences, representing a unique way of thinking, solving problems, and representing knowledge. The Cartesian notion of a mind-body dualism, which had at one time been a prevalent way of thinking, has been rejected by many who contend that bodily movement can represent important forms of knowing and thinking (Dura, 1998; Juntunen and Hyvonen, 2004; Reimer, 2003; Seitz, 2005). Some assert that purposeful movements or gestures are ineffable reflections of a person's knowledge and represent ways ideas can be conveyed without the use of discursive forms (Garber, Alibali, and Goldin-Meadow, 1998; Wis, 1993). Like music, movement and dance are ways of expressing that which words cannot contain (Dura, 1998; Reimer, 2003). Juntunen and Hyvonen (2004) go as far to argue that movement is a metaphor for music and serves as a conceptual bridge to musical learning. While movement might be a unique way of knowing, discrete from music, the evidence seems overwhelming that the two are related. The body can serve as an important medium through which to embody music and demonstrate musical knowledge.

Movement in Music Teaching and Learning

Given the undeniable relationship between music and movement, and the fact that music making requires the simultaneous application of various sensory modalities, including the kinesthetic, it follows that the use of movement would be a logical part of music learning and teaching processes. Its use is suggested in K-8 music textbook series (Bond et al., 2008), as well as music methods texts for preservice educators (Anderson and Lawrence, 2004; Campbell and Scott-Kassner, 2006; Richardson and Atterbury, 2001). It also plays a prominent role in some commonly used music teaching approaches, most notably Dalcroze and Orff. Using movement to develop learning may be done based on the assumption that these experiences help students internalize or reinforce certain music concepts. Pedagogical articles and books advocate for its use in developing rhythmic competence (Dalby, 2005; Shehan, 1987; Weikart, 1989), musical expressivity (Carlson, 1980; Schnebly-Black and Moore, 1997), conceptual knowledge (Neil, 1990), and overall musicality (Campbell and Scott-Kassner, 2006; Woods, 1987). Furthermore, learning dances from specific cultures is thought to deepen understanding of musical practices and people (Longden and Weikart, 1998; McCarthy, 1996; Shehan, 1984).

The pedagogical literature on movement in music education is primarily geared toward working with students at the preschool and elementary levels. And while there is some discussion about using movement with students in instrumental music and/or at the secondary level (O'Toole, 2003; Regelski, 2004; Schleuter, 1997), it is limited in scope and far less prominent. This may be a consequence of the nature of music programs in secondary schools, which are primarily large Western European–style performing ensembles (Abril and Gault, 2008), or the notion that movement is more relevant and effective for use with children than adolescents or adults.

Music and movement are inextricably connected and mutually reinforcing phenomena. This might explain why movement is an inherent part of the musical experience, where it is enacted in culturally specific ways that serve as both ends (e.g., artistic expression, body awareness) and means (e.g., musical skill development, producing music). One area of movement and music that is of particular interest to music educators is how it might be used to facilitate musical learning. This is what the present chapter seeks to examine in further depth.

Purpose, Procedures, and Terminology

While there are pedagogical and theoretical books in which movement is central to the music-learning experience (e.g., Abramson, 1998; Jaques-Dalcroze, 1921; Schnebly-Black and Moore, 1997) and a respectable body of research literature on movement has emerged in the last 30 years, there seem to be no monographs or cohesive book sections in the music education literature that focus on research examining the relationship between movement and music learning. Intuitively, many educators believe that engaging learners in purposeful movement experiences is beneficial to general and specific facets of musical ability and knowledge. Extant research might be able to shed light on these beliefs and practices. The purpose of this chapter is to provide a broad view of the research literature on movement for its potential to inform future research and application in myriad learning settings.

Initial searches for articles and monographs on movement, education, music, understanding, and learning yielded hundreds of citations that were categorized into one of three categories: historical/theoretical, contextual, and empirical. Because the literature on movement was so large and encompassed so many disciplines, documents that did not examine movement in terms of its relationship to music or music-learning processes were not included. Studies were read and judgments were made as to their relevance, importance, and suitability for the chapter. Research on conducting, of which there was a respectable amount, was included only if it examined conducting not as an end, but as a means for developing musical understanding and knowledge. While music education was the primary focus, research in other fields was included if it was thought to shed light on movement's relationship to musical understanding.

The chapter begins by examining the use of movement in music teaching and learning processes from a historical and theoretical perspective. This is followed by a consideration of several contextual issues that influence the ways movement is currently being used by music teachers and the ways learners respond to these experiences. The next major section encompasses a review of evidence-based research literature that relates directly to the music experience. The chapter concludes with a discussion of patterns, implications for practice, and suggestions for future research.

Terminology related to movement and music education has been applied inconsistently in various bodies of literature. In an effort to remain consistent within this chapter, here are some operational definitions of commonly applied terms. *Dance* is thought to be a Western concept with no corollaries in other cultures outside the West (Kaeppler, 2000). While music and dance are seen as one and the same in some cultures (Merriam, 1964; Nettl, 2005), in the West, these two concepts remain distinct. Dance researchers use the term *dance* to include any expressive human movement arising from creative processes (Barr and Lewin, 1994; Hanna, 2008; Kaeppler, 2000). It should come as no surprise, then, that dance is usually viewed as being peripheral to music education. For the purposes of this chapter, dance is a creative process of moving the body in space and time, in structured and culturally recognized ways.

Purposeful movement will be used to refer to external body movements used as a means to a nonmovement or dance end. While purposeful movement can be dancelike, it differs from dance in that it is not created or experienced for its own sake (Hanna, 1982). Purposeful movement, or just *movement* herein, can be a creative manipulation of the body, but the primary function is not centered on movement for its own sake. Purposeful movement can be subdivided into *directive movement*, which is directed and/or planned out by one or more people (i.e., choreographed), and *creative movement*, which is learner-driven, exploratory, and free.

Locomotor refers to any movement in which a person travels through space, from one place to another. Examples of locomotor movement include walking, skipping, crawling, and galloping. *Nonlocomotor* movement takes place around the axis of the body and does not carry a person from one place to another. Examples of nonlocomotor movements include clapping, stomping, and kicking. Other terms are described as they arise in the context of this chapter.

Historical and Theoretical Issues

In a historical study of movement in music education, Campbell(1991) traced the use of movement in American music education to the late-19th- and early-20th-century efforts of educational reformers like John Dewey, Friedrich Froebel, and G. Stanley Hall. These leaders of the progressive movement in education believed that instruction in schools should be child-centered, meaning classroom activities should arise from children's natural interests and curiosities. They advocated for the inclusion of music and movement in the school curriculum because they were considered to be of natural interest to children and a way they learn.

Around the same time, the experiments and writings of Emile Jaques-Dalcroze were noticed by music educators in the United States (Lewis, 1998; Mark and Gary, 2007). Jaques-Dalcroze developed a system of rhythmic training through movement called Eurhythmics, which is just one part of a three-pronged approach commonly referred to as "Dalcroze." The other parts of this approach to music education include solfège *rhythmique* and improvisation. The games, exercises, and activities used in this approach are thought to help students develop musicianship by the internalization of sounds through muscles and nerves and externalizations through bodily movements. Seitz (2005) provides some examples of Dalcroze-type activities: "students will toss bean bags or balls across the floor in rhythm...tap on the piano to different rhythms in unison, [or] clap their hands together while making lower leg movements in different meters" (p. 423).[1] Jaques-Dalcroze theorized that people should develop their musicality and kinesthetic awareness through active sensory experiences before more cerebral musical training begins (Schnebly-Black and Moore, 1997). He believed that the use of movement served as primary vehicle to access musical understanding and as a way to connect the mind, body, and spirit in the musical experience (Jaques-Dalcroze, 1921). The Dalcroze approach continues to be discussed and practiced in music education around the world today. Many consider it to be a viable approach for facilitating the development of musical skill, knowledge, and understanding for children and adults.

In 1908, Charles Farnsworth traveled to Europe to study innovative music education practices of the time. That is where he first observed Dalcroze teaching approaches in practice and recognized its potential for use in American music education (Mark and Gary, 2007). In a book published one year later, he advocated using movement in music education as a way to motivate children to focus on songs and to develop rhythmic competence (Farnsworth, 1909). In the 1920s, Mabelle Glenn was responsible for incorporating many of the movement-based ideas of Dalcroze Eurhythmics in the textbook series she edited, *World of Music* (Mark and Gary, 2007). Another influential leader in music education, James Mursell (1937), asserted that muscular responses to music were essential to learning rhythm. Specifically, he believed that movement was necessary for developing an understanding of melodic rhythms (phrasing) (Campbell, 1991). In the United States, the work of the aforementioned individuals helped to provide a theoretical, practical, and empirical basis for using movement in music classrooms.

While there was a momentum toward including movement in classrooms, there was some resistance to its application in the music curriculum (Campbell, 1991). In the early 20th century, Thaddeus Giddings (1929) asserted that movement was not an effective or efficient way of using time during music instruction, believing efforts should focus on developing students' ability to read music instead. He recommended that rhythmic movement be taught within the physical education curriculum. Although there were some exceptions, music textbooks at the time focused primarily on singing, with few to no pedagogical suggestions for the use of movement (Campbell, 1991). In most schools of the early 20th century, dance and rhythmic movement education fell under the auspices of physical education, not music education (Carter, 1984; Volk, 1998).

Rudolf von Laban was another major figure in movement and dance education who had an impact on music education. He believed that movement should be learned by all people as a way to develop self-awareness and creativity (Laban and Ullmann, 1971). Although his theories of movement (developed before 1950) were more typically applied in dance and physical education, they eventually made their way into music teaching and learning practices (Brooks, 1993; Gordon, 2007; Lewis, 1998). Laban asserted there were four factors of bodily movement (time, space, flow, and weight) and eight basic actions (punch, slash, dab, flick, press, wring, glide, and float) (Laban and Ullmann, 1971). These concepts were thought to encompass a movement vocabulary that could be notated or used pedagogically. The application of Laban's ideas to music education came in interpreting movements through music and expressing music perceptions through movement, using the aforementioned factors and actions as guiding prompts or conceptual frames (Gordon, 2007; Nash, 1974; Woods, 1987). In recent years, there has been an emerging interest in applying Laban's ideas to conducting (e.g., Billingham, 2009; Gambetta, 2005).

Music educator and composer Zoltan Kodály sought to apply movement as a means to better singing in his method of music education (Choksy, 1981; Johnston, 1986). This primarily entailed the use of hand signs (commonly attributed to John Curwen and Sarah Glover), which represented different solfège syllables that could be used in conjunction with singing (Landis and Carder, 1990). Engaging the visual and kinesthetic modalities was thought to help children develop a better sense of intervallic relationships (Choksy, Abramson, Gillespie, Woods, and York, 2001; Choksy, 1999). While folk dances, action songs, and other forms of movement might be used as part of the Kodály method, they are considered tangential, not fundamental (Choksy et al., 2001). Kodály believed that movement should be used only as a means to help children develop musical knowledge and eventually be weaned away. In the words of Kodály: "You can truly understand music only if you hear music with no bodily movement at all—only in your brain, only if the music is flying freely in your head without any touch to the earth" (Johnston, 1986, p. 14).

The Orff approach to music teaching and learning evolved, in part, based on the assumption that dance arises from music and music arises from dance. In the early years of its development, Carl Orff and his collaborators experimented with integrating dance and musical arts by providing dancers with the opportunity to make music and musicians the opportunity to dance (Choksy et al., 2001; Shamrock, 1997). Carl Orff and Gunild Keetman (his close collaborator) were greatly influenced by the ideas of Jaques-Dalcroze and Laban (Orff, 1977). Many years after these initial experiments in music and dance education, Orff continued to posit that movement was a vital component of the music-learning experience. He stated that music should not be taught on its own; he believed that it should be a "unity with movement, dance, and speech" (1977, p. 6). Much like proponents of the progressive movement in education, Orff (1977) believed that movement was important in the education of children because it was a natural way they responded to their world in general and music in particular. An underlying assumption of the Orff approach is that movement is inextricably linked with music and that the two are mutually reinforcing (Frazee and Kreuter, 1987). Orff (1977) asserted that Western society generally stifled the innate human need to move to music, which limited people's ability to fully develop as human beings. In the Orff approach, movement is used to provide students with opportunities to move in free, creative, and expressive ways (creative movement), as well as in structured and planned ways (directive movement) (Choksy et al., 2001). Today, teachers who seek certification in the Orff approach are required to successfully complete course work in movement, among other areas of study.

Physical education specialist Phyllis Weikart developed a teaching approach called education through movement. It is grounded in the belief that movement serves as a way to enhance learning in many subjects, including music (Weikart, 1989). She describes key movement experiences as an important grounding for music learning. The key experiences are acting upon directions for movement, describing movements, moving in both nonlocomotor and locomotor ways, and moving with objects. It is primarily focused on children in preschool through grade three. Weikart's teaching model includes three components meant to be applied in sequence: (1) separate, or teach movement through modeling using only one of three modes of presentation at a time (visual, aural, or kinesthetic); (2) simplify, or teach movement by starting with the simplistic actions and gradually building on them; and (3) facilitate, or provide students with opportunities to engage with movement ideas such that they construct knowledge for themselves. Weikart (1989) also developed a detailed hierarchy of movement types, based on their level of difficulty. In their book on elementary music education, Carlton and Weikart (1994) assert that a foundation in movement (the Weikart method) is essential in laying a foundation for musical development.

Edwin Gordon's music learning theory (MLT) has been characterized as a comprehensive method for developing audiation, a term used to describe hearing and comprehending music cognitively, without the presence of the sound (Gordon, 2007). The application of movement in MLT has been strongly influenced by the work of Laban, Jaques-Dalcroze, and Weikart and is thought to serve as a vehicle for facilitating musical thinking (Valerio, Reynolds, Taggart, Bolton, and Gordon, 1998). Claiming that rhythm is not an intellectually processed concept (unlike audiation), Gordon (2007) contends it is best learned kinesthetically—through body movements. Specifically, movement is used as a way to develop awareness of rhythmic concepts (i.e., meter, macro and micro beats, melodic rhythms), which are thought to improve musical performance. Like many music educators before him, Gordon asserts that movement is an essential means to improved musicianship. He states that "young children depend on uninhibited movement to grasp meaning of and to eventually audiate meter in a consistent tempo. Thus, when children are given freedom to explore movement, they develop a relaxed feeling as they move, which is the best foundation for formal music instruction" (Gordon, 1997, p. 247).

The National Standards in Music Education (Consortium of National Arts Education Associations, 1994) do not include movement as one of nine content standards, but it is addressed as one of several fundamental ways students can respond to music, as well as develop skills and knowledge in music. More specifically, movement is described as a way children (K-4) can demonstrate their perceptions of music and learn music through direct sensory experiences. Interestingly, involving students in movement experiences is not included in the standards above the fourth grade. Dance, however, is mentioned in reference to one of many arts forms students should be able to relate to music. Active experiences moving in the classroom may be seen as more relevant and/or effective for use with children in music instruction than it is for use with adolescents or adults.

Movement has played a role in American music education from as far back as the early 20th century. It has been applied in myriad ways to reach the specific learning goals that align with a given music education philosophy. Many teaching approaches and methods consider the use of purposeful movement as a means to help learners reach specific goals (e.g., better singing, rhythm, expression). This speaks to the somewhat pervasive pedagogical assumptions among advocates for movement in music education, that movement is an effective tool for developing skills, knowledge, and understanding.

Contextual Issues

Developmental Issues in Young Children

It seems clear that humans are predisposed to physically move to music, yet many questions remain: What is the nature and context of those movements? How do they change as people mature? Researchers have examined spontaneous movements to music in the earliest years of life, a period that is least affected by culture. This knowledge might provide educators and researchers with a better understanding of the ways humans process and come to understand music, which have implications for practice and research.

The first human responses to music are manifest through movements of the body. Researchers have found that infants respond to music-like sounds through movements of their heads and eyes, as ways of orienting toward a given sound source (Papousek, 1996; Pouthas, 1996; Trehub, 2003). These physical responses are thought to serve as indicators of music perception, including preference and attention (Ilari, 2002). Although movement in the earliest months of life does not seem to reflect specific properties of music, movement toward a sound source is a purposeful physical response to music.

The music-like sounds infants choose to move to provide clues about their perceptions. Research has found a strong relationship between a mother's speech, which is quite music-like (Ilari, 2009), and an infant's movements (Condon and Sander, 1974; Gruhn, 2002). Some have theorized that elemental syntactic and prosodic language structures are innately processed by infants through bodily movements (Condon, 1975). Interestingly, Nakata and Trehub (2004) noted decreased limb movements and increased attentiveness (measured through visual fixation) when infants were presented with audiovisual displays of maternal singing. Researchers claim that decreased spontaneous movement is a direct result of increased attention. Another theory is that children feel comforted by the sounds of their mothers' voices, which leads to reduced heart rates, associated with decreased body movements. These studies suggest links between infants' movements to sound and cognition.

Other researchers have studied the nature of movement responses to music in the first months of life. In a classic study of young children, Moog (1976) found that the first physical movements to music included limb extensions, bouncing, and swaying; prior to the 18th month, children moved to music in repetitive but unsynchronized ways. As the infants matured, however, they became better able to control their movements, which permitted them to respond to music in ways that seemed (to observers at least) to reflect the music. Hicks (1993) also found that children 6 and 14 months of age responded to music most often through physical responses but noted a sequence of movement types. Children most commonly and first moved through orienting responses, followed by nonpulsating, then pulsating movements in the body. These purposeful physical responses were found to precede vocal responses to music, furthering the case that movement is a primary form of response to music. These two observational studies note developmental trends in the ways children move to music, indicating greater direct relationships between musical stimuli and movements.

Movement and musical production also seem to be closely related in young children. In their landmark study of young children's unhampered music making, Moorhead and Pond (1978) stated: "The constant simultaneous occurrence of musical production and rhythmically bodily movement, as beating a drum or ringing a bell while marching, led to the belief that the rhythmic factors of physical movement and musical production are related if not identical" (p. 31). At times, music seemed to spark movement; at other times, movement seemed to invoke music making. Children moved for the sheer enjoyment of moving; at other times, they seemed to move as a means of making sounds. For example, children stomped to make sounds with their feet. Similar reasons for moving were observed and described in a more contemporary ethnographic study of children's music making in the United States (Campbell, 1998).

Moorhead and Pond (1978) noted patterns in the unique, recurring movement habits of individual preschool children as they engaged with music. Some children moved in ways that reflect scenes from life (someone swimming or driving a car). Other children moved in more stylized and dance-like ways to music that was being played or to music they produced. Rhythmic movements observed seemed to be reproductions or interpretations of the rhythmic qualities of music. Other times, they were performed for the purpose of creating sound. Children were often observed chanting and singing softly as they walked around the room, yet running was often accompanied by louder chants. Movement speed (or intensity) may be a way children naturally express dynamics (or intensity) of music they produce. We can speculate that this might be the same for music transmitted through another performer or a recording.

Children's creative movement responses to music were examined in another observational study (Sims, 1985). Children between the ages of 3 and 5 were asked to move freely to three different musical experts in an experimental environment that controlled for peer or adult modeling. Music excerpts lasted a little under a minute each and were chosen to represent a variety of styles and tempi. Responses were videotaped, and two observers were asked to analyze the type of movements in 5-second intervals based on the following a priori movement categorizations: locomotor, axial movements (nonlocomotor, large body movements), and small motor movements (nonlocomotor, small body movements). Among all 22 children tested, the frequency of movement types was distributed almost equally: locomotor movements (28.69 percent), axial movements (21.88 percent), small motor movements (21.67 percent), and no movements (27.33 percent). Most individual children limited their movement types to a few. Older children who moved rhythmically were found to synchronize with the beat more often than young children. There were no significant differences in movements by gender. These findings might not be indicative of the way children move in naturalistic settings. Children are likely to move very differently when they are in their bedrooms listening to music or making music by themselves or in more social environments. Nonetheless, it is interesting that children were rather limited in their movement vocabularies, and their abilities to express music through movement continued to develop with age.

In a study of preschool children's creative movements to music in free play conditions of a classroom, Metz (1989) observed that children were in tune to certain elements of the music heard. For example, children would cease movement during silences and resume when the music played again. Although the speed and intensity of their creative movements changed for each musical example, indicating they were aware that the music was different, their movements did not always correspond to the style, pitch, or dynamics of the music. Curiously, Moorhead and Pond (1978) noted that children were able to perceive dynamic changes as inferred by changes in their movements. It may be that children are able to encode and express through movement, music they produce more effectively than music they hear. Findings suggest that certain music elements or ways music is transmitted are more easily perceived or naturally expressed through movement than are others.

Sociocultural Factors

The social environment plays a role in the ways children respond to music through movement. One study reported that children with severe intellectual disabilities responded with movements to music sung or played by a caregiver more frequently than to other nonhuman music stimuli, such as music recordings and music toys (DeBedout and Worden, 2006). Metz (1989) reported that when adults provided verbal suggestions, descriptions, or encouragement, children's physical responses became more aligned with the musical elements. Teacher modeling and verbal prodding were also found to be effective in increasing the diversity of movement responses in young children. Children are also affected by those they observe. From as young as 18 months, children copy movements they see modeled by teachers and caregivers when listening or performing music (Metz, 1989; Reynolds, 1995). Research findings indicate that preschool (Flohr and Brown, 1979) and upper elementary students (Ferguson, 2004) are highly influenced by their peers when moving creatively to music. Clearly, the ways humans move are highly influenced by individuals in their social environs.

Researchers have sought to determine if there are gender differences in the ways children move to music. In an observational study of 3- through 5-year-old children, Miller (1983) found that girls had a tendency to move to music more often than boys. The older girls were found to imitate one another's movements more often than boys. In another observational study of children's natural music-making behaviors, Campbell (1998) noted that "both boys and girls exhibited continuous motor activity, but while boys typically used their whole bodies, the movement of girls often showed an isolation of one or two body parts, such as clapping and stamping" (p. 18). Other gender differences were noted by Boone and Cunningham (2001) in the ways that boys and girls expressed emotion in music through movement (described further in the section on expressivity). In contrast to these studies, Sims (1985) found no differences in movement type by gender—possibly explained by the experimental testing conditions or the *a priori* categories used to measure and classify movements. Despite these findings, the research suggests gender differences in the quality and effort of movements.

The studies of children described in this section provide a window into the ways humans spontaneously move to music. Despite common beliefs, research has demonstrated that from the earliest years of life, children move in purposeful ways to music. Although those movements might not be directly or obviously reflective of music to an adult observer, even from the earliest months of life, they do serve a purpose. A lack of movement, while not indicative of the music elements, might be an indicator of increased attention to music. There seem to be developmental trends, where movements are more closely related to music elements with maturity. These responses can come into greater alignment with music with suggestions or through modeling provided by a teacher or other caregiver.

Children's movements to music are diverse and unique to each individual but are also highly dependent on and mediated by social context. Obviously, as children mature, their environment has an increased impact on how they choose to move (or not move) with and to music. The body of research on spontaneous movements to music made and heard in the preschool years suggests a number of movement categories that might be helpful for purposes of classification: (1) *functional*, or movement that serves a specific function (e.g., orienting one's head or eyes to a sound source) and is not an expression or interpretation of the music heard or performed; (2) *rhythmic*, or movement that is reflective of the rhythmic elements of the music produced or heard that might be realized for the sounds it produces (e.g., stomping feet) or the kinesthetic feeling it induces; (3) *creative*, or movement that expresses a combination of elements (e.g., dynamics, melody, expression) in music produced or heard, freely created by the mover; (4) *dramatic*, or movement that imitates some scene from life experience (e.g., someone cooking or swimming); and (5) *dance*, or stylized movement that is culturally recognized as dance. Any of these five movement categories can be nonlocomotor, locomotor, or a combination. They have all been commonly observed in children's natural engagements with music.

Time and Nature of Instruction

Given humans' propensity to move to music and the historical preponderance of pedagogical endorsements regarding the use of movement in music instruction, one might assume that its use is pervasive in music education practices. A number of studies have measured the amount of time devoted to movement in the music classroom. About 30 years ago, researchers found that movement was commonly used in many elementary music classrooms, although it only comprised a small proportion of class time (Forsythe, 1977; Moore, 1981; Wagner and Strul, 1979). In another study examining uses of music class time, researchers reported that elementary music teachers trained in Orff Schulwerk used movement an average of 26.14 percent, which was more than any other music activity (Wang and Sogin, 1997). It should be noted that there was a high degree of variability among teachers across all music activities that were observed. Connors (1995) reported that elementary specialists in a large urban school district used movement in their music classes with all grade levels, although it was used more often in lower than upper elementary grades. In addition to knowing "if," "how much," and "with whom," some researchers have questioned "how" and "to what ends" movement is being applied in practice.

In a recent study, American preschool teachers surveyed claimed to use directive movement activities with preschool students in conjunction with singing (Nardo, Custodero, Persellin, and Fox, 2006). The majority of these teachers (72 percent) reported teaching movement by serving as models and asking students to imitate them. The most common use of movement was in relation to action songs. Movement was important to teachers because they believed it was a reflection of students' ethnic cultures and it helped them develop their kinesthetic intelligence. Temmerman (2000) studied Australian preschool programs to observe how movement was being utilized in music instruction and what meaning it had for children. Movement was found to be an integral part of preschool music curricula and was used for a variety of means and ends. For example, it was used during listening activities, to accompany singing, to reinforce music concepts, to develop bodily awareness, and to develop social skills. The children in these programs were asked to describe their preference for myriad music classroom activities. Of all music activities that were part of these programs, movement and dance were ranked most positively among students. In describing why, the children referred to the active nature of movement and the joy they felt moving freely and creatively to music.

Student Attitudes and Preferences

Researchers studying student attitudes and preferences have found that movement is a classroom activity generally enjoyed by students. Carlson (1983) studied the effects of a movement-based instructional curriculum on fifth-grade students' attitudes toward the music program. Results indicated that students in the movement group were more positive toward overall music instruction than those in a control group (no movement). Males in the treatment group responded more positively to movement-based instruction than did their female counterparts. Besides the gender difference, similar results were reported for high school students in a choral ensemble (McCoy, 1989). It should be noted that these results might be explained by the Hawthorne effect, which suggests any new or special treatment will yield a positive result. Bowles (1998) found that students were more positive toward moving creatively than toward moving in a directive, dance-like manner, across and within grade levels (K-5). While playing instruments was the preferred music activity (chosen by 50 percent of students), dancing/ moving was ranked second (15 percent), followed very closely by singing (14 percent).

Some researchers have examined students' preferences for various presentation modalities (i.e., visual, kinesthetic, aural). When asked to interpret music through listening experiences, Kerchner (2000) found that second- and fifth-grade students preferred using visual (iconic images representing music) to kinesthetic (creative movements representing music) modes of representation. Similarly, Dunn (1994) found that students preferred to have music presented through visual rather than kinesthetic modalities in a classroom setting. It would be interesting to know if the preference for visual modalities noted in these studies can be explained by the manner in which music is transmitted and/or experienced in contemporary culture. Alternately, visual modes of presentation or representation might seem more valuable to children because of their permanence. In contrast, kinesthetic modes of representation are temporal and fleeting. Children might also be more self-conscious about using kinesthetic representations in the company of their peers.

Research confirms that movement is being used in music instruction, especially at the preschool and elementary levels. The reasons for using movement in music instruction vary, from developing body awareness, to honoring student cultures, to reinforcing music concepts. While movement is not necessarily the preferred music classroom activity or mode of representation or presentation, there is evidence that students express positive attitudes toward movement throughout various grade levels. Students' preferences for movement activities are likely to be dependent on the nature of the experiences provided by teachers. It should be noted that with the exception of one, all of the studies in this section on uses and attitudes focused on formal learning experiences of elementary and preschool age children.

Research on Movement and Music Learning

Rhythm

Musical rhythm has many direct corollaries to movement. For example, when people talk about moving their bodies to music, they rarely say they are moving to a melody or a particular harmony; people move to the beat or rhythm. Furthermore, the ability to synchronize to music is a necessary skill for both music and dance—two inextricably linked art forms. From the fine motor skills needed to play the sitar, to the gross motor skills needed to play a marimba, the very nature of performance depends on one's ability to move rhythmically. Aware of these connections, Jaques-Dalcroze (1921) went as far as to claim that musical rhythm is movement and movement is rhythm. It should come as no surprise that experiences moving may serve as a way to develop or reinforce rhythmic skills or perceptions. A number of studies have examined the relationship between movement and rhythm, as well as the viability of using movement as an instructional tool for rhythmic learning.

Personal Tempo

Personal tempo is the natural pulse or beat created by an individual through locomotor or nonlocomotor movements (e.g., walking or clapping) without any music stimuli. Knowledge of personal tempo is thought to be important because it provides instructors with a baseline understanding of natural rhythmic tendencies. Walters (1983) reported that personal tempo was fairly consistent for individuals but highly variable among individuals. Kindergarten through third-grade students were found to have personal tempi that ranged from 40 beats per minute (bpm) to 210 bpm. Research findings consistently indicate that increases in age correspond with decrease in personal tempo, for both locomotor and nonlocomotor movements (Drake, Jones, and Baruch, 2000; Frego, 1996; Loong, 1999; Walters, 1983). Physical (limbs) and physiological (heartbeat rates) differences might explain these maturation differences.

Like Walters (1983), Loong (1999) found that individual children were fairly consistent in their personal tempi for a given performing task. However, tempi performed by these preschoolers varied according to the task and were found to be less variable among individuals. There were significant differences in mean beats per minute between instrument types used to create a beat. The following are personal tempo ranges by instrument type: scraping instruments (111.09–113.53 bpm), striking instruments (140.18–142.39 bpm), and shaking instruments (162.90–167.93 bpm). This is likely to be a result of the size of the movements required to make a sound on each of the instrument types and the greater complexity of playing a scraping or striking instrument, which involve two hands, each responsible for different types of movement. It is interesting to note the small variability among children on a given instrument type.

Beat   Synchronization studies have examined the ways people maintain a beat to music using movements. Synchronization refers to the "coordination of rhythmic movement with rhythmic sensory stimuli" and is considered fundamental to both music and dance (Repp, 2006, p. 55). People have been found to have a tendency to anticipate the beat when synchronizing taps (small motor, nonlocomotor movements) to a metronome, yet when the stimulus includes additional tones in between the beat, or when additional movements are inserted between taps, the anticipation tendency disappears (Repp, 2006; Snyder and Krumhansl, 2001). Trained musicians also anticipate the beat when tapping, although their asynchrony is far less pronounced than it is for nonmusicians (Aschersleben, 2002). In reviewing a large body of literature on synchronization, Aschersleben (2002) surmised that "synchronization error is in no way an artifact of the experimental situation but seems to be necessary for persons to gain the subjective impression of being in synchrony" (p. 67). These studies might help to explain the general tendency people have of rushing a pulse expressed through locomotor and nonlocomotor movements.[2]

Several studies have examined the relationship between personal tempo and the ability to synchronize to a beat. Children of various ages (6, 8, and 10) and adults with and without formal musical training were tested on beat-tapping ability (with and without a musical stimulus) and tempo discriminations (Drake, Jones, and Baruch, 2000). Researchers reported developmental changes corresponding with increased age and amount of music training, which included a decreased personal tempo and an improved ability to synchronize with music and discriminate tempi. Results also indicated that children were more successful on a synchronization task when the music was closest to their personal tempo. Slower tempi were generally more challenging for students than were faster tempi. This particular finding is consistent with an earlier study of preschool children (Frega, 1979). Furthermore, students classified as having a consistent personal tempo were found to be significantly more successful on the synchronization test than those classified as having an inconsistent personal tempo. Both of these studies suggest that maturation plays a role in ability to synchronize to a beat. As such, performance improvements in moving to a beat might be expected with advanced age, as well as music training.

Clearly, certain movements of the body are going to pose a greater challenge than others for students. In her teaching method, Phyllis Weikart (1989) recommends that children experience keeping a steady beat in a variety of ways but that they should follow a particular sequence, which she posited moved gradually from simple to more complex. One study sought to measure the validity of this sequence by testing children from 3 through 7 years of age (Jordan, 1994). Beat coordination was found to be significantly more difficult using the lower body movements (stomps) than upper body movements (claps); movements without an end point were significantly more difficult than those with an end point; movements asymmetrical to the body were more difficult than symmetrical movements. As found in many prior studies, ability to keep a beat improved with each successive age level. These findings were confirmed by a similar study in physical education research (Derri, Tsapakidou, Zachopoulou, and Gini, 2001). Both of these studies served to validate the sequence of movement types (by level of difficulty), as recommended by Weikart in her education through movement teaching method (Weikart, 1989).

Some studies have examined the different means through which children can express rhythm through movement. In a study of preschool children's rhythmic abilities using different movement types, researchers concluded that large motor movements were more challenging to control than small motor movements (Rainbow and Owen, 1979). This is supported by another study that found that kindergarten through third-grade students had more difficulties echoing rhythmic patterns through stepping than for clapping or chanting (Schleuter and Schleuter, 1985). As in other studies, there was a positive relationship between rhythmic test scores and grade level, suggesting maturation and/or training effect. Rainbow (1980) found that 3- and 4-year-old children are more successful at performing rhythms when doing so through vocalization rather than movement tasks. The addition of speech while moving during music training might also improve the rhythmic accuracy and expressivity of rhythmic movements performed by children (McFarland, 2006). Larger movements of the body seem to be more difficult for children to control with the precision required of rhythmic or synchronized movements. That might explain why children were more successful chanting or speaking rhythms than moving the rhythms through small or large motor movements.

Impact of Instruction on Rhythmic Skills   A large number of studies have sought to determine the impact of movement instruction on rhythmic performance skills. Dalcroze Eurhythmics has been used as an instructional treatment in several of these studies. Rose (1995) measured the effects of Eurhythmics on the beat competency of students in kindergarten, first grade, and second grade. Three classes received music instruction through a Dalcroze approach, and three classes (control groups) received music instruction primarily through verbal explanations and no movement. At the conclusion of the 32-week treatment period, a test of beat competency was administered. Results revealed a significant difference between groups, in favor of those who received the movement training through a Dalcroze approach. Other studies have found that using a movement approach in music instruction (Dalcroze or Laban) had a positive effect on 4- and 5-year-old children's ability to perform macro and micro beats with a song (Blesedell, 1991). No differences were found between the two teaching approaches. It may be that these two approaches were not distinct enough as they were applied in the instructional treatment. In another study, sixth-grade students who received 10 weeks of movement instruction in the instrumental music classroom were significantly better at a synchronization test than were students who received traditional rhythm instruction, without the use of movement (Rohwer, 1998).

One study tested the effect of instruction customized to students' personal tempi on a variety of synchronization tasks (Nelson, 1990). Results indicated that there was no significant difference between those who received the treatment and those who received training in beat keeping that was not customized to students' personal tempi. This finding stands in contrast to a prior study that did find that children were more successful when tasks were closer to their personal tempi (Drake, Jones, and Baruch, 2000). Another study found no difference in synchronization abilities if young children were trained primarily through locomotor or nonlocomotor movements (Croom, 1998). It seems that any training or movement experiences maintaining a steady beat on one's body can result in an increase in kinesthetic synchronization abilities. Maturation and other informal experiences with music seem to be the primary explanation for these results. Maturation is a significant factor leading to improvements in motoric music abilities (Gilbert, 1980; Zimmerman 2002).

Perceiving a steady beat is thought to be fundamental to accurate music performance. Therefore, physically moving one's body to a steady beat while performing seems to be a logical way to ensure beat perception and improve performance. To test this notion, Boyle (1970) studied the effects of foot tapping on 191 high school instrumentalists' sight-reading abilities. In a carefully constructed experimental design, instrumentalists were divided into two groups. All groups received instruction in listening to the beat, as well as playing and practicing rhythmic patterns, but one group was instructed to tap the beat as they performed and the other was not. Results indicated that students who were instructed to tap their feet to the beat were more successful at a rhythmic sight-reading task than those who were not.

Other studies have specifically examined the effect of rhythmic movement training on rhythmic achievement. Children in one study were provided with movement instruction—20 minutes, once a week, for 28 weeks (Douglass,

1977). A control group received rhythmic training using traditional verbal counting systems. Froseth's "Physical Response to Rhythm in Music" (PPR) test was used as pretest and posttest measures to determine the ability to echo rhythms on a woodblock and clapping. Analysis of the results showed a significant difference in rhythmic performance abilities, in favor of the movement group. Moore (1984) also found movement training (through an Orff approach) to have a positive impact on the rhythmic abilities of second- and third-grade students, as measured through an aptitude test. In another study, the use of Laban movement efforts (flow, weight, time, and space) in music instruction was found to improve rhythmic performance skills but not rhythmic perceptions of high school students, as measured by several author-constructed tests (Jordan, 1986).

Most studies examining the impact of movement on rhythmic learning have done so in terms of a particular instructional treatment. Kuhlman (1996), on the other hand, tested the effects of prior participation in a movement-based music instruction on beginning instrumentalists' abilities to express duple and triple meters in performance. One group of instrumentalists had participated in the 3-year, weekly music program that used education through movement (Weikart method) prior to starting the instrumental program. Another group did not have this background. All participated in the same instrumental lessons during the period of the study. Results indicated no significant difference between groups on the ability to express meter in a performance on their instruments. Studying the long-term impact of a particular approach to movement or music education is ripe with possibilities. In this study, the dependent variable might have been too limited in its scope and focus. We can only speculate that a series of varied performance tests may have provided some evidence of the impact of past movement training on current performance skills. Alternately, it is possible that students were not able to make transfers of learning between the 3 years of instruction in general music and the current instruction in learning to play an instrument.

Impact of Instruction on Rhythmic Perception Educative movement experiences with music have been found to shape rhythmic perceptions. In a carefully designed and controlled experiment of rhythmic perception, infants listened to a 2-minute rhythmic pattern without accented beats (Phillips-Silver and Trainor, 2005). As the rhythm played, half of the infants were bounced by an adult on every second beat (duple) and half on every third beat (triple). After the treatment, listening preferences were tested for two versions of the same rhythmic pattern but with accents on every third or second beat added. The experiment was repeated a second time, with infants being blindfolded. Results were consistent for both experiments: infants preferred the version (duple or triple) that corresponded with the way they had been moved. This suggests that experiences of moving to music affect our music perceptions.

Joseph (1982) studied the impact on rhythmic perceptions of kindergarten students of year-long music instruction with a major emphasis on movement through a Dalcroze Eurhythmics approach. Findings indicated that children in the treatment group were more successful in identifying and responding to familiar rhythmic patterns found in unfamiliar musical examples than those in a control group who did not receive movement instruction. Findings from both of these studies suggest that as early as infancy, movement experiences affect rhythmic perceptions and identification skills.

Other studies have yielded confounding results. In one study, sixth-grade beginning instrumentalists who participated in a movement-based instructional treatment were no more successful than the control group (who received traditional beginning instrumental instruction) on a test "that assessed the students' abilities to perceive degrees of steadiness and tempo change in compared isochronous tap sets" (Rohwer, 1998, p. 418). Lewis (1986) found no significant differences in her study evaluating the effectiveness of movement-based instruction on music perceptions of first- and third-grade students. Scores on the rhythmic portions of the dependent measures (i.e., meter, rhythm patterns, and tempo) were no different between the control (no movement) and treatment groups (movement).

Gates (1993) found evidence that a visual-aural mode of instruction was more effective than a kinesthetic-aural mode on first-grade children's rhythmic achievement. Students who participated in the kinesthetic music classes (i.e., movement-based) scored significantly lower on a rhythmic achievement test (aural rhythmic discrimination and rhythmic matching tasks) than those in the visual group. Rhythmic instruction emphasizing movement seemed to be less effective than similar instruction emphasizing visual modalities. These findings might be explained by the tests used to measure achievement, which relied on the kinesthetic less than the aural and visual modalities. Interestingly, other studies have found that children prefer visual modes of representation over kinesthetic modes (Dunn, 1994; Kerchner, 2000).

Rhythmic movement is an essential skill in most music-making endeavors. It is an area of the literature that has been of interest to researchers in both music education and psychology of music. Certain patterns were noted in the literature. First, maturation plays a significant role in myriad rhythmic abilities. As children mature, their ability to synchronize to a beat improves, as do their general rhythmic achievements. Second, when asked to maintain a steady beat to music, people have a tendency to anticipate the beat. Musical training, as well as the type of music stimuli, plays a role in decreasing that asynchrony. Third, certain movements are more challenging to children to perform with precision. Large motor, locomotor movements are more difficult than small motor, nonlocomotor movements. In fact, nonmovement tasks (verbalizations) seem to be the easiest ways of producing rhythm in childhood. This is not to say that they should not perform rhythms through the body at some point, but it might suggest a particular teaching sequence. Fourth, there is no evidence from the research that one movement approach is more effective than another in developing rhythmic skills or perceptions. Studies reviewed indicate that any type of movement training is effective in improving learners' rhythmic skills. The effectiveness of movement instruction in music instruction on rhythmic skills seems to be more convincing than it is for rhythmic perceptions. In part, this might be explained by the fact that movement activities were closely related to the dependent measures, which required movement. In other words, instruction was most closely linked to the test.

Pitch

Many of the English-language terms applied in reference to pitch are metaphorical and suggest space, movement, and time. Terms such as *up*, *down*, *higher*, *lower*, *step*, and *leap* are used refer to both the relative position of pitch and specific movements of the body. While movements of the body are concrete and provide visual and kinesthetic cues, pitch is abstract and has less obvious bearing on the terms used to describe its movement—except maybe in standard notation. Given this semantic relationship, movement might be used as a means for developing understanding of pitch concepts.

Several studies have sought to determine if instruction that includes substantial movement experiences would have an effect on pitch discrimination abilities. One study examined the effect of a Dalcroze-based approach on 76 first-graders' melodic perceptions (Crumpler, 1982). Two intact classes were provided with twelve 30-minute lessons on melodic concepts using lessons from a popular textbook series that included no movement. The other two intact classes received instruction on the same melodic concepts, taught making extensive use of Dalcroze-based instruction (i.e., movement games and activities). After the treatment period, students were tested, using a researcher-developed measure, on their ability to make pitch register and contour discriminations. In contrast to the textbook group, children in the Dalcroze group made significant gains from the pretest to the posttest. While there were significant differences on mean pretest scores between groups (in favor of the textbook group), there were no differences on posttest scores. Results from a similar study with third- and fifth-grade students support these findings (Berger, 1999).

Other studies have also confirmed the positive effects of movement instruction on pitch perceptions. In one study, kindergarten students were provided with either music instruction that included singing and movement or another that only included singing. After 6 weeks of instruction, kindergartners in the movement group performed significantly better than their counterparts on tests of pitch discrimination (Montgomery, 1997). Steeves (1985) examined the effect of using Curwen hand signs[3] on interval identification. Results indicated that children in the hand sign group were more accurate and quicker to identify intervals than children who were in the group that did not use them. In another study, Dunne-Sousa (1988) found that children were able to identify a song most accurately through movement cues (corresponding movements for a song) than through other cues, such as chanted rhythms. These studies provide support for the use of movement in music instruction as a means to improve students' awareness and under-standing of pitch-related concepts.

However, mixed results were reported in one study. Mueller (1993) sought to determine the effect of movement-based instruction on the melodic perception of third-grade students. The instructional treatment, designed to teach melodic concepts through movement, was administered twice weekly (30 minutes) over the period of 9 weeks. A control group received music lessons focused on melodic concepts without the use of movement. The melodic concepts included pitch register (high and low), direction (up, down, and same), and progression (steps, leaps, and repeats). Components of Colwell's (1979) *Silver Burdett Music Competency Test* were used to measure the aforementioned melodic concepts. Results indicated a significant difference between the treatment and control group test scores for melodic progression, in favor of the movement group. However, no significant gain scores were found for either group on measures of pitch reg-ister and direction. One wonders if there was a ceiling effect in this study, given the simplicity of the dependent measure for these children. It may be that any training would have had little impact, one way or another, on test scores.

Vocal Performance

Children have a natural tendency to move as they sing (Campbell, 1998), and singing while moving has been noted to seem more "free" than in other con-ditions (Moorhead and Pond, 1978, p. 41). Several studies have sought to better understand the relationship between movement and singing, two seem-ingly linked phenomena.

In a longitudinal study on the development of young children's musical potential, Gruhn (2002) studied a group of 1- and 2-year-old children in a stimulating musical setting for 15 months, focusing on their attention, movement, and vocalization. One of the most pertinent results of this study was the strong correlation found between the coordination, fluency, and syn-chronization of movements and the accuracy of pitch reproduction in the voice (Gruhn, 2002). Based on the findings of the study and knowledge of the litera-ture, Gruhn stated that "it is difficult to find a neurologically plausible expla-nation because there is no overlap of the cortical areas for movement and voice production, but there is evidence for a neurophysiological link between gross and fine motor control in body movement and in muscles engaged in the vocal apparatus" (pp. 65–66). These results suggest a relationship between fine motor movements that affect singing intonation and pitch accuracy.

Bodily movement might both improve singing and reflect the music sung. In a case study of singer Annie Lenox, Davidson (2001) found evidence to suggest that Lenox's singing voice was physically supported and sustained through the use of certain external body movements. Liao and Davidson (2007) reported that children's movements were reflective of their vocal qual-ities. For example, "the size of the movement reflects the different dynamic levels and the continuity of movement reflects the articulation" (p. 91). One study found a positive correlation between the size of performers' movements and the level of expressive intention (Davidson, 2009). In part, these findings are corroborated by other observational studies in the literature (Campbell, 1998; Moorhead and Pond, 1978). Movements may be used not only as a means to support the singing voice but also as a way to reflect expressive intentions and production.

Movement has also been used as an instructional tool, for the purpose of improving singing. To test its viability, Kim (2000) compared the effects of 10 weeks of singing instruction and singing instruction that included Laban-based movement activities (with a focus on Laban efforts) on first-grade students' singing abilities. A control group received no singing instruction. Children were tested singing a criterion song. Its quality was measured by three evaluators using Rutkowski's "Singing Voice Development Measure" and a researcher-created measure of tonality. Results indicated no significant differences between the two treatment groups (movement and singing-only) and the control group, although there was a small difference in mean group scores between the movement and singing-only groups. It seems that any singing instruction, with or without movement, can positively affect children's singing. Building on this study, Chen (2007) tested the effect of locomotor and nonlocomotor movement activities in music instruction on Taiwanese first-grade children's overall singing performance abilities. Students in the locomotor group were found to significantly outperform their counterparts in the nonlocomotor group.

A similar study was conducted using the high school choral ensemble as the unit of analysis. Holt (1992) tested the effect of Laban-based movement instruction in choral rehearsals on overall group performance. Four choirs received 5 hours of rehearsals and instruction; for two of the choirs, the instruction included Laban-based movement experiences. The researcher controlled for music singers' music aptitudes. Each group's performance on a criterion piece was evaluated by judges using a researcher-designed rating scale. Analysis of the results revealed a significant difference between the groups, in favor of the movement group. One must use caution in generalizing these results, given that the unit of evaluation was the choir, and there were only two choirs in each treatment group. The effects of movement instruction on singing abilities remain inconclusive, given the results of the reviewed studies and limited body of literature in the area of pitch-related concepts.

Expressivity

Bodily movement plays a critical role in musical performance. In fact, it is thought to reflect and generate the sounds being produced (Davidson, 2001, 2009). Surprisingly, however, few empirical studies have examined the direct relationship between movement instruction and the ability to perform expressively or perceive expression in music.

In a unique study, Boone and Cunningham (2001) examined 4- and 5-year-old children's ability to encode emotion in music through creative movements. To do so, researchers provided children with a model of ways they could move a teddy bear to express four different emotions (happiness, sadness, anger, and fear), along with corresponding music. Afterwards, children were asked to move a teddy bear themselves to express the emotions they perceived in eight different music excerpts. Each of their performances was videotaped so that adults could view them (without audio) to determine what emotion each child was attempting to express through the movements of the teddy bear. Results indicated that children were able to accurately express emotional meaning in music through creative movements at a level beyond chance. Subsequent analysis found that children were more successful at expressing sadness and happiness than they were fear and anger. Five-year-old children were more accurate than their 4-year-old counterparts, suggesting developmental differences. Gender differences were also noted. Boys were more apt to express happiness and anger with more intensity through faster tempi and more upward movements than were girls. Girls were found to express happiness through more facial affect than boys. Findings of this study suggest that young children are able to encode emotions in music and express them creatively through movement. A confounding variable in this study was facial affect, which may have provided substantive cues to judges who were charged with determining what emotion children were expressing. In other words, it is not solely movement that was being judged. Given their limited vocabularies at this age, movement might provide children with a way to communicate emotions expressed through music.

In another study examining emotions, Ebie (2004) sought to determine the effect of four different teaching approaches on 56 middle school students' abilities to express four emotions (happiness, sadness, fear, and anger) in their singing. The four instructional approaches were (1) traditional (verbal instructions given by the teacher), (2) aural modeling (the teacher provided examples of how to sing), (3) kinesthetic (students were able to explore different ways of expressing emotions through their bodies), and (4) audiovisual (students viewed pictures while listening to pieces of music representing each of the four emotions). Results indicated a significant difference between the traditional approach and the other three approaches, in favor of the latter three. No differences were found among those three approaches. Findings from this study indicate that instruction that includes movement explorations in the choral classroom is more effective in facilitating expressive singing than verbal directions alone. With that said, aural modeling and audiovisual approaches were just as effective as movement.

Another study examined the effect of Laban-based practices and ideas (i.e., effort and shape) in conducting instruction, on college-age students' abilities to perceive expressivity in various performances (Neidlinger, 2003). Students who received the Laban-based conducting instruction applied a greater number of movement terms to describe and distinguish between various levels of expressive movement in four movement-based performances than did those students in a control group. However, there were no significant differences on their general perceptions of expressivity in the various movement-based arts forms. It seems logical that, given the Laban instruction, participants would apply newly learned terminology in a judgment task. Results of this study are inconclusive as to how Laban methods in conducting instruction might affect students' perceptions of expressivity. These findings might be a result of the short treatment period (approximately 3 hours and 20 minutes). Future research on the application of Laban ideas and practices on learners' perceptions of expressive performance and performance expressivity are warranted.

Music Listening and Perception

Movement experiences may affect the ways people perceive and represent music while and after listening. In a study of preschool children, Sims (1986) found that children who were engaged in movement experiences that corresponded to the music were more attentive during music-listening experiences than those children who listened passively. While these findings stand in contrast to those of a previously reviewed study with infants (Nakatta and Trehub, 2004), there may be differences in the ways children of these diverse age groups respond to and process music. Gromko and Poorman (1998) sought to compare (1) the effect of listening to music while following a visual map with (2) listening while moving to the music with a teacher in terms of perceptions of form. Children who moved to the music scored significantly better on the measure of form perception than their visual-map counterparts. These findings are corroborated by a similar study (Sutter, 1999).

Experiences of moving spontaneously (i.e., creatively) to music were found to improve children's ability to create graphic notation representing rhythm and phrasing in a piece of music (Fung and Gromko, 2001). In contrast, findings from a carefully controlled study measuring three instructional treatments (passive, creative movement, structured movement) on listening map-reading skills showed no significant difference by treatment group (Gromko and Russell, 2002). These results do not support the findings of the aforementioned studies. Given that the treatment provided only one listening of the musical work before map-reading skills were assessed, the researchers suggested that future work on the effectiveness of movement and aural experiences on music perception provide participants with at least one trial before administering a test.

Although there is one study that does not corroborate the others, evidence leans in favor of using movement with children during listening tasks. Movement experiences, whether directive or creative, may provide children with opportunities to process the music on their own terms and construct understanding of the music they hear. Passive listening may not be the most effective in facilitating children's thinking about and/or symbolically representing music. While anecdotal evidence seems to suggest that children enjoy moving as they listen to music, future research might consider ways to uncover how and why kinesthetic experiences add to the construction of musical meaning or identity. It would also be interesting to know the long-term effects of such experiences on students' music perceptions and abilities to listen to music attentively.

Creative Thinking

In the only empirical study found examining movement, music, and creativity, Gibson (1988) compared the impact of 10 weeks of music instruction (focused on improvisation) with music instruction including movement and visual art on sixth- and seventh-grade students' creativity, as measured by Webster's "Thinking Creatively with Music" and the *Torrance Tests of Creative Thinking* (Torrance, 1999). Students in the multiple arts group made significant gains from pretest to posttest on both measures; students in the music-only group also made gains, but they were not significant. Results of this study suggest that providing students with opportunities to incorporate various artistic media, learning modalities, and senses may be beneficial for improving their creative thinking. It cannot be determined from this study if the movement components, the visual arts components of the lesson, or both made the difference. Research that isolates factors could be helpful in pinpointing what impact, if any, movement has on creativity.

Patterns and Future Directions

The striking connections between music and movement have not gone unnoticed in music education. For centuries, music educators have intuitively believed that movement could be a way to develop and reinforce music skills and understandings, as well as a way students can demonstrate their knowledge. Movement continues to be an area of great interest to music educators, as evidenced by the number of pedagogical materials, workshops, and practices that include movement. Its application, however, has mostly been limited to use with children in formal learning settings. Concomitantly, a body of research on movement and music learning has emerged, mostly focusing on the aforementioned age groups and settings. This is the literature's strength, as well as its limitation. Movement, as a teaching and learning tool, may contain untapped potential for use with adolescents, adults, and older adults in myriad music-learning settings.

The ways humans respond to music through movements of the body vary greatly by culture as early as childhood (Blacking, 1973), and there are likely to be marked differences in people's attitudes, behaviors, and learning styles depending on their cultural backgrounds. The majority of studies on movement and learning in the English-language literature were conducted in North America and Europe, so caution should be used in generalizing these findings beyond their cultural contexts. Future research in music education might examine movement and music learning from diverse cultural perspectives, as a way to better understand human cognition and uncover commonalities and differences among cultures. Given the increasing diversity of students in schools across North America and the globe, music education research might seek to examine the relationship of culture and the ways people respond to and learn music through movement. These findings could suggest new culturally informed pedagogical practices.

Many studies reviewed in this chapter compared "traditional" lessons or curricula with those that included movement. In reading some of the studies, movement treatments seemed to be more innovative and dynamic than those provided to control groups. Future research should carefully examine the reliability of the planned and implemented treatments, which might reflect researcher or implementer biases, respectively. This could also help to control for the Hawthorne effect, which posits that any new or special treatment will yield positive results. In some studies, it was difficult to discern if it was participation in movement activities, the innovative nature of the movement lessons, the implementer's bias for a particular treatment, or some other factor that explained the positive effects on musical skills and perceptions.

Studies that use instructional treatments as their independent variables should describe these lessons or curricula in as much detail as possible. Otherwise, replications and application are next to impossible. Furthermore, to say that a control group received "traditional" instruction is not enough to know what we are comparing. Some studies were excluded from this chapter because there was little way of discerning the nature of the instructional treatment provided. Detailed descriptions can better serve educators who might seek to apply these ideas in their own teaching.

Studies measuring the effect of movement instruction on rhythmic performance seemed to be more conclusive than those measuring rhythmic perceptions. This may be because the former used dependent variables for the measures that were more closely related to the independent variable. In other words, there were fewer transfers of learning required of participants. Those treatments that are further removed from the chosen measures may require an extended treatment period. Alternately, the instructional treatment should provide participants with trials in making relevant transfers. Measures are likely to be most effective when all forms of validity, as well as reliability, have been considered.

There are still important questions that remain unanswered: Does movement have a different impact on music learning in childhood than in adolescence or adulthood? If so, what is the nature of these differences, and how might this knowledge reshape music education practices in secondary and tertiary schools? How can expanded forms of movement (beyond foot tapping and rhythm clapping) be applied in instrumental music settings as a way to develop music skills, improve expressivity, and deepen understanding of music? Given limited classroom contact time, one might ask if movement is the most effective use of time. How do people, of various cultures, use movement as a way to facilitate learning in their everyday lives? Can transfers be made to music teaching and learning? Can movement serve as a way to spark creativity? How and to what ends? To date, we cannot answer these questions. Future research might seek to fill these and other lacunae in the literature.

Summary and Implications

Patterns in the research findings of this chapter suggest implications for music teaching and learning. Research has consistently shown that children have a natural need and desire to move to music. Teachers from preschool on should capitalize on this knowledge by providing students with myriad opportunities to move to music. This can give teachers a window into children's music perceptions and also help them develop their understandings of music. While initial experiences of moving freely and creatively to music may yield limited responses, teachers can expand the range of movement types by providing verbal suggestions and visual models, which might draw attention to specific elements of music. Moreover, movement can provide children with opportunities to show what they know through nonverbal means, which might provide an equally valid way of demonstrating knowledge. This is especially pertinent for students who have difficulties or are unable to communicate through a given language (Abril, 2003).

Studies examining personal tempo and synchronization offer some implications for practice. Research suggests that children are more successful at rhythmic tasks when they are within a reasonable range of their personal tempo. Therefore, teachers should take general tempo ranges into consideration when asking children to play instruments or move in certain ways. Tasks required of music students should be sequenced from simple to more complex. Various studies support the application of Weikart's (1989) hierarchy of movement types with children. Maturation does seem to play a significant role in both an individual's personal tempo and beat-keeping abilities. Research overwhelmingly supports the case that children will naturally improve their synchronization and rhythmic abilities with age and experience. It may be that teachers do not need to spend exorbitant amounts of time developing skills in keeping a beat when holistic experiences engaging with music through listening, moving, playing, and singing may suffice.

No clear differences in the impact of various movement-music approaches (i.e., Dalcroze, Kodály, Orff, Laban) on learning were noted in the literature. With the exception of a few studies, it seems that any form of movement instruction was effective in affecting positive changes in participants' rhythmic performance abilities and in some facets of perception. As such, teachers should consider their curricular objectives and goals, consider if movement experiences closely relate to them, and make a decision as to the suitability of incorporating movement experiences in instruction. The particular approach to movement instruction may be less important than its actual alignment with specific learning outcomes.

As compared with rhythmic concepts, the literature examining the impact of movement instruction on pitch is less developed. However, there is support for the application of movement in developing pitch perception. Given the abstract nature of pitch, and the need for learners to perceive pitch changes, movement experiences might provide more concrete ways (visual and kinesthetic) of developing conceptual understanding. The use of Curwen hand signs and other movements of the body that represent the movement of pitch might be effectively used in a variety of learning settings. While there does seem to be some positive relationship between movement and singing performance, the impact of movement instruction on singing abilities is not well established as of yet.

Creative and directive movements in the classroom seem to provide children with opportunities to develop a heightened understanding of the music. Actively listening to music through movement has been found to be more effective than passive listening in getting children to attend, perceive, and represent music iconically. Furthermore, lessons that include a variety of media (movement and visual arts) are thought to be beneficial for improving children's creativity. Teachers might design listening lessons that actively engage students through movement. The literature on expressivity suggests that movement can be an effective way for children to represent the emotions they encode in music listening. As an instructional tool, movement can also serve to make singing more expressive. Teachers might consider creating lessons that incorporate a variety of modalities (kinesthetic, aural, visual) to develop their students' expressivity and general creativity.

Research finds that students are generally positive about movement's applications in their music learning. This might be because of the physical nature of movement or the change of pace it provides for students who spend the majority of a school day sitting at desks. But is that enough? The fact that children enjoy movement activities should not be the primary reason to include it in music instruction. Teachers should know why and how to use movement such that it has the greatest impact on their pupils' music learning. Research reviewed in this chapter provides clues as to why, how, and to what ends. Developing musical skills, knowledge, and understanding should be the primary reason to incorporate the use of movement in music instruction. Ultimately, involving students in instructional experiences they enjoy can motivate them and prime them for music learning.

ACKNOWLEDGMENT

I would like to acknowledge R. J. David Frego for his assistance in initial conceptualizations of the chapter, in locating a number of the empirical studies reviewed, and in contributing to this project in its infancy.

NOTES

1. See the following references for more examples: Abramson, 1998; Boyarsky, 2009; Schnebly-Black & Moore, 1997.

2. For a more detailed review of literature on synchronization from a psychological perspective, see Repp (2006).

3. A system of using hand gestures and movements to represent pitch, commonly applied in the Kodaly teaching method.

REFERENCES

Abramson, R. M. (1998). *Alfred Feel it! Rhythm games for all*. Miami, FL: Warner Brothers.

Abril, C. R. (2003). No hablo ingles: Breaking the language barrier in music instruction. *Music Educators Journal, 89*(5), 38–43.

Abril, C. R., & Gault, B. (2008). The state of music in secondary schools: The principal's perspective. *Journal of Research in Music Education, 56*(2), 68–81.

Anderson, W. M., & Lawrence, J. E. (2004). *Integrating music into the elementary classroom* (6th ed.). Belmont, CA: Thomson Schirmer.

Aschersleben, G. (2002). Temporal control of movements in sensorimotor synchronization. *Brain and Cognition, 48*, 66–79.

Barr, S., & Lewin, P. (1994). Learning movement: Integrating kinaesthetic sense with cognitive skills. *Journal of Aesthetic Education, 28*(1), 83–94.

Berger, L. M. (1999). *The effects of Dalcroze Eurhythmics instruction on selected music competencies of third- and fifth-grade general music students*. Unpublished doctoral dissertation, University of Minnesota, Minneapolis.

Billingham, L. (2009). *The complete conductor's guide to Laban movement theory*. Chicago: GIA.

Blacking, J. (1967). *Venda children's songs: A study in ethnomusicological analysis*. Johannesburg, South Africa: Witwatersrand University Press.

Blacking, J. (1973). *How musical is man?* Seattle: University of Washington Press.

Blesedell, D. S. (1991). *A study of the effects of two types of movement instruction on the rhythm achievement and developmental rhythm aptitude of preschool children*. Unpublished doctoral dissertation, Temple University, Philadelphia, PA.

Bond, J., Boyer, R., Campbelle-Holman, M., Crocker, E., Davidson, M., DeFrece, R., Ebinger, V., Goetze, M., Henderson, B., Jacobson, J., Jothen, M., Judah-Lauder, C., King, C., Lawrence, V., McCullough-Brabson, E., McMillion, J., Miller, N., Rawlins, I., Snyder, S., & Soto, G. (2008). *Spotlight on music*. New York: Macmillan/McGraw-Hill.

Boone, R. T., & Cunningham, J. G. (2001). Children's expression of emotional meaning in music through expressive body movement. *Journal of Nonverbal Behavior, 25*(1), 21–41.

Bowles, C. L. (1998). Music activity preferences of elementary students. *Journal of Research in Music Education, 46*(2), 193–207.

Boyarsky, T. (2009). Dalcroze Eurhythmics and quick reaction exercises. *Orff Echo, 41*(2), 15–19.

Boyle, J. D. (1970). The effect of prescribed rhythmical movements on the ability to read music at sight. *Journal of Research in Music Education, 18*(4), 307–318.

Bowles, C. L. (1998). Music activity preferences of elementary students. *Journal of Research in Music Education, 46*(2), 193–207.

Brooks, L. M. (1993). Harmony in space: A perspective on the work of Rudolf Laban. *Journal of Aesthetic Education, 27*(2), 29–41.

Bumanis, A., & Yoder, J. W. (1987). Music and dance: Tools for reality orientation. *Activities, Adaptation, and Aging, 10*(1/2), 23–33.

Campbell, P. S. (1991). Rhythmic movement and public school music education: Conservative and progressive views of the formative years. *Journal of Research in Music Education, 39*(1), 12–22.

Campbell, P. S. (1998). *Songs in their heads*. New York: Oxford University Press.

Campbell, P. S., & Scott-Kassner, C. (2006). *Music in childhood: From preschool through the elementary grades* (3rd ed.). Belmont, CA: Thomson Schirmer.

Carlson, D. L. (1980). Space, time, and force: Movement as a channel to understanding music. *Music Educators Journal, 67*(1), 52–56.

Carlson, D. L. (1983). *The effect of movement on attitudes of fifth grade students toward their music class*. Unpublished doctoral dissertation, University of Tennessee, Knoxville.

Carlton, E. B., & Weikart, P. S. (1994). *Foundations in elementary education. Music*. Ypsilanti, MI: High/Scope.

Carter, C. L. (1984). The state of dance in education: Past and present. *Theory into Practice, 23*(4), 293–299.

Chen, R. M. (2007). *Effects of movement-based instruction on singing performance of first grade students in Taiwan*. Unpublished doctoral dissertation, Temple University, Philadelphia, PA.

Choksy, L. (1981). *The Kodály context: Creating an environment for musical learning*. Englewood Cliffs, NJ: Prentice-Hall.

Choksy, L. (1999). *The Kodály method: Comprehensive musicianship* (3rd ed.). Upper Saddle River, NJ: Prentice Hall.

Choksy, L., Abramson, R. M., Gillespie, A. E., Woods, D., & York, F. (2001). *Teaching music in the twenty-first century* (2nd ed.). Upper Saddle River, NJ: Prentice Hall.

Colwell, R. (1979). Silver Burdett Music Competency Tests. Morristown, NJ: Silver Burdett Company.

Condon, W. S. (1975). Speech makes babies move. In R. Lewin (Ed.), *Child alive: New insights into the development of young children* (pp. 77–85). London: Temple Smith.

Condon, W. S., & Sander, L. W. (1974). Neonate movement is synchronized with adult speech: Interactional participation and language acquisition. *Science, 183*(4120), 99–101.

Connors, D. N. (1995). *The use of movement by elementary general music specialists in the Los Angeles Public Schools*. Unpublished doctoral dissertation, University of Cincinnati, Cincinnati, OH.

Consortium of National Arts Education Associations. (1994). *Dance, music, theatre, visual arts: What every young American should know and be able to do in the arts*. Reston, VA: Music Educators National Conference.

Croom, P. L. (1998). *Effects of locomotor rhythm training activities on the ability of kindergarten students to synchronize non-locomotor movements to music*. Unpublished doctoral dissertation, Temple University, Philadelphia, PA.

Crumpler, S. E. (1982). The effect of Dalcroze Eurhythmics on the melodic musical growth of first grade students. Unpublished doctoral dissertation, Louisiana State University, Baton Rouge.

Dalby, B. (2005). Toward an effective pedagogy for teaching rhythm: Gordon and beyond. *Music Educators Journal, 92*(1), 54–60.

Davidson, J. W. (2001). The role of the body in the production and perception of solo vocal performance: A case study of Annie Lenox. *Musicae Scientiae, 5*(2), 235–256.

Davidson, J. W. (2009). Movement and collaboration in musical performance. In S. Hallam, I. Cross, & M. Thaut (Eds.), *The Oxford handbook of music psychology* (pp. 364–376). Oxford: Oxford University Press

Davies, S. (2003). *Themes in the philosophy of music.* Oxford: Oxford University Press.

DeBedout, J. K., & Worden, M. C. (2006). Motivators for children with severe intellectual disabilities in the self-contained classroom: A movement analysis. *Journal of Music Therapy, 43*(2), 123–135.

Derri, V., Tsapakidou, A., Zachopoulou, E., & Gini, V. (2001). Complexity of rhythmic ability as measured in preschool children. *Perceptual and Motor Skills, 92*, 777–785.

Douglass, J. A. (1977). *Rhythmic movement and its effect on the music achievement of fourth-grade children.* Unpublished doctoral dissertation, University of Michigan, Ann Arbor.

Drake, C., Jones, M. R., & Baruch, C. (2000). The development of rhythmic attending in auditory sequences: Attunement, referent period, focal attending. *Cognition, 77*(3), 251–288.

Dunn, R. E. (1994). *Perceptual modalities in music listening among third-grade students.* Unpublished doctoral dissertation, Northwestern University, Evanston, IL.

Dunne-Sousa, D. (1988). *The effect of speech rhythm, melody, and movement on song identification and performance of preschool children.* Unpublished doctoral dissertation, Ohio State University, Columbus.

Dura, M. T. (1998). *The kinesthetic dimension of the music listening experience.* Unpublished doctoral dissertation, Northwestern University, Evanston, IL.

Ebie, B. D. (2004). The effects of verbal, vocally modeled, kinesthetic, and audiovisual treatment conditions on male and female middle-school vocal music students' abilities to expressively sing melodies. *Psychology of Music, 32*(4), 405–417.

Farnsworth, C. H. (1909). *Education through music.* New York: American Book Company.

Fassbender, C. (1996). Infants' auditory sensitivity towards acoustic parameters of speech and music. In I. Deliege & J. Sloboda (Eds.), *Musical beginnings: Origins and development of musical competence* (pp. 56–87). Oxford: Oxford University Press.

Ferguson, L. S. (2004). *I see them listening: A teacher's understanding of children's expressive movements to music in the classroom.* Unpublished doctoral dissertation, University of Illinois at Urbana-Champaign.

Flohr, J. W., & Brown, J. (1979). The influence of peer imitation on expressive movement to music. *Journal of Research in Music Education, 27*(3), 143–148.

Forsythe, J. L. (1977). Elementary student attending behavior as a function of classroom activities. *Journal of Research in Music Education, 25*(2), 228–239.

Frazee, J., & Kreuter, K. (1987). *Discovering Orff.* New York: Schott.

Frega, A. L. (1979). Rhythmic tasks with 3-, 4-, and 5-year-old children: A study made in Argentine Republic. *Bulletin of the Council for Research in Music Education, 59,* 32–34.

Frego, R. J. D. (1996). Determining personal tempo in elementary-aged children through gross motor movements. *Southeastern Journal of Music Education, 8,* 138–145.

Frego, R. J. D. (2009). Dancing inside: Dalcroze Eurhythmics in a therapeutic setting. In J. L. Kerchner & C. R. Abril (Eds.), *Musical experience in our lives: Things we learn and meanings we make* (pp. 313–330). Lanham, MD: Rowman & Littlefield.

Fung, C. V., & Gromko, J. E. (2001). Effects of active versus passive listening on the quality of children's invented notations and preferences for two pieces from an unfamiliar culture. *Psychology of Music, (29)*2, 128–138.

Gambetta, C. L. (2005). *Conducting outside the box: Creating a fresh approach to conducting gesture through the principles of Laban movement analysis.* Unpublished doctoral dissertation, University of North Carolina at Greensboro.

Garber, P., Alibali, M. W., & Goldin-Meadow, S. (1998). Knowledge conveyed in gesture is not ties to the hands. *Child Development, 69*(1), 75–84.

Gardner, H. (1983). *Frames of mind: A theory of multiple intelligences.* New York: Basic Books.

Gates, C. A. (1993). *The effect of perceptual modality on rhythmic achievement and modality preference of first-grade children.* Unpublished doctoral dissertation, University of Kentucky, Lexington.

Gibson, S. M. (1988). *A comparison of music and multiple arts experiences in the development of creativity in middle school students.* Unpublished doctoral dissertation, Washington University, Seattle.

Giddings, T. P. (1929). Seeing rhythm. *Music Supervisors' Journal, 15*(3), 23–27.

Gilbert, J. (1980). An assessment of motor music skill development in young children. *Journal of Research in Music Education, 28*(3), 167–175.

Gordon, E. (1997). *Learning sequences in music: Skill, content, and patterns: A music learning theory.* Chicago: GIA.

Gordon, E. (2007). *Learning sequences in music: A contemporary music learning theory.* Chicago: GIA.

Groene, R., Zapchenk, S., Marble, G., & Kantar, S. (1998). The effect of therapist and activity characteristics on the purposeful responses of probable Alzheimer's disease participants. *Journal of Music Therapy, 35*(2), 119–136.

Gromko, J. E., & Poorman, A. S. (1998). Does perceptual-motor performance enhance perception of patterned art mussic? *Musicæ Scientiæ, 2*(2), 157–170.

Gromko, J. E., & Russell, C. (2002). Relationships among young children's aural perception, listening condition, and accurate reading of graphic listening maps. *Journal of Research in Music Education, 50*(4), 333–342.

Gruhn, W. (2002). Phases and stages in early music learning. A longitudinal study on the development of young children's musical potential. *Music Education Research, 4*(1), 51–71.

Hanna, J. L. (1982). Is dance music? Resemblances and relationships. *World of Music, 23*(1), 57–71.

Hanna, J. L. (2008). A nonverbal language for imagining and learning: Dance education in K-12 curriculum. *Educational Researcher, 37*(8), 491–506.

Hicks, W. K. (1993). *An investigation of the initial stages of preparatory audiation.* Unpublished doctoral dissertation, Temple University, Philadelphia, PA.

Holt, M. M. (1992). *The application to conducting and choral rehearsal pedagogy of Laban effort/shape and its comparative effect upon style in choral performance.* Unpublished doctoral dissertation, University of Hartford, CT.

Hsu, G. O. B. (1981). Movement and dance are child's play. *Music Educators Journal, 67*(9), 42–43.

Ilari, B. S. (2002). Music perception and cognition in the first year of life. *Early Child Development and Care, 172,* 311–322.

Ilari, B. (2009). Songs of belonging: Musical interactions in early life. In J. L. Kerchner & C. R. Abril (Eds.), *Musical experience in our lives* (pp. 21–38). Lanham, MD: Rowman & Littlefield.

Janata, P., & Grafton, S. T. (2003). Swinging in the brain: Shared neural substrates for behaviors related to sequencing and music. *Nature neuroscience, 6*(7), 682–687.

Jaques-Dalcroze, E. (1921). *Rhythm, music and education.* Trans. H. Rubinstein. London: Dalcroze Society.

Johnston, R. (1986). *Kodály and education: Monograph III.* ªOntario, Canada: Avondale.

Jordan, F. L. (1994). *A validation of the Weikart sequence of levels of beat coordination for children aged 3–7.* Unpublished doctoral dissertation, Indiana University, Bloomington.

Jordan, J. M. (1986). *The effects of informal movement instruction derived from the theories of Rudolf von Laban upon the rhythm performance and discrimination of high school students.* Unpublished doctoral dissertation, Temple University, Philadelphia, PA.

Joseph, A. S. (1982). *A Dalcroze Eurhythmics approach to music learning in kindergarten through rhythmic movement, ear-training and improvisation.* Unpublished doctoral dissertation, Carnegie Mellon University, Pittsburgh, PA.

Juntunen, M.-L., & Hyvonen, L. (2004). Embodiment in musical knowledge: How body movement facilitates learning within Dalcroze Eurhythmics. *British Journal of Music Education, 21*(2), 199–214.

Kaeppler, A. L. (2000). Dance ethnology and the anthropology of dance. *Dance Research Journal, 32*(1), 116–125.

Kerchner, J. L. (2000). Children's verbal, visual, and kinesthetic responses: Insight into their music listening experience. *Bulletin of the Council for Research in Music Education, 146,* 31–50.

Kim, S. (2000). *The effects of sequential movement activities on first-grade students' solo singing abilities.* Unpublished doctoral dissertation, University of Southern Mississippi, Hattiesburg.

Kuhlman, K. L. (1996). *The effects of movement-based instruction, meter, and rhythmic aptitude on beginning instrumental music students' abilities to communicate metric structure in performance.* Unpublished doctoral dissertation, University of North Carolina, Greensboro.

Laban, R., & Ullmann, L. (1971). *The mastery of movement.* London: MacDonald & Evans.

Landis, B., & Carder, P. (1990). The Kodály approach. In P. Carder (Ed.), *The eclectic curriculum in American music education* (pp. 55–74). Reston, VA: MENC, Music Educators National Conference.

Levitin, D. J. (2006). *This is your brain on music: The science of a human obsession*. New York: Dutton.

Lewis, B. (1998). Movement and music education: An historian's perspective. *Philosophy of Music Education Review, 6*(2), 113–123.

Lewis, B. E. (1986). *The effect of movement-based instruction on the aural perception skills of first- and third-graders*. Unpublished doctoral dissertation, Indiana University, Bloomington.

Liao, M.-Y., & Davidson, J. W. (2007). The use of gesture techniques in children's singing. *International Journal of Music Education, 25*(1), 82–96.

Longden, S. H., & Weikart, P. S. (1998). *Cultures and styling in folk dance*. Ypsilanti, MI: High/Scope Educational Research Foundation.

Loong, C.-Y. (1999). *The effects of tempo in rhythm of young children under five years old*. Unpublished doctoral dissertation, Kent State University, Kent, OH.

Mark, M. L., & Gary, C. L. (2007). *A history of American music education*. Lanham, MD: Rowman & Littlefield Education.

McCarthy, M. (1996). Dance in the music curriculum. *Music Educators Journal, 82*(6), 17–21.

McCoy, C. W. (1989). The effects of movement as a rehearsal technique on performance and attitude of high school choral ensemble members. *Contributions to Music Education, 16*, 7–18.

McFarland, A. L. (2006). *Effects of overt speech upon accuracy and expression of rhythmic movement*. Unpublished doctoral dissertation, Temple University, Philadelphia, PA.

Merriam, A. (1964). *The anthropology of music*. Evanston, IL: Northwestern University Press.

Metz, E. R. (1989). Movement as a musical response among preschool children. *Journal of Research in Music Education, 37*(1), 48–60.

Miller, L. B. (1983). *Music in early childhood: Naturalistic observation of young children's musical behaviors*. Unpublished doctoral dissertation, University of Kansas, Lawrence.

Montgomery, A. J. H. (1997). *The influence of movement activities on achievement in melodic pitch discrimination and language arts reading readiness skills of selected kindergarten music classes*. Unpublished doctoral dissertation, University of Southern Mississippi, Hattiesburg.

Moog, H. (1976). *The musical experience of the pre-school child*. Trans. C. Clarke. London: Schott.

Moore, J. L. S. (1984). *Rhythm and movement: An objective analysis of their association with music aptitude (Orff Schulwerk, Weikart movement)*. Unpublished doctoral dissertation, University of North Carolina, Greensboro.

Moore, R. S. (1981). Comparative use of teaching time by American and British elementary music specialists. *Bulletin of the Council for Research in Music Education, 66–67*, 62–68.

Moorhead, G. E., & Pond, D. (1978). *Music of young children*. Santa Barbara, CA: Pillsbury Foundation.

Mueller, A. K. (1993). *The effect of movement-based instruction on the melodic perception of primary-age general music students*. Unpublished doctoral dissertation, Arizona State University, Tempe.

Mursell, J. L. (1937). *The psychology of music*. New York: W. W. Norton .

Nakata, A., & Trehub, S. E. (2004). Infants' responsiveness to maternal speech and singing. *Infant Behavior and Development, 27*(4), 455–464.

Nardo, R. L., Custodero, L. A., Persellin, D. C., & Fox, D. B. (2006). Looking back, looking forward: A report on early childhood music education in accredited American preschools. *Journal of Research in Music Education, 54*(4), 278–292.

Nash, G. C. (1974). *Creative approaches to child development with music, language and movement.* Van Nuys, CA: Alfred.

Neidlinger, E. J. (2003). *The effect of Laban Effort/Shape instruction on young conductors' perception of expressiveness across arts disciplines.* Unpublished doctoral dissertation, University of Minnesota, Minneapolis.

Neill, J. (1990). Elementary music con moto. *Music Educators Journal, 76*(5), 29–31.

Nelson, D. D. (1990). *Personal tempo as a consideration in the rhythmic training of first-grade students.* Unpublished doctoral dissertation, University of Florida, Gainesville.

Nettl, B. (2005). *The study of ethnomusicology: Thirty-one issues and concepts.* Champaign: University of Illinois Press.

Orff, C. (1977). Orff-Schulwerk: Past & future. In I. M. Carley (Ed.), *Orff Re-Echoes: Book I* (pp. 3–9). Cleveland, OH: American Orff Schulwerk Association.

O'Toole, P. A. (2003). *Shaping sound musicians: An innovative approach to teaching comprehensive musicianship through performance.* Chicago: GIA.

Papousek, H. (1996). Musicality in infancy research: Biological and cultural origins of early musicality. In I. Deliege & J. Sloboda (Eds.), *Musical beginnings* (pp. 37–55). Oxford: Oxford University Press.

Phillips-Silver, J., & Trainor, L. J. (2005). Feeling the beat: Movement influences infant rhythm perception. *Science, 308*(5727), 1430.

Pouthas, V. (1996). The development of the perception of time and temporal regulation of action in infants and children. In I. Deliege and J. Sloboda (Eds.), *Musical beginnings* (pp. 115–141). New York: Oxford University Press.

Rainbow, E. (1980). A final report on a three-year investigation of rhythmic abilities of preschool aged children. *Bulletin of the Council for Research in Music Education, 66/67,* 69–73.

Rainbow, E. L., & Owen, D. (1979). A progress report on a three year investigation of the rhythmic ability of pre-school aged children. *Bulletin of the Council for Research in Music Education, 59,* 84–86.

Regelski, T. A. (2004). *Teaching general music in grades 4–8: A musicianship approach.* New York: Oxford University Press.

Reimer, B. (2003). *A philosophy of music education: Advancing the vision* (3rd ed.). Upper Saddle River, NJ: Prentice Hall.

Repp, B. H. (2006). Musical synchronization. In E. Altenmueller, J. Kesselring, & M. Wiesendanger (Eds.), *Music, motor control and the brain* (pp. 55–76). Oxford: Oxford University Press.

Reynolds, A. M. (1995). *An investigation of the movement responses performed by children 18 months to three years of age and their caregivers to rhythm chants in duple and triple meters.* Unpublished doctoral dissertation, Temple University, Philadelphia, PA.

Richardson, C. P., & Atterbury, B. W. (2001). *Music every day: Transforming the elementary classroom.* Boston: McGraw Hill.

Rohwer, D. A. (1998). Effect of movement instruction on steady beat perception, synchronization, and performance. *Journal of Research in Music Education, 46*(3), 414–424.

Rose, S. E. (1995). *The effects of Dalcroze Eurhythmics on beat competency performance skills of kindergarten, first-, and second-grade children.* Unpublished doctoral dissertation, University of North Carolina, Greensboro.

Sacks, O. W. (2007). *Musicophilia: Tales of music and the brain.* New York: Alfred A. Knopf.

Schleuter, S. L. (1997). *A sound approach to teaching instrumentalists: An application of content and learning sequences* (2nd ed.). New York: Schirmer.

Schleuter, S. L., & Schleuter, L. J. (1985). The relationship of grade level and sex differences to certain rhythmic responses of primary grade children. *Journal of Research in Music Education, 33*(1), 23–29.

Schnebly-Black, J., & Moore, S. F. (1997). *The rhythm inside: Connecting body, mind, and spirit through music.* Portland, OR: Rudra.

Seitz, J. A. (2005). Dalcroze, the body, movement and musicality. *Psychology of Music, 33*(4), 419–435.

Shamrock, M. (1997). Orff-Schulwerk: An integrated foundation. *Music Educators Journal, 83*(6), 41–44.

Shehan, P. (1984). Teaching music through Balkan folk dance. *Music Educators Journal, 71*(3), 47–51.

Shehan, P. (1987). Movement: The heart of music. *Music Educators Journal, 74*(3), 24–30.

Sims, W. L. (1985). Young children's creative movement to music: Categories of movement, rhythmic characteristics, and reactions to changes. *Contributions to Music Education, 12,* 42–50.

Sims, W. (1986). The effect of high versus low teacher affect and passive versus active student activity during music listening on preschool children's attention, piece preference, time spent listening, and piece recognition. *Journal of Research in Music Education, 34*(3), 173–191.

Snyder, J., & Krumhansl, C. (2001). Tapping to ragtime: Cues to pulse finding. *Music Perception, 18*(4), 455–489.

Steeves, C. (1985). *The effect of Curwen-Kodály hand signs on pitch and interval discrimination within a Kodály curricular framework.* Unpublished master's thesis, University of Calgary, Canada.

Sutter, J. (1999). *Kinesthetic analogues: Perception of patterned art music among public school general music students.* Unpublished master's thesis, Bowling Green State University, Bowling Green, Ohio.

Temmerman, N. (2000). An investigation of the music activity preferences of preschool children. *British Journal of Music Education, 17*(1), 51.

Torrance, P. E. (1999). *The Torrance Tests of Creative Thinking: Norms and Technical Manual.* Bensenville, IL: Scholastic Testing Service. (Original work published in 1966.)

Trehub, S. E. (2003). The developmental origins of musicality. *Nature Neuroscience, 6*(7), 669–673.

Valerio, W. H., Reynolds, A. M., Taggart, C. C., Bolton, B. B., & Gordon, E. E. (1998). *Jump right in! The early childhood music curriculum, music play.* Chicago: GIA.

Volk, T. M. (1998). *Music, education, and multiculturalism.* New York: Oxford University Press.

Wagner, M. J., & Strul, E. P. (1979). Comparisons of beginning versus experienced elementary music educators in the use of teaching time. *Journal of Research in Music Education, 27*(2), 113–125.

Walters, D. L. (1983). *The relationship between personal tempo in primary-aged children* and *their ability to synchronize movement with music*. Unpublished doctoral dissertation, University of Michigan, Ann Arbor.

Wang, C. C., & Sogin, D. W. (1997). Self-reported versus observed classroom activities in elementary general music. *Journal of Research in Music Education, 45*(3), 444–456.

Weikart, P. S. (1989). *Teaching movement & dance: A sequential approach to rhythmic movement*. Ypsilanti, MI: High/Scope.

Wis, R. M. (1993). *Gesture and body movement as a physical metaphor to facilitate learning and to enhance musical experience in the choral rehearsal*. Unpublished doctoral dissertation, Northwestern University, Evanston, IL.

Woods, D. G. (1987). Movement and general music: Perfect partners. *Music Educators Journal, 74*(3), 35–36, 41–42.

Zimmerman, M. P. (2002). Musical characteristics of children. In M. R. Campbell (Ed.), *On musicality and milestones* (pp. 127–150). Urbana, IL: School of Music, University of Illinois at Urbana-Champaign.

Self-Regulation of Musical Learning

4

A Social Cognitive Perspective on Developing Performance Skills

GARY E. MCPHERSON

BARRY J. ZIMMERMAN

Every year, millions of children around the world begin learning a musical instrument and embark on an aspect of skill acquisition that not only is complex and time-consuming but also requires years of dedicated practice and commitment in order to achieve success. A major challenge for research, therefore, is to find better and more efficient ways for developing the range of skills required to perform proficiently.

Over the past two decades, researchers have taken various approaches to studying how musicians acquire and refine their skills as performers. Some of the most important research has been compiled by music psychologists who study the quantity and quality of experts' practice (Ericsson, Krampe, and Tesch-Römer, 1993; Sloboda, Davidson, Howe, and Moore, 1996). Evidence across other pursuits such as poetry, painting, mathematics, chess, and sports (Bloom, 1985; Ericsson, 1996; Chase and Simon, 1973; Hayes, 1989) confirm findings in music (Ericsson, Krampe, and Tesch-Römer, 1993; Lehmann and Gruber, 2006; Sloboda, Davidson, Howe, and Moore, 1996) that experts undertake vast amounts of practice over a period of more than 10 years to perfect their skills to mastery level (Hayes, 1989; Weisberg, 1999). In music, international-level concert violinists invest about 10,500 hours of "deliberate practice" on their instrument by the age of 20 (an average of almost 2 hours per day across a 15-year period), in contrast to about 8,000 hours for professional players and 4,000 hours for music teachers (Ericsson, Krampe, and Tesch-Römer, 1993).

One could assume from these findings that practice does indeed make perfect. However, although research on prodigies and elite performers provides valuable insight into the nature of expertise in music, more work is needed on normal, everyday performance before researchers will be in a position to more accurately determine what happens during the many years that it takes to develop instrumental skill, and how different levels of motivation might affect an individual's practice across any given time period. Clearly, in the current video game age in which children have many distractions and only a small percentage of school instrumentalists go on to perform professionally or as amateurs after leaving school, there is a need for more research over the entire range of abilities to clarify more precisely what teachers can do to improve their students' abilities (McPherson, 1995, 2005). This research is more urgent if one compares the advances in other areas of academic and motor learning over recent decades with the less developed research base that currently exists in music.

In contrast to the expertise-oriented perspective studied by music psychologists (e.g., Lehmann and Davidson, 2002; Lehmann and Gruber, 2006), an important body of educational research has focused on the processes students adopt or acquire as they mature into independent learners. *Self-regulated learning*, a field in which some of the most important recent advances in the study of cognitive development have occurred, is a useful paradigm from which to study how learners acquire the tools necessary to monitor and control their own thoughts, emotions, impulses, performance, and attentional resources to improve their performance (Bandura, 1991; Vohs and Baumeister, 2004; Zimmerman, 2008). Like any academic or motor task, learning a musical instrument requires a great deal of self-regulation, which is evident when students become "metacognitively, motivationally, and behaviorally active participants in their own learning process" (Zimmerman, 1986, p. 308).

Self-regulation is cyclical because feedback obtained from prior performance helps learners to adjust their current performance and future efforts. Adjustments of this type are necessary because personal, behavioral, and environmental factors are constantly changing during learning and performance. According to Zimmerman (2000a), these factors are observed and monitored using the three self-oriented feedback loops shown in figure 4.1.

Behavioral self-regulation involves self-observation to strategically adjust one's performance processes or method of learning, whereas *environmental self-regulation* refers to observing and adjusting environmental conditions and outcomes (e.g., finding somewhere quiet to practice). *Covert self-regulation* occurs as a result of monitoring and adjusting cognitive and affective states, such as consciously focusing attention on the music instead of the audience, in order to relax and perform better. How productively learners self-monitor these three sources of self-control influences both the effectiveness of their strategic adjustments and the nature of their self-beliefs. According to this perspective, the triadic feedback loops are assumed to be

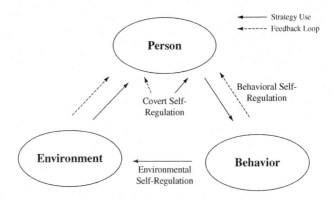

Figure 4.1 Triadic Forms of Self-Regulation.

Note: A social cognitive view of self-regulated academic learning. From B. J. Zimmerman (1989), *Journal of Educational Psychology, 81*, p. 330. Copyright 1989 by the American Psychological Association. Reprinted with permission from the author.

open, because self-regulated learners proactively increase performance discrepancies by raising goals and seeking more challenging tasks. For example, when musicians decide to perform more challenging literature, they make success more difficult to achieve but use the outcome discrepancies to motivate themselves to attain higher level skills. In this way, self-regulation involves triadic processes that are proactively as well as reactively adapted for the attainment of personal goals (Zimmerman, 2000a). This is why researchers need to be sensitive to the influence of variations in context and personal experience (Butler 2002; Zimmerman, 1989), because students' personal capacity to self-regulate depends on learning and development, with older and more experienced learners more able to self-regulate their own learning (Bandura, 1986).

This self-regulation view of teaching and learning holds great potential for research in music education, because efficient learning in music requires at least as much self-regulation as any academic subject or other area of motor learning. In addition, learning to play a musical instrument may require more self-regulation than most other domains, particularly in the early stages of development where there are many difficulties to overcome, and when children often experience confusion and failure. Unlike most academic subjects, music involvement is also frequently optional. It relies on a great deal of autonomy, especially in situations where it is up to the child to decide when and where they will practice, in addition to choosing whether to practice or avoid new, difficult, or unlearned repertoire (Austin, Renwick, and McPherson, 2006; O'Neill and McPherson, 2002).

Relatively few studies have been undertaken on self-regulation in music, in contrast to a growing body of literature available in academic and motor domains. Therefore, many gaps still exist, with many issues remaining to be resolved. A primary aim of this chapter, therefore, is to generate interest on this topic in music education by providing a framework from which future research might be conducted. Where relevant, we will outline studies that have compared novice players with experts and professionals. However, our main intention is to focus our discussion on studies with school-age musicians, rather than college or professional performers, in order to differentiate the model proposed here with the strand of research in music psychology that has sought to clarify higher levels of professional and expert performance. Our chapter, therefore, focuses on the *self-regulatory processes* that shape and influence the learning of a musical instrument and is organized according to two major sections. The first provides a review of existing literature in music according to six key self-regulatory processes; the second presents practical and theoretical implications for music teaching and learning.

A Framework for Studying Self-Regulated Learning in Music

We do not view self-regulation as a fixed characteristic, such as a personality trait, ability, or stage of development, but rather as a context-specific set of processes that students draw on as they promote their own learning (Zimmerman, 1998a, 1998b). These processes affect one or more of six dimensions of musical self-regulation, as shown in table 4.1. Column 1 identifies the essential scientific question that can be used to underpin research related to the six psychological dimensions shown in column 2. Column 3 describes the socializing processes that facilitate the development of the self-regulatory processes listed in column 4. Taken together, these four columns provide the basis for studying key processes involved in efficient musical learning and also for devising strategies that can optimize music teaching.

Motive

To learn a musical instrument, a child must be able to concentrate and move through different tasks in the face of many potential distractions. Environmental factors, such as peer intrusions and a noisy work environment, and personal factors, such as inappropriate practice strategies, confusion, and changing interests and goals, can all too easily distract a young child. Maintaining concentration in the face of these obstacles requires a great deal of volition and personal self-motivation, which researchers (Corno, 1989; Zimmerman, 1998b) believe kick in to control concentration and aid progress when different types of environmental and personal obstacles conflict with learning. Volition and self-motivational processes are an implicit part of explanations concerning how a young child's initial enthusiasm for learning an instrument can, over time, become self-regulating. The motive dimension of our model, therefore, explains how children come to value their learning, choose to continue learning, and persist with their musical practice

Table 4.1 Dimensions of Musical Self-Regulation

Scientific Question	Psychological Dimensions	Socialization Processes	Self-Regulation Processes
Why?	Motive	Vicarious or direct reinforcement by others	→ Self-set goals, self-reinforcement and self-efficacy
How?	Method	Task strategies are modeled or guided socially	→ Self-initiated covert images and verbal strategies
When?	Time	Time use is socially planned and managed	→ Time use is self-planned and managed
What?	Behavior	Performance is socially monitored and evaluated	→ Performance is self-monitored and evaluated
Where?	Physical environment	Environments are structured by others	→ Environments are structured by self
With whom?	Social	Help is provided by others	→ Help is sought personally

(McPherson and Renwick, 2000). As shown in table 4.1, others' vicarious or direct reinforcement provides a foundation from which young learners can develop the types of self-regulatory processes needed for them to develop the self-motivation to persist with their efforts. Although exceptions like Louis Armstrong can be easily found, music psychologists generally agree that parental support is a major ingredient in this process (Gembris and Davidson, 2002; McPherson, 2009). We begin our review, therefore, with an explanation of how parents, guardians, and other caregivers can support their child's home practice. This is followed with a section on self-motivation, which surveys some of the issues relevant to understanding how music learners come to be able to set goals for themselves, evaluate and reinforce their own learning, and gain an understanding of their own ability as a musician.

Parental Support

During their early years, children come to learn that they must take responsibility for their own actions. Their earliest experiences are regulated by their parents, who enforce rules of behavior for everyday tasks that provide the context to acquire knowledge, attitudes, and skills that will eventually enable them to cope with more formal aspects of learning after they start school (Corno, 1995; Goodnow and Warton, 1992; Warton, 1997; Warton and Goodnow, 1991). Corno (1989, 1994, 1995; Xu, 2004) believes that these socialization practices help children acquire an awareness of their own functioning in terms of the cognitive, motivational, and affective resources they will use to guide their subsequent learning.

The parents' role in the process leading to how quickly a child will develop self-regulatory behaviors does not diminish when the child enters school but continues well into adolescence (Warton, 1997). This is because children do not always make a link between remembering to do certain activities and the need to take personal responsibility to do these without being reminded. One U.S. study shows that fewer than 10 percent of parents of fifth-grade children viewed homework as their child's sole responsibility (Chen and Stevenson, 1989). In Australia, Warton (1997) interviewed 98 children about their home-work practices. Questions focused on the children's knowledge of the purpose and value of homework, the types of homework activities they were normally asked to complete at home, and their understandings of and feelings toward having to complete homework. An important component of Warton's inter-view focused on aspects of self-regulation, particularly in terms of reminders. Results show that fewer than a third of her second-graders viewed homework as their own responsibility and something that they must remember to complete themselves. Around 76 percent of the second-grade children reported being reminded by their parents to do their homework, with one girl stating: "It would be a favor to Mum if I remember without her having to tell me" (Warton, 1997, p. 219). By fourth grade, 72 percent still reported being reminded, and by sixth grade, 50 percent of the children reported that they still received such parental support. Warton's results show that children receive constant support in the form of reminders and checking from both parents and teachers to complete homework and that this is maintained across the entire elementary school grades. These results are consistent with a study of fifth-grade American children (Chen and Stevenson, 1989), which found that fewer than 10 percent viewed homework as their own responsibility.

Families where homework is a priority, and where parents are actively involved in facilitating their child's out-of-school work, provide a conducive environment for young children to develop the skills that enable them to eventually take charge of their own learning (Warton, 1997). Hoover-Dempsey and Sandler (1995) believe that such parental involvement in home-work activities occurs in three ways: (1) modeling, by demonstrating how to work through assignments; (2) reinforcement, through praise, encourage-ment, and passive involvement; and (3) direct instruction, by drilling and other activities designed to promote factual learning.

These points highlight important similarities, as well as some interesting differences, between school homework and musical practice. While most parents would feel comfortable engaging in each of these three ways to help their own child's homework, few parents have the requisite knowledge and background in music to assist their child through modeling or direct instruction. So, for many parents, reinforcement is the primary means by which they help their child cope with the continual demands of maintaining a regular practice schedule, particularly after the early weeks of instruction when the novelty of learning an instrument starts to diminish and the reality of maintaining a consistent practice schedule starts to set in (McPherson and Davidson, 2002, 2006).

The nature of a parent's help with learning an instrument is therefore different from the way they will help their child with homework, especially if they have not learned music themselves. In such cases, parents tend to help their child through reinforcement rather than through explicit modeling or direct instruction. This was shown in case studies of the home practice of children who began band instruments in Australian schools (McPherson and Renwick, 2000). The researchers obtained home practice videotapes from 27 of a larger sample of 157 third- and fourth-grade children who were involved in a 3-year longitudinal study that sought to clarify the environmental and personal catalysts that shape their musical development. After careful viewing of the videotapes to cull out children who were irregular with their videotaping or who seemed to be unduly influenced by having a camera on them while they practiced, seven children were selected for more extensive analysis using the software package *The Observer* (Noldus, Trienes, Hendriksen, Jansen, and Jansen, 2000). Using this technique, which allows the researcher to watch and code observed behaviors directly onto a computer for subsequent analysis, the researchers were able to compile a detailed record of each child's practice. Results from this analysis of young beginners show that in the first year of their learning, their parents were in close proximity about 65 percent of the time they spent practicing. Eighty-one percent of this time was spent listening, 12 percent guiding (e.g., asking what piece the child would play next), and only 6 percent in an active teaching role (1 percent of the time was spent distracting the child from practice). By the third year of the study, a higher level of autonomy was observed in the children, with parents present only 22 percent of the time. Almost all (97 percent) of this time was spent listening to the child's practice rather than guiding or actively teaching.

Many children view practicing as a chore or boring in the same way that they view their school homework (McPherson and Davidson, 2002; McPherson and Renwick, 2001; Pitts, Davidson, and McPherson, 2000). McPherson and Davidson (2002) report that more than 80 percent of the 157 third- and fourth-grade beginning band students who were involved in the same longitudinal study needed some sort of reminder from their parents to do their practice in the month after taking up their instrument. But by the end of their first 9 months, the mothers' reports of whether they were reminding their child to practice had dropped to 48 percent. Citing comments obtained from structured interviews with the parents during the period studied, McPherson and Davidson conclude that by this time, the mothers had made an assessment of their child's ability to cope with practice, as well as their own capacity to devote energy into regulating their child's practice through continual reminders and encouragement to practice. Some mothers continued to support practice schedules, even though the child's interest had decreased markedly. Other mothers started to withdraw their reminders, possibly based on an assessment that their child may not be able to cope emotionally, that if he or she were really interested practice would be done anyway, or because they were unwilling to invest the time and effort needed to regulate their child's daily schedule. It is not surprising, therefore, that with so much variability in parental involvement, wide differences in performance ability and intrinsic motivation appeared soon after the children started learning their instruments (McPherson and Davidson, 2002, 2006; Pitts, Davidson, and McPherson, 2000; see also Zdzinski, 1996).

Studies of child prodigies show that most had parents who systematically supervised their practice (Lehmann, 1997; Sosniak, 1985, 1987). They also became accustomed to performing in front of their family and friends before giving their first recital. Their parents and teachers' interest in their development helped them to gradually build the confidence, motivation, and persistence that would eventually distinguish them as performers (Sosniak, 1987). In these ways, the encouragement and support the parents provided were important as the prodigies developed the personal discipline necessary to persist with the many hours of practice needed to develop their skill to an elite level. The parents not only applauded and rewarded their child's initial attempts to perform in front of their family and friends but also supported and encouraged their efforts when interest flagged or skills stalled (Sosniak, 1990). Less than successful efforts were seen as a challenge to be overcome rather than as a debilitating failure (Sosniak, 1990). According to Sosniak (1987):

> Parents kept students practicing an hour a day, for instance, until the students began to work consistently on their own initiative. As the youngsters increased their time at the keyboard parents learned to place higher priority on the practice than on having the child wash the dinner dishes or take out the garbage. They also learned to live with, and enjoy, the noise of music-making at all hours of the day and night. The parents' respect for and appreciation of the child's music-making inspired the child further, and so on. (p. 528)

One might assume that the family background of young prodigies is entirely different from the normal population of children who succeed musically, albeit at a lower level. However, a study of 257 English students (age 8 to 18) drawn from a variety of musical backgrounds demonstrates that many of the elements cited for prodigies are also common in the normal population (Davidson, Sloboda, and Howe, 1995/1996; Sloboda and Davidson, 1996). In broad terms, this evidence suggests that high-achieving student musicians tend to have parents who actively support their child's practice, especially during the initial stages where the parents either sat in on lessons or actively sought regular feedback from the child's teacher. They also supported their child's practice by verbal reminders to practice, encouragement, moral support, and in some cases, direct supervision. Their involvement was most evident in the early stages of development, when the children's ability to self-regulate their own learning was least evident. Then, as each child's developing self-motivation started to increase and he or she became increasingly autonomous in lessons and practice, the parents, many of whom did not have a musical background, started to withdraw their direct involvement, even though they still maintained a high level of moral support for their child's increasing involvement with music. In contrast, low-achieving student musicians tended to receive little parental support during their early years, but during their teenage years, parental pressure to motivate practice and attend lessons increased markedly. The researchers viewed this as a last effort by the parents to keep their child learning (Davidson, Howe, Moore, and Sloboda, 1996; see also, Davidson, Howe, and Sloboda, 1997; Davidson, Sloboda, and Howe, 1995/1996; Sloboda and Davidson, 1996).

Results of these Australian and British investigations run parallel with evidence from Zdzinski (1994, 1996) in the United States. He studied 406 instrumental music students from five band programs in rural New York and Pennsylvania and found that parental involvement was significantly related to the students' performance level and to their affective and cognitive musical outcomes. These effects were more evident at the elementary level than for junior and senior high school. This result is consistent with a study by O'Neill (1996, 1997), who studied 6- to 10-year-old instrumentalists. She reports a significant relationship between the parent's involvement in lessons and children's progress. Abler students tended to have parents who were more likely to seek information from the child's teacher about how to assist their child and also talk with the teacher about how their child's home practice was progressing.

According to O'Neill (1997), high-achieving students are not necessarily innately talented or "clever." Rather, they work harder and with more self-discipline than their less capable peers (Csikszentmihalyi, 1990). But as the previous survey has shown, parental involvement may facilitate the self-regulatory processes needed for children to eventually take charge of their own learning. Indeed, McPherson (2009) has proposed a framework for studying parent-child interactions in music, based on evidence that the goals and aspirations parents hold have an impact on the types of styles and practices that shape children's sense of competence, musical identity, and accomplishment, plus their continuing desire to participate, exert effort, overcome obstacles, and succeed musically. Aligned with this view, Creech (2001) suggests that parents who possess a strong sense of self-efficacy for their child's musical learning construct a role for themselves within the learning process (e.g., attending lessons), keep in contact with the teacher, help to instill discipline and focus in practice sessions, and support their child emotionally during difficult or taxing periods (see also Creech and Hallam, 2003; Costa-Giomi, 2004). Nurturing children's motive to continue learning an instrument therefore implies providing them with an environment that offers some degree of challenge within a loving, supportive atmosphere where high but realistic aspirations are encouraged. As McPherson (2009) stresses, these effects are reciprocal, because parents often respond positively when their child displays curiosity and a willingness to engage in new activities, especially those that are aligned with what parents themselves value and wish to encourage.

Accepting that parent-child interactions are pivotal to children's musical development, our literature survey continues with other key variables related to the motive dimension.

Self-Motivation

According to self-regulated learning theory, understanding why some students and not others decide to engage in an activity such as learning an instrument and practicing regularly involves studying the causes of students' self-motivation and a number of key self-motivation beliefs and processes, such as goal setting, self-efficacy perceptions, intrinsic interest, and attributions (Zimmerman and Schunk, 2007).

The music literature includes many references indicating how effective expert musicians are at setting daily practice session goals. Gellrich and Parncutt (1998), for example, cite Clara Schumann, whose "passage work and exercises changed from day to day, depending on which aspect of her technique she wished to work on" (p. 9), while Mach's (1991) interview with the concert pianist Misha Dichter shows that he would often practice awkward musical passages by isolating them and turning them into daily exercise goals to work on intensively. Recent attempts to scientifically validate this largely anecdotal literature suggest that as performance skills develop, musicians increasingly employ higher level strategies to organize their practice (Gabrielsson, 1999). For example, Hallam (1994, 1997a) compared differences between novice and professional performers using interviews and analysis of the novices' practice sessions. Her analyses show that more capable musicians are aware of their own strengths and weaknesses, possess extensive knowledge about the nature of different tasks and what they need to do to complete them, and are able to adopt a range of strategies in response to their needs. In this way, professional musicians are able to set short- and long-term goals for themselves and to mentally note what they want to accomplish during each daily practice session or over the weeks or months leading up to a professional performance. These are exactly the types of characteristics that educational researchers (Zimmerman, 1998a) believe typify self-regulated learners.

Obviously, the highly regulated practice habits of expert musicians result from many years of deliberate practice and are also influenced by a variety of intrinsic and extrinsic motivations, such as wishing to perform well or needing to master new repertoire for an upcoming concert. In contrast, typical beginning musicians will need to be supported as they learn how to define their own practice goals. Barry and McArthur (1994) cite evidence that practice is more effective when it is goal oriented and directly related to the task being practiced. In their survey of 94 applied music teachers, 66 percent reported always or almost always asking their students to set specific goals for each of their practice sessions. However, only 14 percent reported always or almost always requiring their students to keep a written record of their practice objectives (see also Barry, 1992).

According to Lehmann and Ericsson (1997), teachers should use a range of pedagogical and technical devices to encourage student goal setting and subsequent self-monitoring in order to improve practice. Although much research needs to be undertaken to validate this claim, McPherson (1989) speculates that asking students to evaluate their own and others' performance will not only help to keep them on task but also develop their capacity to internalize goals and monitor their own progress. After reviewing literature, he concluded that one strategy for achieving this would be for students to use a practice diary in which they set their own goals for practice completion and write in any problems they have encountered between lessons. McPherson advises teachers to review the student's comments at some point during each lesson and also write in comments that help focus the learner's attention on weekly goals, specific instructions that help focus their attention on how they are supposed to play the repertoire being learned, what parts need most practice, practice strategies (e.g., slow versus fast practice), and other self-reflective strategies that encourage learners to develop the kinds of goal-setting and monitoring strategies needed for them to be able to manage their own learning in ways that will eventually become self- rather than teacher-regulated. Empirical evidence for these teaching suggestions has been found in McPherson's (2005) longitudinal study with young learners. Learners who used a practice diary to keep track of what they were learning and take notes about what needed to be practiced during the week scored significantly higher on the performing rehearsed music measure for each of the 3 initial years of their learning than learners who did not use a practice diary. Likewise, students who practiced strategically, by focusing on the repertoire they needed to learn before moving on to pieces they enjoyed playing (in comparison with the other way around) progressed at a faster rate across their first 3 years of learning.

Self-Efficacy

Related to learners' ability to set goals for themselves and to reinforce their own learning is their sense of competence or self-efficacy. Bandura (1997) defines *self-efficacy* as "the conviction that one can successfully execute the behavior required to produce the outcomes" (p. 79). Self-efficacy is a key component of self-beliefs, because students who believe in their own capacity are more likely to persist despite obstacles, encouragement, and confirmatory feedback (Schunk and Pajares, 2004; Zimmerman, 2000a). Studies on academic achievement show that perceptions of personal competence "act as determinants of behaviour by influencing the choices that individuals make, the effort they expend, the perseverance they exert in the face of difficulties, and the thought patterns and emotional reactions they experience" (Pajares, 1996a, p. 325; see also Bond and Clark, 1999; Hackett, 1995; Pajares, 1996b). Indeed, research in academic subjects suggest that students with high self-efficacy are more likely to be more confident, choose more challenging tasks, exert more effort, persist longer, and be less likely to experience debilitating anxiety (Bandura, 1986; Pajares, 1996a; Zimmerman, 2000b). Importantly, these studies also show that students avoid tasks and situations in which they feel they are inadequate and tend to concentrate on tasks and activities in which they feel they can cope (Pintrich and Schunk, 1996).

Examining these findings for music performance, McPherson and McCormick (1999) theorized that music students who display high self-efficacy expectations would be more likely to achieve in a physically and emotionally demanding performance environment, such as a formal music examination, than their peers who display the same level of skill but lower personal expectations. Results with two different types of graded music examination systems were consistent with the researcher's predictions (McCormick and McPherson, 2003, 2007; McPherson and McCormick, 1999, 2006). In the structural equation models for both studies, self-efficacy accounted for the greatest part of the variance of the students' examination results, a finding that highlights the importance for musicians to enter a stressful music examination with a positive belief in their own capacity to succeed. This finding is in accord with educational research showing that students who display high self-efficacy expectations tend to perform at a more advanced level in examinations than their peers who display the same level of skill but lower personal expectations (Pintrich and Schunk, 1996). It also complements work by Nielsen (2004, 2008) with older musicians, in which positive relationships between personal beliefs for completing a task and the use of cognitive, metacognitive, and resource management strategies while practicing have been reported.

Self-Beliefs

According to Zimmerman (1998a), understanding why some learners are more self-motivated than others involves differentiating between the various levels of self-beliefs and values that students bring to their learning. Education research shows that even elementary school children can differentiate levels of intrinsic motivation for different school subjects (Jacobs, Lanza, Osgood, Eccles, and Wigfield, 2002), but that a general motivational orientation can also be found for each individual that is less domain-specific (Gottfried, 1985).

In McPherson's longitudinal study cited earlier, 157 third- and fourth-grade children were interviewed immediately before they commenced learning a band instrument in eight different school instrumental programs (McPherson, 2001). The questionnaire McPherson devised included a range of dimensions theorized to influence their subsequent learning. As part of the interviews, children were asked open-ended questions concerning how long they thought they would continue playing their new instrument. Later in the same interview, they were asked to identify whether they thought they would play their instrument "just this year," "all through primary [i.e., elementary] school," "until I'm an adult," or "all of my life." Information obtained from both the open-ended and circled responses was condensed into short-, medium- and long-term categories of commitment to playing. Results show that even before commencing lessons, 7- and 8-year-old children were able to differentiate between their interest in learning a musical instrument, the importance to them of being good at music, whether they thought their learning would be useful to their short- and long-term goals, and also the cost of their participation, in terms of the effort that they felt would be needed to continue improving. For many of these children, learning an instrument was no different from participating in a team sport, taking up a hobby, or other recreational pursuits. Many were intrinsically interested in learning an instrument but did not see it as important to their long-term future careers. Others were less intrinsically motivated but recognized the utility value of learning in terms of their overall education. For the majority of children, learning an instrument was something useful to do while they were at school but of far less value in later life. Only a handful viewed their involvement as something that could possibly lead to a future career. The children's predictions of how long they expected to play immediately before they commenced learning their instrument were then compared with their results on the *Watkins-Farnum Performance Scale* (Watkins and Farnum, 1962), obtained 9 months after they started learning, and their yearly practice, as assessed by averaging their parents' reports of how much practice they were doing at three evenly spaced periods across their first 9 months of learning. Students who displayed short-term commitment were the lowest achievers, irrespective of whether they were undertaking low, moderate, or high levels of musical practice. Students who expressed medium-term commitment achieved at a higher level according to the amount of their practice during their first 9 months of playing. The highest achieving students, however, were those who displayed long-term commitment to playing, coupled with high levels of practice. Similarly, O'Neill (1996, 1997), who worked with 60 English student musicians, shows that her subjects' perception of the importance of a musical task predicted the amount of practice they undertook, and Hallam (1998), who worked with 109 violin and viola students (age 6–16), found that her subjects' attitude about practice was a crucial factor for whether they dropped out of instruction (see also Renwick, 2008; Schmidt, 2005).

Taken together, these studies suggest that children bring to their instrumental learning clear expectations about how hard they are prepared to work and that the level of their intrinsic motivation is highly associated with their subsequent achievement. One of the greatest challenges for music researchers is to further our understanding of the role of children's motivational beliefs, to be able to assess their presence, and to know how they might be facilitated by teachers. This is at the very heart of self-regulated learning theory in terms of understanding why some children are sufficiently self-motivated to take charge of their own learning, while others lack the determination and commitment to achieve at even a mediocre level.

Method

Summarizing her extensive research, Hallam (1997a) suggests that practice becomes purposeful and self-determined only when a student acquires a range of *task-oriented strategies* to draw on. Thus, to understand the method dimension, it is important to consider the types of skills, knowledge, and understandings that allow children to choose or adapt one particular method over others when engaging with music. As table 4.1 and the discussion that follows indicates, task strategies are often modeled or guided socially and, as a result of increasing experience with the discipline, become more and more self-initiated. At the highest level are self-regulated learners who are methodical in the way they approach their learning and not only plan how they will practice but "spontaneously invent increasingly advanced strategies to improve their performance" (Nielsen, 1999, p. 275).

Developing Task-Oriented Strategies

One of the ways to study task-oriented strategies is to map out the different stages of development as skills improve. Studies of this type suggest that distinct changes occur as expertise develops (Barry and Hallam, 2002; Gruson, 1988; Hallam, 1994; Miksza, 2007). For example, McPherson and Renwick's (2000) analysis of seven beginning band students' home practice reveals that more than 90 percent of practice time was spent simply playing through a piece from beginning to end, without adopting a specific strategy to improve performance. Their analyses, using the computer interface described previously, showed that specific strategies, such as singing, silent fingering, and silent inspection of the music, each accounted for less than 2 percent of the beginners' total practice time (see also McPherson and Renwick, 2001; Leon-Guerrero, 2008; Miksza, 2007). Barry and Hallam (2002), who reviewed literature on this issue, suggest that many beginners are not always aware of where they are going wrong, perhaps because they have not developed appropriate internal aural schemata to identify and monitor their own mistakes. Slowly, as their skills develop, they begin to identify errors using what Williamon and Valentine (2000) refer to as a musical "stutter," by stumbling over and correcting individual notes. Finally, as their growing awareness of larger structures develops, they begin to repeat slightly larger units of note patterns until they are able to focus their attention on identifying and improving difficult sections. The tendency for young musicians, therefore, is to focus on getting the notes correct, but as their expertise develops, they start attending more and more to rhythm, other technical aspects of their playing, and finally to the expressive dimensions of musical performance (Barry and Hallam, 2002).

These results are in accord with Gruson's (1988) pioneering study with 43 pianists, aged between 6 and 46. Separating the players into 11 levels, based on the syllabus of the Toronto Royal Conservatory of Music, Gruson recorded their first practice sessions on previously unlearned repertoire and then analyzed these using an observational scale with 20 categories. As expected, the players made fewer errors as they became more familiar with each piece. However, players in the more proficient levels tended to use more self-guiding speech and verbalizations, as well as strategies such as practicing both hands separately and rehearsing sections longer than a measure. Gruson's interviews with the subjects about their practicing habits confirmed her analysis of the practice session recordings that the reported frequency and cognitive complexity of strategies increased according to musical expertise.

Practicing for Yourself Compared with Practicing for the Teacher

It has been known for some time that one way of fostering positive motivation lies in designing programs for students that take advantage of their own individual goals, interests, and self-perceptions (Eccles-Parsons, 1983). To date, most studies of children's practice have examined repertoire that the student has been assigned by a teacher, with almost no effort to study how choice might affect a student's sense of mastery, confidence, and persistence in learning new material. However, a study investigating this issue was undertaken by Renwick and McPherson (2000, 2002), who used the computer interface described earlier to compare a 12-year-old clarinetist practicing pieces that had been assigned by her teacher with her work on a piece that she had asked her teacher to learn. In one practice session, the young player spent on average 0.9 seconds practicing per note in the score for her teacher-assigned repertoire. With the piece that she wanted to learn, this increased to 9.8 seconds per note: an 11-fold increase. A number of other remarkable differences were also observed. For example, when playing teacher-assigned repertoire, the girl practiced almost exclusively using her "default" play-through approach, by correcting errors en route as she worked her way through the piece. In contrast to her efforts on the teacher-assigned repertoire, the young girl's self-regulatory approach to the work she wished to learn scaffolded her to the types of behaviors that Gruson (1988), Miklaszewski (1989), and Nielsen (1999) suggest typify the deliberate practice strategies employed by experts, such as increasing her use of silent fingering and silent thinking, singing, deliberate alteration of tempo when repeating sections, and practicing longer sections.

Theoretically, we speculate that the young clarinetist engaged in such high-level practice on the self-selected repertoire because of two critical aspects: her will to more generally improve her playing and her determination to fully master the piece. This is in contrast to the girl's practice of the teacher-assigned pieces, where she demonstrated some commitment to improving her playing but far less focus and determination to master each piece she was practicing. Close examination of the videotaped practice sessions shows that this focus in concentration and determination to master the self-selected piece was critical in propelling her to a much more sophisticated level of self-regulation (see further, de Bruin, Rikers, and Schmidt, 2007; McPherson, 1989; Renwick, 2008).

Although a great deal more work needs to be done to investigate this more thoroughly, the results are consistent with other disciplines, where studies indicate that allowing students to choose what to work on and which method to use can increase their intrinsic motivation and task involvement (see further, Pintrich and Schunk, 1996; Stipek, 1998). If this is true, then music teachers need to offer students real choices between the best possible materials and methods. Students who are always learning pieces that are selected by their teacher may be likely to feel that they are learning these pieces to satisfy their teachers rather than because they themselves want to learn them. Allowing some choice with regard to the types of pieces a child will learn could be an important dimension of helping to instill the feeling that they are in control of their own learning and therefore an active participant in the learning process (McPherson, 1989).

Mental Strategies and Self-Instruction

Tentative findings in music are consistent with research across academic learning and motor areas of skill development that suggest self-regulated learners actively choose to employ learning strategies such as task strategies, imagery, and self-instruction (Weinstein, Husman, and Dierking, 2000; Zimmerman, 2000b). Working with 101 high school wind players, McPherson (1993, 1997) undertook a content analysis of their reflective comments to describe what they were doing in their mind before they began playing, which he could compare with their scores on measures designed to test their ability to perform by sight, by ear, from memory, and by improvising. For example, on the sight-reading measure, students were scored higher if they mentioned looking to remind themselves of the key or time signature of the music they were about to start playing, analyzed the first section of the music, or scanned the music to identify possible obstacles. Content analysis of the playing by ear and from memory tasks coded responses according to whether the musicians reported strategies that were independent of the instrument or sound of the item, independent of the instrument but involving singing inwardly, or involved kinesthetic recall on an instrument linked with sound. For the improvisation items, student responses were separated into four categories: no plan, the first note or pattern dictating the final shape and course of the improvisation; a vague conception of what might be achieved, but this idea was not always adopted once the improvisation had commenced; some idea for shaping the improvisation, such as thinking about the range and style that could be used; or a distinct preconceived plan for shaping the response and moving fluently between ideas.

Self-regulated musicians on each of the measures consciously employed more sophisticated and musically appropriate strategies as they prepared their performance. For example, the highest scoring student on the playing from memory test displayed a mature level of metacognitive ability. First, he chanted the rhythm of the melody to himself to establish an appropriate tempo and feel. He then sang the melody through once before mentally rehearsing it a few times from beginning to end. To check that he had memorized the melody correctly, he then looked away for a brief period to rehearse the melody in his mind. This was followed by a brief period when he isolated and practiced a problem section before returning to mentally rehearse the melody in its entirety. McPherson (1997) reports a significant correlation ($p < .001$) between scores on each of the measures he administered and the learning strategies the students used to prepare for and monitor their performance.

In a follow-up study, McPherson (2005) examined similar mental strategies with a sample of 157 beginning instrumentalists. While accumulated practice explained part of the variance in the children's ability to perform repertoire they were practicing, mental strategies were consistently a more powerful predictor for explaining their ability to sight-read, play from memory, and play by ear. In this sense, understanding children's musical progress involves more than documenting the amount of practice they have accumulated. As reported by McPherson (2005):

> Watching the children develop across the three years and analysing their responses provided ample evidence that better players possessed more sophisticated strategies for playing their instrument very early in their development and that these players were the ones who went on to achieve at the highest level. Importantly, these were the players who knew when and how to apply their strategies (especially when asked to complete the more challenging musical tasks), possessed the general understanding that their performance was tied to the quality of their effort (particularly effort expended in employing appropriate strategies to complete individual tasks), and were able to coordinate these actions to control their own playing. (p. 27)

These results are in some ways similar to those of Cantwell and Millard (1994), who studied six 14-year-old students selected on the basis of their extreme scores on a learning process questionnaire, which identified whether they tend to adopt a deep or surface approach to learning. Findings indicate that students who adopted a deep approach defined the problem in musical rather than technical terms, although they knew that they needed to achieve automaticity in technical matters. Students who adopted a surface approach tended to use rote-learning strategies and sought external feedback. The authors suggest that "technically skilled musicians who approach the task of learning new music with surface motivations and strategic behaviours may be less likely to incorporate the high-order attributes associated with competent musicianship" (p. 62).

The Norwegian music educator Siw Nielsen (1997, 1998, 1999, 2000, 2008) is one of the first researchers to complete a doctorate on musical performance that is specifically based on principles of self-regulated learning theory. In an English-language article (Nielsen, 1999), she explored and identified the learning strategies of two organ students as they prepared a complex piece for performance. Her description of how the two organists prepared their performance provides a fascinating account of how they were able to use learning strategies "to select relevant areas, to join parts of the piece as a whole, and to relate auditive 'pictures' beyond the score to the performing of the piece" (Nielsen, 1999, p. 289). Nielsen's detailed analysis enabled her to compile a preliminary scheme for classifying learning strategies in musical practice. She concluded that "students' need to reflect on their use of strategies during practice as a prerequisite for being able to use a range of skills systematically" (Nielsen, 1999, p. 289).

Finally, Gabrielsson's (1999) extensive review of research on the performance of music provides additional support that successful musicians strategically plan how they will control and monitor their playing when practicing and performing. Varied practice, mental rehearsal, motor exercises, memorization techniques, responding to perceptual feedback, and building a mental representation that can be easily translated into sound are some of the many strategies that are integrated into the armory of expert performers. As a supplement to Gabrielsson's survey, Wilson (1997) suggests that stage fright can be controlled when musicians cognitively restructure their own thoughts and feelings about their public performances by anticipating the symptoms of their anxiety and turning them into constructive use. Self-regulated musicians are therefore more likely to psyche themselves up for a performance by using positive inner talk and other optimistic strategies. In contrast, musicians without these skills tend to be so afraid of failure that they deliberately think of excuses for a poor result prior to their performance (Wilson, 1997; Wilson and Roland, 2002).

Time

According to educational theorists, self-regulated students are able to plan and manage their time more efficiently than unregulated learners (Zimmerman, 1994, 1998a). In relation to music, the time dimension of musical self-regulation (see table 4.1) refers to how a learner's use of time moves from being socially planned and managed to self-planned and managed.

Tentative findings suggest that young musicians' practice becomes increasingly more efficient as they develop their skills on an instrument. McPherson and Renwick (2000) found that 73 percent (range 57–82 percent) of their first-year students' videotaped home practice, measured from the first to the last note of each practice session, was spent playing their instrument. This rose to 84 percent (range 76–90 percent) by Year 3, suggesting that these beginners were starting to use their time more efficiently. However, as the ranges in parentheses indicate, there were also large differences between students. The majority of the students' playing time was spent on repertoire (Year 1: 84 percent; Year 3: 93 percent). Technical work (scales and arpeggios) took up the remainder. Interestingly, the rest (Year 1: 27 percent; Year 3: 16 percent) of these musicians' practice time was spent on nonplaying activities, such as looking for printed music, talking or being spoken to, daydreaming, responding to distractions, and expressing frustration. Less than 6 percent of nonpracticing time was spent resting.

Research on academic subjects shows that many non-self-regulating children actively avoid studying or use less time than allocated (Zimmerman and Weinstein, 1994). This was also true in McPherson and Renwick's analysis of beginners' practice. The least efficient learner spent around 21 percent of his total practice sessions talking with his mother about his practice tasks and expressing displeasure at his repeated failure to perform correctly, while others were seen to call out to a parent to ask, "Am I allowed to stop yet?"

From a different perspective, Sloboda and Davidson (1996) describe "formal" and "informal" aspects of home practice. In their study of 257 school-age students, drawn from various levels of music training, high-achieving musicians tended to do significantly greater amounts of "formal" practice, such as scales, pieces, and technical exercises, than their less successful peers. But the high achievers were also likely to report more "informal" practice, such as playing their favorite pieces by ear or improvising. Sloboda and Davidson conclude that these "informal" ways of practicing contribute to musical success because the highest achieving students are able to find the right balance between freedom and discipline in their practice. Similarly, using a self-report questionnaire administered to 190 pianists (age 9 to 18) that was designed to explore motivational and self-regulatory components of instrumental performance, McPherson and McCormick (1999) employed factor analysis to group three aspects of practice they defined as *informal creative activities* (playing by ear for enjoyment, improvising music), *repertoire* (learning new pieces, performing older familiar pieces), and *technical work* (using a warm-up routine, practicing scales, studies, and sight-reading music). Results showed that the amount of time students report practicing each week in each of these three areas was significantly related to the quality of their cognitive engagement during their musical practice and also to how much they reported enjoying music and playing their instrument. In this study, pianists who achieved higher levels of practice were more likely to rehearse music in their minds and to make critical ongoing judgments concerning the relative success of their efforts. They were also more capable of organizing their practice in ways that provide for efficient learning, such as practicing the pieces that need the most work and isolating difficult sections of a piece that need further refinement. Although much work is needed to validate and clarify these findings, the results suggest that students who are more cognitively engaged while practicing not only tend to do more practice but also enjoy learning their instrument more and are more efficient with their learning.

Musicians also need to be able to pace and manage the use of their time. For example, even young musicians increase the quantity and quality of the time they spend practicing in the weeks leading up to a significant performance, such as a music recital or examination (Hallam, 2000; Sloboda and Davidson, 1996). This is often what expert musicians report. Misha Dichter, for example, spent as much as 12 hours a day practicing when young but practiced only 4 hours per day when touring and 6 hours when learning new repertoire at home, while Glenn Gould believed that excessive practice beyond 4 hours a day diminished his effectiveness as a performer (Mach, 1991). However, in terms of self-regulated musical learning, many issues remain to be solved, particular in terms of how young musicians manage their practice time and why some do this more effectively than others. Sloboda and colleagues (1996) found increasing levels of practice from the most capable players across the various age groups. However, some of their musicians managed to obtain high externally assessed performance examination results with very little practice, in contrast to their peers who reported doing four times as much practice to achieve the same results. As we will see in the section on motivational orientations, some learners tend to avoid practicing difficult repertoire, relying instead on strategies they feel comfortable with to practice pieces they can already play. In contrast, others enjoy the challenge of learning and actively adapt their practice habits to improve their own performance (see also O'Neill and McPherson, 2002).

Behavior

A distinguishing characteristic of self-regulated learners is that they notice when they do not understand something or when they are having difficulty learning a particular skill (Thomas, Strage, and Curley, 1988). The ability to react by choosing, modifying, and adapting one's performance based on feedback obtained when performing is therefore central to the process of self-regulation (Zimmerman, 2000a). In terms of the dimensions of self-regulation proposed in table 4.1, students' performance can be socially monitored and evaluated by knowledgeable others (e.g., teachers and parents) but needs to become self-monitored and evaluated to be truly self-regulating. The following review provides a tentative analysis of some of the important elements in this process, according to three categories: metacognition, self-evaluation, and motivational orientations.

Metacognition

One of the principal means by which students monitor and control their performance is metacognition, which refers to thinking about thinking. It occurs in two ways during learning: the thoughts students have about what they know and do not know and the thoughts they have about regulating their own learning (Shuell, 1988). As students become more self-regulated, they develop along both dimensions, first by becoming more aware of their abilities to remember, learn, and solve problems and second by developing more strategic efforts to manage their cognitive activities when learning, thinking, and problem solving (Bruning, Schraw, and Ronning, 1999). For example, as musicians gain experience, they become more aware of how much time they will need to learn a new piece, different strategies that will help them perform correctly, and what they need to do to improve their playing (Barry and Hallam, 2002). Although this growing awareness of knowledge and skills is important, unless students elect to monitor and control their own cognitive processes, they are unlikely to become effective learners (Brunning, Schraw, and Ronning, 1999; see also Miksza, 2006, 2007).

For teaching, an important component of helping students acquire metacognitive abilities is to encourage them to describe what goes on in their minds as they think. Pogonowski (1989) suggests that a good metacognitive analogy to practicing the piano would involve making yourself aware of how you want a particular phrase to sound and controlling and monitoring your cognitive resources to make it sound the way that you feel makes the most sense musically. On the other hand, not using metacognitive awareness would involve thinking about something else either during or at the end of the performance. While the fingers may have had a workout, you would not have been using your metacognitive processes to monitor and control the product.

Hallam's (1997a, 2000) studies of string players show that expert musicians have developed extensive metacognitive skills that enable them to make accurate assessments of their own strengths and weaknesses. These skills allow them to respond to different performance situations and to draw on a range of strategies that they can employ to overcome a variety of technical and expressive problems. The experts' metacognitive abilities seem to be highly individual, and although there were similarities across some aspects of their practice, there was also considerable variation between individuals. For example, Hallam (2000) reports a number of differences in the regularity of her experts' practice, the way they structure their practice, and the manner in which they approach warming up and refining their technique. They also used a wide variety of ways to prepare for a performance. Some developed their interpretation as their playing became more fluent, others made detailed plans of how they were going to learn a piece in advance, while still others made changes to their interpretation along the way. In contrast, Hallam's school-age students showed little evidence of specific performance preparation. Although 92 percent of her sample reported undertaking more focused and technically oriented practice leading up to a music examination, their practice usually depended on task requirements. In stressful performance situations such as a recital or music examination, the students employed various self-monitoring and evaluative strategies, such as treating the performance as though it was a lesson, consciously avoiding thinking about it, and actively focusing their concentration and attention on the music rather than on their feelings about how they were being assessed (Hallam, 2000). They also devoted more time to self-guiding speech as their fluency to perform a work increased (Hallam, 1997a).

The studies by Hallam (1997, 2000) provide important data on the individual variation of school-age string players as they manage and control their own practice. Some completed all task requirements and could quickly identify difficulties as they practiced, concentrate their efforts on the difficult sections, and integrate these into their whole performance. Other students completed task requirements but tended to work on large sections of a work rather than focus on difficulties. The least self-regulating students did not complete task requirements, tended to practice only the first and not subsequent sections of the music, and wasted considerable amounts of time during their practice.

Self-Evaluation

In what ways do students respond to feedback, monitor their own progression, and evaluate how effectively they are learning? Although few music studies have been undertaken to determine how and in what ways musicians self-evaluate their own progression, available evidence does suggest that successful instrumentalists employ a distinct self-regulatory approach when completing challenging tasks. For example, McPherson (1993, 1994) administered the *Watkins-Farnum Performance Scale* (WFPS; Watkins and Farnum, 1962) to 101 high school wind players who were asked, immediately after they completed the test, to explain to the researcher exactly how they prepared for their performance of each exercise. A comparison of the highest and lowest scoring students revealed distinct differences in the way these musicians prepared for their performance. Low-scoring students tended not to seek information that might assist their performance, such as checking the key or time signature of the work. Typical of their explanations were comments such as "I was looking to see what note it started on and singing the rhythm of the first part in my mind." In a separate research example, very few were able to remember the key and time signature of the music when the researcher unexpectedly covered the music immediately before they were asked to perform. Likewise, when the music was covered unexpectedly immediately after they completed the example, only a couple of students were able to remember any of the dynamic markings in the three-line example that had two dynamic indications (*mp* and *f*) and a crescendo.

In contrast, content analysis of comments on the same tasks by the highest scoring students showed that they made themselves more aware of these important details before commencing their performance. One had even been taught by his teacher to state aloud the key and time signature of each example before commencing to perform. Another student stated: "I first look at the key and time signatures, and then try and run over the harder sections by singing them in my mind as I finger them on my instrument." These comments were typical of the highest scoring students, all of whom mentioned taking note of the key and time signature, as well as scanning the music to find and mentally rehearse difficult obstacles before they started to play (see also McPherson, 2005). This finding is consistent with comments by Salis (1977), Stebleton (1987), and Wolf (1976) that competent sight-reading depends on the ability to identify familiar patterns and to spend time evaluating the musical material before beginning to perform.

Other evidence of high school musicians' ability to respond to feedback and self-monitor their playing is also reported by McPherson (1993, 1994, 2005). He reports evidence that more self-regulated players were more capable of adjusting and correcting their performance after playing a wrong note that was not in the key of the music. In these cases, aural feedback seemed to act as a cue for the correction of the error, such as a piece in F major where a B-flat was sometimes played as a B-natural. More self-regulated students monitored their playing to correct errors in subsequent sections of the piece.

Finally, various descriptions of experts' musical practice reinforce the view that they are characteristically meticulous in the way they evaluate and regulate their own learning. A good example is the pianist Misha Dichter, who analyzed recordings of himself in order to perfect his style (Mach, 1991):

> Initially, all the things that sounded fine in the practice room sounded quite different in the play-backs; this caused me to rethink many things and has been a very rewarding process. (p. 67)
>
> There's something marvellous about being able to hear yourself and study from your own mistakes, from your own performance, and to hear and to study others on records as well. (p. 72)

Based on his analysis of educational research on this issue, Zimmerman (2000a) proposed that there are essentially four general criteria people use to evaluate themselves: mastery, previous performance, normative, and collaborative. Mastery criteria involve the use of a graduated sequence from easy to hard, evident in graded music examinations or instrumental method books that are carefully structured and sequenced according to increasing difficulty. The use of such process goal hierarchies predisposes a learner to adopt mastery criteria when self-evaluating because the sequential order of the subgoals provides a ready index of mastery. The learner knows, for example, that repertoire at the front of a book is easier than pieces toward the back of the book, and also that book 1 is easier than book 2. Previous performance or self-criteria involve comparing one's current level of achievement with earlier levels. The benefit of this type of evaluation is that it highlights learning progress resulting from repeated practice.

Whereas mastery and previous performance evaluations involve judging changes in your own performance, normative criteria involve comparing your own progression with the progress of others (e.g., other members of an ensemble). The main drawback of this type of self-evaluation is that it focuses learners' attention on social factors, such as how well they are doing in comparison with their peers. Normative criteria also tend to emphasize negative aspects of functioning, such as when an ensemble loses a music competition despite having improved in comparison with their previous efforts. Collaborative criteria are relevant to group activities. In some ways, the role of a tuba player in an ensemble is distinctly different from that of a clarinetist because each instrument fulfills a different role in the ensemble. The criteria of success for tuba players are different than those used for other sections of an ensemble, and how well a tuba player can work cooperatively with the rest of the ensemble becomes the ultimate criterion of success. A review of research on these four evaluative standards (Covington and Roberts, 1994; Zimmerman, 2000a) suggests that mastery criteria enhance motivation and achievement more than normative criteria.

Motivational Orientations

Dweck (1986, 2000), a leading researcher in the area of motivation, believes that children's motivational patterns influence their behavior in predictable ways. For example, *adaptive mastery-oriented* students tend to continue working hard when faced with failure and enjoy putting effort into achieving their goals. These types of learners remain focused on trying to achieve, despite difficulties that might come their way. In contrast, *maladaptive helpless-oriented* students often fail to establish reasonable goals for themselves, or goals that are within their reach. When they feel that the situation is out of their control and that nothing they can do will help, they tend to avoid further challenges, lower their expectations, experience negative emotions, give up, or perform more poorly in the future (Dweck, 1986, 2000; Dweck and Leggett, 1988; Grant and Dweck, 2003; Henderson and Dweck, 1990; see also O'Neill and McPherson, 2002).

These motivational patterns were studied in music by O'Neill (1996, 1997), who examined the cognitive-emotional-performance patterns of 46 children (age 6 to 10) during their first year of learning an instrument. Before beginning instruction, the children were administered a problem-solving task and procedure used to assess their motivational patterns (O'Neill and Sloboda, 1997). Eighteen children were defined as maladaptive helpless-oriented because they avoided challenges, showed low persistence, and performed poorly when faced with failure. Before they commenced learning, this group was compared with another 28 children who were defined as adaptive mastery-oriented in that they were more inclined to persist with their efforts following failure. O'Neill believes that studying these two motivational patterns is important because bright and skilled children can display either orientation. Her results provide convincing evidence of how children who displayed mastery-oriented motivational patterns on a problem-solving task before commencing their instrument progressed to a higher level of achievement at the end of their first year of learning than children who displayed maladaptive helpless motivational patterns. According to O'Neill (1997):

> Helpless children evaluate achievement situations in terms of performance goals where the aim is to display their competence and avoid failure and negative judgments of their performance. In contrast, mastery children tend to choose learning goals which emphasise the need to increase their competence.

As a result, mastery children tend to view failure as merely part of the learning process, rather than something to be avoided. (p. 65)

Physical Environment

Self-regulated learners know that the physical environment can affect their learning and actively seek to structure and control the setting where their learning takes place (Zimmerman, 1998a). In terms of our proposed model (see table 4.1), children come to realize the importance of these skills every time a teacher demonstrates good posture or a parent turns off the television so they won't be distracted from their practice. To date, very little research attention in music has been focused on this issue and the ways in which some children and not others structure their environment to ensure more effective learning.

Obviously, some students have little control over the setting where they can practice. For example, placing a piano in a family room close to a television can result in tension between siblings, especially in situations when one child wishes to practice at the same time that another wants to relax in front of the television. However, results of the McPherson and Renwick (2000) study of practice videotapes provide some tentative clues to how beginning band instrumentalists structure their environment. Their instrumentalists chose a wide variety of locations when practicing, ranging from the privacy of a bedroom to a busy family living room. Some even appeared in different rooms on different days, which the researchers suggest might mean that they were consciously choosing an appropriate place to practice depending on the family situation for that particular day. While this might enable them to obtain help from other family members whenever needed, it also meant that they were more likely to be distracted by others members of the family, pets, or even the television. Additional data obtained from child and parent interviews supported their conclusion that the physical environment was mostly well equipped with a music stand and an appropriate chair. However, distinct differences between children were noticeable. Some held their instrument correctly while seated or standing with a straight back and appropriate playing position, in contrast to others who were much less consistent with their posture. In one practice video, a young learner even sat cross-legged on his pillow with the bell of his instrument resting on his bed. From the first day they took their instruments home to practice, the children differed quite markedly in the way they structured their environment (see further, Pitts, Davidson, and McPherson, 2000; Austin and Berg, 2006).

Work by Hallam (2000) also provides further tentative evidence concerning how some musicians employ environmental structuring to help them learn. Her interviews with 22 professional musicians and 55 student musicians age 8 to 16, reports various strategies for coping with practice. One very perceptive self-regulating player even commented:

I get the metronome out. I'm a great believer in the metronome. Well it's a discipline... if you're not feeling like practicing... the metronome concentrates your mind in a way that nothing else seems able to do, because you've got to concentrate on it. (Hallam, 2000)

In music, the use of an "idealized model," such as CD recordings plus interactive, computer-based practice systems aimed at helping students improve and enjoy their practice, is becoming increasingly common to aid students' performance (Barry and McArthur, 1994; see also SmartMusic at www.smartmusic.com/default.aspx). Many band and string methods now incorporate play-along recordings, while Suzuki's talent education program has long employed recordings that children are asked to listen to repeatedly as an aid to learning repertoire on their instrument. Such devices help focus children's attention on what they are doing and also make learning more enjoyable and productive.

These comments suggest that the physical environment is probably more important than previously imagined in children's musical development. For this reason, a great deal more research is needed to tease out the detail of how self-regulated learners structure their physical environment in ways that assist their learning.

Social Factors

When faced with difficulties, socially self-regulated learners rely on and actively seek help from knowledgeable others, in addition to available resources. Understanding this dimension of table 4.1 involves examining the subtle distinction between help that is provided by others and help that is sought personally.

Parents   The importance of parental involvement has been mentioned earlier as it applies to supporting and nurturing young children's motivation for homework and musical practice. Taken together, these findings suggest that parents play an important role in facilitating the self-regulatory mechanisms that eventually allow their children to take control of their own learning (McPherson, 2009; see also Green, Walker, Hoover-Dempsey, and Sandler, 2007).

Recent evidence by Hallam (2000) provides some additional evidence of how novice musicians use social factors to regulate their learning as they consciously attempt to overcome nerves, particularly when preparing to perform at an externally assessed music performance in front of an examiner whom they have not met before. Almost 70 percent of her 55 novice string musicians adopted some kind of strategy as they prepared for their examination. Some of the more self-regulated players asked to play in front of parents or other family members, or arranged to be tested by someone else in a mock examination, in the weeks leading up to their examination.

Teachers   Hays, Minichiello, and Wright (2000) suggest that effective music teachers act like mentors to their students by stimulating and guiding their cognitive and technical skills in a nurturing but rigorous environment. The relationship between student and teacher can be intense, thereby affecting developing musicians' conceptualization of themselves and their musical goals. Other studies (Davidson et al., 1998) support these results and will be of no surprise to music educators. A good teacher contributes significantly to a child's desire to learn by providing an external source of motivation that eventually develops into a deep intrinsic love of music as the young musician becomes more actively engaged in learning and playing music. Sloboda and Davidson (1996) report on interviews they completed with 257 young musicians age 8 to 18. They used bipolar rating scales to measure the students' perception of their teachers' personal, teaching, and performance characteristics. Findings showed that the students' first teacher was perceived differently across the sample. High-achieving students typically regarded their first teacher as chatty, friendly, and a good player, in contrast to students who ceased playing, who often regarded their first teacher as unfriendly and a bad player. According to these researchers, as students mature and become more competent players, they start to differentiate more and more between the professional and personal qualities of their teachers, such that they may feel, for example, that their teacher is condescending and strict but a brilliant player. The researchers suggest that the most important qualities of a child's first teacher are to be able to communicate well and to pass on their love of music. Teachers who display these qualities are more likely to increase motivation because their students perceive learning as something that is fun and enjoyable. Later, after the child has started to develop his or her skill on the instrument, the externally reinforced support received from parents and teacher develops into an intrinsic desire to learn that is focused more on improving and extended skills. Self-motivation of this sort means that students perceive learning as something they can control themselves, with subsequently less need to rely on the external reinforcement provided by either parents or teacher (Sloboda and Davidson, 1996).

Based on this, teachers have a responsibility to create a learning environment that is conducive to the promotion of self-regulation. This conclusion has been reported in a study by Anguiano (2006) involving 290 middle school instrumental students, which shows that the motivational style of a teacher is directly linked to the quality of his or her student's motivation, which then mediates the young musician's desire to continue learning, in addition to music achievement. More specifically, Austin and Berg (2006) outline the imperative for the good teaching practice of explicitly teaching students ways of engaging in strategic practice, as well as ways they might utilize a greater variety of practice strategies. Their work parallels more general research showing that when students like their teacher, then they are more likely to experience motivational and achievement benefits (Montalvo, Mansfield, and Miller, 2007).

Siblings and Peers   To date, the influence of siblings and peers has not received the same attention from researchers as parents and teachers, although there is a growing interest in group cooperation and peer-directed learning with regard to informal learning in the music classroom demonstrating that peers, in certain situations, can be better at explaining difficult ideas because they are "better at getting inside each others' 'zones of proximal development,' to use Vygotskian terminology, than teachers are" (Green, 2008, p. 184; see also Slavin, 1995, p. 4). It would be unwise, therefore, to conclude that the influence of siblings and peers is any less than for teachers, given also Davidson, Howe, and Sloboda's (1997) comments that older siblings often take on the role of a teacher for their younger brother or sister, although rivalry and personality conflict between siblings can also hinder or stimulate a young child's musical development. Likewise, the influence of peers and older role models a student may strive to emulate has received virtually no attention from music researchers, although it is highly likely in certain instances that their impact might be profound. Even asking advice from another player in the ensemble indicates a readiness to seek information that can benefit one's performance.

In the child development literature, Azmitia and Hesser (1993) demonstrate the unique and shared influence of older siblings and peers on young children's cognitive development. They explain how young children confer on their siblings "a special role by selecting them as models and guides and prompting them to use effective teaching strategies such as explaining and transferring responsibilities" (pp. 442–443). In their study, siblings generally provided more guidance, explanations, and positive feedback than did older peers, and young children were more inclined to observe, imitate, and seek help from siblings as well. In contrast to self-regulated learners, however, non-self-regulated children tend to be reluctant to seek advice because they are unsure of what to ask or perhaps afraid of how they might appear (Newman, 1994).

Other Resources

Finally, a self-regulated student musician will actively seek information and help from other sources such as recordings and books. Although we could find no specific research that mentions this issue in music (in contrast to various reports in academic learning; see for example, Newman, 1994; Zimmerman and Martinez-Pons, 1986, 1988), quite a lot of anecdotal evidence is available. For example, the first author has vivid memories of growing up in a small country town without a teacher. Whenever he became frustrated with his lack of progress on the trumpet, he would go to his room and play recordings of works he was learning. Such instances of self-regulation not only helped to clarify aspects of performance technique and expression that he needed to improve or develop but also sustained his motivation during the difficult period when he was without a teacher who could direct his learning.

Practical and Theoretical Implications for Music Teaching and Learning

Possessing the self-regulatory skills to get a job done is one thing, but it is an entirely different matter to "apply them persistently in the face of difficulties, stressors, or competing distractions" (Zimmerman, 1995, p. 219). Consequently, studying self-regulatory process also involves trying to understand the processes whereby students learn to mobilize, direct, and sustain their efforts.

Self-Regulation as a Cyclical Process

Zimmerman (1998b, 2000a, 2004) views self-regulated learning as an open-ended cyclical process that occurs in three phrases: forethought, performance control, and self-reflection (figure 4.2).

Forethought refers to the thought processes and personal beliefs that precede efforts to engage in a task and therefore influence subsequent learning. *Performance/volitional control* involves processes that occur during learning that affect concentration and performance. After learning has occurred, *self-reflection* influences the learner's reaction and subsequent response to the experience. As shown in figure 4.2, these processes are cyclical, because the learner's *self-reflection* feeds back into forethought to influence future learning efforts (Zimmerman, 2000a).

Forethought can occur in two major ways as a student learns a musical instrument (see figure 4.2). Setting both short- and long-term goals enables learners to establish standards for their performance and is therefore an important motivational process. Students who set clear goals for themselves are more likely to gain pleasure and feel confident about their abilities, focus their efforts as they learn, work harder, and persist with instruction, particularly when faced with difficulties (Pintrich and Schunk, 1996; Zimmerman, 2007). The essence of goal setting is being able to break larger goals into manageable ones, such as spending time learning a new technique on an instrument (e.g., triple tonguing on flute or trumpet) in order to master more difficult repertoire, which in turn can subsequently expand one's performance opportunities. To facilitate these processes, students are encouraged to strategically plan their learning behavior by devising methods that are appropriate for the task and setting and to focus on what they are doing now to work toward their larger goals (Hofer, Yu, and Pintrich, 1998).

As skills develop, their effectiveness often declines, and another strategy becomes necessary. An example would be a novice musician switching from the strategy of performing warm-up material from the printed score to a strategy of playing it from memory. Because intrapersonal, interpersonal, and contextual conditions are so diverse and changeable, self-regulated musicians need to continuously adjust their goals and choice of strategies

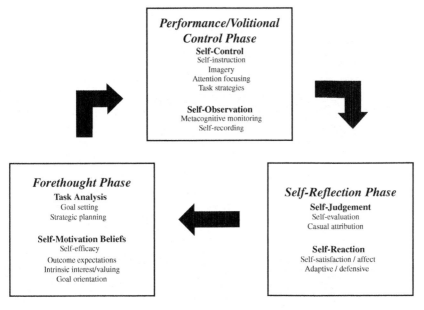

Figure 4.2 Self-Regulated Learning Cycle Phases.

Note: Motivating self-regulated problem solvers. From Zimmerman & Campillo (2003). Copyright 2003 by Cambridge University Press. Reprinted by permission from the authors.

(Zimmerman, 2000a). Students' goal orientations also affect their motivation to self-regulate (Nielsen, 2008). For example, Dweck and Leggett (1988) summarized research indicating that mastery goals account for between 10 percent and 30 percent of students' use of learning strategies.

These processes are affected by a number of personal beliefs that motivate self-regulated learners using these skills. Self-efficacy is also of critical importance, because it is particularly salient in specific performance activities (Bandura, 1997; Zimmerman, 2000b). Self-efficacy may seem closely tied to theories of self-concept and self-competence in that it does include personal judgments of ability (Pintrich and Schunk, 1996). Where it differs, however, is that self-efficacy also includes being able to organize and execute the actions or skills necessary to demonstrate competent performance. For example, self-efficacy for music performance implies not only a self-recognition of being a good instrumentalist but also explicit judgments for possessing the skills necessary to perform in front of others, such as in a music recital or concert.

Another important distinction is that self-efficacy judgments are made in relation to a specific type of performance (Pintrich and Schunk, 1996; Stipek, 1998). A trumpeter might lower his or her efficacy judgments for playing a high note in a particular piece because of a sore embouchure, or a pianist may display lower self-efficacy when faced with the challenge of learning a difficult piece in what he or she feels is too short a time frame. These self-efficacy judgments subsequently interact with the learner's outcome expectations. While a student musician might feel confident of obtaining an "A" for the performance requirements of a course, outcome expectations refer to the consequences this grade might have in the future, such as deciding whether to go on to study music after leaving school (Zimmerman, 2000a). As Zimmerman (2000a) explains, "The more capable people believe themselves to be, the higher the goals they set for themselves and the more firmly committed they remain to those goals" (p. 18). Self-regulated learners also tend to believe in their own abilities because they adopt hierarchical process goals that are personally satisfying and see these as milestones in a lifelong mastery process. This is evident when musicians come to value performing not for the external rewards, such as parental praise or obtaining a high grade at school, but rather for the sheer intrinsic pleasure of performing masterfully. In this way, the level of a student's *intrinsic interest* influences whether a learner will continue making efforts to learn, without the need to receive tangible rewards (Zimmerman, 1998a).

For *performance/volitional control*, researchers focus on two processes that are believed to enable learners to optimize their performance. First, self-control processes help musicians focus on their performance and what they are playing. These processes help musicians optimize their efforts through such means as self-instruction (overtly or covertly describing how to execute a task), imagery, attention focusing, and task strategies. For example, musicians can instruct themselves through the use of self-talk to reinforce how they should master a difficult passage that needs to be learned during a practice session. *Self-instruction* of this type helps students to monitor and control their concentration during learning (Vygotsky, 1962). On other occasions, musicians will use a form of inner self-speech (e.g., "I can do this!") to psyche themselves up before or during a major performance. These types of processes strengthen a musician's ability to focus attention on the performance and can also alleviate performance anxiety. Mental imagery, according to Kohut (1985), involves creating mental blueprints of specific performance goals or tasks. Their application in music perceptual-motor activities is particularly important. Musicians, for example, often use mental imagery to plan, enhance, and model what they are learning to perform physically.

Self-regulated learners use a variety of resources to focus their attention, thereby blocking out distractions and concentrating more effectively on what they are doing. Efficient musical practice would seem reliant on how well a musician is able to attend to his or her performance and also on task strategies that affect the learner's implementation of strategic or other learning methods. For example, young musicians who break down a difficult work into smaller units that can be isolated and practiced separately are more likely to be more successful and attentive as they practice than similar student musicians who perform the same piece from beginning to end without more concentrated efforts to refine the sections in which they are having difficulty.

A second type of performance process involves self-observation, which helps inform a learner about his or her progress, or lack of progress. *Metacognitive* or *self-monitoring* refers to mentally tracking one's performance, whereas *self-recording* refers to keeping a physical record of one's performance. Researchers who study self-observation as it relates to motor skills recommend limiting metacognitive monitoring to key processes or outcomes, as too much monitoring can interfere and disrupt one's performance. (Barry Green's *Inner Game of Music,* 1986, provides practical advice on this matter; see also Renwick, McPherson, and McCormick, 2008.) Self-monitoring can be complicated even further by the fact that as skills are acquired, less intentional monitoring is required, particularly as skills become automatic. Carver and Scheier (1981) recommend encouraging students to shift their self-monitoring to a more general level, such as from the action itself to the immediate environment and the outcomes of that action. A good example would involve shifting attention from interpreting the visual symbols used to represent crescendos and diminuendos in music notation to an inward feel for how the music should and could be expressed. Self-recording, although rarely used by musicians, is an effective way to monitor one's progress. For example, musicians who record and then analyze repertoire they are preparing for a recital are able to use this information as a means of assessing what sections of the pieces they need to work on most and how much they have improved since their last recording (see earlier quotation from Misha Dichter). Similarly, musicians can self-experiment with pieces they already know how to play to evaluate whether a piece might work better at a faster tempo, whether the dynamic shadings could be further exaggerated, or whether the use of subtler tonal colors might enhance their performance. Ways of focusing one's attention, such as these forms of metacognitive monitoring, assist concentration and help to block out distractions (Corno, 1994).

Self-reflection can occur in four ways: self-evaluation, causal attributions, self-satisfaction/affect, and adaptivity. Self-evaluation is usually one of the initial self-reflective processes to occur and can involve comparing information with some sort of standard or goal, such as judging feedback given by an ensemble director, comparing one's performance with peers, or reacting to an examiner's written assessment after a music performance or recital. Self-regulated learners are often keen to evaluate how well they are doing in comparison with their peers and resort to comparing their performance with others when no formal standards are available. These self-evaluations typically lead to attributions about the causal meaning of the results. Although attributional beliefs are discussed in the motivation chapter in this volume, it is important to note here that these processes are pivotal to learning aspects of self-reflection, as well as motivational aspects. When students attribute their failure to ability rather than effort, they are more likely to give up trying to improve. Typical self-regulated musicians attribute both their success and failure to correctable causes that can be improved through more effort, even during long stretches when their practice produces meager results (Zimmerman, 2000a).

These self-judgments are integrally related to the satisfaction or dissatisfaction derived from performing well or poorly and the conclusions a person then makes for improving future efforts to learn or perform. Self-satisfaction perceptions are important because learners choose to engage in activities and learning experiences that are satisfying and make them feel good and avoid activities and learning experiences that they do not find satisfying, that do not make them feel good, and that result in anxiety (Bandura, 1991). According to Zimmerman (2000a):

> When self-satisfaction is made conditional on reaching adopted goals, people give direction to their actions and create self-incentives to persist in their efforts. Thus, a person's motivation does not stem from the goals themselves, but rather from self-evaluative reactions to behavioral outcomes. (p. 23)

When self-regulated learners draw conclusions about their efforts, they make adaptive or defensive inferences that subsequently influence their future efforts. Adaptive inferences can direct learners to new or better forms of performance self-regulation, such as choosing a better or more effective strategy (Zimmerman and Martinez-Pons, 1992). On the other hand, defensive inferences tend to limit personal growth, especially in situations where the learner feels helpless, procrastinates, avoids tasks, or ceases active engagement due to apathy (Garcia and Pintrich, 1994).

Self-reactions affect forethought processes and can therefore dramatically affect future courses of action toward a musician's most important goals (Zimmerman, 2000a). For example, self-satisfaction can strengthen a musician's self-efficacy beliefs for mastering challenging new repertoire, learning goal orientations, and intrinsic interest in the task. When musicians' self-motivational beliefs are enhanced, they are more likely to feel inclined to continue their cyclical self-regulatory efforts to attain their goals. In contrast, when they are reduced, musicians are less likely to feel confident about their ability and less intrinsically motivated to devote further energy to improving their performance. The road to achieving musical excellence as a performer is long and arduous, and there will be times in every musician's life when feelings of self-efficacy will dramatically alter after a particularly rewarding or disappointing performance. The social cognitive model shown in figure 4.2 is therefore useful in helping to explain the cyclical processes across the life span whereby achievers persist and feel fulfilled, as well as the avoidance and self-doubts of nonachievers (Zimmerman, 2000a).

Various recommendations can be drawn from the discussion to this point concerning how future research in music education might draw on the self-regulatory perspective outlined in this chapter. One of the most important needs is studies using the cyclical model depicted in figure 4.2 to determine how practice processes become self-enhancing and self-sustaining. In academics and sports, goal setting and strategy choice training have been found to affect not only students' performance effectiveness but also their self-monitoring, attributions, self-satisfaction, self-efficacy, and intrinsic interest. Students who set strategic process goals to monitor those processes tend to make attributions regarding their effectiveness (Zimmerman and Kitsantas, 1997). This increases many self-motivational beliefs (self-satisfaction, self-efficacy, outcome expectations, and intrinsic interest). By contrast, untrained students typically set outcome goals, lack defined strategies, attribute outcomes to a lack of ability, and tend to make defensive self-reactions rather than adaptive ones (Zimmerman and Kitsantas, 1997). In this way, multidimensional research based on a cyclical model of self-regulation has the potential of explaining how self-enhancing as well as self-defeating cycles of musical practice are established.

Development of Self-Regulatory Skill

This perspective might be criticized by those who would argue that young children are unable to self-regulate their own learning. Like most generalizations, this view is partially true. However, as many parents can testify, children as young as 3 sing songs louder and softer to attract or avoid parental attention, which is certainly evidence of self-regulation at a basic level. Research on academic subjects shows that developmental changes in self-regulatory behavior occur during the early years of schooling. Although second-graders display some basic forms of self-regulation such as simple strategies, the processes are not fully integrated in self-regulatory cycles until around eighth grade (Bonner, 1998). Current evidence suggests that there is an intermediate level of integration (e.g., goal setting predicting strategy use and self-efficacy judgments) around fifth grade. The available evidence suggests, therefore, that the acquisition of self-regulatory processes starts early and then becomes integrated into cycles with increasing age and experience.

Several developmental theories of self-regulation regarding young children (between birth and approximately age 6) such as Kopp's (1982) and Vygotsky's (1962) theories deal with relatively simple motoric acts. However, as shown in table 4.2, the self-regulatory view proposed here to describe complex skills in music asserts that self-regulation has social origins and shifts to self sources in a developmental sequence involving four distinct dimensions: observation, emulation, self-control, and self-regulation (see Schunk and Zimmerman, 1997, 2003; Zimmerman, 2000a). Technically, this is not a developmental model but rather a hierarchical learning model that is based on the proposition that learners who follow the sequence will learn more effectively and in a more self-regulated way. Data to verify this assumption have recently been building in both sports and academic writing (Kitsantas, Zimmerman, and Cleary, 2000; Zimmerman and Kitsantas, 1999). For music, this four-level model posits that a novice learner would learn most quickly when exposed to effective teaching, social modeling, task structuring, and encouragement (Schunk and Zimmerman, 2003). At this observational level, young musicians might be able to induce features of learning strategies from observing models such as their teacher or other stu-

Table 4.2 Developmental Levels of Regulatory Skill

Level of Development	Description	Social Influences	Self Influences
Observational	Vicarious induction of a skill from a proficient model	Models Verbal description	
Emulative	Imitative performance of a general pattern or style of a model's skills with social assistance	Social guidance Feedback	
Self-controlled	Independent display of the model's skill under structured conditions		Internal standards Self-reinforcement
Self-regulated	Adaptive use of skill across changing personal and environmental conditions		Self-regulatory processes Self-efficacy beliefs

dents. They will need to practice, however, to fully integrate the skills they are learning into their behavioral repertoires. Improvement during practice occurs when learners have opportunities to observe models that provide guidance, feedback, and social reinforcement and respond to students' needs to refine aspects of the skill they are attempting to master. During this process, strategies and feedback are based on the learner's efforts to imitate a desired model. As an example, skills (such as triple-tonguing on a trumpet) should be initially acquired cognitively through observing (including listening to) a model.

Learners move to the emulative level once they are able to perform at an approximate level to the model they are trying to imitate. To follow our example, at this stage the trumpeter's triple-tonguing would not be at the same level as the teacher's demonstration but would nonetheless exhibit the basics of the skill, though the rhythm and syllables used for triple-tonguing may not yet be fully automatic or consistent. At the observational and emulative stages, learning is primarily social. Self-control emerges at the third stage, when learners start to adopt strategies independently while performing transfer tasks, even though their use of these strategies, though internalized, are affected by representational standards they attempt to duplicate (Schunk and Zimmerman, 2003). To expand our example further, the trumpeter would now be able to triple-tongue independently, having mastered the basic physical skills required to perform this technique on the instrument, but would still rely on aural images of modeled performances and other internalized representations, plus self-reinforcement processes. Self-controlled efforts at this level involve practicing the skill in solitary but structured contexts, such as working through triple-tonguing examples from a relevant practice book. When the skill becomes automatized, the learner can practice varying it (e.g., for speed and dynamics) according to changing contexts (e.g., a Sousa march versus "The Trumpeter's Lullaby"). At this point, the learner shifts to personal outcomes as the criterion to modulate the skill, such as one's personal reaction or an audience's reactions. Self-regulated learning at this fourth level occurs when learners respond to differing personal and situational conditions by modifying learning and performing strategies and making adjustments depending on differing situations. Running in parallel, self-set goals and perceptions of self-efficacy motivate students to achieve (see table 4.2).

Conclusions

This chapter has outlined how theories of self-regulated learning can provide an overarching framework for studying how instrumental students acquire the skills, knowledge, and attitudes to take control of their own learning. We have argued that self-regulation can be viewed as a socially embedded cognitive construct, based on our belief that research using this paradigm would significantly enhance present knowledge on how children acquire the complex range of skills needed for them to persist and succeed with their music learning.

Practical and theoretical implications abound, particularly as very little research currently exists using this framework, in contrast to the wealth of information in academic subjects and motor domains. For example, expert-novice studies could be conducted to investigate differences in specific self-regulatory processes for different types of musical instruments. Like experts in other disciplines, musicians have highly refined self-regulatory techniques (goals, strategies, methods of self-monitoring, types of attributions, and adaptive judgments) that need to be identified for each instrument or choral training. By contrast, novice learners tend to focus unsystematically on performance outcomes rather than specific techniques, and this leads them to make ability attributions and self-defensive reactions. This research could lead to systematic efforts to train students to focus on these self-regulatory processes. For example, beginning brass players could be taught to focus on such sound-enhancing techniques as forming a correct embouchure, abdominal breathing, and sustained air columns, rather than on outcome-driven methods such as pressing to hit notes. By investigating improvements not only in playing skill but also in students' acquisition of cyclical self-regulatory processes, music teachers will have a much better sense of whether students can practice effectively on their own and whether they are being self-motivated to continue their musical development. Investigation of planned practice episodes and daily self-recording accomplishments may yield benefits in music as it has in academic and sport functioning. Addressing research studies such as these will lead to a better understanding of how these processes work in music and may ultimately account for and redress the problem of why some gifted students underachieve in music.

Research that clarifies more precisely how students develop into self-regulated musicians therefore deserves special attention from music education researchers who are capable of drawing on and integrating into their studies some of the major developments in educational research. Adapting and expanding current theories on this issue and drawing on and integrating information from other areas of educational psychology will enable music education researchers to develop more sophisticated theories of musical development that can be used to underpin future teaching and learning in music.

Ultimately, we will probably have to wait another decade to see if researchers have taken up the challenge of focusing their research on the types of questions that have, for the past couple of decades, dominated so much of the literature on academic learning. Our view is that such an emphasis would significantly strengthen music education research, in part because it would help to broaden the paradigms from which the environmental and personal catalysts that shape teaching and learning in music have traditionally been studied.

REFERENCES

Anguiano, K. R. (2006). *Motivational predictors of continuing motivation and achievement for early adolescent instrumental music students.* Unpublished doctoral dissertation, University of Iowa, Iowa City.

Austin, J. R., & Berg, M. (2006). Exploring music practice among sixth-grade band and orchestra students. *Psychology of Music, 34*(4), 535–558.

Austin, J. R., Renwick, J., & McPherson, G. E. (2006). Developing motivation. In G. E. McPherson (Ed.), *The child as musician: A handbook of musical development* (pp. 213–238). Oxford: Oxford University Press.

Azmitia, M., & Hesser, J. (1993). Why siblings are important agents of cognitive development: A comparison of siblings and peers. *Child Development, 64,* 430–444.

Bandura, A. (1986). *Social foundations of thought and action: A social cognitive theory.* Englewood Cliffs, NJ: Prentice-Hall.

Bandura, A. (1991). Self-regulation of motivation through anticipatory and self-reactive mechanism. In R. A. Dienstbier (Ed.), *Nebraska symposium on motivation: Vol. 38. Perspectives on motivation* (pp. 69–164). Lincoln: University of Nebraska Press.

Bandura, A. (1997). *Self-efficacy: The exercise of control.* New York: Freeman.

Barry, N., & Hallam, S. (2002). Practicing. In R. Parncutt & G. E. McPherson (Eds.), *The science and psychology of musical performance: Creative strategies for teaching and learning* (pp. 151–165). New York: Oxford University Press.

Barry, N. H. (1992). The effects of practice strategies, individual differences in cognitive style, and gender upon technical accuracy and musicality of student instrumental performance. *Psychology of Music, 20,* 112–123.

Barry, N. H., & McArthur, V. (1994). Teaching practice strategies in the music studio: A survey of applied music teachers. *Psychology of Music, 22,* 44–55.

Bloom, B. S. (Ed.). (1985). *Developing talent in young people.* New York: Ballantine.

Bond, M., & Clark, R. E. (1999). Comparison between self-concept and self-efficacy in academic motivation research. *Educational Psychologist, 34,* 139–153.

Bonner, S. (1998). *Developmental changes in self-regulated learning during a multi-trial sort-recall task.* Unpublished doctoral dissertation, City University of New York.

Bruning, R. H., Schraw, G. J., & Ronning, R. R. (1999). *Cognitive psychology and instruction* (3rd ed.). Upper Saddle River, NJ: Prentice-Hall.

Butler, D. L. (2002). Qualitative approaches to investigating self-regulated learning: Contributions and challenges. *Educational Psychologist, 37,* 59–63.

Cantwell, R. H., & Millard, Y. (1994). The relationship between approach to learning and learning strategies in learning music. *British Journal of Educational Psychology, 64,* 45–63.

Carver, C. S., & Scheier, M. F. (1981). *Attention and self-regulation: A control-theory approach to human behavior.* New York: Springer-Verlag.

Chase, W. G., & Simon, H. A. (1973). Perception in chess. *Cognitive Psychology, 4,* 55–81.

Chen, C., & Stevenson, H. W. (1989). Homework: A cross-cultural examination. *Child Development, 60,* 551–561.

Cleary, T. J., & Zimmerman, B. J. (2001). Self-regulation differences during athletic practice by experts, non-experts, and novices. *Journal of Applied Sport Psychology, 13,* 61–82.[d]

Corno, L. (1989). Self-regulated learning: A volitional analysis. In B. J. Zimmerman & D. H. Schunk (Eds.), *Self-regulated learning and academic achievement: Theory, research, and practice* (pp. 111–141). New York: Springer-Verlag.

Corno, L. (1994). Student volition and education: Outcomes, influences, and practices. In D. H. Schunk & B. J. Zimmerman (Eds.), *Self-regulation of learning and performance* (pp. 229–251). Hillsdale, NJ: Erlbaum.

Corno, L. (1995). Comments on Winne: Analytic and systematic research are both needed. *Educational Psychologist, 30,* 201–206.

Costa-Giomi, E. (2004). "I do not want to study piano!" Early predictors of student dropout behavior. *Bulletin of the Council for Research in Music Education, 161/162,* 57–64.

Covington, M. V., & Roberts, B. (1994). Self-worth and college students: Motivational and personality correlates. In P. R. Pintrich, D. R. Brown, & C. E. Weinstein (Eds.), *Student motivation, cognition, and learning: Essays in honor of Wilbert J. McKeachie* (pp. 157–187). Hillsdale, NJ: Erlbaum.

Creech, A. (2001). *Play for me: An exploration into motivation, issues and outcomes related to parental involvement in their children's violin study.* Unpublished masters thesis, University of Sheffield, UK.

Creech, A., & Hallam, S. (2003). Parent-teacher-pupil interactions in instrumental music tuition: A literature review. *British Journal of Music Education, 20*(1), 29–44.

Csikszentmihalyi, M. (1990). *Flow: The psychology of optimal experience.* New York: Harper & Row.

Davidson, J. W., Howe, M. J. A., Moore, D. G., & Sloboda, J. A. (1996). The role of parental influences in the development of musical performance. *British Journal of Developmental Psychology, 14*, 399–412.

Davidson, J. W., Howe, M. J. A, & Sloboda, J. A. (1997). Environmental factors in the development of musical performance skill over the life span. In D. J. Hargreaves & A. C. North (Eds.), *The social psychology of music* (pp. 188–206). Oxford: Oxford University Press.

Davidson, J. W., Moore, J. W., Sloboda, J. A., & Howe, M. J. A. (1998). Characteristics of music teachers and the progress of young instrumentalists. *Journal of Research in Music Education, 46*(1), 141–160.

Davidson, J. W., Sloboda, J. A., & Howe, M. J. A. (1995/1996). The role of parents and teachers in the success and failure of instrumental learners. *Bulletin of the Council for Research in Music Education. 127*, 40–44.

De Bruin, A. B. H., Rikers, M. J. P., & Schmidt, H. G. (2007). The influence of achievement motivation and chess-specific motivation on deliberate practice. *Journal of Sport and Exercise Psychology, 29*, 561–583.

Dweck, C. S. (1986). Motivational processes affecting learning. *American Psychologist, 41*, 1040–1048.

Dweck, C. S. (2000). *Self-theories: Their role in motivation, personality and development.* Philadelphia: Psychology Press.

Dweck, C. S., & Leggett, E. (1988). A social-cognitive approach to motivation and personality. *Psychological Review, 95*, 256–273.

Eccles-Parsons, J. (1983). Children's motivation to study music. In *Motivation and creativity: National symposium on the applications of psychology to the teaching and learning of music* (pp. 31–40). Washington, DC: Music Educators National Conference.

Ericsson, K. A. (Ed.). (1996). *The road to excellence.* Mahwah, NJ: Erlbaum.

Ericsson, K. A., Krampe, R. T., & Tesch-Römer, C. (1993). The role of deliberate practice in the acquisition of expert performance. *Psychological Review, 100*(3), 363–406.

Gabrielsson, A. (1999). The performance of music. In D. Deutsch (Ed.), *The psychology of music* (2nd ed., pp. 501–602). San Diego, CA: Academic Press.

Garcia, T., & Pintrich, P. R. (1994). Regulating motivation and cognition in the classroom: The role of self-schemas and self-regulatory strategies. In D. H. Schunk & B. J. Zimmerman (Eds.), *Self-regulation of learning and performance: Issues and educational applications* (pp. 127–153). Hillsdale, NJ: Erlbaum.

Gellrich, M., Parncutt, R. (1998). Piano technique and fingering in the eighteenth and nineteenth centuries: Bringing a forgotten method back to life. *British Journal of Music Education, 15*, 5–24.

Gembris, H., & Davidson, J. W. (2002). Environmental influences on development. In R. Parncutt & G. E. McPherson (Eds.), *The science and psychology of musical performance: Creative strategies for music teaching and learning* (pp. 17–30). New York: Oxford University Press.

Goodnow, J. J., & Warton, P. M. (1992). Understanding responsibility: Adolescents' views of delegation and follow-through within the family. *Social Development, 1*, 89–106.

Gottfried, A. E. (1985). Academic intrinsic motivation in elementary and junior high school students. *Journal of Educational Psychology, 77*, 631–645.

Grant, H., & Dweck, C. (2003). Clarifying achievement goals and their impact. *Journal of Personality and Social Psychology, 85*, 541–553.

Green, B. (1986). *The inner game of music*. New York: Anchor Doubleday.

Green, C. L., Walker, J. M. T., Hoover-Dempsey, K. V., & Sandler, H. M. (2007). Parents' motivations for involvement in children's education: An empirical test of a theoretical model of parental involvement. *Journal of Educational Psychology, 99*(3), 532–544.

Green, L. (2008). Group cooperation, inclusion and disaffected pupils: Some responses to informal learning in the music classroom. *Music Education Research, 10*(2), 177–192.

Gruson, L. M. (1988). Rehearsal skill and musical competence: Does practice make perfect? In J. A. Sloboda (Ed.), *Generative processes in music* (pp. 91–112). Oxford: Clarendon.

Hackett, G. (1995). Self-efficacy in career choice and development. In A. Bandura (Ed.), *Self-efficacy in changing societies* (pp. 232–258). New York: Cambridge University Press.

Hallam, S. (1994). Novice musicians' approaches to practice and performance: Learning new music. *Newsletter of the European Society for the Cognitive Sciences of Music, 6*, 2–10.

Hallam, S. (1997). Approaches to instrumental music practice of experts and novices: Implications for education. In H. Jorgensen Jørgensen & A. C. Lehmann (Eds.), *Does practice make perfect? Current theory and research on instrumental music practice* (pp. 89–108). Oslo, Norway: Nørges musikkhøgskole.

Hallam, S. (1998). The predictors of achievement and dropouts in instrumental tuition. *Psychology of Music, 26*, 116–132.

Hallam, S. (2000). The development of performance planning strategies in musicians. In C. Woods, G. B. Luck, R. Brochard, S. A. O'Neill, & J. A. Sloboda (Eds.), *Proceedings of the Sixth International Conference on Music Perception & Cognition*. Keele, Staffordshire, England: Keele University Department of Psychology (CD-ROM).

Hayes, J. R. (1989). Cognitive processes in creativity. In J. A. Glover, R. R. Ronning, & C. R. Reynolds (Eds.), *Handbook of creativity* (pp. 135–145). New York: Plenum.

Hays, T., Minichiello, V., & Wright, P. (2000). Mentorship: The meaning of the relationship for musicians. *Research Studies in Music Education, 15*, 3–14.

Henderson, V. L., & Dweck, C. S. (1990). Motivation and achievement. In S. S. Feldman & G. R. Elliott (Eds.), *At the threshold: The developing adolescent* (pp. 308–329). Cambridge, MA: Harvard University Press.

Hofer, B. K., Yu, S. L., & Pintrich, P. R. (1998). Teaching college students to be self-regulated learners. In D. H. Schunk & B. J. Zimmerman (Eds.), *Self-regulated learning: From teaching to self-reflective practice* (pp. 57–85). New York: Guilford.

Hoover-Dempsey, K. V., & Sandler, H. M. (1995). Parental involvement in children's education: Why does it make a difference? *Teachers College Record, 97*, 310–331.

Jacobs, J., Lanza, S., Osgood, D. W., Eccles, J. S., & Wigfield, A. (2002). Ontogeny of children's self-beliefs: Gender and domain differences across grades 1 through 12. *Child Development, 73*, 509–527.

Kitsantas, A., Zimmerman, B. J., & Cleary, T. (2000). The role of observation and emulation in the development of athletic self-regulation. *Journal of Educational Psychology, 91*, 241–250.

Kohut, D. L. (1985). *Musical performance: Learning theory and pedagogy.* Englewood Cliffs, NJ: Prentice-Hall.

Kopp, C. B. (1982). Antecedents of self-regulation: A developmental perspective. *Developmental Psychology, 18,* 199–214.

Lehmann, A. C. (1997). The acquisition of expertise in music: Efficiency of deliberate practice as a moderating variable in accounting for sub-expert performance. In I. Deliege & J. Sloboda (Eds.), *Perception and cognition of music* (pp. 161–187). Hove, England: Psychology Press.

Lehmann, A. C., & Davidson, J. W. (2002). Taking an acquired skills perspective on music performance. In R. Colwell & C. Richardson (Eds.), *The new handbook of research on music teaching and learning* (pp. 542–560). New York: Oxford University Press.

Lehmann, A. C., & Ericsson, K. A. (1997). Research on expert performance and deliberate practice: Implications for the education of amateur musicians and music students. *Psychomusicology, 16,* 40–58.

Lehmann, A. C., & Gruber, H. (2006). Music. In K. A. Ericsson, N. Charness, P. J. Feltovich, & R. R. Hoffman (Eds.), *The Cambridge handbook of expertise and expert performance* (pp. 457–470). Cambridge, UK: Cambridge University Press.

Leon-Guerrero, A. (2008). Self-regulation strategies used by student musicians during music practice. *Music Education Research, 10*(1), 91–106.

Mach, E. (1991). *Great contemporary pianists speak for themselves* (Vols. 1–2). Toronto, Ontario: Dover.

Mantalvo, G. P., Mansfield, E. A., & Miller, R. B. (2007). Liking or disliking the teacher: Student motivation, engagement and achievement. *Evaluation and Research in Education, 20*(3), 144–158.

McCormick, J., & McPherson, G. E. (2003). The role of self-efficacy in a musical performance examination: An exploratory structural equation analysis. *Psychology of Music, 31*(1), 37–51.

McCormick, J., & McPherson, G. E. (2007). Expectancy-value motivation in the context of a music performance examination. *Musicæ Scientiæ, Special Issue,* 37–52.

McPherson, G. (1989). Cognitive mediational processes and positive motivation: Implications of educational research for music teaching and learning. *Australian Journal of Music Education, 1,* 3–19.

McPherson, G. E. (1993). *Factors and abilities influencing the development of visual, aural and creative performance skills in music and their educational implications.* Unpublished doctoral dissertation, University of Sydney, Australia.

McPherson, G. E. (1994). Factors and abilities influencing sight-reading skill in music. *Journal of Research in Music Education, 42*(3), 217–231.

McPherson, G. E. (1995). Redefining the teaching of musical performance. *Quarterly Journal of Music Teaching and Learning, 6,* 56–64.

McPherson, G. E. (1997). Cognitive strategies and skills acquisition in musical performance. *Bulletin of the Council for Research in Music Education, 133,* 64–71.

McPherson, G. E. (2001). Commitment and practice: Key ingredients for achievement during the early stages of learning a musical instrument. *Bulletin of the Council for Research in Music Education, 147,* 122–127.

McPherson, G. E. (2005). From child to musician: Skill development during the beginning stages of learning an instrument. *Psychology of Music, 33*(1), 5–35.

McPherson, G. E. (2009). The role of parents in children's musical development. *Psychology of Music, 37*(1), 91–110.

McPherson, G. E., & Davidson, J. W. (2002). Musical practice: Mother and child interactions during the first year of learning an instrument. *Music Education Research, 4*(1), 141–156.

McPherson, G. E., & Davidson, J. W. (2006). Playing an instrument. In G. E. McPherson (Ed.), *The child as musician: A handbook of musical development* (pp. 331–351). Oxford: Oxford University Press.

McPherson, G. E., & McCormick, J. (1999). Motivational and self-regulated learning components of musical practice. *Bulletin of the Council for Research in Music Education, 141,* 98–102.

McPherson, G. E., & McCormick, J. (2006). Self-efficacy and performing music. *Psychology of Music, 34*(3), 321–336.

McPherson, G. E., & Renwick, J. (2000). Self-regulation and musical practice. In C. Woods, G. B. Luck, R. Brochard, S. A. O'Neill, & J. A. Sloboda (Eds.), *Proceedings of the Sixth International Conference on Music Perception & Cognition.* Keele, Staffordshire, England: Keele University Department of Psychology (CD-ROM).

McPherson, G. E., & Renwick, J. (2001). A longitudinal study of self-regulation in children's musical practice. *Music Education Research, 3*(2), 169–186.

Miklaszewski, K. (1989). A case study of a pianist preparing a musical performance. *Psychology of Music, 63,* 81–97.

Miksza, P. (2006). An exploratory investigation of self-regulatory and motivational variables in the music practice of junior high band students. *Contributions to Music Education, 33*(2), 9–26.

Miksza, P. (2007). Effective practice: An investigation of observed practice behaviors, self-reported practice habits and the performance achievement of high school wind players. *Journal of Research in Music Education, 55*(4), 359–375.

Newman, R. S. (1994). Academic help seeking: A strategy of self-regulated learning. In D. H. Schunk & B. J. Zimmerman (Eds.), *Self-regulation of learning and performance: Issues and educational applications* (pp. 283–301). Hillsdale, NJ: Erlbaum.

Nielsen, S. G. (1997). Self-regulation of learning strategies during practice: A case study of a church organ student preparing a musical work for performance. In H. Jørgensen & A. C. Lehmann (Eds.), *Does practice make perfect? Current theory and research on instrumental music practice* (pp. 109–122). Oslo, Norway: Norges musikkhøgskole.

Nielsen, S. G. (1998). Selvregulering av læringstrategier under øving: En studie av to utøvende musikkstudenter på høyt nivå. [Self-regulation of learning strategies during practice: A study of two gifted church organ students possessing a high level of technical skill]. Unpublished doctoral dissertation, Norwegian Academy of Music, Oslo, Norway.

Nielsen, S. G. (1999). Learning strategies in instrumental music practice. *British Journal of Music Education, 16*(3), 275–291.

Neilsen, S. G. (2000). Self-regulated use of learning strategies in instrumental practice. In C. Woods, G. B. Luck, R. Brochard, S. A. O'Neill, & J. A. Sloboda (Eds.), *Proceedings of the Sixth International Conference on Music Perception & Cognition.* Keele, Staffordshire, UK: Department of Psychology (CD-ROM).

Nielsen, S. G. (2004). Strategies and self-efficacy beliefs in instrumental and voice individual practice: A study of students in higher music education. *Psychology of Music, 32*(4), 418–431.

Nielsen, S. G. (2008). Achievement goals, learning strategies and instrumental performance. *Music Education Research, 10*(2), 235–247.

Noldus, L. P. J. J., Trienes, R. J. H., Hendriksen, A. H. M., Jansen, H., & Jansen, R. G. (2000). The Observer Video-Pro: New software for the collection, management, and presentation of time-structured data from videotapes and digital media files. *Behavior Research Methods, Instruments & Computers, 32,* 197–206.

O'Neill, S. A. (1996). *Factors influencing children's motivation and achievement during the first year of instrumental music tuition.* Unpublished doctoral dissertation, Keele University, Keele, UK.

O'Neill, S. A. (1997). The role of practice in children's early performance achievement. In H. Jørgensen & A. C. Lehmann (Eds.), *Does practice make perfect? Current theory and research on instrumental music practice* (pp. 53–70). Oslo, Norway: Norges musikkhøgskole.

O'Neill, S. A., & McPherson, G. E. (2002). Motivation. In R. Parncutt & G. E. McPherson (Eds.), *The science and psychology of musical performance: Creative strategies for teaching and learning* (pp. 31–46). New York: Oxford University Press.

O'Neill, S. A., & Sloboda, J. A. (1997). The effects of failure on children's ability to perform a musical test. *Psychology of Music, 25,* 18–34.

Pajares, F. (1996a). Self-efficacy and mathematical problem-solving of gifted students. *Contemporary Educational Psychology, 21,* 325–344.

Pajares, F. (1996b). Self-efficacy beliefs in academic settings. *Review of Educational Research, 66,* 543–578.

Pintrich, P. R., & Schunk, D. H. (1996). *Motivation in education: Theory, research and applications.* Englewood Cliffs, NJ: Prentice-Hall.

Pitts, S., Davidson, J., & McPherson, G. E. (2000). Developing effective practise strategies: Case studies of three young instrumentalists. *Music Education Research, 2*(1), 45–56.

Pogonowski, L. (1989). Metacognition: A dimension of musical thinking. In E. Boardman (Ed.), *Dimensions of musical thinking* (pp. 9–19). Reston, VA: Music Educators National Conference.

Renwick, J. (2008). *Because I love playing my instrument: Young musicians' internalised motivation and self-regulated practising behaviour.* Unpublished doctoral dissertation, University of New South Wales, Australia.

Renwick, J., & McPherson, G. E. (2000). "I've got to do my scale first!" A case study of a novice's clarinet practice. In C. Woods, G. B. Luck, R. Brochard, S. A. O'Neill, & J. A. Sloboda (Eds.), *Proceedings of the Sixth International Conference on Music Perception & Cognition.* Keele, Staffordshire, England: Keele University Department of Psychology (CD-ROM).

Renwick, J., & McPherson, G. E. (2002). Interest and choice: Student-selected repertoire and its effect on practising behaviour. *British Journal of Music Education, 19*(2), 173–188.

Renwick, J. M., McPherson, G. E., & McCormick, J. (2008). Effort management, self-monitoring and corrective strategies in the practising behaviour of intermediate instrumentalists: Observations and retrospective think-aloud protocols. Paper presented at the International Society for Music Education world conference, July 21–25, 2008, Bologna, Italy.

Salis, D. L. (1977). *The identification and assessment of cognitive variables associated with reading of advanced music at the piano.* Unpublished doctoral dissertation, University of Pittsburgh, PA.

Schmidt, C. P. (2005). Relations among motivation, performance achievement, and music experience variables in secondary instrumental music students. *Journal of Research in Music Education, 53*(2), 134–147.

Schunk, D. H., & Pajares, F. (2004). Self-efficacy in education revisited: Empirical and applied evidence. In D. McInerney & S. Van Etten (Eds.), *Big theories revisited* (Vol. 4, 115–164). Greenwich, CT: Information Age.

Schunk, D. H., & Zimmerman, B. J. (1997). Social origins of self-regulatory competence. *Educational Psychologist, 32,* 195–208.

Schunk, D. H., & Zimmerman, B. J. (2003). Self-regulation and learning. In W. M. Reynolds & G. E. Miller (Eds.), *Handbook of psychology: Educational psychology* (pp. 59–78). Hoboken, NJ: John Wiley & Sons.

Shuell, T. J. (1988). The role of transfer in the learning and teaching of music: A cognitive perspective. In C. Fowler (Ed.), *The Crane symposium: Toward an understanding of the teaching and learning of music performance* (pp. 143–167). Potsdam, NY: Potsdam College of the State University of New York.

Slavin, R. E. (1995). *Cooperative learning: Theory, research and practice.* 2nd ed. New York: Allyn & Bacon.

Sloboda, J. A., & Davidson, J. W. (1996). The young performing musician. In I. Deliege & J. A. Sloboda (Eds.), *Musical beginnings: Origins and development of musical competence* (pp. 171–190). New York: Oxford University Press.

Sloboda, J. A., Davidson, J. W., Howe, M. J. A., & Moore, D. G. (1996). The role of practice in the development of performing musicians. *British Journal of Psychology, 87,* 287–309.

Sosniak, L. A. (1985). Learning to be a concert pianist. In B. S. Bloom (Ed.), *Developing talent in young people* (pp. 19–67). New York: Ballantine.

Sosniak, L. A. (1987). The nature of change in successful learning. *Teachers College Record, 88,* 519–535.

Sosniak, L. A. (1990). The tortoise, the hare, and the development of talent. In M. J. A. Howe (Ed.), *Encouraging the development of exceptional skills and talent* (pp. 477–506). Leicester, England: British Psychological Society.

Stebleton, E. (1987). Predictors of sight-reading achievement: A review of the literature. *Update, 6,* 11–15.

Stipek, D. (1998). *Motivation to learn* (3rd ed.). Needham Heights, MA: Allyn & Bacon.

Thomas, H. W., Strage, A., & Curley, R. (1988). Improving students' self-directed learning. *Elementary School Journal, 88,* 313–326.

Vohs, K. D., & Baumeister, R. F. (2004). Understanding self-regulation. In R. F. Baumeister & K. D. Vohs (Eds.), *Handbook of self-regulation: Research, theory, and applications* (pp. 1–9). New York: Guilford.

Vygotsky, E. (1962). *Thought and language.* Cambridge, MA: MIT Press.

Warton, P. M. (1997). Learning about responsibility: Lessons from homework. *British Journal of Educational Psychology, 67,* 213–221.

Warton, P. M., & Goodnow, J. J. (1991). The nature of responsibility: Children's understanding of "your job." *Child Development, 62,* 156–165.

Watkins, J. G. and Farnum, S. E. (1962). The Watkins-Farnum Performance Scale (Forms A and B). Milwaukee, WI: Hal Leonard.

Weinstein, C. E., Husman, J., & Dierking, D. R. (2000). Self-regulation interventions with a focus on learning strategies. In M. Boekaerts, P. Pintrich, & M. Zeidner (Eds.), *Handbook of self-regulation* (pp. 728–747). San Diego, CA: Academic Press.

Weisberg, R. W. (1999). Creativity and knowledge: A challenge to theories. In R. Sternberg (Ed.), *Handbook of creativity* (pp. 226–250). Cambridge: Cambridge University Press.

Williamon, A., & Valentine, E. (2000). Quantity and quality of musical practice as predictors of performance quality. *British Journal of Psychology, 91*, 353–376.

Wilson, G. D. (1997). Performance anxiety. In D. J. Hargreaves & A. C. North (Eds.), *The social psychology of music* (pp. 227–245). New York: Oxford University Press.

Wilson, G. D., & Roland, D. (2002). Performance anxiety. In R. Parncutt & G. E. McPherson (Eds.), *The science and psychology of musical performance: Creative strategies for music teaching and learning* (pp. 47–62). New York: Oxford University Press.

Wolf, T. (1976). A cognitive model of musical sight-reading. *Journal of Psycholinguistic Research, 5*(2), 143–172.

Xu, J. (2004). Family help and homework management in urban and rural secondary schools. *Teachers College Record, 106*, 1786–1803.

Zdzinski, S. F. (1994). Parental involvement, gender, and learning outcomes among instrumentalists. *Contributions to Music Education, 21*, 73–89.

Zdzinski, S. F. (1996). Parental involvement, selected student attributes, and learning outcomes in instrumental music. *Journal of Research in Music Education, 44*(1), 34–48.

Zimmerman, B. J. (1986). Becoming a self-regulated learner: Which are the key subprocesses? *Contemporary Educational Psychology, 11*, 307–313.

Zimmerman, B. J. (1989). A social cognitive view of self-regulated academic learning. *Journal of Educational Psychology, 81*, 329–339.

Zimmerman, B. J. (1994). Dimensions of academic self-regulation: A conceptual framework for education. In D. H. Schunk & B. J. Zimmerman (Eds.), *Self-regulation of learning and performance: Issues and educational applications* (pp. 3–21). Hillsdale, NJ: Erlbaum.

Zimmerman, B. J. (1995). Self-efficacy and educational development. In A. Bandura (Ed.), *Self-efficacy in changing societies* (pp. 202–231). Cambridge: Cambridge University Press.

Zimmerman, B. J. (1998a). Academic studying and the development of personal skill: A self-regulatory perspective. *Educational Psychologist, 33*(2/3), 73–86.

Zimmerman, B. J. (1998b). Developing self-fulfilling cycles of academic regulation: An analysis of exemplary instructional models. In D. H. Schunk & B. J. Zimmerman (Eds.), *Self-regulated learning: From teaching to self-reflective practice* (pp. 1–19). New York: Guilford.

Zimmerman, B. J. (2000a). Attaining self-regulation: A social cognitive perspective. In M. Boekaerts, P. R. Pintrich, & M. Zeidner (Eds.), *Handbook of self-regulation* (pp. 13–39). San Diego, CA: Academic Press.

Zimmerman, B. J. (2000b). Self-efficacy: An essential motive to learn. *Contemporary Educational Psychology, 25*, 82–91.

Zimmerman, B. J. (2004). Sociocultural influence and students' development of academic self-regulation: A social-cognitive perspective. In. D. McInerney &

S. Van Etten (Eds.), *Big theories revisited* (Vol. 4, 139–164). Greenwich, CT: Information Age.

Zimmerman, B. J. (2007). Goal setting: A key proactive source of academic self-regulation. In D. H. Schunk & B. J. Zimmerman (Eds.), *Motivation and self-regulated learning: Theory, research, and applications* (pp. 267–295). Mahwah, NJ: Erlbaum.

Zimmerman, B. J. (2008). Investigating self-regulation and motivation: Historical background, methodological developments, and future prospects. *American Educational Research Journal, 45*(1), 166–183.

Zimmerman, B. J., & Campillo, M. (2003). Motivating self-regulated problem solvers. In J. E. Davidson & R. J. Sternberg (Eds.), *The nature of problem solving* (pp. 233–262). New York: Cambridge University Press.

Zimmerman, B. J., & Kitsantas, A. (1997). Developmental phases in self-regulation: Shifting from process to outcome goals. *Journal of Educational Psychology, 89,* 29–36.

Zimmerman, B. J., & Kitsantas, A. (1999). Acquiring writing revision skill: Shifting from process to outcome self-regulatory goals. *Journal of Educational Psychology, 91,* 1–10.

Zimmerman, B. J., & Martinez-Pons, M. (1986). Development of a structured interview for assessing student use of self-regulated learning strategies. *American Educational Research Journal, 23,* 614–628.

Zimmerman, B. J., & Martinez-Pons, M. (1988). Construct validation of a strategy model of student self-regulated learning. *Journal of Educational Psychology, 80,* 284–290.

Zimmerman, B. J., & Martinez-Pons, M. (1992). Perceptions of efficacy and strategy use in the self-regulation of learning. In D. H. Schunk & J. Meece (Eds.), *Student perceptions in the classroom: Causes and consequences* (pp. 185–207). Hillsdale, NJ: Erlbaum.

Zimmerman, B. J., & Schunk, D. H. (2007). Motivation: An essential dimension of self-regulated learning. In D. H. Schunk & B. J. Zimmerman (Eds.), *Motivation and self-regulated learning: Theory, research, and applications* (pp. 1–30). Mahwah, NJ: Erlbaum.

Zimmerman, B. J., & Weinstein, C. E. (1994). Self-regulating academic study time: A strategy approach. In D. H. Schunk & B. J. Zimmerman (Eds.), *Self regulation of learning and performance: Issues and educational applications* (pp. 181–199). Hillsdale, NJ: Erlbaum.

Research on Elementary and Secondary School Singing

5

KENNETH H. PHILLIPS

SANDRA M. DONESKI

Singing at the elementary and secondary levels in the United States continues to be a major emphasis in the school music curriculum. The first of the national standards in music education (Consortium, 1994) states that all children should be able to sing, alone and with others, a varied repertoire of music.

The research in the area of school singing continues to grow. However, as with most other areas, there remain many questions. Perhaps the most basic question is why the music education profession has been unsuccessful in producing a society that can sing. The 1997 National Assessment of Educational Progress (*NAEP 1997 Arts Report Card: Eighth-Grade Findings from the National Assessment of Educational Progress*, 1998) reports that for eighth-grade students singing "Twinkle, Twinkle, Little Star," only "25 percent of the students performed the pitches at an Adequate level or above" (p. 36). Clearly, there is much room for improvement.

An understanding of how to teach singing has made considerable advancement since the 1980s, when the children's choir movement in the United States expanded rapidly. The idea that voice instruction for children was inappropriate was shown to be false; children involved in professional community ensembles were demonstrating healthy singing voices, even when singing demanding literature. The American Academy of Teachers of Singing (2002) reversed an earlier statement cautioning against child vocal instruction to state that:

Acutely aware of the physical damage improper excessive or ill-advised singing can cause, the Academy in the past has recommended that children not engage in formal voice studies. However, upon further investigation, no scientific, pedagogical, or psychological evidence indicates that child voice pedagogy is inherently harmful to children's bodies, minds, or spirits. The Academy now recognizes that there are benefits to teaching children to sing. In fact, well-trained singers of any age are less likely than untrained singers to hurt their vocal instruments or to allow their instruments to be hurt by others. (p. 1)

*vocal instruction is not harmful

This statement should put an end to the belief that systematic vocal instruction for children is harmful or inappropriate.

The idea that children can be taught to sing using age-appropriate vocal pedagogy has begun to make an impact on the way singing is taught in schools. Music teachers are learning how to work with the child voice, and singing is no longer viewed as a recreational activity but as a skill that can be developed. Research into the physiological and psychological parameters of singing is ongoing, and much of what is presented in this chapter advances the understanding of this psychomotor process. These studies do not venture into the area of clinical research, which is oriented toward vocal studio teachers. The majority of research presented here involves children in school settings, and most of this research is quantitative in nature. Singing has not been the topic of much qualitative research, although qualitative investigation could be helpful in discovering why many children's positive attitudes toward singing seem to decrease as they mature.

skill

Singing takes many forms across diverse cultures, and this research review does not address this issue. Rather, singing in this chapter relates to a general American style that Ross (1948) identifies as having "a ringing-resonant quality, which makes use of the pharynx as the primary resonator and enunciator, amplified or modified by the nasal passages and the mouth" (p. 11). This style also makes use of upper, middle, and lower vocal registers, as opposed to the one-register, chest-voice approach used by most pop vocal artists. This style often leads to vocal abuse and vocal nodules.

The first *Handbook of Research on Music Teaching and Learning* (Colwell, 1992) contains a chapter on child and adolescent singing (Phillips, 1992a) that summarizes the known research up to 1990. Goetze, Cooper, and Brown (1990) present an additional review of literature for the same time span on singing in general music. The present chapter explores research related to school vocal music published during the 1990s and into the first decade of the 21st century. The chapter is divided into two main sections: elementary and secondary school singing.

Elementary School Singing

Research at the elementary level (K-6) has identified numerous topics that affect children's singing. Those areas presented here are as follows (in alphabetical order): accompaniment, assessment, attitude, audiation, home environment, individual or small-group versus large-group singing, Kodály instruction, modeling, psychomotor coordination, song acquisition, and song literature. Some articles appear under more than one heading in that research questions for these studies focus on more than one area.

Accompaniment

Recent research suggests that instruction with harmonic accompaniment does not have an effect on singing accuracy, at least singing from a traditional perspective. Atterbury and Silcox (1993a) found no significant difference between treatment (n = 96) and control groups (n =109) in an investigation of the effect of piano harmonic accompaniment on the singing of kindergarten students. The authors state, "The narrow range (1–4) of the rating scale may have been responsible for the lack of difference observed in the statistical analysis" (p. 45). It also could be that piano accompaniment serves to distract kindergarten children. Phillips (1992b) suggests that teachers not use the piano to accompany children's singing, especially in the primary grades. This helps the teacher to better hear the children's voices and enables the children to more readily hear themselves.

Guilbault (2004) also studied the effects of harmonic accompaniment on singing achievement among kindergarten and first-grade students and included tonal improvisation as an additional dependent variable. As with Atterbury and Silcox (1993a), no significant difference was found between groups for song singing. There was a significant difference (p < 0.05) for tonal improvisation. The author states:

> Children who received song instruction with root melody accompaniment achieved significantly higher tonal ratings when improvising than children who did not have such instruction. Implied harmonic functions within the original tonic pitch and tonality occurred most often in the melodic improvisations of children in the experimental group. (p. 74)

Guilbault's study stretches the concept of singing beyond rote performance of songs and tonal patterns to include tonal improvisation, which is not something often found in kindergarten music curricula. Kindergarten music teachers might want to explore the possibility of beginning this skill among young children as a means of laying a foundation for more advanced improvisatory singing. The development of improvisation among children is the third of the National Standards (Consortium, 1994). Future studies in this area could add to a much-needed knowledge base for developing vocal improvisation, including the role that harmonic accompaniment plays in its development.

Assessment

The literature is replete with studies that compare tonal patterns with song phrases to assess various aspects of children's singing. The types of patterns used are numerous. Some are based on sequential pedagogy, like those associated with Kodály or music learning theory (Gordon), others are specifically melodic or harmonic in function, and some are performed with solfège syllables or neutral syllables and vary in length.

Moore (1994) investigated performance of harmonic (intervals and triads) and melodic tonal patterns among pitch-accurate singers age 8 to 11. Subjects (N = 128) echoed melodic patterns ranging from 2 to 6 tones and sang the upper tone of two-note intervals, the lower tone of another set of two-note intervals, and the middle tone of triads. Ratings were based on the number of trials it took a student to accurately sing the criterion pattern or pitch. Results indicated a significant difference for pitch-matching task and significant interaction for age and singing task ($p < 0.05$). Melodic and upper pitch-matching tasks were not different. Middle tones of triads were most difficult, followed by lower tone of two-note intervals. Based on frequency of errors, older students had an easier time finding lower notes than younger students, and both groups were equally challenged finding the middle tones of triads. None of these results were surprising.

Welch (1994) reviewed the literature regarding assessment of singing to develop a measure to be used in a longitudinal study. The review suggested the following sequence for singing development: (1) words, (2) rhythm, (3) pitch, (4) pitch contour, (5) individual phrase stability, and (6) overall key stability (p. 5). Welch suggested two areas that music educators must take into consideration in developing appropriate assessment tools. First, he cautioned against a "goodness of fit" approach in analyzing children's singing based solely on a Western cultural context. Second, he suggested that some out-of-tune singing is judged as the result of developmentally inappropriate singing tasks for the particular students.

In the 3-year longitudinal study of singing development in early childhood, Welch (1994) utilized both machine-based and human judges to assess the singing of 200 5-year-old children from 10 schools, urban and suburban, in the greater London area. A comparative sample of up to 800 students age 3 to 12, as well as a third sample of cathedral choristers and singers from children's choirs, served to reflect the effects of experienced vocal training. He tested the subjects in their school or rehearsal settings, believing they would be more comfortable singing in familiar environments. Assessment included glides (vocal glissandi between two pitches), patterns, single pitches, and songs, as well as pitch contour, individual phrase stability, and overall key stability. A 13-year-old female served as vocal model and recorded eight composed songs, each with similar melodic contour and direction of intervals. Teachers used the recordings in class for 2 weeks before the individual vocal assessments were made. Professional musicians rated data from the 5-year-old subjects' singing using a 7-point scale. Results confirmed the developmental sequence outlined by Welch and showed "five-year-olds tend to match words better than the melodic contour and that the matching of pitch direction was better for the example melodic fragments (patterns) and single notes compared to the glides and songs" (p. 15).

Regarding human-based versus a machine-based approach to singing assessment, Welch suggests the two procedures are not easily separated: "The sophistication of modern technology allows many of the assessment parameters to be altered by the experimenter and so there is a strong 'human' element which permeates all assessment" (p. 15). In other words, technology is only as good as the person who defines the parameters of the assessment. Welch does note that a machine-based instrument often helps to clean up human perception. Perhaps both modes are equally successful.

As a continuation of the previous study, Welch, Sergeant, and White (1995/1996) investigated the singing competencies of 5-year-old students. Subjects ($N = 186$) performed a series of four vocal tasks: glides, patterns, single pitches, and songs. An 11-year-old chorister sang and recorded the glides, patterns, and pitches; these also were electronically produced and recorded. As in the previous study, teachers played the recorded songs for the subjects during a 2-week period prior to data collection. Students' responses were digitally recorded and rated by professional musicians. Results showed for song performance that words were matched more accurately than contour of melody ($p < 0.0001$). Significant differences were found in favor of pitches/simple glides compared with patterns ($p < 0.001$), in favor of patterns compared with all glides ($p < 0.0001$), in favor of glides compared with songs ($p < 0.0001$), and for songs compared with complex glides ($p < 0.0001$). Each of the three vocal tasks was significantly better than the ratings for the songs ($p < 0.0001$). Welch, Sergeant, and White concluded that "words often have primacy over musical features for young developing singers and this is supported by the song data" (p. 160).

Music teachers know that young children often chant words as a substitute for actual singing. Young singers seemingly do not differentiate between singing voice and speaking voice. For this reason, singing on a neutral syllable is sometimes recommended for learning songs, although research results in this area are mixed and unclear.

Welch, Sergeant, and White (1997) investigated age, gender, and vocal task on children age 5, 6, and 7 ($N = 184$). Based on ratings of students' performances of pitch glides, pitch patterns, single pitches, and songs, significant differences were found for test type ($p < 0.0001$), test year ($p < 0.001$), and test type by test year ($p < 0.001$). Patterns were performed better than songs. In year three, girls performed songs significantly better than boys ($p < 0.016$). The authors concluded:

> There is clear evidence in this first major United Kingdom (UK) longitudinal study of children's singing development that (a) boys and girls enter school at age 5 with broadly similar vocal pitch matching abilities and (b) this similarity is maintained across the first 3 years of schooling, except in relation to song singing. However, this particular difference between the sexes at age 7, although statistically significant, accounts for a relatively small part of the total variation observed in the data. Of far greater significance to vocal pitch accuracy were the nature of the task and the year of testing.... It may be that there is something about the school culture that promotes girls' rather than boys' vocal pitch accuracy in relation to songs as cultural artifacts. The lack of

difference between the sexes in more elemental vocal pitch matching tasks (as exampled by the test battery items) would seem to suggest that any such differences between the sexes in "song" singing is rather more likely to be cultural in origin rather than biological. (p. 158)

The purpose of an investigation by Moore, Fyk, Frega, and Brotons (1995/1996) was to determine how students from various cultures matched melodic intervals. Sixteen two-tone melodies were performed by 480 subjects age 6 and 9. Significant differences were found due to age, gender, and interval ($p < 0.0001$). Results indicated the following hierarchy of intervals from least to most challenging for 6- and 9-year-old children: unison, descending minor third, descending perfect fourth, ascending major second, descending major third, descending major second, ascending minor third, ascending major third, ascending and descending perfect fifth, ascending perfect fourth, octave, minor second, and descending octave. The authors state: "Findings clearly indicate unisons, descending minor thirds, and perfect fourths are easier to match than minor seconds and octaves for these youngsters" (p. 132). When responses were inaccurate, the subjects tended to sing pitches lower than given stimuli and often reduced the size of the intervals. This is similar to a finding by Welch (1994) in which a trend was noted for 5-year-old students to perform patterns below the modeled stimulus. Welch (1996) pointed out when reviewing a study by Wurgler (1990) that "analysis of vocal range data revealed differences between subjects when singing the test songs compared to the pitch patterns; for each grade subjects had a greater vocal pitch range when singing pitch patterns (p. 117)" (Welch, 1996, p. 81).

A study by Moore, Chen, and Brotons (2004) examined singing in relation to xylophone playing among 8- and 10-year-old students in England, Spain, Taiwan, and the United States. A series of six-note patterns were modeled vocally and on a xylophone for participants ($N = 192$) in Taiwan, England, and the United States. Data in Spain were collected in a different manner. The 10 patterns used pitches from C pentatonic including the octave. Subjects were given three opportunities to perform each pattern. Significant differences in the singing task were found, with girls performing better than boys ($p < 0.04$), and no significant difference was found for grade level. Echo singing of xylophone patterns was significantly better than echo singing of patterns ($p < 0.001$).

In a descriptive study by Wolf (2005), 560 participants in kindergarten through second grade echo-sang 40 two- and three-note tonal patterns (Tonal Pattern Performance Test, TPPT). The author-designed TPPT contained patterns commonly found in kindergarten and first-grade published music curricula. "To accommodate for a sparse representation of minor patterns in the curriculums, parallel forms of patterns were presented in both major and minor; thus, TPPT comprised two parallel sections (major and minor)" (p. 63).

Difficulty of performance was determined by intervallic relationships (all easy patterns were thirds), length of pattern (all easy patterns were two-note), and range (almost all easy patterns were low range). Characteristics of modality (major or minor), melodic contour (ascending or descending), and harmonic function (tonic and dominant) did not appear to affect accuracy of performances. (p. 66)

Wolf suggested a sequential approach to tonal pattern development in curricular design for early elementary students, along with more emphasis on performance in minor mode.

Doneski (2005) investigated the effects of wait time on the performance of tonal patterns among second- and fourth-grade students ($N=164$) in an attempt to clarify the physical and psychological constructs associated with children's singing. Patterns that students echoed were rooted in folk songs and chosen for harmonic function: tonic, dominant, and subdominant. Subjects echoed 15 patterns both with and without a wait time of approximately 3 seconds. Five patterns were familiar and practiced in class, five were completely unfamiliar, and five were familiar but in an unfamiliar order. A significant difference was found in favor of patterns performed without wait time ($p < 0.001$). Subjects performed familiar patterns significantly better than both unfamiliar patterns and familiar patterns in unfamiliar order ($p < 0.001$) and did not recognize the patterns they had practiced when they were performed out of order. This suggests students were mimicking rather than echo singing with understanding. Correlations among measures (SVDM, tonal music aptitude, pattern performance) revealed uncertain relationships between singing and wait time:

> Because the wait time condition yielded more concurrent validity coefficients above threshold than the no wait condition, there is reason to believe that audiation-based performance was enhanced by the availability of wait time....
>
> These data unequivocally demonstrate that processes underlying the developmental tonal music aptitude were indeed highly associated with tonal pattern singing for the subgroups of children within each grade level, and in turn, completely unrelated in other subgroups, yielding a weak association for the within-grade group as a whole. The data provide direct evidence that it is possible to reproduce tonal patterns in a manner consistent with, or completely independent of, the mental processes associated with tonal audiation, which vary depending upon grade level and a student's degree of singing voice development. (Doneski, 2005, pp. 14–15)

It remains unclear as to what the relationship is among wait time, audiation, and accuracy of singing. This is a research problem much in need of further investigation.

Rutkowski (1990, 1996) provides a research-based tool in the "Singing Voice Development Measure" (SVDM) for teachers who want to assess the progress of children's singing. The author specifically designed the SVDM for measuring the development of children's singing voices (stages) and not intonation. By using category placements (e.g., "limited-range singer") instead of actual pitch scores, the SVDM reflects a broader measure. In its current form

1.0 – **Pre-Singer**: does not sing but chants the song text.

1.5 – **Inconsistent Speaking-Range Singer**: sometimes chants, sometimes sustains tones and exhibits some sensitivity to pitch but remains in the speaking voice range (usually A2 to C3).

2.0 – **Speaking Range Singer**: sustains tone and exhibits some sensitivity to pitch but remains in the speaking-voice range (usually A2 to C3).

2.5 – **Inconsistent Limited-Range Singer**: wavers between speaking and singing voice and uses a limited range when in singing voice (usually D3 to F3).

3.0 – **Limited Range Singer:** exhibits use of limited singing range (usually D2 to F3).

3.5 – **Inconsistent Initial Range Singer**: sometimes only exhibits use of limited singing range, but other times exhibits use of initial singing range (usually D3 to A3).

4.0 – **Initial Range Singer**: exhibits use of initial singing range (usually D3 to A3).

4.5 – **Inconsistent Singer**: sometimes only exhibits use of initial singing range, but other times exhibits use of extended singing range (sings beyond the register lift B3-fla and above).

5.0 – **Singer**: exhibits use of extended singing range (sings beyond the register lift: B3-flat and above).

Figure 5.1 Nine categories of the Rutkowski Singing Voice Development Measure.

Source: Singing Voice Development Measure. Reprinted with permission from Rutkowski, 1996, p. 357.

(1996), Rutkowski uses a tune for assessment that is comprised of eight three-note patterns to be sung with both text and neutral syllable. Administering the SVDM requires the student to echo-sing the teacher model of each unaccompanied pattern. The patterns are in d harmonic minor and range from a lowest pitch of middle C# to B-flat above.

Rutkowski advises raters to focus on the five main levels and to apply the half levels for singers who fall between the categories (see figure 5.1). "Children who fluctuate between any two levels receive a score of the lower of the two plus 0.5" (Rutkowski 1996, p. 365). Of particular interest in the rating scale is level 5, "Singer," in which a student shows consistent use of extended singing range. In the patterns, B^3-flat (diminished seventh above middle C) is the highest pitch and is approached from D^3 both times it appears. For many children, B^3-flat can be produced with the middle or lower vocal registers, especially when approached from below. Without patterns requiring a more consistent use of upper register (perhaps one pattern using B^3-flat to D^4), it would seem a student designated as a level 5 singer may not adequately meet the qualifications of "consistent extended singing range."

Based on a 1984 pilot study and the main study conducted 2 years later, Rutkowski (1990) reported the reliability of the SVDM and made recommendations for revision to the scale. Kindergarten students ($N = 162$) were administered the SVDM both pretest and posttest. The version of the SVDM used for the main study (1986) included individual student performances of the song "Bakerman" (Rutkowski, 1990, p. 86) and five tonal patterns to be echo-sung on text. Intrarater reliability coefficients (based on duplicate performances placed into judges' master recordings) and children's performance consistency reliability coefficients were calculated for patterns, song, and composite both for pretest and posttest. The reliability coefficients were lower for patterns ($r = 0.74$ for each judge) than for songs ($r = 0.93$ and 0.94) for the pretest, but with marked improvement for patterns in the posttest ($r = 0.97$ and 0.91), and song remained relatively stable ($r = 0.92$ and 0.88). Judges commented that patterns were easier to rate than songs once they were familiar with the material. Children's voices were recorded twice over several days for both pre- tests and posttests with high reliability for the children's consistency of performance for pretest (patterns, $r = 0.96$; song, $r = 0.95$; composite, $r = 0.97$) and for posttest (patterns, $r = 0.94$; song, $r = 0.95$; composite, $r = 0.96$).

Rutkowski made several recommendations for improving SVDM based on the results of the 1990 study. She called into question the use of a song for measuring singing development:

> Although singing a song, rather than patterns, is generally considered singing, it seems that performing a song involved aspects other than use of singing voice. These include memorization of text, rhythm patterns, and tonal pat- terns. A child may not be employing singing voice simply because she cannot remember some of these other components. Therefore, measuring use of singing through performance of a song may not yield a valid score. Since the singing of patterns involves echoing, rather than memorization, the role of these other components would be diminished. (pp. 91–92)

Rutkowski (1996) then modified the assessment measure to be a melody or tune comprised of eight three-note patterns to be sung with text and then with neutral syllable. Two of the original patterns that seemed to encourage the use of speaking voice rather than singing voice were dropped from the revised SVDM.

Levinowitz, Barnes, Guerrini, Clement, D'April, and Morey (1998) sought to determine the reliability of the SVDM (Rutkowski, 1990) with students in grades one through six who were rated on performances of two songs (major and minor tonality). The authors chose songs with a range of an octave or more to ensure singing above "the voice lift" and purposefully wanted one song of longer length to encourage audiation (discriminative pitch percep- tion) at a "deeper level" (p. 39). Student solo performances were recorded during the regular music class. With the exception of the second grade's minor song reliability, the authors reported their reliabilities for grades one through five to be in accordance with those reported by Rutkowski (1990) for younger children. Based on combined ratings of both songs by grade level, results indicated no significant difference in the use of singing voice across grades using the SVDM, which was surprising. These results were probably influenced by the use of the wider singing range (one octave, D^3 to D^4) than that used in the SVDM (diminished seventh). Also, Levinowitz and colleagues (1998) used the original 5-point rating scale of Rutkowski (1990) instead of the revised 9-point scale (Rutkowski, 1996), the 5-point scale being, perhaps, a less discriminating measure.

Rutkowski and Miller (2003a) used the SVDM to examine changes in the use of singing voice with a longitudinal study of first-, third-, and fifth-graders ($N = 25$). (The sample was small as only 25 students remained in the study from first to fifth grade.) They also examined the number of children who used the singing voice accurately. Significant differences were found in singing accuracy from the end of first grade to the beginning of third grade and from the beginning of fifth grade to the end of fifth grade ($p < 0.05$), using SVDM with both text and neutral syllable. The first-grade findings were similar to those in Rutkowski and Miller (2003b), where there were no significant differences in children's SVDM ratings from the beginning to the end of the first grade. Regarding the use of the singing voice at particular grades, the authors found the average child in first grade to be a "limited-range singer," in third grade moved from an "initial-range singer" to an "inconsistent singer," and in fifth grade began as an "initial-range singer" and moved to an "inconsistent singer." Using neutral syllables, 76 percent of students were considered "singers" by the end of fifth grade. These findings are contrary to Levinowitz, and colleagues (1998), where the majority of students were found to be in the nonsinger categories.

The authors (Rutkowski and Miller, 2003b) make a distinction between using the SVDM for determining the use of singing voice as opposed to a scale for measuring singing accuracy. Levinowitz and colleagues (1998) did not follow the procedures outlined by Rutkowski for echoing a tune comprised of patterns with text and neutral syllable. Instead, the subjects performed rote songs from memory, and as noted previously, the singing range was wider in the latter study, requiring students to sing above the voice "lift" in an upper vocal register.

Rutkowski and Chen-Haftek (2001) used the SVDM (1996) to compare singing voice development between first-grade students from the United States ($n = 38$) and China ($n = 30$). Results showed a significant difference between cultures for both native text ($p < 0.0001$) and neutral syllable ($p < 0.031$). Mean scores for the Chinese students were higher than those of the American students on both subtests. The authors stated:

> Since the Chinese children scored higher than the American children, it is difficult to conclude whether the lowest singing behaviors on SVDM were not exhibited by Chinese children at all or whether these children gained use of their singing voice earlier than American children. The pitch range of the speaking voice of these children would be of interest. Perhaps they scored higher due to higher-pitched speaking voice, which would result in more vocal flexibility. Or perhaps cultural differences regarding singing contributed to their earlier acquisition of a singing voice.... (pp. 40–41)

Interrater reliabilities were high for judges from both countries on both subtests, with the lowest for the U.S. judges for text ($r = 0.85$) and the highest for

Chinese judges for text ($r = 0.93$). The authors concluded: "Based on results of this study, it appears that SVDM is a reliable measure to assess Chinese as well as American children's use of singing voice" (p. 40).

Gault (2002) investigated assessment of singing accuracy when using both text and neutral syllable. For kindergarten and first-grade subjects, a significant interaction for song and text condition ($p < 0.001$) indicated that subjects performed one song better with text. "While the two songs in the present study contained the same tonal and rhythmic elements, the song-specific combination of these elements seemed to be a determining factor in the degree of importance that text played in the ability of subjects to perform the song accurately" (p. 61). In other words, the text itself could have been a determining factor as to whether the children were comfortable with it and thus able to sing more accurately using text. This is a confounding variable not disclosed in other research.

Guerrini (2006) investigated the performance of fourth- and fifth-grade students ($N = 174$) using three-note patterns from the SVDM (Rutkowski), a familiar song, and a newly learned song. The SVDM was used to rate the singing accuracy of students on the three tasks. Results indicated a significant difference ($p < 0.0001$) for pattern singing over both a familiar song and a newly learned song. This finding corroborates those of Welch (1994) and Welch, Sergeant, and White (1997), in which tonal patterns were performed better than learned songs. Guerrini also made a new application of the SVDM based on high interjudge reliability using the rating scale for student performance of "America"—a familiar song for participants. The author states:

> This is particularly interesting, because this meant that the inter-judge reliability was at its highest when two judges were rating the performance of "America." It would be expected that the highest reliabilities would appear in the ratings of the SVDM patterns because Rutkowski designed her scale with the purpose of measuring the accuracy of children singing these particular patterns. It was therefore gratifying to discover that in this study a...song yielded even greater inter-judge reliability than the melodic patterns. I concluded that the SVDM is a useful tool for music educators. It can be relied on when measuring fourth and fifth grade students singing "America" and "Path to the Moon," as well as the eight measure patterns that were used in this study. (p. 29)

There is credible research that suggests using patterns for vocal assessment is superior to using song phrases. Research prior to 1990 also suggests this, but conflicting evidence exists. Gault (2002) raises the issue that a song phrase may be just as good when assessing singing accuracy when the text is "comfortable" for the children. Guerrini's finding that interjudge reliability for the song "America" was higher than what Rutkowki reports for tune/tonal patterns using the SVDM cannot be ignored. Then there is the issue of using words versus a neutral syllable. Goetze (1985/1986) was the first to report the use of a neutral syllable as superior to words for vocal assessment. Later research did not support this finding. Rutkowski (1996) in the SVDM uses both words and a neutral syllable to assess vocal development. Boardman

(1964) suggested that words be used with song phrases because she believed children associated words with music. A very early study by Updegraff, Heiliger, and Learned (1938) showed the "phrase test" to be the most discriminating test of singing ability among 3-, 4-, and 5-year-old children. Clearly, uncontrolled variables abound, not the least of which is "what constitutes accurate singing?" The research base for future studies in vocal assessment is becoming larger, and those wishing to pursue this topic will make a valuable contribution to the profession.

Attitude

Research in the area of children's attitudes toward vocal music instruction is scant. Phillips (2003/2004) identifies only eight studies prior to 1990, and fewer since that time.

Austin (1990) investigated the relationship of music self-esteem to participation in school and out-of-school musical activities among fifth- and sixth-grade students ($N = 252$). The author noted: "Research suggests that several individual difference and school environmental variables may mediate the influence of music self-esteem on attitude, motivation, and achievement" (p. 22). The Self-Esteem of Musical Ability scale (Schmitt, 1979) and an experimenter-devised background questionnaire were administered. Music self-esteem for females was found to be significantly greater than for males ($p < 0.01$), and music self-esteem was a significant predictor of participation in both school and out-of-school music activities. "The data indicate that one-third of all subjects have no involvement in music activities and an additional one-third of the sample participated in one school music activity but engaged in no form of music activity outside of the school" (p. 29). Austin recommends that teachers encourage active music participation at the elementary level, "with particular attention paid to young males" (p. 29).

Mizener (1993) investigated attitude toward vocal music among 542 subjects in grades three through six. Subjects completed a questionnaire, and 23 percent were assessed for individual singing skill via singing two songs. The survey addressed five areas: singing interest, choir participation, classroom singing activities, out-of-school singing, and self-perception of singing skill. Results showed the majority of students were positive toward singing, but positive responses decreased as grade level increased.

Phillips and Aitchison (1998) studied attitude toward singing instruction among 269 students in grades four through six. As with Mizener (1993), the investigators found that interest in singing and general music declined as students advanced by grade ($p < 0.001$). Interestingly, students who received specific vocal music instruction demonstrated a more positive attitude toward general music ($p < 0.01$) but not to singing itself. The authors concluded:

> It...may be that students who do not like to sing, especially males in the upper grade levels...may respond negatively to all singing instruction. If this is the case, early intervention strategies are necessary so that students arrive

in the intermediate grades feeling that they are confident and successful singers. (p. 41)

A large study by Scott Phillips (2003/2004) investigated the attitudes of students in grades six through eight ($N = 2,180$) in relationship to self-concept in music. Three surveys elicited responses to 83 items on music attitude, music background, and self-concept in music. Results showed a slight decrease in music attitude by grade for all students and a significant decrease ($p < 0.05$) for low socioeconomic students. Girls' attitudes were found to be significantly higher ($p < 0.05$) than boys' for all grades and socioeconomic levels. Self-concept in music significantly decreased ($p < 0.05$) as grade level increased.

This study by Phillips (2003/2004) brings together the disciplines of social psychology and music education in meaningful and important ways. There is much to be learned in attitude assessment from the field of social psychology, which has a history of developing sophisticated attitude measures. Those doing research on music attitude could find reading Phillips's study helpful in learning how attitude assessment is done by experts in a field where such assessment is a dominant theme.

Siebenaler (2008) investigated children's attitudes toward singing and song recordings related to gender, ethnicity, and age. Students in grades three, four, and five ($N = 249$) represented a high ethnicity of Hispanic and African American children. All students had music instruction (with emphasis on group singing) every third day for 45 minutes each session, and all were eligible to participate in a nonauditioned choir. The students completed a brief questionnaire concerning their attitudes toward singing and choir. Each grade then listened to nine songs recorded from the basal series in use: three were of Spanish origin, three were African American game songs, and three songs were of European origin. Upon listening, students were directed to mark their preference for each song on their response sheet.

Results for gender showed significant differences ($p < 0.05$) for two statements: girls (74.5 percent) liked to sing along with the radio more than boys (64.2 percent), and more girls (66.4 percent) than boys (56.7 percent) thought they were good singers. However, few significant differences between boys and girls were found in their overall attitudes toward singing. The author states that "there were still strongly positive responses from the boys" (p. 54).

Ethnicity showed that significantly more ($p < 0.05$) African American (72.2 percent) than Hispanic (50 percent) students enjoyed singing in music class, and more African American (75.7 percent) than Hispanic (54.6 percent) students thought they were good singers. The author notes that while Hispanic students replied significantly lower, positive responses were still in the majority. Results also showed that a "decline of positive attitudes toward school music was found primarily with the fifth graders" (p. 49). Among the significant results ($p < 0.05$) for attitudes toward choir, more African Americans (71 percent) belonged to choir than did Hispanics (30 percent), and African American students believed that singing was just as much for boys as girls (85.4 percent) than did Hispanic students (79.6 percent).

The relationship of attitude toward music involvement basically confirms something that music teachers know by casual observation—students' positive attitudes to school music decrease with age, and the fifth grade seems to be pivotal. What is needed is research that demonstrates a cause-effect relationship for factors hypothesized to change negative music attitudes to positive music attitudes, especially as students mature.

Audiation

Hearing, remembering, and discriminating pitch are aural skills believed to be related to accurate singing. The term *audiation* has become commonly accepted in reference to these aural discrimination skills (Gordon, 1989).

Shuler (1991) studied the effects of Gordon's learning sequence on the singing performance of third-grade subjects ($N = 109$) and found no significant differences between treatment and control groups. "The effects of learning sequence activities on performance achievement appear to vary depending upon the teacher" (p. 128).

A study by Atterbury and Silcox (1993b) seems to suggest a weak relationship between singing accuracy and audiation skills for students in kindergarten ($N = 66$). No significant difference was found between singers and presingers on the *Primary Measures of Music Audiation*, PMMA (Gordon, 1979). "For the children in this sample, musical aptitude and singing ability were not complimentary attributes" (p. 20).

Music aptitude served as a dependent variable in studies by Rutkowski (1996) and Rutkowski and Miller (2003b, 2003c). In the earlier study, Rutkowski (1996) investigated whether kindergarten children ($N = 99$) would benefit from a small-group approach to singing as opposed to the typical large-group approach. The dependent measures included the PMMA, tonal (Gordon, 1979), which was administered three times during the treatment period. The treatment group scored significantly higher ($p < 0.03$) on a measure of singing accuracy. However: "No significant tonal aptitude differences existed between groups, although both groups had gains in tonal aptitude mean scores during the treatment period" (pp. 360–61). Rutkowski and Miller (2003b, 2003c) found similar results (no difference) between first graders' singing accuracy and developmental music aptitude (Gordon, 1982).

Mota (1997) conducted a 3-year longitudinal study comparing scores on the PMMA with three measures of musical performance among 6- to 9-year-old subjects ($N = 100$). The hypothesis was that musical aptitude tests serve only limited purposes and cannot reflect the variety of manifestations that children's musical behavior can take. There was no significant relationship found between performance on Gordon's PMMA and the three performance tasks.

Hornbach and Taggart (2005) investigated the relationship between singing achievement and developmental tonal aptitude (PMMA) among subjects ($N = 162$) in kindergarten through third grade. Correlations between singing achievement scores and the PMMA reflected no meaningful relationships. The authors concluded: "Singing voice use and tonal aptitude are apparently separate constructs and develop independent of one another" (p. 327).

Jones (1993) assessed the audiation skills of pitch accurate (n = 72) and pitch inaccurate (n = 72) singers in first, second, and third grade. Data were collected using the PMMA (Gordon, 1979). For all three grades, the mean scores for the accurate groups were slightly higher than those of the inaccurate groups. Analyses showed significant differences for all nine comparisons among the three primary grades. In this study, there appeared to be a direct relationship between audiation and singing accuracy, although the mean scores of inaccurate singers were not especially low.

Phillips and Aitchison (1997a) studied the relationship of singing accuracy to pitch discrimination and tonal aptitude among third-grade students. Subjects (N = 72) were tested individually and assigned to either accurate or inaccurate groups. Test measures included the *Music Achievement Test*, Part I, Test 1 (Colwell, 1969) and PMMA, tonal (Gordon, 1979). Results revealed no significant differences on pitch discrimination (MAT) between groups or males and females, but a significant difference (p < 0.013) for tonal aptitude (PMMA) in favor of the accurate singers. Both Jones (1993) and Phillips and Aitchison (1997a) found that accurate third-grade singers had a mean score of 37 on the PMMA, tonal. Inaccurate singers for Jones had a mean score of 33, while for Phillips and Aitchison, inaccurate subjects had a slightly higher score of 34.82. Phillips and Aitchison (1997a) state:

> A raw score of 33 is given by Gordon as being at the 45th percentile, while the score of 34.82 is close to the 56th percentile. In both cases, these scores fall within "average" percentile rankings as given by Gordon for the tonal portion of the PMMA. According to Gordon, one would have to score at the 26th percentile to be in the "low category" of tonal aptitude. Given that both groups of inaccurate singers scored within the "average" category, it would appear that their tonal aptitude was not as sufficiently poor as one might imagine. (p. 18)

The authors conclude that inaccurate singers are not "tone deaf" or lacking in sufficient musical aptitude to match pitch.

In a similar study, Phillips, Aitchison, Bergman, and Western (1999) investigated the relationship of singing instruction, pitch accuracy, and gender to musical aptitude and vocal achievement among another group of third-grade general music students. The study involved a static-group comparison design (Campbell and Stanley, 1963) in which the treatment group (n = 66) received weekly vocal instruction (26 weeks) based on the vocal method in *Teaching Kids to Sing* (Phillips, 1992b); the control group (n = 72) sang songs but received no formal vocal instruction. Results showed no significant difference in musical aptitude between groups by treatment condition or by gender. As in the earlier study (Phillips and Aitchison, 1997a), a significant difference was reported in favor of all accurate singers (p < 0.01) on the PMMA, tonal.

Another study by Phillips and Aitchison (1999) was a continuation of Phillips and colleagues (1999), when students were in third grade. In this study, the same students were now in fourth grade. Results showed no significant difference for musical aptitude (Gordon, 1982) between accurate and inaccurate singers or between males and females. "There appeared to be very little difference between means of accurate and inaccurate singers (33.81 vs. 32.83), and males and females (33.42 vs. 33.37) on a test of aural acuity" (p. 77). Once again, inaccurate singers appeared to be somewhat lagging in audiation skills. Where subjects in earlier studies (Phillips and Aitchison, 1997a; Phillips et al., 1999) were significantly different on the PMMA in third grade, they were not on the *Intermediate Measures of Music Audiation,* IMMA (Gordon, 1982) in fourth grade. Maturation must be considered a factor.

In the third of a series of studies, Phillips, Aitchison, and Nompula (2002) again investigated the relationship of music aptitude to singing achievement, this time among fifth-grade students (the same students from earlier studies, when subjects were in the third and fourth grades). As with the previous study, no significant difference was found between accurate and inaccurate singers on a test of music aptitude (IMMA, tonal, rhythm, composite). The authors state:

> Perhaps grade three (approximately age 9) is the pivotal year before and during which aural skills are developing, and after which they have developed in most children to the point where aural acuity is no longer a detriment to accurate pitch matching. If true, this finding would affirm what Edwin Gordon (1987) has called *developmental music aptitude* (a state of aptitude in flux until the age of nine years) and *stabilized music aptitude* (a state of aptitude which is fixed after age nine). (p. 55)

The authors further state: "It may be that persons who complain of having a 'tin ear' actually hear better than what they think. What they may be lacking is the skill to turn an aural image into a viable product" (p. 55).

A study by Aaron (1993) adds further evidence to the idea that inaccurate singers in the intermediate grades are not lacking in audiation skills. Subjects ($N = 109$) in grades four, five, and six were tested for pitch accuracy; the inaccurate singers served as the sample ($n = 71$) and were assigned at random to treatment or control groups. Following a 16-week period of vocal instruction, all subjects were measured for pitch discrimination using the *Music Achievement Test* (Colwell, 1969) and for tonal memory using the *Wing Standardized Test of Musical Intelligence* (1957). No significant differences were found between groups for either pitch discrimination or tonal memory.

The research on audiation skills seems to suggest that inaccurate singers may be lagging in aural discrimination, especially at the primary level. Mean scores of inaccurate singers, however, tend to be only slightly lower than those of accurate singers and typically fall within the normal range on the PMMA and IMMA. Therefore, for inaccurate singers, especially those in the intermediate grades (4 to 6), singing skill does not appear to be related to low tonal aptitude. The fact that a number of studies report a lack of significant difference between accurate singers and inaccurate singers on audiation measures does not mean that tonal aptitude is unrelated to accurate singing. Rather, it indicates that mean scores of both groups are so close as to deny the finding of a significant difference. The earlier statement by Hornbach and Taggart (2005) that the skill of singing and tonal aptitude are separate constructs and develop independently is not supportable by the research findings in this review.

Home Environment

Research by Persellin (2006) reveals a strong relationship between a child's singing accuracy and home musical environment. The author concludes: "A significant positive relationship was found between the home musical environment and improvement in vocal accuracy ($p < 0.0148$). While the home environment score significantly affected the pre-test to posttest score change, the teaching technique did not" (p. 44). Persellin found that significance in home environment was due mainly to kindergartners who played CDs and tapes at home and whose parents had experience playing a musical instrument.

In a study reviewed earlier, Atterbury and Silcox (1993b) also investigated the effects of home musical environment on the musical aptitude of kindergartners ($N = 66$). Parents completed a musical background form that assessed attitude toward music and musical involvement with children, concert attendance, ownership and playing of audio recordings, and playing of a musical instrument. The data were analyzed for differences between inaccurate ($n = 33$) and accurate ($n = 33$) singers. Significant difference ($p < 0.02$) was found between groups for home environment in favor of the accurate singers. Regarding the influence of home environment on creating accurate singers, the researchers state: "We believe that the public relations agenda for the music education profession needs to be expanded to include preschool musical environment. Parents need to be made aware of the impact of musical experiences during the preschool years upon later development" (p. 20).

Phillips (2003/2004), in a study presented earlier, found in a survey of sixth- through eighth-grade students that 40 percent of the variance in music attitude could be attributed to home musical background. The correlation was stronger for boys ($r = 0.64$) than girls ($r = 0.58$). High socioeconomic students reported significantly richer ($p < 0.05$) home musical environments than low socioeconomic students. "The present study confirms the findings of previous research and establishes that girls' attitudes, home musical environments, and self-concepts in music are significantly higher than boys' for all middle school grade levels and for all SES levels" (p. 117).

How can the music education profession make parents aware of the impact that a positive home musical environment has on a child's musical development and attitude? This is a question that needs to be addressed more fully. Perhaps research in this area could lead to developing some type of communication vehicle that would have a positive impact on the way parents think about the home environment in relation to the musical opportunities made available in the home. Could parents be more inclined to foster a better home musical environment when informed how to do so? Would involving more parents in school-based musical activities have a carry-over effect on the home environment? Perhaps an intergenerational band or choir would enliven musical discussion at home? This could make for an interesting research agenda.

Individual or Small-Group versus Large-Group Singing

There is some evidence that students sing inaccurately because they cannot hear their own voices within a group or class setting (Goetze, 1985/1986). Most singing done in the elementary school tends to be in a group. Should teachers be doing more individual singing with students? This is an important question in classroom singing research, and one that has yet to be resolved.

Green (1994) investigated the effects of unison singing versus individual singing on pitch accuracy among subjects in grades one two, three, and five (N = 241). Results showed children sang more accurately in a group than individually ($p < 0.0001$). The author states: "Subjects in the current study sang together in groups of eight, which is not representative of a normal class size for a typical elementary class. In larger groups, children might have more difficulty hearing themselves and singing accurately" (p. 112).

Cooper (1995) also studied group versus individual responses on singing accuracy among subjects in grades one through five (N = 169). No significant difference between settings was found. Cooper cites the following factors that must be accounted for when comparing research studies on this topic: choice of vocal model, pattern length, and differences in vocal registers needed to match criterion patterns (pp. 228–229).

Rutkowski (1996) investigated individual or small-group voice instruction versus regular large-group singing on effects of singing accuracy among kindergarten children (N = 99). Following 9 months of vocal instruction, the treatment (individual/small group) and control (large group) were posttested using the author's Singing Voice Development Measure (Rutkowski, 1990). Results showed a significant difference between groups ($p < 0.03$) in favor of the treatment group. However, the control mean decreased from pretest to posttest, and Rutkowski noted this confounding problem. "Significant differences between the groups may have been a result of this decrease in singing-voice achievement for the control group rather than the effectiveness of individual/small group singing" (p. 362). This could also be interpreted to mean that effects of large-group singing had a detrimental effect on the control group while the treatment group maintained consistency.

In a study reviewed earlier, Rutkowski and Miller (2003a) followed students' singing achievement from the first through the fifth grades (N = 25) to "investigate the feasibility of helping all children learn to use their singing voices within the traditional general music class setting" (pp. 5–6). Vocal instruction included large-group, small-group, and individual singing activities. Based on the results of the study, it was concluded that by the end of fifth grade 76 percent of the subjects were found to be "singers," exhibiting use of consistent extended singing range. The authors state: "These results were very different from those of Levinowitz et al. (1998), in which only 10–25% of the first- through sixth-grade sample were 'initial range singers'" (Rutkowski and Miller, p. 10). It appears for the Rutkowski and Miller study that the combination of singing approaches (large-group, small-group, individual) was beneficial for students' singing success.

There are many factors affecting children's singing accuracy, and it is difficult to draw any conclusions from the studies just discussed when compared with earlier research on individual versus group singing. Clearly, more research is needed that controls for the factors mentioned by Cooper (1995). Common sense indicates, however, if a child cannot hear or "connect" to his or her own voice in a group setting that the feedback loop necessary to complete the psychomotor process will not be established. Having children sing alone in class is something that provides the opportunity for each child to connect to his or her voice. Echoing tonal patterns is a safe way to begin solo singing, whereas singing a song in front of the class is likely to traumatize many students. Most important, no child should ever be permitted to laugh at another singing alone. The music room must be a safe environment in which the individual, and the singer's voice, is protected. A child who is laughed at most likely will not develop confidence in singing.

Kodály Instruction

The Kodály method is a well-established instructional sequence for the teaching of music and singing in the elementary curriculum. Unfortunately, as with many other vocal approaches, there is a paucity of research related to this popular method.

The effects of hand signs on inaccurate singers in kindergarten through third grade and in seventh and eighth grades ($N = 163$) was investigated by Yarbrough, Green, Benson, and Bowers (1991). All subjects received the same instruction by grade, based on the Kodály use of hand signs. After 8 weeks, students were divided into three response-mode groups for data collection: one group used hand signs, one group used traditional solfège syllables, and the third group used the neutral syllable "la." No significant difference for response mode was found ($p > 0.05$).

Martin (1991) found no significant differences in the singing accuracy of first-grade students ($N = 65$) who had been instructed (1) aurally, (2) aurally with hand signs, and (3) aurally with hands and visual representations of tonal patterns. "Because of the loss incurred by subjects in group 1 (who only echoed with tonal syllables) and the gains made by students in Groups 2 and

3 (who echoed with tonal syllable and used additional visual aids), one may conjecture that the instructional method did affect performance, though not in a statistically significant manner" (p. 167).

Olsen (2003) sought to explore reading, math, and music achievement among first-, second-, and third-grade subjects ($N = 96$) through Kodály music and singing instruction. Olsen hypothesized that subjects in the treatment group would score significantly higher on tests of reading, math, and music achievement following 26 weeks of Kodály instruction that included parallel concepts for reading, math, and music. Subjects in the control group also received Kodály instruction but without mention of parallel concepts. Results showed a significant difference between groups for first-grade math achievement ($p < 0.05$), a significant difference for females at all grade levels in math achievement ($p < 0.05$), and a significant difference for first- and second-grade males in reading ($p < 0.05$) in favor of the treatment group. No difference was found between groups on a test of music achievement. The author concluded:

> The present study represents an attempt to teach music while incorporating reading and mathematics in a meaningful way. It demonstrates that attention to other curricular areas does not have to detract from the teaching of music (no significant difference was found in music achievement by group, grade, or gender). The results indicate that music mastery is not compromised while affirming parallel curricular concepts in the Kodály music classroom. (p. 148)

Olsen's attempt to connect the music curriculum to that of the entire school is an idea worth considering by the profession. All too often, music is viewed as a recreational activity with no academic merit. However, music teachers are (or should be) as interested in producing mature learners who can read and compute as are teachers of those specific subjects. The entire school curriculum can be found within the study of music: reading, math, science, history, foreign language, and so forth. It may be that the future of elementary music education in the United States will depend on how well music can be connected to other academic curricular areas. Music teachers teach reading, but they do not make an issue of it. Perhaps they should. Their jobs may depend on it. This is an area of research in much need of further study.

Modeling

A number of research studies exist on the topic of vocal modeling as affecting children's singing accuracy (Dickey, 1992). Green (1990) tested 282 subjects in first through sixth grade for singing accuracy. Subjects were tested three times individually, each time using a different vocal model (child, adult female, adult male). Data were analyzed by model, sex, and grade level. Results showed more correct responses to the child model ($p < 0.05$), followed by the female and male models. Boys and girls sang more correct responses for the child model, while boys "sang consistently flat with the male model, suggesting a pitch-matching problem unique for boys with this model" (p. 230).

Yarbrough, Green, Benson, and Bowers (1991) also investigated the effect of female versus male vocal modeling on the pitch-matching accuracy of 163 subjects in kindergarten through third grade and in seventh and eighth grades (all inaccurate singers). They found a significant difference in favor of females ($p < 0.05$) and also an interaction effect indicating "the extremely low percentage of correct responses to the male model by the seventh grade compared to the much higher percentage of correct responses by this grade to the female model" (p. 29).

Vibrato as part of the vocal model was investigated by Yarbrough, Bowers, and Benson (1992). Two hundred subjects in kindergarten through third grade responded by singing to three different models: child, female with vibrato, and female without vibrato. The analysis included a four-factor design (certain and uncertain singers, grade level, sex, and models).

> [Results showed] a significant difference between correct responses to vibrato versus nonvibrato models with a greater percentage of correct responses to the nonvibrato model, as well as no significant differences between correct responses to child versus vibrato or child versus nonvibrato responses. (p. 34)

The authors conclude: "At least for younger children and especially for certain singers, the presence of vibrato in the voice of the teacher should be reserved for solo work and should be kept out of the elementary classroom" (p. 37).

Sherburn-Bly (2007) recommends that when less vibrato is warranted, the singer use what she calls "simple tone." Her article, which appears in the *Choral Journal*, is a valuable source for learning to control the vocal vibrato when singing.

The previous three studies were cited by Price, Yarbrough, Jones, and Moore (1994) as precursors to this fourth study examining models that affect pitch-matching accuracy among children, in this case, 216 inaccurate singers in kindergarten through eighth grade. Subjects responded vocally to six models: tenor and bass singing in their regular male voice and in falsetto, and two sine-wave stimuli in the two octaves. The researchers found "no significant differences in accuracy to overall responses between girls and boys, among grades, or to different octaves" (p. 275). A significant interaction ($p < 0.005$) showed that girls responded more accurately in the higher octave and boys more accurately in the lower octave. The authors state that "music teachers need to be cognizant of the octave they are modeling in, with regard to gender and age of students. This is not a novel idea, but now there appear to be more data to support this common pedagogical suggestion" (p. 281).

Continuing in this line of investigation, Yarbrough, Morrison, Karrick, and Dunn (1995) studied the effect of male falsetto modeling on pitch accuracy among uncertain male singers in kindergarten through eighth grade

(N = 108). Models were intervals sung by a tenor and bass in their regular voices and in falsetto and two sine wave stimuli presented in the same octaves. Except for eighth-grade boys, "All other grade levels responded more accurately to higher octave and falsetto models" (p. 9).

Hendley and Persellin (1996) also studied the effects of lower adult male voice and male falsetto models on children's singing accuracy. Subjects were first-, third-, and fifth-graders (N = 152) who were randomly assigned by class to either the tenor or falsetto groups for 8 weeks of vocal instruction. Results indicated that vocal accuracy improved significantly (p < 0.02) for falsetto modeling, while "tenor modeling appeared to hinder pitch-matching accuracy with the younger and more inexperienced singers (the first and third graders)" (p. 13). These findings confirm other research that has found the adult male voice to be a poor vocal model for pitch-matching accuracy among children.

Rutkowski and Miller (2003c) investigated the female teacher's voice as the model in a study of first-grade singing achievement (N = 38). For the treatment group, the teacher gave feedback using her own singing voice as the model for students to echo. The control group received verbal feedback only as to correctness of response. No significant difference was found between groups: "the higher percentage of students in the treatment group whose singing voice achievement improved when compared with the control group suggests that further study of this treatment with a larger sample size be conducted" (p. 1).

Persellin (2006) investigated the effects of three teaching styles involving vocal modeling on 134 kindergartners' singing accuracy: (1) the teacher sang for but never with the children, (2) the teacher sang with but never for the children, and (3) the teacher sang both with and for the children. Treatments were randomly assigned to nine classes and subjects were pretested and posttested using the investigator-designed "Vocal Accuracy Assessment Instrument" (Youngson and Persellin, 2001), in which the voice of an 11-year-old girl was used as a stimulus model. All three treatments were found to improve vocal accuracy, but no significant differences were revealed. "It is possible that young children learn to adapt to whatever teaching style is presented to them when taught by skilled teachers" (Persellin, p. 47).

Research on vocal modeling as it affects singing accuracy has led to these conclusions: (1) children match pitch better when responding to models in the children's own singing range, (2) the child voice and female voice are the best models, and (3) the male model presenting in the "falsetto" (male alto) is better than the male model in the natural voice.

While the term "falsetto" is commonly understood to denote the upper male singing voice, it is also a style of singing often characterized by a strained, pinched sound resulting from an elevated larynx. However, men are capable of singing as male altos, a sound that is more open and free. It might serve the profession well to use the term "male alto" instead of "falsetto" when describing the male model appropriate for children's singing. It is a more natural and pleasing sound. Singing in the male alto voice is important for male teachers to use with beginning singers.

As children become accustomed to singing in the upper register, a male teacher can sing in a light modal voice without students being drawn to imitate the sound an octave lower (Phillips, 1992b).

Psychomotor Coordination

A number of research studies have demonstrated a strong link between psychomotor coordination and singing accuracy. Aaron (1993) sought to determine the effects of a vocal coordination treatment (Phillips, 1992b) among inaccurate singers ($N = 71$). Vocal measures included pitch accuracy and range. Following 16 weeks of instruction, results showed the experimental group improved significantly ($p < 0.05$) in range and pitch accuracy. Analysis found the psychomotor coordination instruction to be significantly more effective for boys in the treatment group. Aaron states: "One additional point, based on personal experience is notable: vocal coordination exercises are fun. Students enjoy beginning classes with 3 or 4 minutes of this physical activity" (p. 12).

A similar study by Henry (1995) used the Phillips method (1992b) to determine its effectiveness with fifth-grade students. Results showed the treatment group (psychomotor coordination) matched pitch significantly better ($p < 0.05$) than the control group when using either text or neutral syllables.

Replicating an earlier study (Phillips, 1985), Phillips and Aitchison (1997b) investigated the effects of vocal coordination instruction on the singing performance of students in fourth through sixth grade. A posttest-only control group design was used with intact classes randomly assigned to either experimental ($n = 127$) or control ($n = 142$). Results showed the treatment (Phillips, 1992b) to be effective for breath management ($p < 0.01$), duration ($p < 0.002$), and vocal range ($p < 0.001$). Pitch accuracy was significant for all girls ($p < 0.011$). The authors state: "Students' singing skills in general music can be improved through vocal instruction that moves beyond the song approach" (p. 195).

Phillips and Aitchison (1998) investigated the effects of a year-long program of psychomotor coordination instruction on attitude toward singing and general music. Subjects were fourth-, fifth-, and sixth-grade students ($N = 269$). Results showed no significant difference between groups ($p < 0.001$) on attitude toward singing, but students who received the formal singing instruction were generally more positive in their attitude toward general music than those in the control group who just sang songs. For the treatment group, singing in general music seemed to make the curriculum more interesting.

Phillips, Aitchison, Bergman, and Western (1999) continued to investigate the relationship of vocal coordination instruction and vocal achievement. Subjects were two intact classes of third-grade subjects assigned as either treatment ($n = 66$) or control ($n = 72$). The treatment group received formal vocal instruction (Phillips, 1992b) over a 26-week period, while the control group sang only songs. Results of a two-way analysis of variance for the author-designed Singing Techniques Test showed a significant difference for the treatment group ($p < 0.003$) and no gender effect. Vocal range (high, low, total) also was found to be significantly different ($p < 0.000$) in favor of all accurate singers. "While the causes of accurate singing are complex, there seems to be strong evidence that students who have mastered certain singing techniques are more likely to sing with greater accuracy and vocal range" (p. 37).

In a second-year study of the effects of vocal instruction on vocal achievement, Phillips and Aitchison (1999) investigated fourth-grade subjects ($N = 85$) who had begun formal voice instruction in the third grade. Following 27 weeks of instruction based on *Teaching Kids to Sing* (Phillips, 1992b), all students were individually tested for pitch accuracy, vocal range, and breathing mode. Significant differences were reported for all three measures of vocal range ($p < 0.001$) in favor of the accurate singers. Results of a Chi-square analysis for breathing mode found a significant difference ($p < 0.001$) in favor of accurate singers. No gender effects were noted. These results demonstrated the effectiveness of psychomotor coordination instruction on children's singing accuracy.

A study by Wurgler (1990) reported on the vocal registers found in K-6 children's singing voices ($N = 285$). In this descriptive investigation, subjects were tested individually singing a simple song in a variety of keys and series of pitch patterns. Results indicated that 85 percent of the subjects exhibited two distinct vocal registers, "chest" and "head" (p. 76), that overlap, producing a secondary or middle register. This is rather common knowledge among elementary music teachers who produce good singers. Among many interesting findings, Wurgler found that subjects who sang predominantly in a chest/lower register had intonation problems and made gross changes to the vocal tract by pushing the lower jaw forward. Subjects who were able to exhibit a "pure head tone" were judged to have had the greater registration options. She also found: "Rarely could head tone be found by ascending to it, especially when the ascent was by step" (p. 113). The singing of descending pitch patterns from higher pitches was more successful in helping students blend vocal registers.

Wurgler reports important information that needs to find its way into the hands of those elementary vocal music teachers who continue to permit children to force the chest register too high, resulting in loud and coarse singing and even vocal nodules. Cultivation of the upper or "head" voice in children is paramount to producing a beautiful singing tone. Wurgler has produced a volume of data that empirically confirm control of vocal registration to be an important part of developing the child singing voice and range. Unfortunately, popular vocal models in the media, with the emphasis on lower or chest voice production continue to provide the wrong models for children's singing. Wurgler highly encourages the use of a balanced register approach (lower, middle, upper). It is the vocally healthy mode of singing.

Song Acquisition

Although the traditional phrase-by-phrase approach to teaching a song is a common pedagogical approach, researchers have begun to examine the most effective ways songs should be taught and learned in the music classroom. Moore, Brotons, Fyk, and Castillo (1997) investigated rote-song learning among 6- to 9-year-old students (N = 600) from England, Poland, Panama, Spain, and the United States. Significant differences were found for culture, age, gender, and melodic material. In this posttest-only design, subjects performed a newly composed two-phrase song using the additive, rote phrase-by-phrase approach. "The contrast between the two phrases indicated that predominate stepwise motion in phrase A was easier to match than phrase B that had more melodic leaps" (p. 87). The authors noted that 45 percent of the subjects struggled recalling phrase A in the composite echo phrase of the song. The learning of phrase B appeared to interfere with recalling phrase A. There also was not a trend toward improvement based on the number of trials. Twenty-eight percent of students made their best performance in the second and third trials, respectively, while 45 percent of subjects made their best performance in trial one. Girls consistently performed better than boys, and country rankings were Spain, Panama, England, Poland, and the United States (p < 0.0001).

> Findings from this study lead to the conclusion that (a) stepwise melodies are easier than those with several leaps, (b) rote song singing improves from age 6 to 9, (c) girls have better responses than boys to learning a new tune, (d) children learn to repeat rhythms more accurately before they can pitch match melodic contours and precise pitches, and (e) although cultural influences are real, increased exposure to music seems likely to improve everyone's singing. (pp. 87–88)

A qualitative study of participants age 2 to 8 (Stadler Elmer, 1997) used structure-genetic constructivism as the paradigm for investigating song acquisition. "In this view, musical development is conceived as an individual's active construction of structures that are inherent in production, perception, and understanding, and which slowly adapt to the conventions of the sociocultural environment" (p. 130). A microanalytic approach was undertaken to investigate "all possible kinds of relevant components and rules of song singing, accompanying activities, and instructional implications of the social setting" (p. 131). The process included (1) detailed description of the natural setting and process involved in children's song learning, (2) computer analysis of recorded singing producing the fundamental frequency by time, and (3) application of an eight-part symbol system that allowed for coding of musical events over time. Findings included the use of joint singing as a scaffold in song learning, suggesting a coconstructive process, as well as the importance of individual differences in song acquisition.

In a study by Klinger, Campbell, and Goolsby (1998), two second-grade classes (N = 39) were taught songs using immersion (whole song) and phrase-by-phrase approaches in a counterbalanced design. A significant difference in favor of immersion ($p < 0.0001$) was found. "Although the children satisfactorily learned the songs through either method, significantly fewer performance errors were made by children taught by the immersion method (across both songs) than when taught using the phrase-by-phrase method" (p. 30).

Marshall (2002) investigated the effect of four presentation modes for song (whole song and text, whole song and neutral syllable, song by phrase and text, song by phrase and neutral syllable) on the singing accuracy of third-grade children. Instruction lasted for 6 weeks, following which subjects were individually tested and audiotaped singing a final criterion song. Two judges rated the singing samples using two rating scales. Results showed that subjects who learned whole songs with text sang most accurately, but no statistical difference was found.

In a study reviewed earlier, Gault (2002) replicated and expanded on the study of Klinger, Campbell, and Goolsby (1998). One hundred twelve kindergarten and first-grade students were randomly assigned by class to one of four treatment groups by pedagogical approach based on song, holistic (immersion), or phrase-by-phrase teaching technique. Results showed a significant difference ($p < 0.018$) in favor of the echo-phrase procedure for only one of the songs. Gault concluded:

> These findings seem to indicate that the efficacy of teaching songs to young school-aged children with or without text or through the use of holistic or echo-phrase teaching procedures depends upon the song to be taught. Furthermore, these findings suggest that the efficacy of the pedagogical procedure used to teach a song may depend on the level of music aptitude of the student learning the song. Thus, rather than relying on pedagogical ideology, careful analysis and understanding of a song's music and text content combined with the teacher's specific instructional objectives may be required to determine the most effective teaching strategy. (p. 61)

What Gault concludes makes sense to most veteran music teachers. There is no "one way" to teach a song—it depends on the nature and complexity of the music. However, having a variety of techniques by which to teach is important knowledge, and research that involves teaching practices and methodologies is rarely found in the literature. There is much need for curricular research and research on teaching practices.

Song Literature

There is a small but growing amount of research that identifies songs common to the heritage of the United States. With the growing emphasis on world music in music education, research into what America's children should be singing as part of American culture is a welcome addition to this discussion of children's singing.

Killian (1993, 1996) studied children's song literature known to third-grade students, college undergraduates, and adults. In her second study (1996), Killian compared verbal recognition of song titles with the ability to sing the songs. Results indicated that "Both adults and children sang fewer songs than they circled..." (p. 222). Out of 1,487 song titles marked "known," an average of only 27 songs in common were sung by both adults and children. Most of these songs could be identified as common to American folk song literature (pp. 220–221).

Prickett and Bridges (1998) investigated whether college music majors and elementary education majors could identify standard children's song literature upon hearing it. Half the students in either group could not identify several songs that music educators have stated are very important for children to learn.

McGuire (2000) studied previous children's song-literature research and other resources to find songs that were common across geographical boundaries in the United States. He classified songs into two categories: devised lists (what people "should know") or authentic lists (what people "do know"). McGuire identified 13 "Songs Common to All Authentic Lists" (p. 315), 16 "Songs from the Authentic Lists Not Listed in Either the *All-America Song Book* or *The Golden Book of Favorite Songs*" (p. 316), and 11 "Songs Common to All Devised Lists" (p. 317). McGuire states: "There seems to be a discrepancy between songs that people actually know and songs that experts are suggesting that people learn" (p. 318). The author states:

> Concerning MENC's "common song repertoire" list, the fact that 16 of the 42 songs on the list (38%) failed to appear on any other list or songbook provides perplexing questions for those interested in this subject. It seems reasonable that if we are to expect people to learn songs that are supposedly standard, these same songs should appear elsewhere in studies systematically examining song repertoire. (p. 319)

McGuire suggests that future research investigate the disparity between what experts say is important for people to know and what people actually know.

The children's choir movement has produced a strong base of quality choral literature. However, only one annotated listing is known (Rao, 1990). Research into high-quality children's choral literature could help the profession learn if this music is known and being used by vocal music educators in the schools.

Summary of Elementary School Singing Research

The following is a summation of results reported in the review of research literature in this chapter. Conclusions are given with caution, for many results are based on only one study. However, it is encouraging to find strands of research in which a number of studies have been conducted, building upon and sharing results that begin to bring clearer vision to important research questions.

- Evidence that piano accompaniment aids students' pitch accuracy when measured is uncertain.
- Evidence suggests that root-oriented, harmonic accompaniment may help develop tonal improvisation skill in young children.
- Strong evidence suggests that tonal patterns are useful for assessing pitch accuracy for singing.
- Strong evidence suggests that 5-year-old children confuse words with melody when tested for pitch accuracy using songs.
- Evidence suggests that descending patterns/intervals are vocally matched better than ascending ones.
- Evidence suggests the xylophone to be a useful model for presenting tonal patterns for pitch-matching development and assessment.
- Evidence suggests the relationship among wait time, audiation, and accuracy of singing remains unclear.
- Strong evidence suggests the "Singing Voice Development Measure" (Rutkowski) to be a useful measure for assessing child vocal development.
- Evidence suggests that familiar songs, "comfortable" for children to sing, can be used successfully to measure pitch accuracy.
- Strong evidence suggests that girls' attitudes toward school music are more positive than boys' attitudes.
- Strong evidence suggests that students' attitudes toward school music declines with maturity.
- Strong evidence suggests that students with greater music self-esteem are more likely to participate in both school and out-of-school music activities.
- Evidence suggests that primary-age children who sing inaccurately may be lagging but not deficient in the development of audiation skills.
- Strong evidence suggests that after the third grade, no significant difference between accurate and inaccurate singers can be found for audiation skills.
- Strong evidence suggests that intermediate-age children who are inaccurate singers are not tone-deaf or weak in music aptitude.
- Strong evidence suggests that a good musical home environment is likely to affect students' participation and success in music.
- Evidence suggests it is unclear as to whether individual or group singing is more conducive to children's pitch accuracy.
- Evidence suggests it is unclear as to whether hand signs are a beneficial aid in encouraging children's singing accuracy.
- Evidence suggests that Kodály music instruction is useful in affirming parallel concepts across music, reading, and mathematics.
- Strong evidence suggests that children match pitch better in their own singing range.
- Evidence suggests the child voice and female voice are the best models for teaching children to match pitch.
- Strong evidence suggests the adult male voice, modeling in the male alto register, is easier for younger children to match pitch than the modal voice of the adult singer.

- Evidence suggests that vocal vibrato in the model of the adult teacher can be a deterrent to accurate pitch matching among younger children.
- Strong evidence suggests that vocal pedagogy involving motor coordination skills is beneficial for children's singing accuracy and vocal range.
- Strong evidence suggests that children are capable of singing in two distinct vocal registers (upper and lower), which can be blended in the middle voice using descending pitch patterns or vocalizes.
- Evidence suggests that songs can be taught successfully using both the "immersion in the whole song" and the "phrase-by-phrase" approaches, depending on the nature of the difficulty of the song literature.
- Evidence suggests little agreement between what experts say is the important song literature for people to know and what people know.
- Evidence that elementary music teachers are using high-quality vocal literature is nonexistent.

Secondary School Singing

A review of literature for choral music education exists for the years 1982 to 1995 (Grant and Norris, 1998). Because of space limitations, most research reviewed in that article is not discussed here. The following topics are covered in this review of secondary school singing research (in alphabetical order): assessment, attitude, changing voice (female, male), choral sound, cultural impact on singing, curriculum, literature, modeling, reflective thinking, rehearsal strategies/techniques, sight singing, and teacher preparation.

Assessment

The area of assessment in choral music education is an important one, but the research is scant on student grading. Kotora (2005) surveyed assessment practices of Ohio high school choral music teachers ($N = 608$) and Ohio college choral methods professors ($N = 38$). Response rates were 43 percent for high school teachers and 54 percent for college professors. Of the 12 grading strategies identified for high school directors, the top three were concert performances (87 percent), student participation (86 percent), and student attendance (85 percent), all nonmusical criteria. However, 77 percent did assess singing, and 74 percent used written tests. A surprising finding was that of the 12 assessment strategies taught by college choral methods teachers, only 55 percent recommended written tests, and worse yet, only 50 percent taught the need for singing tests.

It would seem that college and university choral music education faculty must do a better job of teaching assessment strategies to undergraduate choral methods students if reliance on nonmusical criteria is to cease. Choir is an academic subject, and achievement should be based primarily on knowledge and skills. Some schools continue to discount ensembles for academic credit because ensembles are not seen as academic subjects with academic rigor.

Assessment instruments used in choral festival audiations typically lack standardized measures of validity and reliability. Norris and Borst (2007) sought to compare the criteria and reliability of a commonly used adjudication form with an author-designed form, the Choral Festival Rubric. Both forms contained the same criteria for evaluation: tone quality, diction, blend, intonation, rhythm, balance, and interpretation. Data collection involved four experienced choral directors who evaluated two performances of the same choirs using the traditional and rubric-designed forms. (The rubric form contains qualifying statements; for example, a 5 in tone quality might state: "full, robust sound equally balanced with depth and projection.") Significant differences ($p < 0.05$) were found in favor of the rubric form for all measures except interpretation. The rubric form also showed a higher level of interrater reliability except for the dimension of rhythm. The authors conclude that:

> rubrics containing dimension-specific descriptors could be better suited for the purposes of evaluating performances than instruments containing scant language (words such as excellent, fair, unsatisfactory, etc.), as the descriptors, whereby the adjudicators assign evaluative numbers based on their individual standards. (p. 249)

Choral directors in charge of choral adjudication would benefit from reviewing the Choral Festival Rubric in the article by Norris and Borst (2007, p. 244). Rubrics are becoming popular in all avenues of educational assessment because they more specifically delineate the characteristics of any assigned numerical rating.

Attitude

Two studies by Stamer (2004, 2006) examined student attitudes toward the music contest experience. In the first study (2004), freshmen, sophomore, junior, and senior choral music students ($N = 268$) were surveyed; in the second study (2006), those students who were sophomores ($N = 93$) in the first study were surveyed again as seniors ($N = 62$). Results from both studies showed that significant changes occurred in choral students' perceptions of contests as they matured. Sophomores in both studies attached greater importance to the music contest experience than did seniors. Seniors, in general, were not excited about contests, did not believe contests were fun, and placed less emphasis on contest ratings. The author states: "However, it appears that these actions are more effective with sophomores who are motivated to excel by the external rewards contests provide rather than the internal rewards of excellent music making" (2006, p. 53).

Ensemble directors should take note that extrinsically designed competitions (e.g., "winner takes all") do not meet the needs of all students. In some cases, competition can decrease the interest of intrinsically motivated students (e.g., "doing your individual best").

Kennedy (2002) used qualitative inquiry to examine factors motivating junior high boys to participate in choir. Participants included 11 males, 3 females, and their choral director. Data collection included interview, observation, participant observation, and material culture, which was triangulated accordingly. Factors found to motivate boys' membership in choir were love of singing, teacher influence, and peer influence. The author states: "With respect to musical attitudes, teacher and student responses highlighted the importance of professionalism, presentation, and musical sensitivity" (p. 31). The author concluded:

> A surprising finding was the small degree of importance that the boys placed on range-appropriate repertoire. They handled the notes out of their ranges with apparent ease, devising inventive and practical coping strategies. Far more important to them was repertoire they liked. (p. 35)

Kennedy's study reminds teachers that the key to attracting and keeping singers is a high-quality choral program. Students are attracted by professionalism.

Changing Voice: Female

Williams (1990) studied the characteristics of premenarcheal ($n = 17$) and postmenarcheal ($n = 16$) girls' speaking and singing voices (ages 11 to 15) in relation to pitch range, pitch consistency, and tone quality. Results showed (1) postmenarcheal girls were significantly taller and weighed more ($p < 0.05$), (2) girls in both groups were diagnosed by an otolaryngologist as having incomplete closure of the posterior region of the vocal cords (breathiness), (3) no significant difference in vocal range, (4) no significant difference in tone quality, (5) no significant difference in fundamental speaking pitch, and (6) no significant difference in the frequency of experiencing sore throats or voice cracks when singing. Breathiness appeared to be the major vocal problem of these adolescent females; the voice change was not found to be a traumatic event.

Phillips and Fett (1992) investigated the respiratory patterns and tone quality of adolescent female singers. A *CSpeech*® computer program designed for vocal spectral analysis was used to assess signal-to-noise ratio (i.e., tone and breathiness). Results showed a fair amount of breathiness in the singing voices of girls ages 14 and 15 and the use of spectral analysis to be an excellent means of assessing vocal tone quality.

In an experimental study, Fett (1993/1994) examined the effects of vocal skills instruction (Phillips, 1992b) on measures of singing performance and vocal coordination among adolescent females. Subjects were 45 ninth-grade girls assigned at random to either treatment ($n = 24$) or control ($n = 21$). The treatment period consisted of daily choral rehearsals over 22 weeks, with the treatment group receiving a warm-up inclusive of vocal skills instruction; the control group used general vocalizing. Data analysis revealed significant differences in favor of the treatment group on breathing measures ($p < 0.001$) and vocal performance measures (tonal quality, $p < 0.05$; pitch range, $p < 0.05$; tonal duration, $p < 0.02$). Fett reported that breathiness in the female voice was reduced by specific vocal skills instruction. "A review of means indicates that the treatment group experienced less breath in the tone over time, while the control group's breathiness increased slightly" (p. 75).

The tradition of having only male choristers sing in English cathedral choirs has changed since 1991, with more than 20 cathedral choirs in the United Kingdom accepting female singers. In a descriptive, 3-year longitudinal study, Howard and Welch (2002) observed adolescent female voice changes in a professional choral context at Wells Cathedral in the United Kingdom. The authors found a wider variation of individual vocal function than might be expected in a normal group response. Specifically, the common factor of breathiness in the adolescent female voice was present, but "the acoustic data analyses... suggest that it can be modified by education in this specialized performance context" (p. 65). It also is suggested that individual voice differences can be neglected in a choral setting where emphasis is on the collective voice.

Choral directors often assume that adolescent female voices are breathy and that little can be done except wait for the voice to mature. However, the studies by Fett (1993/1994) and Howard and Welch (2002) suggest that vocal skills instruction is effective in teaching adolescent females to sing with clearer tone quality. Middle school choral directors would do well to explore means by which to help adolescent girls sing with less breathiness.

Changing Voice: Male

Adolescent boys often perceive the change in their voices as traumatic and embarrassing. This was confirmed in a study by Killian (1997), who examined the voice-change process among 141 males (both changing-voice singers, adults, singers and nonsingers). Data were collected via audiotaped interviews, which were scripted and verbal content analyzed. Results revealed (1) boys had a more vivid memory of the voice change than did adult men, (2) singers noticed the voice change more than nonsingers, (3) singers noticed the voice change affected both singing and speaking more than nonsingers, (4) boys mentioned voice pain or thinking they were ill at onset of the voice change more than did adult men, and (5) no significant difference was found across groups as to the overall effect of the change process (pp. 527–528). The author concluded: "Given the number of negative experiences mentioned [by boys] that actively involved choir directors, it seems advisable to disseminate information to future choral educators about the musical expectations and sensitivity necessary to instruct changing-voice boys more effectively" (p. 534).

In another study of the male changing voice, Killian (1999) explored the hypothesis that boys' voices may be changing earlier than typically expected. Singing and speaking voices of fifth- ($n = 56$) and sixth-grade ($n = 43$) boys were categorized and compared. Results (percentages) showed (1) voice change was occurring among many of the fifth- and sixth-grade boys, (2) voices seemed to be changing earlier than indicated in previous research, (3) pitch (singing and speech) lowered as the voice change process advanced, (4) overall range narrowed as the process progressed, (5) speaking pitch remained two to three semitones above the lowest singing pitch, and (6) the majority of boys believed their voices were different than a year before (pp. 362–363).

Many elementary general music teachers know that more boys are experiencing the voice change in elementary school. This factor creates a problem since K-6 singing is traditionally treble-voice. Should boys with changing or changed voices sing an octave lower than the class? Can boys continue to sing in a male alto register that is basically treble voice? Is two- and three-part music advisable to accommodate boys with changing voices? The answers all depend on the predisposition and the flexibility of the boys in any given class, but all three of these solutions are tenable.

Phillips and Emge (1994) sought to determine if the vocal registers used by boys with changing voices had an impact on their singing ranges. Subjects were seventh- ($n = 26$) and eighth-grade ($n = 26$) boys enrolled in choral programs whose directors assigned all boys to a limited, changing-voice part. The hypothesis of the study was that adolescent boys can sing with wider vocal ranges when taught how to sing with distinct vocal registers. Results demonstrated that both seventh- and eighth-grade boys sang with significantly higher, lower, and total overall ranges ($p < 0.001$) when introduced to singing in the chest/modal and male alto vocal registers. The results of this study support the belief that a limited vocal range for adolescent males does not make use of their vocal potential. "The subjects in this study were capable of demonstrating an average range of two octaves when they were singing in both lower and upper registers" (p. 16).

In a similar study, Emge (1998) again investigated the impact of vocal registers on the singing performance of eighth-grade boys ($N = 61$). Group A ($n = 19$) sang in a limited, mid-range part, while group B ($n = 42$) sang traditional tenor and bass ranges. Both groups, however, were trained in the use of different vocal registers. Results showed the limited-range group to have a significantly higher and total range ($p < 0.05$), while both groups significantly increased highest and lowest pitches sung ($p < 0.05$). The author states:

> [Proponents of the limited-range technique] suggest that singing ranges for the majority of adolescent males prior to, during, and immediately following the voice change are between 16 and 20 half-steps. By the end of the present study, however, 100% of the subjects in group A and 77% in group B had total singing ranges of 20 to 35 half-steps. (p. 10)

Emge suggests that teachers of adolescent males not limit these students to singing a limited-range part, but consider traditional tenor and bass parts that explore wider ranges. This requires "that directors are willing to train their male singers in the use of different vocal registers" (p. 12).

Cooksey and Welch (1998) are critical of the national music curricula of the United Kingdom for its lack of directives to music teachers on issues of the adolescent singer:

> It is a weakness of the revised National Curriculum for Music (1995) that it makes no appropriate reference to this unique period of adolescent voice change and, as a result, teachers receive inadequate statutory guidance on the development of singing at Key Stage 3. (p. 99)

This article reviews the information that the authors believe music teachers in the United Kingdom should be able to find in the National Curriculum for Music:

- while voice development follows a predictable sequence of stages, individuals begin and follow the pattern at variable times;
- age is a poor criterion for voice classification;
- the rate of physiological growth can vary greatly during each stage;
- there is variability between individuals within each voice classification stage, depending upon which of the determining stage criteria are being examined;
- at any point during years 7 to 9 (ages 12–14), the music teacher will typically encounter a variety of voice change stages in each classroom setting;
- while a linear pattern of development occurs, individual profiles vary considerably within the overall scheme. Growth rates and pubertal entry points are not predictable;
- singing habits (and perceptions about singing as a personal activity) acquired during adolescence can be long-lived, so it is important that such habits are healthy and successful in matching musical with developing physiological and psychological needs. (p. 116)

These points are based on Cooksey's earlier descriptive research that reflects the adolescent voice "as is" rather than what "could be" with proper instruction. Cooksey has not researched the impact of vocal register development on the singing of adolescent males.

In a qualitative study similar to that of Killian (1997), Kennedy (2004) studied the process of the male voice change from the point of view of the boys ($N = 60$) in the American Boychoir School (Princeton, New Jersey). Participants (sixth-, seventh-, and eighth-graders) in the study ($N = 36$) were interviewed in small groups; the interviews were recorded and transcribed. Triangulation of data was effected through the cross-referencing of interview transcripts, observations, and material culture. Five results were presented: (1) while patterns of voice-change experience were evident, each young man's experience was unique, (2) exploring and using a wide singing range seemed to have no detrimental effect on the voice, (3) teaching boys in a single-sex environment may be beneficial during the voice change, (4) singers need to learn good vocal technique to keep from harming their voices, and (5) helping young men navigate through the frustration of the voice change appears critical (pp. 76–77).

Freer (2006) encourages the use of narrative inquiry to "provide a framework for investigations of how the social, academic, and musical needs of adolescents can inform the process of teaching choral music in the middle grades" (p. 69). The author uses his own self-story "to suggest that listening to the stories of young adolescent boys about their singing experiences may provide a more complete understanding of how success and persistence can be planned for within the choral environment of middle schools" (p. 69).

A descriptive study by Demorest and Clements (2007) examined the influence of perceptual ability, task demands, and singing range on the pitch-matching achievement of adolescent boys in various stages of the voice change. Subjects were boys in sixth through ninth grade ($N = 60$) who were assigned to three groups based on a pitch-matching assessment task (certain, $n = 36$; inconsistent, $n = 12$; uncertain, $n = 12$). Results revealed a significant difference in perceptual pitch-matching based on vocal matching ability ($p < 0.01$) in favor of certain and inconsistent singers over uncertain singers. It seems that perceptual tonal deficiency affected the singing accuracy of the uncertain group. Significant difference ($p < 0.05$) also was found for test type in favor of the context-pitch over single-pitch. This difference was due mainly to the inconsistent singers. The results replicate the findings of an earlier study by Demorest (2001a). "These results support the speculation that perception and production may be more related for older singers, at least for adolescent boys going through the voice change" (p. 124). Of question, however, is the author-designed, computerized "Pitch Matching Perception Test," for which validity is not addressed. It would seem appropriate that the opinions of experts might have been sought to determine whether the task involved was a valid measure of pitch perception or something else (e.g., ability to make a visual decision about an aural phenomenon).

Adler (1999) surveyed choral directors in the United States ($n = 22$) and Canada ($n = 48$) as to their practices for working with male singers before and during the voice change. Among the many findings, the author reported:

> Of the respondents in this survey, 85.3% had received some kind of formal training about changing male voices. Of the respondents with formal training, 84.8% felt that their formal training had **not** prepared them adequately to teach boys with changing voices. Only 70.6% of respondents taught their students about the voice change process. (p. 30)

Adler notes the need for research that addresses the social psychology of male singers. He concludes that "research has failed to assist teachers in stopping the exodus of male singers from choral programs" (p. 32).

Helping the male with changing voice continues to present challenges for middle school and junior high choral directors. Research suggests that boys can learn to sing through this adolescent period with vocal instruction that includes psychological understanding and encouragement and psychomotor coordination. Understanding vocal registers is of paramount importance if choral directors are to unify boys' voices before, during, and following the voice change.

Choral Sound Quality

Choral directors have long debated the relationship of singers' spacing and standing formation to sound quality. Daugherty (1999) investigated these variables by assessing the preferences of auditors ($N = 160$) to taped excerpts of one high school choir (SATB) singing the same homophonic choral selection in two choral formations (block/sectional and mixed) and three spacings (close, lateral, circumambient). Preferences also were solicited from the choristers ($n = 46$). Results showed both auditors and singers significantly preferred ($p > 0.05$) spread spacing over close. Auditors showed no significant preference between the two formations, but the singers significantly preferred ($p < 0.05$) the mixed standing formation (women more than men). Singers attributed better hearing of self and ensemble to spread spacing. "In light of such results, the sometimes frenetic and conflicting discussions of choral formations (section versus mixed, etc.,) in many methods textbooks possibly constitute a misplaced debate" (p. 236). The choir's spacing was shown to be the significant preference factor in this study.

Ekholm (2000) studied the effects of soloistic versus blended choral singing and random versus acoustic (matching by similarity of vocal sound) choral seating on blend and overall choral sound. Choral conductors ($n = 37$), voice teachers ($n = 33$), and nonvocal musicians ($n = 32$) rated performances of four choral selections sung by a college choir of 22 voice majors. Eight choristers were recorded individually and their solos evaluated by 12 voice teachers. All choristers were asked to rate the experimental conditions for vocal comfort and choral sound. Results indicated that choral conductors significantly preferred blended over soloistic singing ($p < 0.001$); no significant difference was found on this variable for voice teachers or nonmusicians. A significant main effect ($p < 0.005$) in favor of the acoustic seating arrangement was found for all judges ($N = 102$; 37+33+32). Among the 12 voice teachers, solo singing was ranked significantly higher than soloistic choral singing ($p < 0.002$). Choristers' choral sound preference revealed a significant main effect for singing mode in favor of blended singing ($p < 0.001$) over soloistic, and a significant main effect for acoustic ($p < 0.009$) over random seating. Choristers commented that acoustic seating permitted them to hear themselves and other singers better, they were less apt to oversing, it was easier to sing in tune, they had a greater feeling for blend, and it allowed for greater vocal freedom. "Positive comments on blended singing mentioned increased ability to attend to dynamics, intonation, and vocal tone and not having to compete with other singers to be heard" (pp. 131–132). The author concluded: "Further research on choral sound is needed to study optimal spacing of choristers and development of strategies to adapt solo vocal technique to a choral setting" (p. 134).

The debate between choral camps as to blended versus soloistic singing comes down to preference. There will never be a right answer when it comes to matters of taste. However, Ekholm (2000) presents an interesting finding in that choristers preferred blended singing and acoustic seating/voice matching. Do choral directors ever ask singers if they have a preference for the style of singing they use and how they stand in formation? Perhaps choral directors should ask!

Cultural Impact on Singing

A study by Chinn (1997) provides insight into the problems African-American girls can have when singing in environments that are primarily Caucasian populated. The subjects were 44 African American females enrolled in choral music classes in grades 9 to 12. A "Cultural Mistrust Inventory" was used to determine the subjects' vocal model acceptance and vocal self-concept in relation to a culturally "white" singing environment. Results of this inventory showed 23 subjects were in the "high-mistrust" group and 21 subjects in the "low-mistrust" group. Results indicated significant differences between groups on each vocal characteristic measure ($p < 0.01$) in favor of the high-mistrust group, who "demonstrated more characteristics associated with the African-American culture than did the low-mistrust group" (p. 636). The author concluded:

> The present study demonstrated that cultural mistrust is related to singing tasks. Thus it might prove beneficial for choral music educators to consider how cultural mistrust might influence student responses to instructional practices and literature when they plan their teaching. (p. 647)

Ensemble directors of highly ethnic, diverse groups know that Chinn's conclusions are vitally important to the success of any musical group. Teachers teach people, and knowing the cultural background that students bring to the classroom can make or break the success of any music group.

Curriculum

Hamann (2007) conducted a survey of middle school choral directors in Minnesota ($N = 200$) to determine those factors that influenced the choices made for choral music curriculum. The response rate was low (16 percent), jeopardizing the results. However, the question is important, and one main finding is worth considering: There was no clear vision found for middle school choral curriculum. "Until choral music educators form a clearer vision of what components are vital to an appropriate, high-quality choral music education at the middle level, teachers will continue to struggle to balance the many voices competing for attention" (p. 70). The author states that this is a preliminary study leading to others for helping to define an appropriate choral curriculum. She and others are encouraged to do research in this area that is almost void of substantial knowledge. While Hamann cautions against generalizing the results, it is probably safe to say that choral music education lacks unity; choral music educators focus mainly on preparing for concerts.

Hamann concludes: "With the growing influence of the national standards comes a prime opportunity for choral music in the middle to demonstrate its value to the growth and education of the middle level learner" (p. 71).

Literature

Forbes (2001) surveyed and interviewed high school choral directors to determine the literature they chose and the criteria by which they chose that literature for their top mixed choirs. Two groups supplied the data: outstanding choral music educators ($N = 89$) in five southern states ($N = 59$, response rate of 50.1 percent) and directors not nominated ($N = 202$) as outstanding ($N = 59$, response rate of 28.7 percent). Numerous statistical differences were found between groups, but results showed no uniformly structured criteria for selecting repertoire. "Although this writer believes in the importance of inspiration in the repertoire selection process, the current unstructured approach to repertoire selection may be problematic, especially for young and inexperienced conductors" (p. 118). One interesting finding showed that directors tended to think more about educational value when choosing classical literature but more about entertainment value when choosing popular music.

> This finding calls into question the educational validity of programs that focus primarily on the performance of popular music and lends support to the stated concerns of many directors regarding the perceived proliferation of choral programs that focus on the performance of popular music to the exclusion of music of other styles. (p. 118)

The proliferation of popular music in today's culture makes it difficult for choral directors to stand against the trend of taking the easy way out by choosing music of little lasting or educational value. Those who do program for educational objectives are to be commended.

In a survey of Virginia choral directors ($N = 263$), Reames (2001) investigated the literature performed by beginning high school choirs. Findings were based on a response rate of 75 percent. Only one significant relationship was found between teacher experience and literature selection: experienced teachers chose more Baroque literature for beginning high school choirs ($p < 0.05$). Contemporary music was the most often performed.

> MENC encourages the use of a broad repertoire, and many choral experts believe that high-quality choral music representative of all periods, though not necessarily difficult music, is attractive to all students and should be the basis of the music program. Choral directors may want to expand beginning choir literature choices to promote positive musical experiences with a balanced variety of styles and historical periods. (p. 131)

The survey also revealed that Virginia choral directors found college methods classes to be the least valuable source for finding beginning high school choral literature. "Preservice teachers need to be given the tools to work effectively with choirs of every age and level, and the skills to appropriately select and locate music materials" (p. 131). Based on the findings of the two studies in this section, it would seem that those at the college and university level who prepare future choral music educators must communicate that all music chosen for performance should have educational value.

Modeling

While the effects of vocal modeling have been researched repeatedly at the elementary level, almost nothing has been done at the secondary level. Williams (1994) investigated the effects of gender modeling on the pitch-matching accuracy of high school students ($N = 67$). Subjects were recorded in two sessions responding to either male or female vocal models. Significant main effect differences were found for both gender models: males sang better with the male model ($p < 0.036$), and females sang better with the female model ($p < 0.037$). A significant difference also was found ($p < 0.008$) on overall pitch matching in favor of males. (Males in most choirs tend to be fewer and more self-selected.) The findings of this study were "consistent with the results of earlier studies of young children in finding that singers match more accurately with voices like their own" (p. 43). The author advises choral directors: "In situations where the gender of the teacher is not the same as the student gender, another student who is of the appropriate gender might serve as a better model than the teacher" (p. 43).

In a qualitative study, Grimland (2005) analyzed modeling as a teaching tool used by three choral directors over a 14-week period of rehearsals. Data included transcriptions of 20 percent of the rehearsals, field notes from observations, and interviews with the directors (triangulation). Modeling was found to be characteristic of all three teachers' instruction. These models were identified as audible, visible, and process oriented. The author states:

> There were several pedagogical purposes in terms of the choice of modeling as an instructional strategy. For example, each teacher used modeling to prepare students for a musical task, and all modeled examples to refine musical performances. As a point of emphasis, each teacher imitated incorrect aspects of performances in an effort to clarify what not to do, and sometimes this mimicry was exaggerated. In addition, all three teachers used modeling simultaneously with student singing to reinforce and guide appropriate performances. (p. 8)

Grimland concludes by stating the importance of undergraduate choral methods students learning to model effectively in the three forms identified in the study. "Prospective teachers should be encouraged to develop and apply modeling skills" (p. 12).

Modeling is such a valuable technique for choral directing success, and Grimland's recommendation should be heeded by those who teach under-graduate choral methods classes. Preservice teachers need to learn more than just audible modeling (vocal demonstration). Visible (e.g., phrase shaping) and process-oriented modeling (e.g., learning to "think through" the preparation of a musical score) are techniques equally of importance. It should not be assumed that students know how to model in these modes.

Reflective Thinking

Reflective thinking has become a topic of considerable discussion and research in education. Stevens (2001) used a qualitative design to determine if a sample of 20 high school choral students drawn from his own choral program (N = 115) were better choral students for having used reflective thinking (Arts-Propel model) via journaling as part of their choral experience. Results showed that all five measures of reflective thinking (ensemble rehearsal critique, beginning of semester questionnaire, tape-recorded peer-student critiques, student journals, taped interviews) were successful for capturing reflective thought. "This supplemental activity heightens student self-awareness in the choral ensemble, which in turn promotes richer reflective activity" (p. 194). Stevens recommends the use of the processfolio to "move from a paper and tape collection to an electronic portfolio" (p. 206).

In another qualitative study, Butke (2006) involved five middle and high school choral teachers in a reflective process for 9 weeks. "The five participants were asked to keep daily reflective journals, write an autobiographical narrative, and complete reflective narrative exercises" (p. 59). Results showed (1) all teachers used new approaches in the pedagogical, curricular, personal/professional, or critical categories, (2) teachers encountered varying levels of success when initiating change, (3) teachers became more self-motivated as the study progressed about conversing and writing in more detail, (4) the richness of past experience and support of influential people contributed to teachers' desire and ability to reflect, and (5) teachers became empowered in a way that altered their perceptions of what was possible in the way of change (p. 63). The author developed "The Cyclical Model of Reflection" as a summative outcome of the study (p. 65).

Reflective thinking has shown itself to be a beneficial tool in helping teachers understand themselves in relation to the work environment. More teachers should be encouraged to use this process. Unfortunately, time restraints often keep teachers from keeping a journal.

Rehearsal Strategies and Techniques

Teacher feedback is an important element of the teaching process. Schmidt (1995) examined the responses of 120 high school students in grades 7 through 12 enrolled in a summer music camp. He wanted to determine students' approval and disapproval behaviors as a function of difference in internal and external attributions in vocal music, grade level, and gender. Data were responses to 29 audiotaped excerpts of applied vocal music instruction. The sole significant effect was for gender ($p < 0.001$): females rated each of the approval factors higher than males, and males rated disapproval factors higher than females. It seems that "girls were more responsive to adult praise than to praise from peers, whereas the opposite was found for boys" (p. 326). Schmidt recommends:

> Choral teachers should likely reconsider the ways in which disapproval or negative feedback is used. The results indicate that male singers (particularly at the high school level) might respond more positively to negative feedback than female singers; thus different ratios of positive to negative feedback for male and female students are implied. (p. 326)

Schmidt also found that students tended to view success as largely due to internal factors (e.g., effort and ability) rather than external factors, such as teacher, task, or mere luck.

Dunn (1997) included teacher reinforcement or feedback as a variable in his study of performance improvement of two high school choirs ($N = 60$). One choir ($n = 31$) received instruction with feedback, and the second ($n = 29$) received the same instruction without verbal or facial reinforcement. Forty performances were evaluated by three expert judges for (1) improvement of 10 music concepts (sequenced and structured in a hierarchy), (2) effects of teacher reinforcement on student attentiveness, and (3) performance achievement and attitude. Results showed musical concept performance gains were similar for all excerpts. A surprise finding was that subjects in the feedback group were consistently more off-task than subjects in the no-feedback group. "Perhaps the focus of instructor feedback on musical performance rather than social behavior such as attentiveness was a factor in student on/off-task" (p. 564). Student attitude ratings were significantly higher for the feedback group ($p < 0.001$). No statistical analysis was computed for the difference between groups on performance achievement, but the feedback group scored more than 11 points higher than the no-feedback group on this measure. "These results support the idea that given equivalent amounts of teacher instruction and performance time, the addition of teacher academic reinforcement might produce better musical performance" (p. 564).

Skadsem (1997) investigated the effects of conductor verbalization, dynamic markings, conductor gesture, and choir dynamic level on singers' dynamic responses. Subjects ($N = 144$) were undergraduate and graduate music students (conductors, $n = 48$; choral singers, $n = 48$; high school choral students, $n = 48$). Each subject was audiotaped singing nine renditions of a folk tune while watching a videotape of a conductor, listening to a choir through headphones, and viewing the music. Three judges evaluated the audiotapes. Results indicated that verbal remarks from the conductor were significantly better than written, gesture, and choral listening in soliciting dynamic responses from all singers ($p < 0.05$). "The verbal instructions used in this study were extremely concise...and, when evaluated, proved to be effective in eliciting the most dynamic response" (p. 517). One factor not mentioned by the author is that choral students could be so unaccustomed to seeing choral conductors vary the size of the conducting pattern to match dynamic level that singers are not sensitized to respond dynamically to the conducting gesture. Thus, conductors talk dynamics.

Freer (2003) studied the effects of teacher discourse (scaffolding and non-scaffolding language) on middle school choral students' responses ($N = 88$). Scaffolding language involved transitional statements connecting or building from one idea to another. Qualitative data included student reflective reports completed after each of five rehearsals. Analysis involved looking for correlations with the structural statements of the teachers, both of whom were known to use scaffolding and nonscaffolding language. Results showed the teachers used scaffolding language 25 percent of the time, mostly for transferring responsibility for learning from teacher to students and for task-based support (reinforcement), which was overwhelmingly positive. Freer found a strong positive relationship between teacher use of scaffolding language, complete sequential units of instruction, and quality of student experience during middle school choral rehearsals.

Yarbrough and Madsen (1998) investigated attributes of effective choral rehearsing from videotaped excerpts of a university choral conductor rehearsing a university choir over one semester. Subjects ($N = 89$) were graduate ($n = 47$) and undergraduate ($n = 42$) music majors who evaluated seven videotapes of choral rehearsal excerpts (two selections) that focused only on the conductor. Data were gathered using observation forms developed in previous research. Results found no significant differences between graduates and undergraduates or vocal and instrumental students on rehearsal evaluations. There was a significant difference among excerpt ratings ($p < 0.0001$) in favor of excerpt 5, which "contained less off-task student behavior, a higher percentage of approvals, more eye contact and student activities from 5–6 seconds" (p. 475). The highest rated excerpt received the most positive comments from the students as to student attentiveness, enthusiasm, pacing, and overall teaching effectiveness. The authors conclude: "In choral conducting and methods classes we strongly encourage prospective conductors to maintain a fast pace, to allow singers maximum performance time, and to keep our instructions brief and to the point" (p. 477).

A study by Yarbrough and Henley (1999) was "the third in a series of studies designed to study effective choral rehearsal techniques" (p. 310). The purpose of the study was to determine if focusing evaluators' attention on students versus conductor would affect assessment of teaching in choral rehearsing. Subjects ($N = 176$) were university music education majors randomly assigned to one of two experimental groups: (1) focus on the conductor and (2) focus on the choral students. Data were gathered from subjects' viewing of seven rehearsal excerpts involving two selections. No significant differences between groups were found for gender, major (vocal or instrumental), and level (graduate or undergraduate). There was a significant difference between groups ($p < 0.0001$) for observation focus in favor of the conductor group, although significant interactions tended to confound this finding. The highest rated excerpt contained a high percentage of approvals, moderate eye contact, many activity changes, a high percentage of student response time, and rapid pacing (p. 313). The authors concluded: "Ratings in this study were lower across all categories for both student and teacher behavior when the evaluators' attention was focused on the students in the ensemble" (p. 314). "Regardless of the difficulties, there is now enough extant research showing the importance and effectiveness of these variables [student attentiveness, positive reinforcement, pacing] to more vigorously encourage their emphasis in music teacher training programs" (p. 317).

Knowing good rehearsal techniques and strategies is important to conducting an effective rehearsal, and research has provided knowledge of what it takes to conduct an efficient rehearsal. Unfortunately, this information is often unknown by many choral directors. Disseminating results of research to teachers continues to challenge the teaching profession.

Sight-Singing

A review of literature by Demorest (1998) on sight singing in the secondary choral ensemble is available for research published through 1998. Again, because of space constraints, research in that article is not explored here. Topics presented by Demorest include instructional time devoted to sight-singing, methods and materials, student achievement, group achievement, individual achievement, and experimental, descriptive, and predictive studies.

The assessment of sight-singing was the focus of a study by Henry (2001) in which she formulated the Vocal Sight-Reading Inventory (VSRI) as a test for secondary choral students. Tonal patterns were constructed and content validity established in reference to secondary choral literature. Test reliability was high ($r = 0.97$), and a strong correlation was shown between the pitch skills of the test and the skills required to sight-read tonal music ($r = 0.96$). In the main study, 183 students in five high schools participated in individual sight-reading assessment. Results showed:

> Subjects from grades 9–12 obtained a mean score of 10.70, or roughly 38% accuracy in sight-reading the pitch skill patterns included in the VSRI. These scores present a considerably more dismal view of student music reading ability than those obtained in previous studies.... (p. 32)

The author also noted the importance of process validity:

> The VSRI was deemed to have process validity because of the brief amount of time required to administer the test, the brief amount of time required to score the test, the potential for self administration, and the ease of recording and tracking student progress. (p. 32)

Henry recommended additional research using the VSRI in longitudinal studies. This could be a worthy pursuit because a standardized test for sight-reading achievement would be of value to choral music educators.

In another study of sight-singing instruction, Henry (2004) sought to determine the effectiveness of using specific pitch skills emphasizing scale degree and harmonic function in both familiar and unfamiliar melodies. Two groups of novice high school singers received 12 weeks of sight-singing instruction using either newly composed melodies ($n = 41$) or familiar melodies that contained the same skills ($n = 26$). Results showed both groups scored significantly higher pretest to posttest ($p < 0.0004$), and there was no significant difference between groups. Henry concluded: "Targeting specific pitch skills in both familiar and unfamiliar melodies shows promise as an effective tool for sight-singing instruction" (p. 206).

Norris (2004) surveyed sight-singing requirements at junior and senior high school large-group ratings-based choral festivals throughout the United States. Data from all 50 states were collected. Results showed that less than half of all states required sight-singing tests at junior high or high school levels. Since vocal music students are notoriously poor sight-readers, it would seem that choral directors would want the added pressure on students to prepare for sight-singing adjudication.

Two recent studies surveyed sight-singing practices in specific states: Florida (Kuehne, 2007) and Kentucky (Floyd and Bradley, 2006). These studies present a wealth of information regarding materials used in sight-singing, elements and skills, time spent, and so forth. One point of particular interest is that both surveys found the majority of choral directors did not think their undergraduate methods courses prepared them to teach sight-singing skills to their choirs. "In fact, around 18% marked no influence at all" (Kuehne, p. 126). Floyd and Bradley (2006) cite the Kentucky Music Educators Association's professional development program as providing an important source of information for choral directors on the teaching of sight-singing. "These findings should encourage KMEA, along with other state music associations, to continue offering high-quality professional development opportunities" (p. 77). Notably, Kuehne's study focuses on middle school choral programs, something of a rarity in this line of survey research.

Practice time prior to a sight-singing assessment was the focus of a study by Killian and Henry (2005). Volunteer singers ($N = 200$) from two high school all-state choir camps ($N = 600$) sang individually at sight one melody after a 30-second study period and then sang a second melody without the study time. Significant difference was found in favor of study time ($p < 0.0083$). Further analysis showed no significant difference for low-accuracy singers—study time tended not to help these students. Practice strategies used by the high-accuracy singers included vocally establishing the key, the use of hand signs, singing out loud during practice, and physically keeping the beat. Results of this study indicate that choral directors should permit students practice time prior to sight-singing evaluation.

Yarbrough, Orman, and Neill (2007) examined teaching process prior to sight-singing adjudication and wanted to know what choral directors say and do in that instructional period. Subjects were 84 high school ($n = 47$) and middle school ($n = 37$) choral directors participating in the sight-singing portion of a districtwide contest. Choral ensembles represented both top-level and second-level groups. "With permission from each of the directors, we videotaped with a camera focused on a director to record verbal instructions" (p. 29). This process was done for each of two instruction periods for a total of 8 minutes of videotaping per director. Verbal instructions and reinforcements by the directors and student responses were scripted, coded, timed, and analyzed. Of the many interesting findings, it was reported that "directors talked about 42.46% of the total time videotaped and allowed 52.54% of the remaining time for students to respond without the teacher talking" (p. 32). It was noted that reinforcement was used by most of the directors and that "reinforcement is more effective if it is specifically related to the musical task" (p. 32). As in previous research, most directors were found to use movable *do* as opposed to fixed *do*.

The research on sight-singing has increased in the last two decades, especially in the area of secondary choral music. Unfortunately, it remains that research has not identified any superior method for teaching this vital skill. It is rare that commercial publications have any research base. At best, the profession might well continue to follow Demorest's advice to choose an instructional approach and use it regularly (Demorest, 2001b). Clearly, research into sight-singing methodology is warranted and needed.

Teacher Preparation

Stegman (1996) investigated six choral music student teachers' perceptions of successes and problems during student teaching through extended interviews, weekly reflection sessions, observations of instruction, and documents. Five general areas emerged as important to students' interactive thought: (1) beliefs about teaching and learning, (2) orientation to subject matter, (3) perspectives regarding curriculum and planning, (4) reflection, and (5) images, models, and metaphors. Much emphasis was noted as being on self; that is, the student teachers tended to be concerned more with their own image than what was happening with the students being taught. Three of the students eventually were able to demonstrate a more global perspective on their role as music educators.

Snow (1998) investigated undergraduate conductor/teacher planning processes and relationships to knowledge of pedagogy as evidenced in teaching. This qualitative study focused on an alternative model that emphasized brainstorming and imagining for teaching as documented by a visually oriented map of student thinking. Participants were six junior-level undergraduate students in a university choral methods class. Data collection over a 15-week semester involved (1) written teaching plans, (2) videotapes of conducting episodes, (3) teacher/researcher field notes, and (4) students' written assignments. Results supported a preparatory brainstorming process based on in-depth score study and analysis. Students demonstrated an expert-like mind-set toward development of expertise, a linking of pedagogical knowledge to teaching, and improved attention to teaching for contextual understanding of the music.

Anyone who has taught a choral methods course at the college or university level knows how difficult it is for students to grasp the process of score study in anticipation of the choral rehearsal. Snow's investigation demonstrates a means by which this can be accomplished through a brainstorming technique that requires students to think out loud in the process of score study. Such a preparatory technique is process oriented and actively engages students in mapping out a score, which then helps to reveal the plan of attack for teaching it. Score study is something every choral methods student should understand, and Snow provides a successful means for implementing this activity.

Summary of Secondary School Singing Research

The following is a summation of results reported in the current review of research literature for secondary school singing. Conclusions are given with caution; most results are based on one study.

- Evidence suggests that high school choral directors continue to rely heavily on nonmusical criteria when grading students.
- Evidence suggests that choral methods instructors at the college and university levels do not uniformly recommend the use of written or singing tests as part of choral assessment.
- Evidence suggests that choral contests appeal to students less as they mature from sophomores to seniors.
- Evidence suggests that choral adjudication forms that use rubrics are more favored by choral adjudicators than forms of a more general nature.
- Strong evidence suggests that breathiness in the voice of the adolescent female can be modified with proper instruction.
- Evidence suggests that adolescent boys' voices are changing earlier than once expected, many in the fifth and sixth grades.
- Evidence suggests that adolescent boys are sensitive to the voice change and need help in navigating the voice-change process.
- Strong evidence suggests that adolescent boys are capable of singing a wider range of pitches with no detrimental vocal effect when taught to sing in chest and male alto registers.
- Evidence suggests that teaching adolescent boys in a single-sex environment can be beneficial during the voice change.
- Evidence suggests that most choral methods instructors at the college and university level do not adequately prepare preservice teachers to work with adolescent singers with changing voices.
- Evidence suggests that choral singers prefer to stand with greater spacing and in a mixed formation, both of which help singers to more easily hear their own voices.
- Evidence suggests that more choral directors prefer a blended versus a soloistic-style choral sound.
- Evidence suggests that both choral directors and singers prefer acoustic voice matching seating arrangements in choir.

- Evidence suggests that understanding cultural mistrust can be an important factor in understanding how it influences students' singing responses in a culturally diverse choral ensemble.
- Evidence suggests little uniformity across middle school choral curricula.
- Evidence suggests that high school choral directors exhibit little uniformity of standards for choosing high school choral literature.
- Evidence suggests that college and university choral methods classes are not strong sources for finding beginning high school quality choral literature.
- Evidence suggests that high school choral directors think more about entertainment value when programming contemporary literature of the popular variety.
- Evidence suggests that male members of high school choirs respond vocally better to a male adult voice, and likewise, females respond vocally better to a female adult voice.
- Evidence suggests that choral directors use three basic forms of modeling: vocal/audible, gesture/visible, and process/thinking oriented.
- Evidence suggests the reflective thinking process to be beneficial for both high school choral students and directors.
- Evidence suggests that female choir members are more responsive to adult praise than praise from peers, while the opposite is true for males.
- Evidence suggests that choral students react positively to verbal and facial feedback from the director, but such feedback can lead to off-task behavior.
- Evidence suggests that choral students respond better to verbal directives regarding dynamics than to the conductor's gesture.
- Evidence suggests that teacher use of scaffolding statements can result in raising the quality of the student experience during middle school choral rehearsals.
- Strong evidence suggests that fast pacing is conducive to efficient choral rehearsing.
- Evidence suggests that choral students, in general, sight-read poorly.
- Evidence suggests that undergraduate choral methods classes typically do not sufficiently prepare preservice teachers to teach sight-reading skills.
- Evidence suggests that giving a student practice time to study a sight-reading example results in better sight-singing accuracy.
- Evidence suggests that more choral directors use movable *do* as opposed to fixed *do*.
- Evidence suggests that choral music student teachers are more concerned with their own images than with assessing choral students' responses.
- Evidence suggests that a brainstorming practice between student and teacher leads to a better understanding of score analysis among students in choral methods classes.

Summary

More than 100 studies are presented in this research review of elementary and secondary school singing. The focus is on studies since 1990, and the majority of citations are from articles appearing in peer-reviewed journals, sources that guided the authors in deciding those studies to include in this chapter.

Kruse, Oare, and Norman (2008) analyzed three refereed journals in music education (*Journal of Research in Music Education*, Volumes 34–53; *Bulletin of the Council for Research in Music Education*, Issues 111–130; *Contributions to Music Education*, Issues 13–32) "to discover the extent to which the *National Standards* have impacted research trends in music education" (p. 54). For the 10-year period spanning 1994 to 2005, 130 of the 637 articles published related to categories of the National Standards, and of these the first standard, "Singing, alone and with others, a varied repertoire of music," ranked first with 26.23 articles (4.12 percent). For the 10-year period prior to the publication of the National Standards (1986–1995), articles on singing ranked third (3.27 percent). A ranking of third with 41.34 articles published (3.76 percent) was reported for the combined years 1986 to 2005 (p. 57). Singing has been and continues to be a major research interest in the field of music education.

Summary statements presented in this chapter show far more "evidence" than "strong evidence" labels, especially at the secondary level. The majority of studies are single investigations with little replication or ongoing discovery. The profession is in need of research findings that are shown to be consistent over a number of investigations. Researchers, especially doctoral students, should consider building on the numerous studies in this chapter by replicating and improving on this research. Perhaps research in the 21st century will provide answers that can change the course of how singing is taught and how students learn to sing. The first of the National Standards is clear: all students are to be able to enjoy singing as a means of music making.

Issues for Future Research

From the time of Lowell Mason to approximately the 1930s, singing was taught in schools as a basic skill—a learned behavior. With the advent of progressive education in the early 1900s, it became the belief that children should not be taught as little adults but rather with a less structured mode of instruction. Hence, formal singing instruction was dropped from the school music curriculum in favor of a more recreational song approach (Gehrkens, 1934, p. 89). Singing has not recovered from this change in teaching mode, and the general population of young adults today does not sing as their parents and grandparents once did. Many elementary general music teachers seem to have little understanding of the child voice and do not know how to develop it. Research is needed to identify (1) what present elementary music teachers believe about teaching all children to sing, (2) what these teachers know and do not know about the child voice, (3) how comfortable they are with their own singing voices, (4) their level of interest in learning more about child vocal pedagogy, and (5) how best to disseminate this knowledge.

It also would be helpful to know if elementary methods classes at the college and university level devote adequate time to child and adolescent vocal pedagogy. What is the status of singing in the curriculum? The future of singing in the United States depends on elementary and middle school general music teachers.

Another important issue for future research is the use of high-quality song literature. The children's choir movement advanced by ACDA has produced a vast quantity of high-quality children's choral literature. How much of this music is being used in the elementary curriculum? What songs are in use by elementary music teachers? Are teachers aware of high-quality song literature that exists outside the basal series?

How beneficial is aural discrimination instruction in developing confident singers? Is it to be taken for granted that children eventually learn to discriminate pitch and rhythm, or can early focused instruction build a bridge to psychomotor coordination? What are the roles of wait time and mental practice in relation to accuracy of pitch?

Do some vocal exercises and vocalizes work better than others in developing a confident child singer? With the small amount of time often accorded singing in elementary general music, what is the most efficient approach to voice-building activity? What areas of instruction should be included in the singing curriculum?

Do schools in America still involve students in assembly singing? Does this practice have a positive effect on students' attitudes toward singing and school music? Is there a basic song literature that could be identified for such a purpose?

How many elementary music teachers also direct elementary choirs? Are these choirs select in nature or do all students have the opportunity to sing in a choral ensemble? Do schools exist in which all students are required to sing in choir? What effect does this have on attitudes toward singing?

Is it better for adolescent boys to be separated from adolescent girls for music class instruction? What do boys think about singing in the presence of girls during the voice-change years and vice versa? Is separation of the sexes for music class a common practice in middle schools?

How can attitudes be improved toward singing as students mature? Is there a cultural bias against the singing of boys in the United States? Can research identify ways in which boys can be encouraged to sing?

Are there ways in which parents and guardians can be encouraged to enrich the musical home environment? Can specific practices be discovered that would help music teachers effectively communicate the benefits of music in the home?

Answers to these questions would not only improve the status of singing in schools but also provide music teachers with the knowledge and techniques for making the next generation one that sings. A praxial approach to music means that all students are practicing music makers.

Importance of Singing in the School Curriculum

Why should music educators be concerned with teaching all children to sing? The following reasons (Phillips, 2007) present a rationale for the importance of singing in the school music curriculum:

- Singing is a means of making music in which everyone can participate: it is a learned behavior.
- Singing enhances the quality of life: those who participate feel better.
- Singing is a basic and powerful form of communication: thoughts, ideas, and feelings transcend words alone.
- Singing creates a community or bond among those who sing: people need connection and cultural identity.
- Singing provides a way for people to celebrate and commemorate life: important events are enhanced by song.
- Singing in a group promotes cooperative learning: working well together is basic to a productive society.
- Singing helps people understand other people: song often captures the essence of various races, cultures, and nationalities.
- Singing develops the aesthetic response: an intrinsic valuing of art defines the high creative level to which humanity can aspire.

These and other reasons provide impetus for researchers and music teachers to continue in their venture of finding ways for teaching all children to sing. This is a worthy challenge to be met if the first of the National Standards is to be realized.

REFERENCES

Aaron, J. (1993). Using vocal coordination instruction to help the inaccurate singer. *Update: Applications of Research in Music Education, 11*(2), 8–13.

Adler, A. (1999). A survey of teacher practices in working with male singers before and during the voice change. *Canadian Journal of Research in Music Education, 40*(4), 29–33.

American Academy of Teachers of Singing. (2002). *Teaching children to sing: A statement by the American Academy of Teachers of Singing.* Available at www.americanacademyofteachersofsinging.org/assets/articles/Teaching Children.pdf.

Atterbury, B. W., & Silcox, L. (1993a). The effect of piano accompaniment on kindergartners' developmental singing ability. *Journal of Research in Music Education, 41*(1), 40–47.

Atterbury, B. W., & Silcox, L. (1993b). A comparison of home musical environment and musical aptitude in kindergarten students. *Update: Applications of Research in Music Education, 11*(2), 18–21.

Austin, J. R. (1990). The relationship of music self-esteem to degree of participation in school and out-of-school music activities among upper-elementary students. *Contributions to Music Education, 17,* 20–31.

Boardman, E. L. (1964). *An investigation of the effect of preschool training on the development of vocal accuracy in young children.* Unpublished doctoral dissertation, University of Illinois at Urbana-Champaign.

Butke, M. A. (2006). Reflection on practice: A study of five choral educators' reflective journals. *Update: Applications of Research in Music Education, 25*(1), 57–69.

Campbell, D., & Stanley, J. (1963). *Experimental and quasi-experimental designs for research.* Chicago: Rand McNally.

Chinn, B. J. (1997). Vocal self-identification, singing style, and singing range in relationship to a measure of cultural mistrust in African-American adolescent females. *Journal of Research in Music Education, 45*(4), 636–649.

Colwell, R. (1969). *Music achievement tests.* Chicago: Follett.

Colwell, R. (Ed.) (1992). *Handbook of research on music teaching and learning.* New York: Schirmer.

Consortium of National Arts Education Associations. (1994). Dance, music, theatre, visual arts: What every young American should know and be able to do in the arts. Reston, VA: Music Educators National Conference.

Cooksey, J. M., & Welch, G. F. (1998). Adolescence, singing development and national curricula design. *British Journal of Music Education, 15*(1), 99–119.

Cooper, N. A. (1995). Children's singing accuracy as a function of grade level, gender, and individual versus unison singing. *Journal of Research in Music Education, 43*(3), 222–231.

Daugherty, J. F. (1999). Spacing, formation, and choral sound: Preferences and perceptions of auditors and choristers. *Journal of Research in Music Education, 47*(3), 224–238.

Demorest, S. M. (1998). Sightsinging in the secondary choral ensemble: A review of the research. *Bulletin of the Council for Research in Music Education, 137,* 1–15.

Demorest, S. M. (2001a). Pitch-matching performance of junior high boys: A comparison of perception and production. *Bulletin of the Council for Research in Music Education, 151,* 63–70.

Demorest, S. M. (2001b). *Building choral excellence: Teaching sight-singing in the choral rehearsal.* New York: Oxford University Press.

Demorest, S. M., & Clements, A. (2007). Factors influencing the pitch-matching of junior high boys. *Journal of Research in Music Education, 55*(2), 115–128.

Dickey, M. R. (1992). A review of research on modeling in music teaching and learning. *Bulletin of the Council for Research in Music Education, 113,* 27–40.

Doneski, S. M. (2005). *The effects of wait time on the tonal pattern performance accuracy of second- and fourth-grade students.* Unpublished doctoral dissertation, University of Hartford, Hartford, CT.

Dunn, D. E. (1997). Effect of rehearsal hierarchy and reinforcement on attention, achievement, and attitude of selected choirs. *Journal of Research in Music Education, 45*(4), 547–567.

Ekholm, E. (2000). The effect of singing mode and seating arrangement on choral blend and overall choral sound. *Journal of Research in Music Education, 48*(2), 123–135.

Emge, S. W. (1998). The adolescent male: Vocal registers as affecting vocal range, register competence, and comfort in singing. *Center Review* (Northeastern State University, Tahlequah, OK), 7(1), 1–12.

Fett, D. L. (1993/1994). *The adolescent female voice: The effect of vocal skills instruction on measures of singing performance and breath management.* Unpublished doctoral dissertation, University of Iowa, Iowa City.

Floyd, E., & Bradley, K. D. (2006). Teaching strategies related to successful sight-singing in Kentucky choral ensembles. *Update: Applications of Research in Music Education, 25*(1), 70–81.

Forbes, G. W. (2001). The repertoire selection practices of high school choral directors. *Journal of Research in Music Education, 49*(2), 102–121.

Freer, P. K. (2003). *Rehearsal discourse of choral conductors: Meeting the needs of young adolescents.* Unpublished doctoral dissertation, Teachers College, Columbia University, New York.

Freer, P. K. (2006). Hearing the voices of adolescent boys in choral music: A self-story. *Research Studies in Music Education, 27*, 69–81.

Gault, B. (2002). Effects of pedagogical approach, presence/absence of text, and developmental music aptitude on the song performance accuracy of kindergarten and first-grade students. *Bulletin of the Council for Research in Music Education, 152*, 54–63.

Gehrkens, K. (1934). *Music in the grade school.* Boston: C. C. Birchard.

Goetze, M. (1985/1986). Factors affecting accuracy in children's singing. Unpublished doctoral dissertation, University of Colorado, Boulder.

Goetze, M., Cooper, N., & Brown, C. (1990). Recent research on singing in the general music classroom. *Bulletin of the Council for Research in Music Education, 104*, 16–37.

Gordon, E. E. (1979). *Primary measures of music audiation.* Chicago: G.I.A.

Gordon, E. E. (1982). *Intermediate measures of music audiation,* Chicago: G.I.A.

Gordon, E. E. (1987). *The nature, description, measurement and evaluation of music aptitude.* Chicago: G.I.A.

Gordon. E. E. (1989). *Learning sequences in music.* Chicago: G.I.A.

Grant, J. W., & Norris, C. (1998). Choral music education: A survey of research 1982–1995. *Bulletin of the Council for Research in Music Education, 135*, 21–59.

Green, G. (1990). The effects of vocal modeling on pitch-matching accuracy of elementary school children. *Journal of Research in Music Education, 38*(3), 225–231.

Green, G. (1994). Unison versus individual singing and elementary students' vocal pitch accuracy. *Journal of Research in Music Education, 42*(2), 105–114.

Grimland, F. (2005). Characteristics of teacher-directed modeling in high school choral rehearsals. *Update: Applications of Research in Music Education, 24*(1), 5–14.

Guerrini, S. (2006). The developing singer: Comparing the singing accuracy of elementary students on three selected vocal tasks. *Bulletin of the Council for Research in Music Education, 167*, 21–31.

Guilbault, D. (2004). The effect of harmonic accompaniment on the tonal achievement and tonal improvisations of children in kindergarten and first grade. *Journal of Research in Music Education, 52*(1), 64–76.

Hamann, K. L. (2007). Influence on the curriculum choices of middle school choir teachers. *Update: Applications of Research in Music Education, 26*(1), 64–74.

Hendley, J. A., & Persellin, D. C. (1996). How the lower adult male voice and the male falsetto voice affect children's vocal accuracy. *Update: Applications of Research in Music Education, 14*(2), 9–14.

Henry, J. E. (1995). *The effectiveness of Kenneth Phillips' strategies on the singing development of students in grade 5.* Unpublished master's thesis, Pennsylvania State University, College Park.

Henry, M. (2001). The development of a vocal sight-reading inventory. *Bulletin of the Council for Research in Music Education, 150*, 21–35

Henry, M. (2004). The use of targeted pitch skills for sight-singing instruction in the choral rehearsal. *Journal of Research in Music Education, 52*(3), 206–217.

Hornbach, C. M., & Taggart, C. C. (2005). The relationship between developmental tonal aptitude and singing achievement among kindergarten, first-, second-, and third-grade students. *Journal of Research in Music Education, 53*(4), 322–331.

Howard, D. M., & Welch, G. F. (2002). Female chorister voice development: A longitudinal study at Wells, UK. *Bulletin of the Council for Research in Music Education, 153/4*, 63–70.

Jones, M. (1993). An assessment of audiation skills of accurate and inaccurate singers in grades 1, 2, and 3. *Update: Applications of Research in Music Education, 11*(2), 14–17.

Kennedy, M. A. (2002). "It's cool because we like to sing": Junior high school boys' experience of choral music as an elective. *Research Studies in Music Education, 18*, 26–36.

Kennedy, M. C. (2004). "It's a metamorphosis": Guiding the voice change at the American Boychoir School. *Journal of Research in Music Education, 52*(3), 264–280.

Killian, J. (1993). A comparison of knowledge of children's songs among older adults. *Missouri Journal of Research in Music Education, 30*, 8–17.

Killian, J. (1996). Definitions of "knowing": Comparisons of verbal report versus performance of children's songs. *Journal of Research in Music Education, 44*(3), 215–228.

Killian, J. (1997). Perceptions of the voice-change process: Male adult versus adolescent musicians and nonmusicians. *Journal of Research in Music Education, 45*(4), 521–535.

Killian, J. (1999). A description of vocal maturation among fifth- and sixth-grade boys. *Journal of Research in Music Education, 47*(4), 357–369.

Killian, J. N., & Henry, M. L. (2005). A comparison of successful and unsuccessful strategies in individual sight-singing preparation and performance. *Journal of Research in Music Education, 53*(1), 51–65.

Klinger, R., Campbell, P., & Goolsby, T. (1998). Approaches to children's song acquisition: Immersion and phrase-by-phrase. *Journal of Research in Music Education, 46*(1), 24–34.

Kotora, Jr., E. J. (2005). Assessment practices in the choral music classroom: A survey of Ohio high school choral music teachers and college choral methods professors. *Contributions to Music Education, 32*(2), 65–80.

Kruse, N. B., Oare, S., & Norman, M. (2008). The influence of the National Standards on research trends in music education. *Bulletin of the Council for Research in Music Education, 176*, 51–61.

Kuehne, J. M. (2007). A survey of sight-singing instructional practices in Florida middle-school choral programs. *Journal of Research in Music Education, 55*(2), 115–128.

Levinowitz, L. M., Barnes, P., Guerrini, S., Clement, M., D'April, P., & Morey, M. J. (1998). Measuring singing voice development in the elementary general music classroom. *Journal of Research in Music Education, 46*(1), 35–47.

Marshall, H. D., III (2002). *Effects of song presentation method on pitch accuracy of third-grade children*. Unpublished doctoral dissertation, Temple University, Philadelphia.

Martin, B. A. (1991). The effects of hand signs, syllables, and letters on first graders' acquisition of tonal skills. *Journal of Research in Music Education, 39*(2), 161–170.

McGuire, K. M. (2000). Common songs of the cultural heritage of the United States: A compilation of songs that most people "know" and "should know." *Journal of Research in Music Education, 48*(4), 310–322.

Mizener, C. L. P. (1993). Attitudes of children toward singing and choir participation and assessed singing skill. *Journal of Research in Music Education, 41*(3), 233–245.

Moore, R. (1994). Effects of age, sex, and melodic/harmonic patterns on vocal pitch-matching skills of talented 8–11 year-olds. *Journal of Research in Music Education, 42*(1), 5–13.

Moore, R., Brotons, M., Fyk, J., & Castillo, A. (1997). Effects of culture, age, gender, and repeated trials on rote song learning skills of children 6–9 years old from England, Panama, Spain and the United States. *Bulletin of the Council for Research in Music Education, 133*, 83–88.

Moore, R., Fyk, J., Frega, A., & Brotons, M. (1995/1996). Influence of culture, age, gender, and two-tone melodies on interval matching skills of children from Argentina, Poland, Spain, and the U.S.A. *Bulletin of the Council for Research in Music Education, 127*, 127–135.

Moore, S., Chen, H., & Brotons, M. (2004). Pitch and interval accuracy in echo singing and xylophone playing by 8 and 10 year-old children from England, Spain, Taiwan, and U.S.A. *Bulletin of the Council for Research in Music Education, 161–62*, 173–180.

Mota, G. (1997). Detecting young children's musical aptitude: A comparison between standardized measures of music aptitude and ecologically valid musical performances. *Bulletin of the Council for Research in Music Education, 133*, 89–94.

NAEP 1997 arts report card: Eighth-grade findings from the national assessment of educational progress (1998), Chapter 2, Music, 1–36. Washington, DC: Author. Retrieved May 1, 2008, from www.nationsreportcard.gov/arts_2008/

Norris, C. E. (2004). A nationwide overview of sight-singing requirements of large-group choral festivals. *Journal of Research in Music Education, 52*(1), 16–28.

Norris, C. E. & Borst, J. D. (2007). An examination of the reliabilities of two choral festival adjudication forms. *Journal of Research in Music Education, 55*(3), 237–251.

Olsen, E. K. B. (2003). *Affirming parallel concepts among reading, mathematics, and music through Kodály instruction*. Unpublished doctoral dissertation, University of Iowa, Iowa City.

Persellin, D. C. (2006). The effects of vocal modeling, musical aptitude, and home environment on pitch accuracy of young children. *Bulletin of the Council for Research in Music Education, 169*, 39–50.

Phillips, K. H. (1985). The effects of group breath control training on selected vocal measures related to the singing ability of elementary students. *Journal of Research in Music Education, 33*(3), 179–191.

Phillips, K. H. (1992a). Research on the teaching of singing. In R. Colwell (Ed.), *Handbook of research on music teaching and learning* (pp. 568–576). New York: Schirmer.

Phillips, K. H. (1992b). *Teaching kids to sing.* New York: Schirmer.

Phillips, K. H. (2007). *Why sing?* Unpublished manuscript, Gordon College, Wenham, MA.

Phillips, K. H., & Aitchison, R. E. (1997a). The relationship of inaccurate singing to pitch discrimination and tonal aptitude among third-grade students. *Contributions to Music Education, 24*(1), 7–22.

Phillips, K. H., & Aitchison, R. E. (1997b). Effects of psychomotor instruction on elementary general music students' singing performance. *Journal of Research in Music Education, 45*(2), 185–196.

Phillips, K. H., & Aitchison, R. E. (1998). The effects of psychomotor skills instruction on attitude towards singing and general music among students in grades 4–6. *Bulletin of the Council for Research in Music Education, 137*, 32–42.

Phillips, K. H., & Aitchison, R. E. (1999). Second-year results of a longitudinal study of the relationship of singing instruction, pitch accuracy, and gender to aural acuity, vocal achievement, musical knowledge, and attitude towards singing among general music students. *Contributions to Music Education, 26*(1), 67–85.

Phillips, K. H., Aitchison, R. E., Bergman, J. F., & Western, B. A. (1999). First-year results of a study relating singing instruction, pitch accuracy, and gender to aural acuity and vocal achievement among general music students. *Research Perspectives in Music Education, 1*, 32–37.

Phillips, K. H., Aitchison, R. E., & Nompula, Y. P. (2002). The relationship of music aptitude to singing achievement among fifth-grade students. *Contributions to Music Education, 29*(1), 47–58.

Phillips, K. H. & Emge, S. (1994). Vocal registration as it affects vocal range for seventh- and eighth-grade boys. *Journal of Research in Singing and Applied Vocal Pedagogy, 18*(1), 1–19.

Phillips, K. H., & Fett, D. L. (1992). Breathing and its relationship to vocal quality among adolescent female singers. *Journal of Research in Singing and Applied Vocal Pedagogy, 15*(2), 1–12.

Phillips, S. L. (2003/2004). *Contributing factors to music attitude in sixth-, seventh-, and eighth-grade students.* Unpublished doctoral dissertation, University of Iowa, Iowa City.

Price, H. E., Yarbrough, C., Jones, M., & Moore, R. S. (1994). Effects of male timbre, falsetto, and sine-wave models on interval matching by inaccurate singers. *Journal of Research in Music Education, 42*(4), 269–284.

Prickett, C., & Bridges, M. (1998). Familiarity with basic song repertoire: Music education/therapy majors versus elementary education majors. *Journal of Research in Music Education, 46*(4), 461–468.

Rao, D. (1990). *Choral music for children: An annotated list.* Reston, VA: MENC.

Reames, R. R. (2001). High school choral directors' description of appropriate literature of beginning high school choirs. *Journal of Research in Music Education, 49*(2), 122–135.

Ross, W. E. (1948). *Sing high, sing low.* Bloomington: Indiana University Press.

Rutkowski, J. (1990). The measurement and evaluation of children's singing voice development. *The Quarterly: Center for Research in Music Learning and Teaching, 1*(1–2), 81–95.

Rutkowski, J. (1996). The effectiveness of individual/small group singing activities on kindergartners' use of singing voice and developmental music aptitude. *Journal of Research in Music Education, 44*(4), 353–368.

Rutkowski, J., & Chen-Haftek, L. (2001). The singing voice within every child: A cross- cultural comparison of first graders use of singing voice. *Early Childhood Connections: Journal of Music- and Movement-Based Learning, 7*(1), 37–42.

Rutkowski, J., & Miller, M. S. (2003a). A longitudinal study of elementary children's acquisition of their singing voices. *Update: Applications of Research in Music Education, 22*(1), 5–14.

Rutkowski, J., & Miller, M. S. (2003b). The effectiveness of instruction and individual/small group singing activities on first graders' use of singing voice and developmental music aptitude. *Contributions to Music Education, 30*(1), 23–28.

Rutkowski, J., & Miller, M. S. (2003c). The effects of teacher feedback and modeling on first graders' use of singing voice and developmental music aptitude. *Bulletin of the Council for Research in Music Education, 156*, 1–10.

Schmidt, C. P. (1995). Attributions of success, grade level, and gender as factors in choral students' perceptions of teacher feedback. *Journal of Research in Music Education, 43*(4), 313–329.

Schmitt, M. (1979). *Development and validation of a measure of self-esteem of musical ability.* Unpublished doctoral dissertation, University of Illinois at Urbana-Champaign.

Sherburn-Bly, R. (2007). Straight tone in the choral arts: A simple solution. *Choral Journal, 47*(8), 61–69.

Shuler, S. C. (1991). The effects of Gordon's learning sequence activities on vocal performance achievement of primary music students. *The Quarterly: Center for Research in Music Learning and Teaching, 2*(1–2), 118–129.

Siebenaler, D. (2008). Children's attitudes toward singing and song recordings related to gender, ethnicity, and age. *Update: Applications of Research in Music Education, 27*(1), 49–56.

Skadsem, J. A. (1997). Effect of conductor verbalization, dynamic markings, conductor gesture, and choir dynamic level on singers' dynamic responses. *Journal of Research in Music Education, 45*(1), 509–520.

Snow, S. L. (1998). *Rehearsing the choral context: A qualitative examination of undergraduate conductor/teacher planning processes and relationship to emergent pedagogical knowledge evidenced in teaching.* Unpublished doctoral dissertation, Michigan State University, East Lansing.

Stadler Elmer, S. (1997). Approaching the song acquisition process. *Bulletin of the Council for Research in Music Education, 133*, 129–135.

Stamer, R. A. (2004). Choral student perceptions of the music contest experience. *Update: Applications of Research in Music Education, 22*(2), 5–12.

Stamer, R. A. (2006). Changes in choral student perceptions of the music contest experience. *Update: Applications of Research in Music Education, 25*(1), 46–56.

Stegman, S. F. (1996). *An investigation of secondary choral music student teachers' perceptions of instructional successes and problems as they reflect on their music teaching.* Unpublished doctoral dissertation, University of Michigan, Ann Arbor.

Stevens, Jr., H. M. (2001). *A teacher/action research study of student reflective thinking in the choral rehearsal.* Unpublished doctoral dissertation, University of Texas, Austin.

Updegraff, R., Heiliger, L., & Learned, J. (1938). Effect of training upon the singing ability and musical interest of three, four, and five-year-old children. *University of Iowa Studies in Child Welfare, 14,* 83–131.

Welch, G. (1994). The assessment of singing. *Psychology of Music, 22,* 3–19.

Welch, G. (1996). A review of a perceptual study of vocal registers in the singing voice of children by Pamela Sewell Wurgler. *Bulletin of the Council for Research in Music Education, 129,* 77–82.

Welch, G., Sergeant, D., & White, P. (1995/1996). The singing competencies of five- year-old developing singers. *Bulletin of the Council for Research in Music Education, 127,* 155–162.

Welch, G., Sergeant, D., & White, P. (1997). Age, sex and vocal task as factors in singing "in tune" during the first years of schooling. *Bulletin of the Council for Research in Music Education, 133,* 153–160.

Williams, B. (1990). *An investigation of selected female singing- and speaking-voice characteristics through a comparison of a group of pre-menarcheal girls to a group of post-menarcheal girls.* Unpublished doctoral dissertation, University of North Texas, Denton.

Williams, T. S. (1994). The effect of gender model on the pitch-matching accuracy of high school choral students. *Contributions to Music Education, 21,* 39–45.

Wing, H. (1957). *Wing standardized test of music intelligence* (rev. ed.). Windsor, England: NFER.

Wolf, D. (2005). A hierarchy of tonal performance patterns for children ages five to eight years in kindergarten and primary grades. *Bulletin of the Council for Research in Music Education, 163,* 61–68.

Wurgler, P. S. (1990). *A perceptual study of the vocal registers in the singing of children.* Unpublished doctoral dissertation, Ohio State University, Columbus.

Yarbrough, C., Bowers, J., & Benson, W. (1992). The effects of vibrato on the pitch- matching accuracy of certain and uncertain singers. *Journal of Research in Music Education, 40*(1), 30–38.

Yarbrough, C., Green, G., Benson, W., & Bowers, J. (1991). Inaccurate singers: An exploratory study of variables affecting pitch-matching. *Bulletin of the Council for Research in Music Education, 107,* 23–34.

Yarbrough, C., & Henley, P. (1999). The effect of observation focus on evaluations of choral rehearsal excerpts. *Journal of Research in Music Education, 47*(4), 308–318.

Yarbrough, C., & Madsen, K. (1998). The evaluation of teaching in choral rehearsals. *Journal of Research in Music Education, 46*(4), 469–481.

Yarbrough, C., Morrison, S., Karrick, B., & Dunn, D. (1995). The effect of male falsetto on the pitch-matching accuracy of uncertain boy singers, grades, K-8. *Update: Applications of Research in Music Education, 14*(1), 4–10.

Yarbrough, C., Orman, E. K., & Neill, S. (2007). Time usage by choral directors prior to sight-singing adjudication. *Update: Applications of Research in Music Education, 25*(2), 27–34.

Youngson, S. C., & Persellin, D. C. (2001). The effect of Curwen hand signs on vocal accuracy of young children. *Kodály Envoy, 27*(2), 9–12.

Music Learning in Special Education

6

Focus on Autism and Developmental Disabilities

ELISE S. SOBOL

Under the rigorous demands of our federal legislation, what should music practitioners and researchers know to optimize their understanding of and work with our most profoundly challenged students? In particular, what evidence do we have to show that music education can help our students with autism and developmental disabilities make adequate yearly progress? This chapter explores these questions from different angles of published research.

I begin with a review of the designated categories in special education in order to place autism and developmental disabilities in context. A section follows that defines autism according to our current practices in special education. A review of some of the most compelling evidence is presented about music learning for students with autism and developmental disabilities, together with some references to writings of importance to practitioners. The chapter then ends with a brief summary, some implications for practice, and a few suggestions for new directions in research.

Designating Categories in Special Education

Our 21st-century school populations include children from diverse backgrounds and cultures. Students who have disabilities may also include English-language learners and socioeconomically disadvantaged students if they require supportive services to succeed in school. The term *exceptional* is used concurrently with *special learners* to define those children whose school performance shows significant discrepancy between ability and achievement and as a result require special instruction, assistance, and/or equipment (MENC, 2004, p. 1; Mixon, 2007, p. 55; Sobol, 2001, p. 8). The term *twice-exceptional* generally refers to those students who are gifted and talented and have physical disabilities, sensory disabilities, emotional and/or behavioral disorders, attention-deficit hyperactivity disorders, or learning disabilities (National Education Association [NEA], 2006, p. 6).

One useful source of definition for designated categories of students requiring special education services is the New York Department of Education's Vocational and Educational Services for Individuals with Disabilities (VESID) documentation, Section 200.1 (part zz),[1] which includes the following: (1) autism, (2) deafness, (3) deaf-blindness, (4) emotional disturbance, (5) hearing impairment, (6) learning disability, (7) mental retardation, (8) multiple disabilities, (9) orthopedic impairment, (10) other health impairment (which includes attention-deficit disorder and attention-deficit hyperactivity disorder), (11) speech or language impairment, (12) traumatic brain injury, and (13) visual impairment including blindness. The U.S. Department of Education posts information about the complete regulations in the Individuals with Disabilities Education Act (IDEA) and its updates.[2]

Since each student is an individual with unique needs, our national and state governments work together to improve ways to identify, redefine, and reach the needs of our special students. Especially when working with a student with autism and/or developmental disabilities, it is important to keep in mind that a disability does *not* affect a student's ability to participate in or make music. A designating category with a specific Individualized Education Program (IEP) is helpful to the music in special education teacher to understand the educational interventions that facilitate learning for students to their best potential (Dark, Graham, Hughes, McCoy, and McKinney, 1996, p. 3). The research summarized in this chapter is focused on autism and related developmental disabilities and may help practitioners and researchers collaborate to recommend use of successful musical interventions to support more effective IEPs for learning in our public school settings.

Autism and Developmental Disabilities

Definition

Historically, it was Leo Kanner in 1943 who first elaborated on what is now known as the syndrome of childhood autism (Volkmar and Klin, 2005, p. 6). Since 1975 and the passage of the Education for all Handicapped Children Act, Public Law 94–142 (renamed the Individuals with Disabilities Education Act (IDEA) in 1989–1990), there has been a steady progression of support for education of every child, including children with autism and developmental disabilities. Through these past 35 years, the scientific, medical, and educational communities have developed a working consensus for the definition of autism and its related disorders. Although this definition will continue to be refined, *The Diagnostic and Statistical Manual of Mental Disorders* (4th ed.) (DSM-IV™), published by the American Psychiatric Association (1994), identifies autism as a pervasive developmental disorder with the following conditions:

> The essential features of Autistic Disorder are the presence of markedly abnormal or impaired development in social interaction and communication and a markedly restricted repertoire of activity and interests. Manifestations of the disorder vary greatly depending on the developmental level and chronological age of the individual. Autistic Disorder is sometimes referred to as *early infantile autism, childhood autism*, or *Kanner's autism*. The impairment in reciprocal social interaction is gross and sustained. There may be marked impairment in the use of multiple nonverbal behaviors (e.g., eye-to-eye gaze, facial expression, body postures and gestures) to regulate social interaction and communication. There may be failure to develop peer relationships appropriate to developmental level that may take different forms at different ages. Younger individuals may have little or no interest in establishing friendships. Older individuals may have an interest in friendship but lack understanding of the convention of social interaction. There may be a lack of spontaneous seeking to share enjoyment, interests, or achievements with other people (e.g. not showing, bringing, or pointing out objects they find interesting). Lack of social or emotional reciprocity may be present (e.g. not actively participating in simple social play or games, preferring solitary activities, or involving others in activities only as tools or "mechanical" aids). Often an individual's awareness of others is markedly impaired. Individuals with this disorder may be oblivious to other children (including siblings), may have no concept of the needs of others, or may not notice another person's distress. (American Psychiatric Association, p. 66)

Both verbal and nonverbal skills are affected in this disorder. An example of this is the lack of or delay in development of spoken language. If an individual is able to speak, prosody (abnormalities of pitch, intonation, rate, rhythm, or stress) is effected. Subleties in language are not understood, and imitation—so natural in typical development—needs to be specifically taught by the caregiver with words such as "you do." Other conditions may include stereotyped patterns of behavior, interests, activities, nonfunctional routines, or rituals.

> Individuals with Autistic Disorder display a markedly restricted range of interests and are often preoccupied with one narrow interest (e.g. with amassing facts about meteorology or baseball statistics). They may line up an exact number of play things in the same manner over and over again or repetitively mimic the actions of a television actor. They may insist on sameness and show resistance to or distress over trivial changes.... Stereotyped body movements include the hands (clapping, finger flicking) or whole body (rocking, dipping, and swaying). Abnormalities of posture (e.g., walking on tiptoe, odd hand movements and body postures) may be present. Individuals show a persistent

preoccupation with parts of objects (buttons, body parts). There may also be a fascination with movements (e.g., the spinning wheels of toys, the opening and closing of doors, an electric fan or other rapidly revolving object.) The person may be highly attached to some inanimate objct (e.g. a piece of string or a rubber band). (American Psychiatric Association, 1994, p. 67)

Autism presents itself in one or more of the abnormal functioning areas (social interaction, communication, symbolic or imaginative play) before the age of 3 years. Associated pervasive developmental disorders include Rett's Disorder, Childhood Disintegrative Disorder, Asperger's Disorder, and Pervasive Developmental Disorder Not Otherwise Specified (PDD-NOS). Autism occurs approximately four times more in males than females. Rett's Disorder differs from Autistic Disorder in that it is found only in females. DSM-IV diagnostic criteria include normal prenatal development and then an appearance between 5 and 48 months of deceleration of head growth, loss of purposeful hand skills with then a subsequent development of stereotyped hand movements (e.g., hand washing or hand-wringing), loss of social engagement, appearance of poorly coordinated gait or trunk movement, and severely impaired expressive and receptive language development with severe psychomotor retardation (American Psychiatric Association 1994, pp. 72–73). Childhood Disintegrative Disorder appears with a developmental regression following 2 years of normal development in both sexes. Other diagnostic features include significant loss of acquired skills in expressive or receptive language, social skills or adaptive behavior, bowel or bladder control, play, and motor skills (American Psychiatric Association, 1994, p. 75.)

Individuals with Asperger's Disorder clinically do not have delay in language or cognitive development. DSM-IV diagnostic criteria for Asperger's Disorder include qualitative impairment in social interaction in at least two of the following: (1) marked impairment in multiple nonverbal behaviors; (2) failure to develop peer relationships appropriate to developmental age; (3) lack of spontaneous seeking to share enjoyment, interests, or achievements with other people; and (4) lack of social or emotional reciprocity (American Psychiatric Association, p. 77).

For autism and its related pervasive developmental disorders, symptoms can range from mild to profound and are experienced throughout an individual's life span. Autism is a spectrum disorder and is often referred to in special education circles as ASD.

Background

Based on prevalence statistics from the Centers for Disease Control and Prevention in 2009, the Autism Society of America (www.autism-society.org/site/PageServer) notes that autism (1) affects 1 in every 1,100 births, (2) occurs in 1.5 million Americans, and (3) is the fastest growing developmental disability. Prior to the Individuals with Disabilities Education Act, approximately 90 percent of children with developmental disabilities were housed in state institutions.[3] Fortunately, due to our educational progress and legal mandates, this situation is no longer the case.

Autism was added as a special education exceptionality in 1991. Since then, students with autism and developmental disabilities are entering all of our school settings. As a result, music teachers are seeing a complex of different behaviors in their inclusion classrooms and performance programs. Characteristic behaviors may include tantrums, excessive ritualistic and stereotyped mannerisms, poor motivation to achieve, and lack of appropriate focus in attention (Lovaas, 1981, p. 29). To a greater or lesser degree, common behaviors of students with autism and developmental disabilities include (1) visual (gazing at lights, fixating on rotating objects, flapping fingers in front of eyes), (2) auditory (vocalizes, hums, clicks tongue, taps furniture), (3) tactile (stroking own body parts, placing fingers in mouth or ears, self-injurious actions such as pinching), (4) vestibular (rocking, bouncing, spinning one's body), and (5) proprioceptive stimulation (child's body assuming various strange positions, toe walking, tilting head to one side) (Lovaas, 1981, p.106). With early intervention and diagnosis, students with autism can experience developmental gain with music learning.

Research

The Theory of Cognitive Modifiability

After studying in Switzerland with Piaget, the Israeli cognitive psychologist Reuven Feuerstein developed his theory that intelligence is dynamic and modifiable, not static or fixed.[4] This made a huge impact when it came to believing in the learning potential of those with low intellectual functioning and developmental levels. The practice of the "Theory of Structural Cognitive Modifiability" (SCM) (Feuerstein and Rand, 1997) is proving to be most beneficial to our music students with moderate to severe autism and developmental disabilities. The principles and teaching methods of "Mediated Learning Experience" (MLE), "Instrumental Enrichment" (IE), and "Learning Potential Assessment Device" are the components of implementation of the "Theory of Cognitive Modifiability" (Feuerstein, Falik, Feuerstein, and Rand, 2002). Powered by the work from the Center for Enhancement of Learning Potential, MLE is seen as a tool for active learning across the globe and has potential to significantly impact our music education and the reversal of underachievement in our urban schools.

Portowitz and Klein (2007) published a two-year study based on Feuerstein's cognitive modifiability. The work was conducted by the research staff at Bar Illan University. The study involved eight children, six with Down Syndrome and two with severe learning deficits, and included a control group. The study evaluated the hypothesis that music learning cultivates cognitive functions that can then be transferred to build skills in other areas, such as language, reading, and writing for students at risk. Outcome expectations were that (1) children in the music group would do significantly better on cognitve function tests than children in the control group, (2) children in the music group would show significantly more improvement in their social behavior than children in the control group, (3) musical understanding of the children in the music group would be significantly improved, (4) children in the music group would significantly improve in their ability to transfer skills acquired during their music lessons to other areas of learning, and (5) children in the music groups would progress more in their school achievement than children in the control group. The study was distinctive because it was designed to promote thinking processes through the study of music by five specific criteria used in mediated learning: focusing, expanding, mediating, rewarding, and mediating self-regulation. Each criterion found a correlating application for music learning: listening to music, encouraging imaginative and associative thinking, expressing enthusiasm for musical material engaging student interest, encouraging the performance and creation of musical patterns, building feelings of competence, and offering excellent opportunities for mediating self-regulation (Portowitz and Klein, 2007, pp. 261–262). Observations of students took place during the weekly one-hour music lesson. In addition to the mediated learning environments set up during the lesson and the correlated music applications, specific learning skills as defined within the 1992 Theory of Structural Cognitive Modification were chosen to be advanced during the music lessons: (1) musical differentiation between pitch, rhythm, dynamics, expression; (2) recognizing patterns like musical theme to enhance perceptual stability; (3) understanding large-scale musical structure by dots and figures to demonstrate parts that make up a whole; (4) precision and accuracy for quality performance; (5) promoting self-regulation for teaching thoughtful action through numerous musical activities alone and in a group; and (6) the ability to engage in multiple representations for learning alternate modalities of communication, such as singing, playing, or improvisation (p. 266).

The results of the two-year music study were reported as follows: "Significant progress was observed in the development of the targeted cognitive functions" and "studies of mediated musical environments could provide important insights into the learning potential of other groups of children with special needs" (Portowitz and Klein, 2007, p. 268).

Portowitz, Lichtenstein, Egorov, and Brand (December, 2009), explored the possible links between cognitive structures, music education, and self-efficacy among high-risk elementary school children The study involved 81 boys and girls, age 7 to 9 years. Again, Feuerstein's Theory of Cognitive Modifiability was used in mediated learning environments (MLEs) to identify three cognitive functions for music-learning activties. The findings suggest that music, used within the mediated learning environment (MLE), does promote cognitive development which can be applied across the curriculum. This study may be helpful in designing similar action-research projects for special educators who work with students with autism and developmental disabilities. The study gives strength to generalizing knowledge from specific music applications to functional and adaptive daily living.

A classroom-tested action plan using mediated learning experiences to enhance literacy, ear training, and classroom behavior for 176 students with developmental and severe learning disabilities is described by Sobol (2001, pp. 66–80; 2008, pp. 54–72). This project took place in a center-based special education facility with student populations from 56 public school districts of varying socioeconomic and cultural backgrounds. Mediated learning techniques (intentionality, meaning, transcendence, competence, sharing, individuation, goal-setting, and challenge) were closely aligned with the four New York state standards for the arts and assessment for students with severe learning disabilities in a six-week sequential lesson structure. The students benefited from mediation on multiple levels. As a result of the approach used and the weekly lesson assessment scales (3-point scale rating with 3 = frequently, 2 = evident, and 1 = developing), all 176 students were seen to improve their individualized cognitive responses with consistent behaviorial improvements. Due to the preparation, the students were able to sustain attention to the material during the culminating school assembly performance, the goal for the action plan. The positive outcomes of using MLE in the special education classroom should stimulate interest for a similar project with inclusion groups in a public school setting, adding a control group to the design.

As a tool for preliteracy competency, Feuerstein's Theory of Structured Modifiability is seen at work in a study by Carmon, Wohl, and Even-Zohar (2008). This research study involved an equal number of 150 5-year-old girls and boys who participated in an educational program titled "Toy Musical Notes" (TMN). The children were of low socioeconomic status and had, in some cases, developmental delays and compromised learning challenges. With the early intervention of TMN, the researchers investigated their process to help prepare these special children for reading readiness. TMN served as a first language that invited children to read and play with only eight signs. The research study used three groups: a TMN intervention group (four kindergarten classes), a conventional music intervention group (three kindergarten classes), and a nonmusical intervention control group (three kindergarten classes) that involved spatial gymnastics and animal care. Pretests and posttests were given to preschoolers in the intervention year, and three follow-up observations were carried out to compare actual reading performance at the beginning, middle, and end of the first grade. The study showed the use of music in the development of prereading skills. The researchers reasoned that music could aid in the cognitive process of text processing and that TMN could help children absorb the complex cognitive processes of reading text. The results of the TMN program confirmed the research assumptions. The five rigorous tests designed to assess reading readiness, reading ability, and cognitive development showed that:

Regarding reading variables, the TMN group achieved the best scores. The conventional music group's results were generally higher than those of the non-music group. Participation in the experimental groups was found to be the best variable for predicting the level of reading in the first grade. (Carmon et al., 2008, p. 92)

These researchers have created important models for music learning. Their work is showing that cognitive modifiability can be used to structure learning experiences for our most vulnerable students. While having our students experience the joy of music learning, educators can find a key to reaching higher levels of functional independence for our students with autism and developmental disabilities through these successful music-learning experiences.

Other Approaches in Special Education Classroooms

The theory of structured modifiability and its instruments of mediated learning experiences are yet to be in widespread use in special education. Special education classroom teachers use a variety of methods to faciliate communication, behavior management, and sensory integration. Based on analysis of data collected, special educators use a mix of different approaches that will optimize the learning potential for each individual student. The third edition of the *Handbook of Autism and Pervasive Developmental Disorders* (Volkmar, Paul, Klin, and Cohen, 2005), in two comprehensive volumes, testifies to the exhaustive research and advances in knowledge that have been made for our children and adults since 1997.

There are numerous methods that are used to enhance early language in children with autism disorders. The intervention methods fall into three different approaches. The first is didactic and is based on behaviorist theories, including massed trials, conditioning, shaping, prompting, and chaining. Reinforcement is used to increase frequency for target behaviors. The approach is based on verbal behavior theory, where all aspects of language are defined as behavior. The sessions are teacher directed and involve repetitive drills and precise antecedent and consequence sequences. Reinforcer tokens, tangible or edible, are used. The second approach is called naturalistic, and it uses intrinsic rather than extrinsic reinforcers. The third approach is called developmental or pragmatic. This approach uses multiple aspects of communication, such as a gaze or a gesture or a vocalization, to encourage communication as a precursor to speech production. More Than Words (Paul and Sutherland, 2005, p. 958) is a pragmatic approach that uses music to support attention to language by embedding simple language in short, slowly produced song formats, with heavy stress placed on important words.

Applied Behavior Analysis   At the special education setting where I teach, Applied Behavior Analysis (ABA) is the technique of choice, combined with all three approaches, for educating our students with moderate to severe autism and developmental disabilities, age 8 to 21. ABA has been used for more than 30 years as a successful intervention for children with autism (Anderson and Romanczyk, 1999). The term *applied behavior analysis* refers to the basic theories of behavior as developed by Skinner (1938) and others, and it is a method of instruction used in conjunction with Strategies for Teaching based on Autism Research (STAR) (Arick, Krug, Fullerton, Loos, and Falco, 2005, p. 1005). ABA is a powerful and successful intervention for curriculum development. Music, which is performed in real time, is compatible with the step-by-step principles of task analysis, completion, and reinforcement found in ABA interventions.

School-Based Programs   Along with Applied Behavior Analysis, other school-based programs used successfully are "Prompts for Restructuring Oral Muscular Phonetic Targets" (PROMPTS) (Paul and Sutherland, 2005, pp. 951–953), "The Social Communication Emotional Regulation Transactional Support" (SCERTS) (Marans, Rubin, and Laurent, 2005, pp. 988–989), and "Treatment and Education of Autistic and Related Communication Handicapped Children" (TEACCH) (Harris, Handleman, and Jennett, 2005, pp. 1049–1050). With familiarization, music educators can adapt strengths from each program to use in the music classroom. We can learn from the progress of evidence-based interventions in music therapy reported here.

Issues of Socialization and Attention

It should be pointed out that every student who has autism and/or developmental disabilities as a primary diagnosis may also have secondary disabilities that could include impairments in the 12 other designating categories in special education noted earlier. With this in mind, practitioners can look to positive findings in various clinical trials to develop new applications in their classrooms. For example, to increase the independence of a 3-year-old boy with autism, a study by Kern, Wakeford, and Aldridge (2007) demonstrated the use of embedded song intervention as a structural prompt to help him learn self-care tasks, such as hand washing and toileting. The teacher presented the tasks both verbally and musically. The results of the study showed both means as effective in increasing the boy's independence, with task-specific differences noted. As a means for social interaction, empowerment, and sense of accomplishment within and outside the school community, music can become a language that helps to develop communication. Playing an instrument in group activities builds self-esteem and social interaction between age-level peers. Shore (2002) described case studies and strategies he formulated with several unique children on the autism spectrum, including a child with Asperger's Syndrome, which is on the high end of the spectrum. One case was a young boy who was diagnosed with Pervasive Developmental Disorder–Not Otherwise Specified (PDD-NOS). For the first three music sessions, there was little musical exchange between teacher and student. On the next session, Shore designed both an activity board, which described the steps necessary to play the drum, and a time board, which identified "1,"

"2," "3," and "all done." With these materials, the child understood what was expected of him and henceforth had rewarding music sessions. The second case was a 12-year-old with Asperger's Syndrome. His mother was a professional musician who wanted him to learn to read music. Traditional methods of teaching notes on the staff did not work for him. A kinesthetic approach did, and the sessions not only evolved to having him read and play notated music but also increased his abilities to communicate and use fine-motor coordination. The third case involved a person who used facilitative communication. Only when the teacher physically held his arm to play the keyboard did he sing songs he had heard as a child.

In addition, three case examples (Register and Humpal, 2007) illustrated the efficacy of music in facilitating transition in early childhood settings. An inclusion toddler class in a public suburban preschool, a Title I kindergarten class, and an early-intervention prekindergarten program were studied. After data were collected and studied in all three settings, the data showed that music helped the children cope with the challenges of transition from one activity to the next.

Understanding that students with autism may have the additional challenge of attention-deficit hyperactivity disorder (ADHD), research about motor impulsivity, as well as emotional, learning, and behavioral difficulties, is quite relevant to music in special education classrooms. A study (Rickson, 2006) of 13 adolescent boys, age 11 to 16, and a control group was undertaken at the Wellington, New Zealand, School of Music to compare the impact of instructional and improvisational music therapy approaches on the the level of motor impulsivity. All participants had a formal DSM-IV diagnosis of Attention-Deficit Hyperactivity Disorder and were being treated with stimulant medication, which continued throughout the study. None of the participants had previously been involved in a music therapy program. Four were Maori, and the rest of the participants were New Zealand European. All students had learning difficulties with mild intellectual disability, and "many had comorbid diagnoses including Oppositional Disorders, Obsessive-Compulsive Disorder, Post-Traumatic Stress Disorder, Mood Disorder, Fetal Alcohol Syndrome, and Intermittent Explosive Disorder" (p. 43). Impulsivity was measured by the Synchronised Tapping Task (STT) and the parent and teacher versions of Conners' Rating Scales Restless-Impulsive (R-I) and Hyperactive-Impulsive (H-I). In the instructional and improvisational models, improvements were noted in both treatment groups' abilities to listen, to attend, and to engage in group activities. It was the music-making opportunities that made the difference to these youngsters. "It was evident that during music-making the students were able to sustain higher levels of attention, concentration and self control than they could maintain between activities" (p. 58). It appeared that specific musical interventions described in the study could reduce a range of ADHD symptoms in the classroom. Studies on a larger scale could prove even more revealing.

In a study by Montello and Coons (1998), active rhythm-based music therapy was compared with passive listening-based group music therapy with preadolescents who had emotional, learning, and behavioral disabilities. The preadolescents were rated by homeroom teachers in attention, motivation, and hostility. Two groups participated in active group therapy, and two groups participated in passive group therapy. The results indicated that subjects improved signifiantly in both music therapy interventions, and the most significant change was on the aggression/hos tility scale.

To an inexperienced teacher of students with autism, it may appear that the students sometimes are not cognizant of what we are doing in the music classroom. Their very nature seems distant and detached. However, landmark medical studies (Evans and Richardson, 1988; Levinson, 1965) of patients under anesthesia have helped us understand that our students indeed are consciously present for our learning activities and that they take in much more than it appears. Significant additional evidence on attention improvement can be found in using music in coronary care practice (Bonney, 1983.)

Music can also be seen as effective for physiological and psychological change, quieting anxious classroom behaviors (Harvey, 2004). To help with focus and attention, classroom design has been shown to improve education results for students with autism by Coventry University's Design Ergonomics Applied Research Group in the United Kingdom (www.coventry.ac.uk/researchnet/SiteCollectionDocuments/Innovate1.pdf). This design has already been implemented with more than a hundred students in public school classrooms.

Work on Literacy and Language Acquisition

Music brings many benefits to students within the autism spectrum, including learning fundamental academic skills while enhancing skills in literacy and language acquisition. Visual prompts and the use of picture books in general music class encourages and contributes to an integrative arts experience (exploring vocal sounds, practicing rhythms, learning musical concepts, play, and dance) with students within the autism spectrum (Hagedorn, 2004). Research-based reports for enhancing language acquisition and literacy skills in students with direct applications to autism and developmental disabilities include work by Braithwaite and Sigafoos (1998); Brownell (2002); Buday (1995); Chen-Hafteck (1997); Hoskins (1988); Jellison (1984); Kern, Wakeford, and Aldridge (2007); Krauss and Galloway (1982); Ma, Nagler, Lee, and Cabrera (2001); Madsen (1991); Rogow (1982); Standley and Hughes (1997); Wallace (1994); Whipple (2004); and Wolfe and Horn (1993).

Correlating with practice in the special education music classroom, the study by Schon, Boyer, Moreno, Besson, Peretz, and Kolinsky (2008) confirmed that language learning was greatly facilitated when sung in song sequences. Facilitation was due to three components present in music learning: (1) the emotional component of the music appears to increase attention, (2) pitch contours help phonological discrimination, and (3) consistent mapping of musical and linguisitic structure may optimize learning (p. 976). The 23 adult participants in the study made significant strides when the emotional and strict repetitive structural properties of music were present, as compared with when only speech sequences were used. The researchers felt that their work would support evidence for language acquisition for use of lullabies and children's songs in language learning. "Learning a new language, especially in the first learning phase wherein one needs to segment new words, may largely benefit of the motivational and structuring properties of music in song" (Schon et al., 2008, p. 975). This is particularly heartening to educators whose students are nonverbal or have developmental language delays. Further, O'Herron and Siebenaler (2007) confirmed through their reported research of Register (2001) and Standley and Hughes (1997) that explicity taught instruction designed to enhance prereading and writing skills of 4- to 5-year-olds effectively increased their reading ability and that developmentally appropriate music materials would enrich this process.

Preschool intervention programs bring opportunities for early music experiences. Colwell and Murlless (2002) developed an interesting pilot study with five children, using singing and chanting as a vehicle for reading accuracy with learning disabilities. In this six-week pilot study, participants' reading accuracy improved each week, as well as their on-task behaviors, during the music conditions. Although there was little significant difference shown between the results of singing and chanting, it was the music participation that assisted the participants to attend longer to learning their vocabulary words. "In the music environment, children participate in multisensory learning that includes seeing, hearing, speaking (singing) and doing. During the music conditions, students actually focused on twice as many words and signs as they normally did during their small group reading sessions" (p. 13). Other important work with preschool children includes Custodero (2006); Gromko and Poorman (1998); Hamann, Lineburg, and Paul (1998); Jackson (2003); Kern, Wakeford, and Aldridge (2007); and Nardo, Custodero, Persellin, and Fox (2006).

Rhythm and rhyme build phonemic awareness and an ability to hear sound syllables. This develops our students' auditory-visual memory and sequential memory. Decoding music symbol to sound and sound to symbol assists in the development of literacy competencies (Hansen, Bernstorf, and Stuber, 2007; McIntire, 2007). Code systems that exist simultaneously between language and music are frequency (pitch), intensity (dynamics), time/duration (meter, rhythm, tempo), and manner (articulation) of individual sounds (Bernstorf, 2004, p. 3). Preliteracy competencies can be taught to individuals who are cognitively low and/or have autism and developmental disabilities by using signs, symbols, and colors that have universal life relevance. It is useful to use the upside-down stoplight as a learning tool. Signifying red for low (stop), green for high (go), and yellow for middle tones, the basics of melody and harmony can be more easily understood. "This step-by-step, audio-visual-tactile-kinestheic approach to learning musical notation establishes a relationship between musical sound discrimination and the tonality of speech in song and literacy" (Sobol, 2008, p. 41).

Sensory Deficits

Working with students who have autism and developmental disabilities with sensory deficits presents a unique set of challenges. Using music and "Mediated Learning Experiences" (MLE), deficient cognitive functions can be strengthened. Portowitz (2001) reports a case study of a young man who was blind and who came to study with Reuven Feuerstein at the International Center for Enhancement of Learning Potential. Musical activities were used as a cognitive tool to strengthen deficits in analytical perception, comparison, and synthesis. The subject had intensive sessions with a tactile version of *i*nstrumental Enrichment to promote his perception, orientation in space and time, and abilities of comparison and classification. Music lessons of different genres were designed to renforce his learning objectives. His impaired cognitive functions were addressed by new sources of information and how to achieve access to the information. He made extraordinary progress simultaneously in tactile and auditory modalities. "By becoming an active, creative partner, [Daniel's] learning experience transcended the immediate task at hand, increasing both his self-esteem and ability to function independently" (Portowitz, 2001).

Hearing-impaired students or students who are deaf and have autism as the primary diagnosis are also included in our music classroom landscapes. Students with autism must be taught to understand and to express emotion. To help us understand how to approach this, Darrow's (2006) work is noteworthy. Sixty-two elementary and junior high school students at a midwestern state school for the deaf and students at neighboring elementary and junior high schools joined together to participate in a study to determine perception of emotion in music. Twelve film score excerpts were selected to depict happiness, sadness, and fear. The analysis showed that the hearing students from the neighboring elementary and junior high schools responded closest to the context of the film score. Darrow suggested that adaptive strategies be used for the participants who were deaf for them to better understand timbre, texture, and rhythm for understanding emotional context.

Studies by Kaiser and Johnson (2000) with 10 elementary children who were deaf describe an interactive adaptive experience used by preservice teachers to promote a positive musical experience for the deaf and hearing-impaired student population. Visual-tactile demonstrations of sound vibrations and pitch (high/low), opportunities to feel and play percussion instruments, and visual performance of a brass choir all contributed to an enriching social, educational, and music-teaching and learning experience (p. 226).

Musical/Rhythmic Intelligence

As noted in other chapters of this book, it is clear that we are each born with an innate musical/rhythmic intelligence (Montello, 2002; Sacks, 2007; Smith, 2002; Welch, 2005). Basic in our development and education as young children, we are wired neurologically for music. "Music offers educators the possibility of energizing or relaxing students, carrying content information, priming certain types of cognitive performance and enhancing phonological awareness" (Smith, 2002, p. 73). "Systematic use of music can be an effective way to conciously manage your mind, body, and mood...music might offer the power to harmonize the cerebral hemispheres" (Miles, 1997, p. 7). The technologies of magnetic resonance imaging (MRI), positron emission tomography (PET), and electroencephalography (EEG) can now show us what parts of the brain light up by receiving blood or registering increased electrical activity (Bragdon, 2000, p. 85). Scientists have discovered that music is a whole-brain intelligence—activating and connecting left and right hemispheres in multiple neural brain sites (Jensen, 2000; Miles, 1997; Smith, 2002). In a study by Pantev, Oostenveld, Engelien, Ross, Roberts, and Hoke (1998), the auditory cortex was enlarged by 25 percent in skilled musicians compared with the control group who had never played an intrument.

> Whilst playing an instrument such as the flute, the motor and supplementary motor cortex on left and right is active. The cerebellum is engaged in eye tracking and anticipating movement. The auditory cortex is listening to the sounds played. The frontal cortex is engaged in planning for the combination of physical moves need to create the desired patterns of sounds. (Smith, 2002, p. 74)

Can this cross-hemispheric activity help music educators reach students with autism and developmental disabilities who have, by the very definition of their disability, developmental delay? This is a most important line of research that bears our close attention.

Literature on Practice

Practitioners recommend that success in teaching students with autism and developmental disabilities include (1) a breakdown of tasks into very small component parts, systematically taught and reinforced; (2) consistent classroom structure; (3) clearly defined routine; (4) songs with imitation and repetition; and (5) material that has functional learning value. Important reinforcers, arranged in consultation with the student's special education teacher and psychologist, should be used for task completion in the music room. Lessons presented in a multisensory manner combining audio-visual-tactile-kinesthetic feedback will reach learners of all capabilities (Sobol,

2008, p. 50). Multisensory music teaching of relevant materials for students with disabilities is recommended by several authors (Ellsworth and Zhang, 2007; Hammel, 2004; Iseminger, 2009; McCord and Fitzgerald, 2006; Mercuri and Smith, 1997; Nocero, 1979; Schaiberg, 1988; Sobol, 2001, 2008; and Zinar, 1987). Valuable practical information for music teaching with the student who is deaf or has hearing impairments can be found in Darrow (2006, 2007b) and Schraer-Joiner (2004). For teaching music for the student who is blind or visually impaired, resources can be found in Portowitz (2001), Siligo (2004), and Strunk (2004).

Assistive technology is used to augment speech communication for our students with autism and developmental disabilities. Instructional adaptations with specific accommodations bring assessibility on many levels to our music programs. It is recommended that an entire chapter be devoted to advances in instructional music technology and assistive technology. Technology in special education has leveled the playing field for our special learners. It encompasses different learning styles, and its approach is universal. Technology in practice has not only been beneficial to those with autism and developmental disabilities but also enriched learning opportunities for all exceptionalities, especially those with severe paralysis, blindness, and deafness. Technology has allowed every child with specially trained instructors to participate in enjoyable and educational music learning activities.

New Directions

Across the globe, we are seeing greater preservice opportunities with field work in classes where students with special needs are placed. Districts are using music therapy consultants to help music educators reach specific goals necessary to enforce the IEPs for their special education students (Hammel, 2001b, 2007; McCord and Watts, 2006; McDowell, 2007; Miceli, 2005; Miceli, Sobol, Makowski, and Mergen, 2006; Smith and Wilson, 1999; Van Weelden and Whipple, 2007; Ward-Steinman, 2006).

In Miceli and colleagues' study (2006), two partnership programs with public schools were described for preservice teachers to get field experience with a variety of special learners. The assessment techniques for students in a middle school special education chime ensemble are described, as is a lesson plan format with instructional adapations for students with learning disabilities, speech/language communication disorders, visual/hearing impairments, orthopedic/physical and other health impairments, and those with behavioral difficulties. This type of partnership model allows our music education students to be better prepared for teaching in inclusion classrooms and leading inclusion performance programs. As better diagnostic techniques are developed and more public school doors open for our most compromised children, our preservice teachers need more hands-on opportunities to learn approaches and techniques for music in special education programs.

Other hands-on opportunities are being given by private piano instructors and other studio teachers, who successfully work one-on-one with our special learners and who offer insights to classroom music teachers (Cestaro, 2008a, 2008b; Costa-Giomi, 1999). Randal (2008) describes several collaborative ways that classroom teachers and private instructors can work together. Three notable public personalities, Temple Grandin (2005a) (*Thinking in Pictures: And Other Reports from My Life with Autism*), Stephen Shore (2003) (*Beyond the Wall: Personal Experiences with Autism and Asperger Syndrome*, 2nd ed.), and Donna Williams (1994) (*Somebody Somewhere: Breaking Free from the World of Autism*), have dedicated their lives to educating the public about their personal and professional development challenged by Autism Spectrum Disorder. Their articles, books, and speaking engagements not only are inspirational but also are leading educational understanding in their respective areas. Our special students are important members of our society. For the low-functioning student with autism and developmental disabilities, the educational community becomes more perceptive and competent by understanding the complexities in each learning task. As a result, educators are challenged to find a way to reach and teach each individual. For the high-functioning person who falls on the autism spectrum, we are awed by the presence of extraordinary abilities to concentrate on minute details. Channeled into productive task-specific careers, these talented individuals can be of great benefit to society. Grandin writes "success was made possible for me through patient efforts of the dedicated people who worked with me" (Grandin, 2005b, p. 1284).

Summary and Recommendations

This chapter has given the current definition of *autism* and its related, pervasive developmental disorders. It has placed autism in context within the 13 present categories for school-age children to receive special education services in our public school settings. New research for music learning using the theory of cognitive modifiability with mediated learning environments has been included, along with supportive music research for special education, which has been shown to enhance language and literacy, as well as social emotional development. The chapter continued with discussion of applied behavior analysis (ABA), which uses various approaches for teaching. Sensory deficits and facilitative communication were covered, along with issues of socialization and attention. Also treated were aspects of current practice and work to further understand the processing of emotions with individuals on the autism spectrum.

It would be helpful for practitioners in the music classroom to join researchers in mapping out a long-term study that would show successful use of ABA in the music classroom and its benefit for the changing academic demands through elementary and secondary school. I was surprised when preparing this chapter that an important special education resource with such international perspectives as the two-volume *Handbook of Autism and Pervasive Developmental Disorders* (3rd ed.) had no mention of music or musical interventions in its subject index. There was, however, an extensive 38-page author index. This fact is evidence of the huge disparity between research and practice in our respective fields.

In music class, a student with autism and developmental disabilities finds what he can do, not what he cannot. In so doing, his quality of life is enhanced immeasurably by the feeling of heightened self-esteem and accomplishment. It is essential, when appropriate to the child, that music be a part of future IEP program goals. As of June 2010, federal reguations (www.idea .ed.gov under 34CFR §300.320 (a) (4)) provides the opportunity for music therapy to be an appropriate related service for the child with a disability. Partnered with a music educator, the music therapy services can enable a child with a disability to advance appropriately towards progress not only in attaining annual goals but to make progress in the general education curriculum. This collaboration could then be a beginning of showing successful musical interventions for teaching and learning in our special education collegial circles. Frequently, an individual with moderate to profound autism is in the same educational facility until the age of 21. This is a perfect environment to design longitudinal music studies.

National and international conference sessions should continue to feature poster sessions on new research for music learning in special education, with focus on autism and developmental disabilities. What aspects of pedagogy will best facilitate musical behaviors? Once a nonverbal student emerges with a singing voice, how can we help the speaking voice to emerge? Topic sessions for professional development should continue to be offered at each music conference for teacher training in special education practice.

More successful stories about students with autism spectrum disorders in public school settings need to be published in our music journals. We need to form collaborations of universities teamed with special education classroom teachers, music educators, occupational therapists, other related service providers, and cognitive scientists who can link musical interventions to special education classroom methodologies. We can then begin to affect standards-based exemplary instruction on a large scale. With identifying new directions for research, each study reviewed in this chapter can become a model for a new study; even the smallest step forward is monumental.

In closing, there is no greater art than music for nurturing the learning potential of a student. Each day, progress is made in strengthening the cognitive abilities of our children with autism and developmental disabilities. Music is, by its nature and ability to communicate to all people, an integral part of the success of this progress. A bridge to understanding between the abstract and the concrete is accomplished through the use of universal signs, symbols, and colors. Through skilled practice, musical interventions will help students with autism and developmental disabilities achieve adequate yearly progress in both cognitive-academic and communicative-social functions. By consistently teaching the arts in an audio-visual-tactile-kinesthetic mode and by concentrating on process not product, even the most impaired can be a full participant in the highest of learning activities. For all of our students with exceptionalities, music is a safe haven for focused learning in education.

NOTES

1. www.emsc.**nysed.gov/specialed**/lawsregs/part200.**htm**
2. http://idea.ed.gov/
3. www.ed.gov/offices/OSERS/Policy/IDEA/overview.html
4. http://www.newhorizons.org/strategies/ie/ue.html

REFERENCES

American Psychiatric Association. (1994). *Diagnostic and statistical manual of mental disorders* (4th ed). Washington, DC: Author.

Anderson, S. R., & Romanczyk, R. G. (1999). *Early intervention for young children with autism: Continuum-based behavioral models.* (ERIC Document Reproduction Service No. EJ599192)

Arick, J. R., Krug, D. A., Fullerton, A., Loos, L., & Falco, R. (2005). School-based programs. In F. Volkmar, R. Paul, A. Klin, & D. Cohen (Eds.), *A handbook of autism and pervasive developmental disorders, volume 2* (3rd ed., pp. 39, 1003–1028). Hoboken, NJ: Wiley.

Bernstorf, E. (2004). Music educators: Hidden allies for poor readers. In *Spotlight on making music with special learners: Selected articles from state MEA journals* (pp. 3–5). Reston, VA: MENC: The National Association for Music Education.

Bonney, H. (1983). Music listening for intensive coronary care units. *Music Therapy, 3*(1), 4–16.

Bragdon, A. D. (2000). *Brains that work a little bit differently.* New York: Barnes & Noble Books.

Braithwaite, B., & Sigafoos, J. (1998). Effects of social versus musical antecedents on communication responsiveness in five children with developmental disabilities. *Journal of Music Therapy, 35*(2), 88–104.

Brownell, M. (2002). Musically adapted social stories to modify behaviors in students with autism: Four case studies. *Journal of Music Therapy, 39*(2), 117–144.

Buday, E. M. (1995). The effects of signed and spoken words taught with music on sign and speech imitation by children with autism. *Journal of Music Therapy, 32*(3), 189–202.

Carmon, Y., Wohl, A., & Even-Zohar, S. (2008). The musical notes method for initial reading acquisition. *Journal of Cognitive Education and Psychology, 7*(1), 81–100.

Cestaro, P. (2008a). How do you teach students who learn at a slower pace? Part One: Using small steps. *Keyboard Companion, 19*(2), 38–43.

Cestaro, P. (2008b). How do you teach students who learn at a slower pace? Part Two: Reading music. *Keyboard Companion, 19*(3), 34–39.

Chen-Hafteck, L. (1997). Music and language development in early childhood: Integrating past research in the two domains. *Early Child Development & Care, 130,* 85–97.

Colwell, C. M., & Murlless, K. D. (2002). Music activities (singing vs. chanting) as a vehicle for reading accuracy of children with learning disabilities: A pilot study. *Music Therapy Perspectives, 20*(1), 13–19.

Costa-Giomi, E. (1999). The effects of three years of piano instruction on children's cognitive development. *Journal of Research in Music Education, 47*(3), 198–212.

Custodero, L. A. (2006). Singing practices in 10 families with young children. *Journal of Research in Music Education, 54*(1), 37–56.

Dark, I. D., Graham, R. M., Hughes, J., McCoy, M.,& McKinney, D. D. (1996). *Music for all children*. Washington, DC: VSA Educational Services/Silver Burdett Ginn.

Darrow, A. (2006). The role of music in deaf culture: Deaf students' perception of emotion in music. *Journal of Music Therapy, 43*(1), 2–15.

Darrow, A. (2007b). Teaching students with hearing losses. *General Music Today, 20*(2), 27–30.

Ellsworth, N. J., & Zhang, C. (2007). Progress and challenges in China's special education development. *Remedial and Special Education, 28*(1), 58–64.

Evans, C., & Richardson, P. (1988). Improved recovery and reduced postoperative stay after therapeutic suggestions during general anesthesia. *Lancet, ii,* 491–492.

Feuerstein, R., Falik, L. H., Feuerstein, R. S., & Rand, Y. (2002). *The dynamic assessment of cognitve modifiability: The learning propensity assessment device:Theory, instruments, and techniques.* Jerusalem, Israel: ICELP.

Feuerstein, R., & Rand, Y. (1997). *Don't accept me as I am.* Arlington Heights, Il.: Skylight Professional Development.

Grandin, T. (2005a). *Thinking in pictures: And other reports from my life with autism.* New York: Doubleday.

Grandin, T. (2005b). A personal perspective of autism. In F. Volkmar, R. Paul, A. Klin, & D. Cohen (Eds.), *A handbook of autism and pervasive developmental disorders, vol. 2* (3rd ed., pp. 1276–1286). Hoboken, NJ: Wiley.

Gromko, J. E., & Poorman, A. S. (1998). The effect of music training on preschoolers spatial-temporal tasks performance. *Journal of Research in Music Education, 46*(2), 173–181.

Hagedorn, V. S. (2004). Special learners: Using picture books in music class to encourage participation of students with Autisitc Spectrum Disorder. *General Music Today, 17*(2), 46–51.

Hamann, D. L., Lineburg, N., & Paul, S. (1998). Teaching effectiveness and social skill development. *Journal of Research in Music Education, 46*(1), 87–101.

Hammel, A. M. (2001b). Special learners in elementary music classrooms: A study of essential teacher competencies. *Update: Applications of Research in Music Education,* Fall/Winter, 20(1), 9–11.

Hammel, A. M. (2004). Inclusion strategies that work. In *Spotlight on making music with special learners: Selected articles from state MEA journals* (pp. 27–30). Reston, Va: MENC: The National Association for Music Education.

Hammel, A. M. (2007). Professional development research in general education. *Journal of Music Teacher Education, 17*(1), 22–32.

Hansen, D., Bernstorf, E., & Stuber, G. M. (2007). *The music and literacy connection.* Lanham, MD: MENC: The National Association for Music Education.

Harris, S. L., Handleman, J. S., & Jennett, H. K. (2005). Models of educational interventions for students with autism: Home, center, and school-based programming. In F. Volkmar, R. Paul, A. Klin, & D. Cohen (Eds.), *A handbook of autism and pervasive developmental disorders, vol. 2* (3rd ed., pp. 1043–1054). Hoboken, NJ: Wiley.

Harvey, W. (2004). Soothing sounds: How to use music with special learners. In *Spotlight on making music with special learners: Selected articles from state MEA journals* (pp. 30–31). Reston, VA: MENC: The National Association for Music Education.

Hoskins, C. (1988). Use of music to increase verbal response and improve expressive language abilities of preschool language delayed children. *Journal of Music Therapy, 25*(2), 73–84.

Iseminger, S. H. (2009). Keys to success with autistic children. *Teaching Music, 16*(6), 28–30.

Jackson, N. (2003). A survey of music therapy methods and their role in the treatment of early elementary school children with ADHD. *Journal of Music Therapy, 40*(4), 302–333.

Jellison, J. (1984). Structuring small groups and music reinforcement to facilitate positive interactions and acceptance of severely handicapped students in the regular music classroom. *Journal of Research in Music Education, 32*(4), 243–264.

Jensen, E. (2000). *Music with the brain in mind.* San Diego, CA.: Brain Store.

Kaiser, K. A., & Johnson, K. E. (2000). The effect of an interactive experience on music majors' perceptions of music for deaf students. *Journal of Music Therapy, 37*(3), 222–234.

Kern, P., Wakeford, L., & Aldridge, D. (2007). Improving the performance of a young child during self-care tasks using embedded song interventions: A case study. *Music Therapy Perspectives, 25*(1), 43–51.

Krauss, T., & Galloway, H. (1982). Melodic intonation therapy with language delayed apraxic children. *Journal of Music Therapy, 19*(2), 102–113.

Levinson, B. (1965). States of awareness during general anaesthesia. *British Journal of Anaesthesis, 37*, 544–546.

Lovaas, O. (1981). *Teaching developmentally disabled children.* Austin, TX: Pro-Ed International.

Ma, Y., Nagler, J., Lee, M., & Cabrera, I. (2001). Impact of music therapy on the communication skills of toddlers with pervasive developmental disorder. *Annals of the New York Academy of Sciences, 930*, 445–447.

Madsen, S. A. (1991). The effect of music paired with and without gestures on the learning and transfer of new vocabulary: Experiment-derived nonsense words. *Journal of Music Therapy, 28*(4), 222–230.

Marans, W. D., Rubin, E., & Laurent, A. (2005). Addressing social communication skills in individuals with high functioning autism and Asperger Syndrome: Critical priorities in educational programming. In F. Volkmar, R. Paul, A. Klin, & D. Cohen (Eds.), *A handbook of autism and pervasive developmental disorders, vol. 2* (3rd ed., pp. 977–1002). Hoboken, NJ: Wiley.

McCord, K., & Fitzgerald, M. (2006). Children with disabilities playing musical instruments. *Music Educators Journal, 92*(4), 46.

McCord, K., & Watts, E. H. (2006). Collaboration and access for our children: Music educators together. *Music Educators Journal, 92*(4). 26.

McDowell, C. (2007). Are they ready to student teach? Reflections from 10 music education majors concerning their threes of field experience. *Journal of Music Teacher Education, 16*(2), 45.

McIntire, J. M. (2007). Developing literacy through music. *Teaching Music, 15*(1), 44–48.

MENC. (2004). *Spotlight on making music with special learners: Selected articles from state MEA journals.* Reston, VA: Author.

Mercuri, C., & Smith, R. A. (1997). *World in tune.* Sparrowush, NY: Carousel.

Miceli, J. S. (Spring, 2005). Providing a model for music learning theory-based collaborative experiences in music teacher education. *GIML Audea, 10,* (2), 5–7.

Miceli, J. S., Sobol, E. S., Makowski, M. T., & Mergen, I. (2006). A four-way perspective on the development and importance of music learning theory-based preK-16 music education involving music for special learners. *Journal of Music Teacher Education, 16*(1), 65–77.

Miles, E. (1997). *Tune your brain using music to manage your mind, body, and mood.* New York: Berkeley.

Mixon, K. (2007). *Reaching and teaching all instrumental music students.* Lanham, MD: Rowman & Littlefield.

Montello, L. (2002). *Essential musical intelligence.* Wheaton, IL: Quest.

Montello, L., & Coons, E. E. (1998). Effects of active versus passive group music therapy on preadolescents with emotional, learning, and behavioral disorders. *Journal of Music Therapy, 35*(1), 49–67.

Nardo, R. L., Custodero, L. A, Persellin, D. C., & Fox, D. B. (2006). Looking back, looking forward: A report on early childhood music education in accredited American preschools. *Journal of Research in Music, 54*(4), 278–292.

NEA. (2006). *The twice-exceptional dilemma.* Washington, DC: Author.

Nocero, S. (1979). *Reaching the special learner through music.* Morristown, NJ: Silver Burdett.

O'Herron, P., & Siebenaler, D. (2007). Intersection between vocal music and language arts instruction: A review of the literature. *UpDate: Applications of Research in Music Education, 25*(2), 16–26.

Pantev, C., Oostenveld, R., Engelien, A., Ross, B., Roberts, L. E., & Hoke, M. (1998). Increased auditory cortical representation in musicians. *Nature, 392,* 811–814.

Paul, R., & Sutherland, D. (2005). Enhancing early language in children with autism spectrum disorders. In F. Volkmar, R. Paul, A. Klin, & D. Cohen (Eds.), *A handbook of autism and pervasive developmental disorders, vol. 2* (3rd ed., pp. 949–976). Hoboken, NJ: Wiley.

Portowitz, A. (July, 2001). Music activities as a cognitive tool for the enhancement of analytical perception, comparison and synthesis for the blind learner. Retrieved from http://home.avvanta.com/~building/strategies/arts/portowitz.html

Portowitz, A., & Klein, P. (2007). MISC music: A music program to enhance processing among children with learning difficulties. *International Journal of Music Education, 25*(3), 259–272.

Portowitz, A., Lichtenstein, O., Egorov, L., & Brand, E. (December, 2009). (Underlying mechanisms linking music education and cognitive modifiability. *Research Studies in Music Education, 31.*107–128.

Randal, M. (2008). Building a united front. *Teaching Music, 16*(3), 39–41.

Register, D. (2001). The effects of an early intervention music curriculum on prereading/writing. *Journal of Music Therapy, 38*(3), 239–248.

Register, D., & Humpal, M. (2007). Using musical transitions in early childhood classrooms: Three case examples. *Music Therapy Perspectives, 25*(1), 25–31.

Rickson, D. J. (2006). Instructional and improvisational models of music therapy with adolescents who have Attention Deficit Hyperactivity Disorder (ADHD): A comparison of the effects on motor impulsivity. *Journal of Music Therapy, 43*(1), 39–62.

Rogow, S. M. (1982). Rhythms and rhymes: Developing communication in very young blind and multi-handicapped children. *Child: Care, Health, and Development, 8*, 249–260.

Sacks, O. (2007). *Musicophilia*. New York: Alfred A. Knopf.

Schaiberg, G. (1988). *TIPS: Teaching music to special learners*. Reston, VA: MENC: The National Association for Music Education.

Schon, D., Boyer, M., Moreno, J., Besson, M., Peretz, I., & Kolinsky, R. (2008). Songs as an aid for language acquisition. *Cognition, 106*(2), 975–983.

Schraer-Joiner, L. E. (2004). Hearing impairments: An alert for all music educators. In *Spotlight on making music with special learners: Selected articles from state MEA journals* (pp. 59–63). Reston, VA: MENC: The National Association for Music Education.

Shore, S. M. (2002). The language of music working with children on the autism spectrum. *Journal of Education, 183*(2), 97–108.

Shore, S. M. (2003). *Beyond the wall: Personal experiences with autism and Asperger Syndrome*. Shawnee Mission, KS: Autism Asperger.

Siligo, W. R. (2004). Teaching music to sighted and visually-impaired students. In *Spotlight on making music with special learners: Selected articles from state MEJ journals* (pp. 63–67). Reston, Va: MENC: The National Association for Music Education.

Skinner, B. F. (1938). *The behavior of organisms: An experimental analysis*. New York: Appleton-Century.

Smith, A. (2002). *The brain's behind it: We are all musical!* Stratford, England: Network Educational.

Smith, D. S., & Wilson, B. L. (1999). Effects of field experience on graduate music educators' attitude toward teaching students with disabilities. *Contributions to Music Education, 26*(1), 33–49.

Sobol, E. S. (2001). *An attitude and approach for teaching music to special learners*. Raleigh, NC: Pentland.

Sobol, E. S. (2008). *An attitude and approach for teaching music to special learners* (2nd ed). Lanham, MD: Rowman & Littlefield.

Standley, J., & Hughes, J. (1997). Evaluation of an early intervention music curriculum for enhancing pre-reading/writing skills. *Music Therapy Perspectives, 15*, 79–86.

Strunk. R. (2004). On teaching and interacting with blind students. In *Spotlight on making music with special learners: Selected articles from state MEA journals* (pp. 76–77). Reston, VA: MENC: The National Association for Music Education.

Van Weelden, K., & Whipple, J. (2007). Preservice music teachers' predictions, perceptions, and assessment of students with special needs: The need for training in student assessment. *Journal of Music Therapy, 44*(1), 74–84.

Volkmar, F.; Paul, R., Klin, A., & Cohen, D. (Eds.). (2005). *A handbook of autism and pervasive developmental disorders* (3rd ed.). Hoboken, NJ: Wiley.

Volkmar, F. R., & Klin, A. (2005). Issues in the classification of autism and related conditions. In F. Volkmar, R. Paul, A. Klin, & D. Cohen (Eds.), *A handbook of autism and pervasive developmental disorders, vol. 2* (3rd ed., pp. 5–42). Hoboken, NJ: Wiley.

Wallace, W. (1994). Memory of music: Effect of melody on recall of text. *Learning, Memory, and Cognition, 20*(6), 1471–1485.

Ward-Steinman, P. M. (2006). The basic IDEA: The individuals with disabilities act in your classroom. *Teaching Music, 14*(3), 22.

Welch, G. F. (2005). We are musical. *International Journal of Music Education, 23*(2), 117–120.

Whipple, J. (2004). Music in intervention for children and adolescents with autism: Meta-analysis. *Journal of Music Therapy, 41*(2), 90–106.

Williams, D. (1994). *Somebody somewhere: Breaking free from the world of autism*. New York: Three Rivers.

Wolfe, D., & Horn, C. (1993). Use of melodies as structural prompts for learning and retention of sequential verbal information by preschool students. *Journal of Music Therapy, 30*(2), 100–118.

Zinar, R. (1987). *Music activities for special children*. West Nyack, NY: Parker.

Music Learning in Early Childhood

7

A Review of Psychological, Educational, and Neuromusical Research

WILFRIED GRUHN

During the last decades, the interest of music education research has turned toward early childhood learning and the unfolding of infants' musical potential. A large body of research has been devoted to the investigation of precocious listening skills, infants' abilities regarding pitch discrimination and rhythm representation, the sensitivity for grouping and segregation, and the discrimination of tempo and timbre; it has focused on the alertness of contour violations, the musical memory and the recognition of familiar sounds, on infants' preverbal vocalizations and emotional communications, and on children's invented notations and spontaneous compositions, as well as on children's harmonic perception and their development of body control and coordination skills, and it has looked at their musical preferences, to name just the most prominent areas (for comprehensive reviews of research literature on early childhood music, see Colwell and Richardson, 2002; Gembris, 2002, 2008; Lehmann, Sloboda, and Woody, 2007; McPherson, 2006; Wirthner and Zulauf, 2002).

Furthermore, trends of recent research methods have also changed and turned from pure observational descriptions and psychometric experiments toward the fascinating area of neuromusical research (see Gruhn and Rauscher, 2008). The development of sophisticated tools in brain imaging (EEG, MEG, MRI, PET, DTI) has shifted the interest of researchers toward the identification of neural correlates and plastic changes in brain development that exhibit measurable effects of learning and perception skills. Therefore, this chapter will especially take notice of recent results in this area of research and present basic knowledge about the developmental growth of musical skills, from prenatal perception to early childhood activities.

Research studies have shown that even young children exhibit remarkable abilities in pitch discrimination and imitative audio-vocal behavior (Patel, 2008; Trehub, 2006). These skills are needed in language as well as song acquisition, both of which call for exact pitch-matching abilities by auditory control. In view of infants' high potential for learning, one can state that the brain is generally optimized for learning from the very beginning. Therefore, the infant should no longer be characterized by deficits, but instead by potential. This is why it has become more common to speak of the "competent infant" (Dornes, 1993; Stone, Smith, and Murphy, 1973) or even of "infants as musical connoisseurs" (Trehub, 2006).

In the following pages, recent studies on early music learning are briefly reviewed, and the results of psychological and neuromusical investigations as they pertain to the development of infants' and young children's musical abilities are summarized. The term *learning* is used in a rather broad sense and includes various kinds of active and conscious responses to environmental and parental stimuli. This conceptualization of learning, therefore, refers to the development of mental representations with regard to music and includes working memory, perception and cognition, and many kinds of performing activities. Finally, we will widen the perspective of music learning from clearly defined, discrete musical skills to include new models of ontogenetic and anthropological aspects, while looking at the development of speech and music (Brown, 2007; McDermott and Hauser, 2005; Molino, 2000; Wallin, 2000; Wallin, Merker, and Brown, 2000).

Prenatal Auditory Sensations

Auditory experience starts before birth. Internal sounds from the mother's body, as well as audible sounds from the extrauterine environment, shape the acoustic experience of the fetus. However, the reception of those acoustic stimuli cannot be referred to as musical perception as much as auditory sensation. The clear sound of words and songs produced by the mother or other people and all kinds of musical and environmental noises to which the fetus is exposed are muffled because high frequencies are attenuated by the mother's body, which acts like a low-pass filter (Parncutt, 2006). In general, frequencies below 300 Hz may not be attenuated, and higher frequencies are increasingly attenuated; those beyond about 2,000 Hz are generally inaudible for the fetus (Abrams, Griffith, Huang, Sain, Langford, and Gerhardt, 1998).

Between the 10th and 20th week of gestation, all hair cells in the cochlea mature, and synapses with the first neurons in the auditory pathway grow (Eliot, 1999). However, the hair cells do not develop simultaneously; they gradually begin to form at the base and finish at the apex of the cochlea. This causes a peculiar situation because hair cells change their frequency response during development.

Cells near the base, which mature first, initially respond to lower frequencies, but as the properties of the basilar membrane change, these cells become sensitive to higher and higher tones, while hair cells farther out in the cochlea, which are just beginning to mature, take over the job of sensing low frequencies. Thus there is a gradual shift in the tonotopic map during development, with lower tones moving out to progressively more distant cochlear locations. (Eliot, 1999, p. 23)

Because of this, pregnant mothers should be very careful to not expose their fetuses to dangerously loud low frequencies that might hurt the basal cells, which later become sensitive to higher frequencies. Such exposure might cause hearing loss.

The hearing system is one of the first completely developed in human brain development. Six weeks after gestation, the auditory nerve, the nucleus cochlearis, and the nucleus olivaris are recognizable. Neurons in the auditory cortex develop later, but earlier than other sensory systems. During the last trimester, the fetal auditory system is anatomically mature, and fetuses can hear in the womb within a range between 200 and 1,000 Hz (Parncutt, 2006). While listening to spoken language, the fetus can easily detect vowels, but consonants in a higher frequency range are largely unavailable (Gerhardt and Abrams, 2000). However, fetal precocious hearings are generally different from perception after birth because the ears of the fetus are filled with liquid, and the surrounding tissues, muscles, and bones of the mother's body attenuate external sounds by 40 to 50 dB (Gerhardt and Abrams, 2000).

Prenatal sound perception is often reflected by movements and heart rate responses. Heart rate accelerations and decelerations in response to sound stimulation are reported for fetuses from about 26 weeks onward (Abrams, 1995; Al-Qahtani, 2005; Lecanuet, 1996; Wilkin, 1991, 1996). Another indication of fetal perceptive faculty is motor response to loud and broadband noises (Lecanuet, 1996) and to any kind of music. These responses become consistent at 28 to 32 weeks (Parncutt, 2006).

Furthermore, changes in maternal emotional state (stress and relaxation) affect fetal behavior response, including heart rate variability, movement intensity, and breathing movements (Van den Bergh, 1992). These effects are biochemically mediated and interact with others, such as acoustic experiences. In general, fetuses are sensitive to changes in patterns of sound and movement and their emotional connotations (Parncutt, 2006).

As one considers the developing auditory perception, the question of prenatal musical learning emerges. This is, of course, limited to memory of sounds that are heard repeatedly during pregnancy. There is some anecdotal evidence that newborns recognize music that they have heard before birth in the womb. Systematic investigations have exhibited that 2- to 4-day-old neonates prefer their mothers' voice to other female voices (DeCasper and Fifer, 1980). Newborns whose mothers had repeatedly sung a melody during pregnancy changed their sucking pattern in order to turn on a recording of this melody more often than the recording of an unfamiliar melody (Panneton, 1985). Similarly, newborns who had heard some specific music regularly before birth responded to the same music after birth with heightened alertness, lower heart rate, and fewer movements (Hepper, 1991).

Animal research has shown that sound stimulation by music, noise, and voice caused morphological effects in chickens and rats (Chaudhury, Nag, and Wadhwa, 2006; Kim et al., 2006; Panicker, Wadhwa, and Roy, 2002; Rauscher, Robinson, and Jens, 1998). In these studies, the exposure to noise during pregnancy had a negative effect and caused growth retardation, decreased neurogenesis in the hippocampus, and impaired spatial learning abilities, whereas the exposure to music increased neurogenesis in the hippocampus and enhanced spatial learning abilities in pups (Kim et al., 2006). Analogously, one can conclude for humans that in general, prenatal music exposure alters the fetal behavioral state, which is carried forward to the newborn period (James, Spencer, and Stepsis, 2002). The evidence of postnatal memory of prenatal sounds and its recognition (Saffran, Loman, and Robertson, 2000) and the preference of familiar tunes provide a first indication of fetal learning. The ability to feel, see, and hear is always associated with remembrance.

Infant Learning

Acculturation: Imitation and Discrimination

An infant's hearing is one of the most important senses since it is vital for speech and song learning and for cognitive and emotional development later in life. Culture and exposure to culturally transmitted sounds determine the development of tonal and rhythmic sensitivities. Therefore, the very first step toward the acquisition of a musical culture is achieved by acculturation. Cultural exposure promotes the development of culture-specific mental representations. Six-month-old infants are able to differentiate meter-disrupting (irregular subdivisions of a regular pulse) from meter-preserving variations (Hannon and Trehub, 2005), but surprisingly, infants adapt to adultlike biases after a relatively limited exposure to their culture-specific music. At the age of 12 months, the ability to differentiate meter-disrupting variations disappears, whereas infants continue to make that differentiation in a metrically simple context (Hannon and Trehub, 2005).

Learning develops by absorbing sound from the environment and by imitation. Even a few days after birth, infants can already imitate facial expressions if they appear in a focal distance (Meltzoff and Decety, 2003). They also imitate the frequency range of their mother's voice in preverbal vocal communication (Leimbrink, 2010,; Malloch, 1999/2000) (see figure 7.1). This can be seen as a result of the attempt to match with the high pitch range of the infant's voice. This reflects the early onset of the perceptive differentiation between *same* and *different*, which is the most fundamental step toward learning. By recognizing something to *be* something, one always relates a perceived object (e.g., a sound) or state (like light or temperature) to a similar

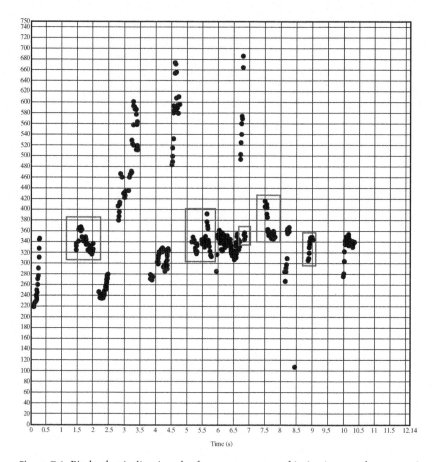

Figure 7.1 Pitch plot indicating the frequency range of imitative vocal communication during mother-infant-interaction with a 4-months old infant.

Note: The infant's reaction is marked by squares.
(From Leimbrink, 2010, p. 175; used with permission.)

or different object or state. One recognizes something to *be* something by comparing it with what it is not. Various degrees of temperature can be felt only as warm or cold in comparison with something that is warmer or colder. A sound is only perceived as loud or soft in comparison with something that is louder or softer. Therefore, in perception and learning, the differentiation between *same* and *different* is crucial.

Although even during the first weeks of life infants' senses are fairly developed, they do not strictly distinguish between the different sensory stimulations, which melt into a unitary perception (Levitin, 2007). Input from the senses is first perceived as an intrabody sensation, which is holistic and engages the entire body. Tactile, visual, acoustic, and other sensory perceptions are not yet diacritically separated from one another. When the baby listens to music, it is not only an auditory experience. The entire body engages in perception: the muscle tonus relaxes, movements get smoother, and the facial expression is gently relieved. This type of intrabody sensation can be referred to the *coenesthetic* organization of the newborn (Spitz, 1965, 1983). As distinguished from the diacritic system, which centers in the cortex, the coenesthetic system is visceral and centers in the autonomous nervous system. Especially during the bonding process, parents attract an infant's attention and stimulate alertness by interventions involving proprioceptive, kinesthetic, tactile, and vestibular stimulation, along with auditory and visual modes (Papoušek, 1996; Papoušek and Papoušek, 1992).

This coenesthetic organization can be traced back to early brain development. The oldest part of the brain, the brain stem, strongly corresponds to body functions. Corporal sensations and movements cause mental models (also referred to as *mental representations*) by afferent stimulus conduction. The neural image of a body action can then activate a particular movement by the efferent nerve conduction (Hüther, 2006). This mutual interaction between body and brain is fundamental for physical, cognitive, and emotional development. What is not experienced by means of the body cannot be mentally represented in the brain. Or the other way around: a functioning brain cannot think without a functioning body connected to it.

Therefore, music perception—especially in infants—involves much more than just acoustic stimulation. Even newborns have already acquired a strong feeling of a regular beat. They are able to detect an omitted beat which is reflected by ERP signals similar to those exhibited by adults when an unexpected event occurs (Winkler, Háden, Ladinig, Sziller, and Honing, 2009). The importance of metric pulse and movement as a means of musical expression and experience has been stressed by psychologists and educators (Flohr and Trevarthen, 2008; Malloch, 1999; Malloch and Trevarthen, 2009; Trevarthen, 1999/2000). Children are much more stimulated to move along with music than with speech (Zentner and Eerola, 2010). Similarly, body movement shapes the ways in which children hear and experience rhythms. Therefore, movement can be seen as the origin of rhythm (Trainor, 2008). This culturally transmitted behavior is also reflected by an old habit of parents and grandparents to rock or bounce babies while they sing to them, which can be observed across all cultures. In one experiment, 7-month-old infants listened to an ambiguous drum rhythm that lacked regular accents. The children were bounced to the rhythm either in duple meter or in triple meter. In a subsequent preferential listening test where the rhythm was performed in a clear duple or triple meter, children preferred the version that corresponded to their previously experienced bouncing pattern (Phillips-Silver and Trainor, 2005). Here, the rhythm perception is primed by movements that infants have experienced. This finding supports the implications of coenesthetic perception.

Development of Musical Abilities: Perception and Recognition

Children are powerful learners and are optimized for learning; their brains work like "learning machines" (Eliot, 1999) that build themselves according to their actual needs or those found in their environment. All important features for survival, orientation, and communication must first be learned to succeed in the physical, visual, and aural world. Communication includes language (speech), music (song), and space (directional hearing) and applies two modes: discrimination of sounds by perception and vocal production of sounds by imitation. Infants are perfectly prepared for both. It seems cogent that the level of musical achievement is directly related to social opportunities to participate in musical activities (songs, chants, dances) with others. It is also crucial for developmental growth that infants build strong personal relations within a social group that provides emotional and physical contact, confidence, safety, and support. More important, there are two poles between which the brain develops: one's own body and an adequate environmental milieu wherein a genetic disposition can develop.

All corporeal sensations and body movements, even at the fetal stage, evoke an arousal pattern in the brain and by this establish neural representations (Hüther, 2006). Whatever is represented in the infant's brain during the process of its maturation originates in a corporeal and sensorial excitement. Correspondingly, this process of developing mental representations will be enhanced within a supportive and propitious milieu. This model is schematically drawn in figure 7.2. It underlines the interactive function of internal

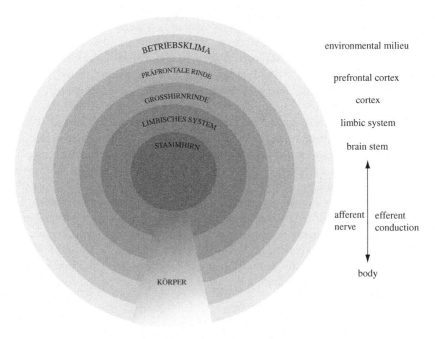

Figure 7.2 Schematic brain model of basic functional layers and their interaction. (Unpublished graph by G. Hüther, used with permission.)

and external factors and makes it clear that genes alone do not determine musical achievement or a musical career. The provision of epigenetic conditions is necessary for a genetic disposition to be expressed.

In this context, music learning can be defined as the development and gradual differentiation of mental representations. In the acoustic domain, mental representations for sound and its functional meaning in a metric and tonal sense are developed through acculturation by ear, that is, by listening to many different forms of music in a given culture, to feel the beat by body interaction and to adjust to a tonal center by vocal exploration (Gruhn, 1997, 1998). Ideally, there should be as much musical input as a child receives in language. More important, the child needs this aural input to initiate a phonological loop (listen and babble), which is a prerequisite to establish mental representations that then are activated in perception.

In language acquisition, infants first learn to separate words from a stream of vocal sounds, then explore and imitate vocal articulation by babbling, and finally attribute a meaning to the words they hear and pronounce. The analogue happens in music. Even young infants are able to detect subtle differences of pitches embedded in a melody (Trehub, Schellenberg, and Kamenetsky, 1999). This aural discrimination is fundamental for imitation during babble and exploration and renders possible the development of mental representations for pitch, timbre, meter, and other aspects. When infants listen to songs and bounce their metric structure, they reinforce that representation by activation and repeated use.

Music learning in early years is always engaged in the development of mental representations. Any repetition of songs and dances strengthens the synaptic connectivity and facilitates further activation. If a mental representation of a tonal or rhythmic pattern can be activated, a process of recognition is initiated that is beyond mere memory of an already heard sound. The activation of already established mental musical representations is called *audiation* in terms of Gordon's music learning theory (Gordon, 1997b, 2001), a concept that has been used more frequently in recent years. Therefore, music learning in infancy and early childhood can be described in general as the process of developing mental representations and their activation through audiation.

Infants are highly competent for aural discrimination and sound segmentation (Fassbender, 1993) and are already sensitive to pitch changes. Two-month-olds respond to pitch changes by an increase of positive slow waves, while 4-month-olds exhibit a negative mismatch similar to adults. At 4 months, infants show robust responses to pitch changes and even to the missing fundamental (Trainor and He, 2008). It is also well known that infants can discriminate melodies. Interestingly, even 7- to 11-month-old infants are able to perceive invariant properties of music such as timbre and melody. Costa-Giomi and collaborators have demonstrated that infants were able to recognize the sound of an instrument playing different melodies but could not recognize a melody played on different instruments (Costa-Giomi, Cohen, and Solan, 2008; Costa-Giomi, Cohen, Solan, and Borck, 2008).

In speech as in song acquisition, infants rely on what they hear. The linguistic environment primes the brain for what one needs in order to discriminate. By 6 months, infants' perceptual abilities are attuned to vowels, and by 10 months, infants have acquired the ability to perceive consonants. Perception is readily attuned to their native language (McMullen and Saffran, 2004).

Furthermore, infants possess an extraordinary ability to discover units and structures in a consistent stream of sound patterns, and they are able to extract words from continuous speech by 7.5 months (Saffran, 2003). To test their statistical learning for word segmentation—that is, the ability to recognize the statistical properties of syllable sequences and to track sequential probabilities—8-month-old infants were exposed to an artificial language such as *golabupabikututibubabupugolabu*...that contains statistically detectable sequence boundaries. The results exhibit that infants use sequential statistics to find word boundaries (McMullen and Saffran, 2004; Saffran, 2003). If this principle is transposed to music and the syllables are replaced by notes (e.g., *golabu* becomes CFE), the infants exhibit the same statistical behavior. In a musical transposition to a different key, infants are more likely to depend on absolute pitch cues than on relative pitch cues (Saffran, 2003; Saffran and Griepentrog, 2001).

For infants, the most salient and attractive feature of a melody is its pitch contour as it is performed in maternal infant-directed speech (*motherese*) (Fernald, 1991). This belongs to the very first aspects of music that are discriminated by infants (Trehub, 2003). In an investigation of 1- to 2-year-old children, it has been demonstrated that children are very sensitive to changes of pitch and tempo (Gruhn, Kiesewalter, Joerger, and Borth, 2005). After a habituation phase when children listened to a melody and a rhythm every day, children were tested by a head-turn method in terms of how they responded to gradually increased changes in pitch (transposition from half a semitone to seven semitones) and gradually accelerated tempo (20 percent to 100 percent). Children recognized small changes (1 to 2 semitones) as "same," as well as tempo modifications of 20 percent. However, if exposed to stronger changes, they pay more attention to the altered melodies and rhythms, indicating that they recognize changes of more than three semitones and an acceleration of more than 50 percent as "different."

Regarding the level of discrimination ability, children show a clear age effect: the older the children have grown, the less they are intrigued by the transposition or the accelerated tempo. However, the opposite is true for the melodic structure. When an acquired melody follows an AAB form that then is altered to an ABA form, only the older children realize that change. Only the switch of two parts—that is, the order of the sequence of the melodic parts—makes the tune "different" to them, whereas younger children just respond to the overall character of the tune and recognize it as "same" (Gruhn et al., 2005) (see figure 7.3).

Very early, infants prefer speech samples where pauses coincide with regular clause boundaries; they have already internalized the syntactic structure

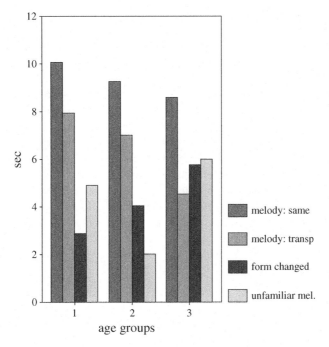

Figure 7.3 Age effects of the attention span for familiar and unfamiliar melodies. (From Gruhn et al., 2005.)

of their mother tongue by the flow of the prosody (Kemler Nelson, Jusczyk, Hirsh-Pasek, and Cassidy, 1989). Similar results emerge from experiments where musical material replaced verbal sentences. Infants listened longer to musical phrases when pauses segmented regular phrases than to those with pauses irregularly placed somewhere within the phrase (Jusczyk and Krumhansl, 1993).

With respect to infants' ability to differentiate between consonant and dissonant music as reported by some researchers (Trainor and Heinmiller, 1998; Trainor, Tsang, and Cheung, 2002), inconsistent results have been discussed, since children's harmonic perception and their understanding of tonal hierarchies remain limited until about age 7 (Trehub, 2006).

Infants' Vocalizations

Preverbal mother-infant communication embraces several communicative modes, such as singing, rhythmic movement, eye contact, touch, expressive gestures, and emotional intonation (Leimbrink, Gruhn, and Hoffmann, 2007). This appears to be culturally universal (Levitin, 2007, p. 262). The mother's infant-directed speech is characterized by a raised pitch level, an exaggerated vocal contour, and an expressive prosody. This supports and intensifies the emotional power and generates a higher level of infant arousal (Trehub, 2006). It is quite natural that infants show more sustained interest in immediate maternal speech and singing than in a recorded audiovisual performance (Nakata and Trebub, 2004).

Adult-infant vocal communication is inseparably connected with social interaction and is based on emotional exchange between the adult and the infant. The highly expressive vocal intonation is employed by the mother to attract her baby's attention (Leimbrink, 2010; Powers and Trevarthen, 2009). For this, she often underlines her vocalization with expressive facial mimicry and gestures, which are first imitated by the neonate even a few days after birth. Very soon, infants also imitate the vocal spectrum of their mother's voice. During the first months of life, body contact often precedes intense eye contact, which then stimulates vocal interaction and imitation. The preferred high pitch range of mother's voice stimulates fast movements in the infant, which reach their peak at 6 months (Leimbrink, 2010). By 7 months, infants start to coordinate the movement of both arms and legs and eventually begin to synchronize hand movements with the rhythm of the mother's speech (Leimbrink, 2010). Generally, one can observe a high level of corporal interaction in connection with vocalizations.

Infants' hearing frequency range diminishes during the first 9 months and eventually stabilizes at a range between 330 and 440 Hz. Interestingly, hearing range does not correspond to the range of mothers' presented vocalizations, which cover a much larger range of 80 to 580 Hz (Leimbrink, 2010). Mothers usually employ a large scale vocal range in combination with exaggerated prosody and stimulating mimicry. However, when a mother talks to the child and engages in communicative alternation with the infant, the range shrinks and comprises a smaller range of only 2 to 4 semitones (Leimbrink, 2010).

At the very beginning, infants seem to develop a protolanguage (Fitch, 2006) that combines musical and linguistic elements. However, the two modes of expression—song and speech, music and language—are not yet separated. Some researchers assume that both grow from the same evolutionary roots of vocalization (Brown, 2000; Marler, 2000; Molino, 2000) because both apply the same neural mechanisms. Here, the most effective learning is based on responsive imitation. Prosodic contours, pitches, and rhythmic articulations are acquired by aural imitation of a perceived auditory pattern. This is the core of audio-vocal learning.

Foundations of Song and Speech Acquisition

During the earliest stage of life, infants apply similar mechanisms for babbling and squealing. The production of pitches and vocal sounds, which precede song and speech acquisition, are learned by an audio-vocal process. This is an imitative behavior that uses aural perception to control vocal production and results in the ability to imitate sound by ear. By contrast, many animals apply *auditory learning*, which means that they are able to understand acoustic signals but can never imitate that signal vocally (Jarvis, 2004, 2006). For example, a well-trained dog understands the command "sit" and responds to it by sitting down. However, a dog cannot imitate that articulated sound of "sit." On the contrary, *vocal learning* means one is able to vocally imitate a perceived sound by a neural mechanism that connects auditory perception with vocal sound production. There are few creatures who have this ability: the three mammalian groups of humans, cetaceans (dolphins, whales, seals), and some bats and the three avian groups of songbirds, parrots, and hummingbirds.

Song learning through vocal imitation is an evolutionary novelty that emerged with the development of a neural control center (Brown, Martinez, Hodges, Fox, and Parsons, 2004). In vocal learners, there is a direct neural link between the larynx representation in the primary motor cortex and the peripheral neural center for vocalization. Furthermore, the supplementary motor area (SMA) plays a key role in motor control. Damage to this area is associated with mutism (Brown et al., 2004). There are two vocal pathways, the anterior and the posterior, that are connected with the human auditory system. The posterior pathway sends information to the vocal part of the brain stem and to the nucleus ambiguus, which controls vocal productions in singing and speaking. The anterior vocal pathway consists of a loop between the motor cortex, basal ganglia, thalamus, and back to the cortex. This pathway connects the language strip of the premotor cortex with the dorsal thalamus (see figure 7.4).

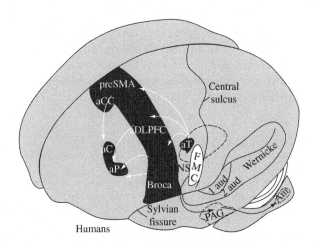

Figure 7.4 Model of the brain pathways for human song and language performance.

Note: Dark gray regions and white arrows indicate anterior vocal pathways; light gray regions indicate auditory regions; dashed lines show connections between vocal pathways. preSMA = presupplementary motor area; aDLPFC = anterior dorsolateral prefrontal cortex; aC = anterior cingulated; aP = anterior putamen (Jarvis, 2004, p. 754).

Additionally and necessarily, these pathways receive information from auditory pathways that enter the anterior and posterior pathways and enable a fine-tuning of motor control in the larynx. Simply put, the auditory information controls muscle tension in the vocal tract. The goal is to match the produced vocal sound with the perceived sound, and this is only possible when one hears one's own voice.

This neural trait makes humans "consummate vocal imitators" (Brown, 2007) who can make use of vocal imitation in learning, as well as in musical performance (song reproduction). The imitative audio-vocal processes are essential for song and speech acquisition. Functional magnetic resonance brain scans during a monotonic vocalization task exhibit activations in exactly those brain areas that are interconnected by the phonological loop: the Broca area (BA 44), the primary auditory area (BA 41), the auditory association cortex (BA 42, 22), and the supplementary motor area (SMA) in connection with deeper structures in the thalamus and the cerebellum.

The structure of this neural mechanism separates the production of emotional screams and squeals in animals from the vocal articulation in human songs and language. However, as mentioned before, this mechanism is not unique to humans; what is unique is the differentiation that develops from infants' early vocalizations to speech. This highlights the complex demands on the imitative behavior, which is structurally similar, but not identical, in language and song acquisition. The vocal task of developing verbal skills requires the ability to match the sound of vocal formants and fit these into alternating communication (*horizontal alternation*). In songs, however, one has to match the exact pitch of a melodic contour and keep a steady pulse (time keeping). Additionally, in group singing and chanting, one must fit into a synchronous pulse taken from the other participants (*vertical integration*) (Brown, 2007). Surprisingly, this ability is performed well even by very young infants. This process of developing song and speech production is not yet separated during the first months but differentiates when in speech a verbal symbol system is gradually established. On the other side, only in music (song) does the vertical integration of pitch (as in a melody) and pulse (as in rhythms) become more crucial.

Table 7.1 Specific Demands in Song and Speech Production

Song	Speech
Hierarchic structure of discrete sounds	
Audio-vocal learning by pitch/sound matching	
Communicative horizontal alternation	
Time keeping maintaining the pulse	Symbolic association of sound and meaning
Keeping a steady beat	
Vertical integration of pulse and pitch;	Horizontal alternation in verbal communication
Polyphonic synchronization in coordinated chorusing	Heterophonic combination in simultaneous speech

As shown in table 7.1, there is no separation between song and speech during the first stages of development; both are part of preverbal or protolinguistic communication. Only when children attribute meaning to words do developmental tracks split and form their own vocal prototypes. Along with the establishment of symbolic associations, a verbal symbol system is acquired that is missing in music. For compensation, a finely tuned imitation of precise pitches and the vertical integration of metric events into an overall time structure come into play in music and determine its characteristic peculiarities. Only the sound matching process, by which auditory input helps to shape the motor activity of the vocal tract, stays the same in song and speech acquisition.

Music Learning of Young Children at Preschool Age

Aptitude

Not just at preschool age the question of aptitude or talent arises. Parents observe their child's behavior and find or do not find indications of musical talent (musicality) or aptitude. Although there is no clear consensus about the differentiation between music aptitude, musicality, musical talent, intelligence, or capacity (Gruhn, 2006), parents intuitively recognize their children as musically gifted or not. Based on their occasional observations and their common understanding of musicality, parents consider formal instruction in music for their children around age 3 to 5. In choosing a musical instrument, music aptitude seems to provide a basis for further achievement. *Music aptitude* may be best defined as the genetically determined potential to process structured and unstructured musical information, whereas musical talent, ability, or capacity refers to achievement as a result or consequence of a given musical potential (Gruhn, 2006).

Infants are well equipped with neural conditions to discriminate aural information and process musical sounds. One may question whether this ability is part of the human biological endowment and to which end this auditory ability is needed in the evolution of humans (Wallin, 2000). One salient aspect is that this ability functions in the development of speech and song in human communication, which fosters emotional and cognitive maturation. Therefore, every child is born with different degrees of musical potential, but this innate disposition needs to be nurtured by musical stimulation if it is not to fade away.

The neural disposition for auditory processing and its development over the life span are grounded in the dynamic process of the growth of synaptic connections (synaptogenesis). The developing fetal and neonatal brain produces a large number of neurons that connect with one another according to environmental stimulation, and these networks stabilize after the age of 8 to 10 to the mature adult level (Chugani, Phelps, and Mazziota, 1987;

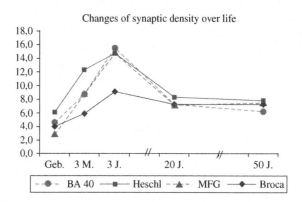

Figure 7.5 Synaptic density of various cortical regions. Based on Huttenlocker.

Note: BA 40 = Brodman Area 40; Heschl = Heschl gyrus, primary auditory cortex; Broca = Brodman Area 44; MFG = mid frontal gyrus.

Huttenlocher, 1979, 1994) (see figure 7.5). The extreme plasticity of the brain enables it to adapt to the environmental demands in the best possible way. If various sounds (pitches, timbres, meters, etc.) are presented and mentally processed, the receptive neurons that are specialized for this particular task connect through synapses and build cell assemblies. The more often these cell assemblies are activated, the stronger the synaptic contact grows and the stronger the neurons fire simultaneously (Hebb, 2002). On the contrary, when children miss or are withheld from musical stimulation, connections get weaker and finally disappear.

The synaptic growth of mental networks in the brain reflects individual experience. The innate disposition offers only the framework within which a potential can develop, and only the actual challenge of social opportunities for musical learning can shape and modulate the potential during the first years of life. According to Gordon, the potential to learn is not a stable factor, but initially a variable process that stabilizes at the age of about 9 (Gordon, 1997a), depending on the environmental support. Therefore, every child is born with some degree of musicality or musical potential (Jacoby, 1984, 2003). Rather, not to be musical is a social artifact (Elschenbroich, 2001) caused by the restraint of opportunities to learn and experience music. The lack of musical stimulation affects the neural networks responsible for musical mental representations; they fail to develop. Consequently, aptitude or talent does not determine whether one will achieve in music. Of course, no high achievement can develop without aptitude. On the other hand, low achievement does not necessarily indicate a low aptitude; often it is only a matter of lacking social opportunities, environmental stimulation, and/or family support. Therefore, children will develop their aptitude if they are informally guided and encouraged to participate in musical activities.

Listening Skills

Initially, young children perceive pitch as a degree of brightness. Therefore, they usually name high pitches as bright and low pitches as dark. Révész (1946) differentiated two components in the perception of pitch: lightness (*Helligkeit*), which is a linear orientation and increases with frequency, and a characteristic tone quality (*Tonigkeit*), which is a cyclic orientation based on the octave similarity. During their first years, children are mainly attentive to the degree of the brightness of a tone. This is what they imitate during babble, no matter what the correct pitch is. Therefore, at that early age, it is not an indication of low aptitude if children do not match the pitch precisely because they listen to and imitate the brightness. This behavior may continue until school age, when they still talk of bright or dark tones although they are already able to match a particular pitch correctly. While children listen to a melody, their listening focuses primarily on contour and brightness (Dowling, 1999). However, preschool children at the age of 3 to 4 start to distinguish roughly between slow and fast (Gembris, 2002), and it appears that slow and fast is a core aspect of their musical experience, even though they are not yet capable of comparative judgments of tempo (Young, 1982).

In a study of six age groups between 5 and 10 years, Minkenberg (1991) found a clear age effect in children's sensitivity to pitch and duration (see figure 7.6). The diagram exhibits a general advantage of rhythm over melody when the children were asked to find errors in a tune or rhythm. Surprisingly,

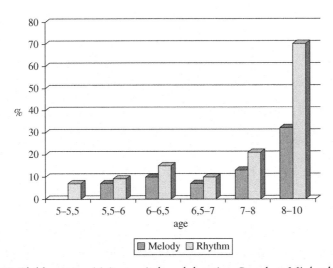

Figure 7.6 Children's sensitivity to pitch and duration. Based on Minkenberg.

Note: The diagram shows the percentage of correct recognitions of changes in pitch (melody) or duration (rhythm) for each age group.

even the 10-year-olds detected less than 50 percent of errors in a melody. These findings deserve replication.

Daily observation tells us that children in Western culture often show better rhythmic ability than tonal abilities. However, rhythm perception during preschool age is quite divergent, depending on extracurricular experiences in the daily life of the individual. Some argue that the synchronization of musical rhythm and movement appears only after children can imitate a rhythm pattern vocally (Gordon, 1997b). Therefore, rhythmic chanting is the most appropriate medium to teach rhythm to 3- and 4-year-olds (Rainbow, 1980). Synchronous clapping to music and metric marching to a given rhythm are difficult tasks that cannot be accomplished before children are able to coordinate body, breath, and voice, which might happen around the age of 4 (Rainbow, 1980). However, other research indicates that more than half of 3-year-old children from different cultural backgrounds are able to tap a steady beat (Flohr, Woodward, and Suthers, 1998).

Even more confusing is our understanding of harmonic relations. Although young children prefer consonant sounds over shrill, dissonant sounds (Trainor and Heinmiller, 1998; Trainor et al., 2002), they have not developed a concept of harmony in early childhood. In experiments with 5- to 10-year-olds, Zenatti (1993) examined the musical preference for tonality versus atonality and consonance versus dissonance. Before the age of 5, she could not find a clear preference, but at the age of 9 to 10, a clear preference for tonal consonant music was established. This confirms the findings of Minkenberg (1991), which profoundly reflect an effect of socialization and acculturation. The older the children grow, the more they have adapted to the values and aesthetic norms of their culture (see figure 7.7).

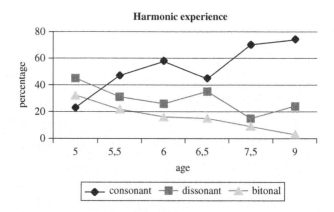

Figure 7.7 Development of preferences for harmony. Based on Minkenberg.

Note: Children between the ages of 5 and 9 show a clear effect of age and enculturation with regard to their evaluation of consonant, dissonant, or bitonal musical examples. The graph shows the percentage of preferences for each age group.

Vocal Development and Song Learning

Studies of vocal development in early childhood confirm the strong impact of maternal prosody on children's vocal activities. During preverbal vocalization, infants alternate with their mother using small patterns of vocal expression. At the end of the first and into the second year, they start to imitate the mother's singing by exploring their own singing voice, which still is not separated from their "speaking" voice in frequency range. This is because children do not generally distinguish between speech and song; they vocalize only in a common "musilanguage" (Brown, 2000). One can talk of "singing" instead of "vocalizing" when the child keeps a consistent pitch longer than in babble, which might match the mother's pitch or come close to its frequency spectrum. When children start to sing, they normally sing *along with* their mother, following the overall melodic contour and seeking to match the brightness (*Helligkeit*) of their mother's voice.

Regarding singing development, different strategies are reported that nurture song acquisition and vocal production in young children. According to Gordon, children should get the opportunity to adapt the sound and rhythmic structure of a song before they are able to sing a song. Therefore, it is important for informal guidance that adults first sing *to* children long before they start to sing *with* them (Gordon, 1997b). Since children can focus their attention on only one aspect of a musical performance at a time, and since they must first learn "same" and "different," adults need to ensure what the children are attending to. This is best achieved by the separation of pitch (tonal patterns) and duration (rhythm patterns) in a learning sequence (Gordon, 1997b). Other pedagogical approaches, such as Orff and Kodály, that are not founded on an empirically proved concept of learning rely on more combined presentations. Regarding vocal accuracy, it has been demonstrated that practicing a variety of different tonalities in combination with body movement separately for tonal and rhythm patterns exhibited the best results (Gruhn, 2002). Even kindergarten children may improve their singing accuracy when they use gestures in combination with neutral syllables (Liao, 2008; Liao and Davidson, 2007).

A situation similar to the separation of tonal and rhythmic aspects can be found in the interference of melodies from words. When adults sing a song with lyrics, children primarily focus on the story given by the text. If one wants them to carefully listen to the melodic properties of a song, one will be more successful in singing a tune with neutral syllables (Gordon, 1997b). In an investigation of first-graders, it appeared that there were slightly better (although not statistically significant) results when the teacher used neutral syllables ("bum") instead of the song text (Rutkowski and Miller, 2003). It was also shown that there was more accurate recognition of songs performed without text and that the melodic properties of a tune influenced song recognition (Feierabend, Saunders, Getnick, and Holohan, 1998). It appears that there may be two different mental organizations that are engaged in the processing of the melodic structure and in learning of the words of a song (Levinowitz, 1989). However, songs with words may facilitate language acquisition because children may benefit from the structuring properties of music included in the song (Schon, Boyer, Moreno, Besson, Peretz, and Kolinsky, 2008).

As children grow older and walk and play with toys, they become able to perform a broad diversity of spontaneous songs. These melodies normally consist of short tonal phrases or repetitive rhythms picked up from songs and chants they have heard. In early studies, researchers observed and documented song development (Metzler, 1961; Werner, 1917), described the ontogenesis of melodic forms that are characterized by small down glides within the range of a minor third and by short repetitions, and framed a typology of early babble songs (*Lallgesänge*) (Werner, 1917). Based on an observational study, Stadler Elmer designed a six-level hierarchy of children's vocal development and introduced a new computer-assisted method to record children's invented songs (Stadler Elmer, 2000; Stadler Elmer and Elmer, 2000) (see figure 7.8). Beyer followed the vocal development of a child in a single case study and presented a valuable body of transcriptions of early songs (Beyer, 1994).

In a free-play day care setting with two 3-year-olds, Young (2002) found that many different types of singing were linked with a particular situation and activity, including (1) free-flow vocalizing (wordless vocal creations), (2)

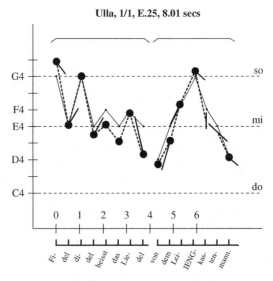

Figure 7.8 Documentation of Ulla's (2 years, 7 months) first presentation of a new song.

Note: Glides (•✑) and fixed pitches (●) following the melodic contour.
(Stadler Elmer, 2000, p. 155; used with permission.)

chanting of repeated phrases, (3) reworking of known songs (remodeling acculturated songs of their environment), (4) singing for animation (associated with play and action), and (5) imitation of actual sounds. At the same time, they learned to sing songs with (at times) distorted lyrics they did not really understand, but they imitated the verbal sound that made sense to them along with the melody. More important, the words represented the melody.

As a diagnostic tool to measure the stages of singing ability, Rutkowski developed a Singing Voice Development Measure (SVDM), employed by many studies to evaluate the singing abilities of preschool and school-age children (Levinowitz, Barnes, Guerrini, Clement, D'April, and Morey, 1998; Rutkowski, 1990, 1997; Rutkowski and Miller, 2003). This measure presents a 5-point scale covering presinger, speaking range singer, limited range singer, initial range singer, and singer. This measure allows one to quantify and rank singing abilities and to compare ability among groups differentiated by age, gender, and cultural background.

Another important dimension of vocal development is its relation to movement. A longitudinal study in which several dimensions of movement (flow, weight, coordination, synchronization) and vocal performance (consistent tempo, rhythmic accuracy, intonation) were measured by ratings on 6-point rating scales (Criterion Based Observation Form or CBOF; see Gruhn, 1999) exhibited a highly significant correlation between vocal control (accuracy, intonation) and movement (flow, coordination) (Gruhn, 2002). This finding supports the importance of the phonological loop in which aural input regulates the fine-tuning of motor activities in the vocal tract. The better consistent tempo, correct intonation, and stable rhythm can be performed vocally, the more coordination children can move with and the more intensely they engage in continuous sustained movement. This has been confirmed by a study on young 4- to 6-year-old children (Gruhn, Haussmann, Herb, Minkner, Gollhofer, in press) who exhibited a clear interaction between their musical abilities (as measured by Gordon's PMMA; Gordon, 1979) and their motion control and body coordination (as measured by a standardized motor test; Zimmer and Volkamer, 1984). Therefore, one can conclude that movement provides an appropriate means to teach vocal tasks when it is related to vocal practice and exploration.

On the contrary, talk and verbal instruction might function as distracters that counteract musical learning. This was investigated by an exploratory case study in which the musical behavior of two toddlers was recorded (Valerio, Seaman, Yap, Santucci, and Tu, 2004, 2006). Both children were exposed to two settings: music play and general play. During music play sessions, there was no verbal instruction, but many different musical stimuli (songs, patterns, improvisations, etc.) instead. In general play sessions, musical stimuli were avoided, but verbal communication was used when introducing games, books, and toys. As a result, it could be shown that both toddlers responded differently to the two conditions, but both performed musical vocal behaviors that were different from nonmusic vocal behaviors.

In general, music play sessions seem to stimulate music-thinking skills that enhance the acquisition of musical syntax (Valerio et al., 2006).

Vocal musical learning in toddlers and preschool children can be best demonstrated by the turn from imitation to anticipation (Faller and Gruhn, 2002). When children imitate a tonal or rhythmic pattern, they must perceive and process the particular aural stimulus, keep it in working memory, retrieve it, and activate a special motor area to perform the same pattern by clapping, chanting, or singing. Necessarily, the imitation will appear delayed because the elapsed time between the presentation of a sensory stimulus and the subsequent behavioral response takes about 150 to 300 ms. If a child simply imitates what has just been heard, an elapsed time span occurs. However, if the child has already learned a pattern, the child will come close to the onset of the presented stimulus or even anticipate it because it has already been developed as a mental representation of that stimulus that only needs to be activated independently of the moment of presentation. This effect was clearly demonstrated in a learning experiment with children between 2 and 6 years of age. The better the children had learned the patterns—that is, the stronger a musical representation was achieved—the closer they came to the stimulus onset time, and finally they became able to anticipate it (Faller, 2001). This turn from imitation to anticipation presents an objective measure of learning.

Invented Notations as a Window into Cognition

Reading and writing music is not a task that can be acquired before the development of an establishment of clear aural representations, which normally starts at school age. However, the early scribbles (invented notations) of preschool children offer simple but intriguing opportunities to examine their musical understanding. Therefore, in this context, we do not review research on how to teach and learn musical notation, but rather view iconographic scribbles as a window into children's musical understanding.

Bamberger (1982) was one of the first who seriously studied how young children represent their musical hearings mentally. For this, she analyzed children's scribbles as a means to understand the development of children's mental representations. The assumption was that children focus their attention on those tonal and rhythmic features that they were able to pick up from a heard or sung pattern. The task of putting down a song or rhythm so that they could remember or show others what they had done provides the researcher with some information concerning the developmental state of children's music cognition. While carefully analyzing the invented notations of a rhythm drawn by 4- to 6-year-old children, Bamberger found two types of notations that can be arranged in a hierarchical order according to the developmental state of the children. She called these types "figural" when children focused on groups or motifs or "figures," and "metric-formal" when the children counted discrete elements in a sequence of sounds (Bamberger, 1982).

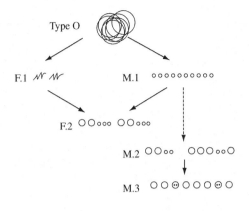

Figure 7.9 Typology of children's drawings.
(Bamberger 1982, p. 194; used with permission.)

However, she insistently stressed that the developmental distinction should not be seen as a linear progression rather than an interacting evolution between two complementary strategies of perception (Bamberger, 1982). Figure 7.9 shows Bamberger's typology of children's drawings; in the diagram, F and M stand for figural and metric-formal.

In a consecutive case study, she described the development of tonal representations as a process from "figural" representations that undergo a transitional phase from which a formal representation will emerge (Bamberger, 1991). The figural strategy focuses on the action-path of events as "a chronological narrative account of the tune" (Bamberger, 1991, p. 184). This characterization comes close to the former metric type with respect to its serial organization. On the contrary, the metric type now becomes "formal," which is seen as a fixed or abstract reference independent of any particular tune (Bamberger, 1991, p. 227ff.).

The differentiation between figural and formal representations becomes extremely important in music learning as it reflects how children typically think. Adults orient themselves in space and time by measuring it. Children are different because they rely on weight and flow as their modes to experience their environment. Measuring time and space relates a perceived event to the next coming event and determines the distance. If we put down a rhythm in a metric notation, we only represent distances and relations symbolically, whereas children relate their perception of a sound event to an anteceding event. Therefore, their perceived grouping of tonal elements is different from what they see in notation. By this, they might get into trouble because they do

Figure 7.10 Simpler rhythm.

not understand the conventions of the standard notation. This becomes very striking in children's drawings of a simple rhythm (figure 7.10).

A metric strategy will focus on a series of 10 sound events, whereas figural perception focuses on two groups that consist of 2 + 3 elements. Because children attend to weight more than to duration, they might find a graphic equivalent to this one seen in figure 7.9 (F.2): O O ooo | O O ooo (Bamberger, 1991; Upitis, 1987). In traditional standard notation, we use the same symbol for the last event of each group (a quarter note) because the duration to the next is the same as the duration between the first and the second. However, musically, we perceive two heavier and three lighter beats because the last of the three elements is more closely related to the anteceding event than to the succeeding.

Similarly, Davidson and Scripp (1988) investigated the pictorial system of four 7-year-olds and found that for children, the text or the story covers the melody. If young children are asked to represent a song they have sung, they draw the story of the text (Davidson and Colley, 1987; Gromko, 1994). Other studies of invented notation confirm that kindergarten children rely on iconic pictures (Barrett, 1997, 2002, 2004). However, if we focus on the action within the drawings, a continuous flow of the sustained movement becomes apparent (Bamberger, 1991). Four- and 5-year-olds can recognize and graphically represent structural chunks (Davidson and Scripp, 1992). However, before they develop a symbolic representation, children focus their attention on movement and weight as the essential modes of their experience; consequently, they apply this body experience to their creative attempts to fix their actions while making music.

Sequential Learning

If one understands learning in terms of a gradual progression through stages of physical, psychological, and cognitive development, a sequential order of steps according to the readiness for proceeding to a next level builds a sequential learning theory. Gordon has devoted a considerable body of research to the clarification of music aptitude and music learning. He has offered a theory of sequential learning (Gordon, 2003, 2007) that is influenced by Gagné's hierarchical structure of learning (Gagné, 1973) and Piaget's stage concept (Piaget, 1947) that has been criticized, in part, because it is biased as biologically determined. However, sequential learning marks an important aspect of cognitive processing and knowledge acquisition. According to Gordon, music learning proceeds in sequential steps. This means that certain levels must be necessarily acquired before one can proceed to the next level.

In early childhood learning, Gordon distinguishes three sequential types of "preparatory audiation," each of which is broken down into subdivisions (Gordon, 1997b):

1. Acculturation
   a. Absorption
   b. Random response
   c. Purposeful response
2. Imitation
   a. Shedding egocentricity
   b. Breaking the code
3. Assimilation
   a. Introspection
   b. Coordination

Gruhn has integrated these phases and stages into a five-level model: (1) enculturation, (2) attention, (3) imitation, (4) coordination, and (5) elaboration (Gruhn, 2002). The learning itself (i.e., the acquisition of musical understanding) follows a sequential order as in language and speech and moves back and forth between discrimination and inference types of learning. In discrimination learning, one has to aurally discriminate between "same" and "different," which provides an essential prerequisite for imitation. In inference learning, a child infers new and extended forms of knowledge from already established knowledge. Inference learning is based on improvisation and creativity, and it applies the familiar structures to new situations by generalization.

Music learning always starts on the *aural/oral* level in which a "vocabulary" of the native culture is established, followed by *verbal association* in which the developed representations are labeled with names such as solfège syllables, and *symbolic association*. Musical elements that can be named are then represented symbolically. This is the level of reading and writing that must be acquired before a child can gain *theoretical understanding*.

In recent times, Gordon has suggested integrating the different levels of preparatory audiation and audiation—as explained in his music learning theory—and the different stages of this learning theory into one comprehensive learning sequence by maintaining the sequential order (Gordon, 2001). A set of sequential stages is needed when teachers are faced with a child's learning difficulties. If a child cannot achieve an intended level, the teacher has to step back to the former lower level. To be able to do this, one has to be fully aware of the sequential steps of learning.

Neural Correlates of Music Learning

Perception and learning always depend on and refer to brain plasticity. The auditory cortex of young infants undergoes remarkable maturational changes. The ability of 4-month-olds to recognize and respond to missing fundamentals reported by Trainor and He (2008) might refer to a plastic modification at an early neural level of auditory processing below the auditory cortex, which results in an adultlike pitch processing behavior. Structural changes and neural connectivity develop according to environmental demands. This is especially true in young children when the brain is in the process of maturation; it adapts to the stimuli to which it is exposed. Music perception therefore calls for new representations that never develop if no musical stimulation is presented. Children's singing is extremely beneficial for children's development. It not only activates emotional centers but also integrates diverging tasks such as pitch control by ear, vocal and motor coordination, and auditory information processing of tonal and rhythmic stimuli. Vocal activity results in a complex feedback between networks of represented patterns and activates sensorimotor patterns. Therefore, musical activities—listening as well as performing—result in a higher connectivity of different brain areas and in a stronger coherence between both hemispheres as obvious neural correlates.

Over the last few years, several longitudinal studies dealing with the effects of formal music instruction on brain development in young children have been conducted (Koelsch, Fritz, Schulze, Alsop, and Schlaug, 2005; Norton, Winner, Cronin, Overy, Lee, and Schlaug, 2005; Overy, Norton, et al., 2004; Overy, Norton, Cronin, Winner, and Schlaug, 2005; Schlaug, Norton, Overy, and Winner, 2005). In one brain-imaging study, 5- to 7-year-old children who started to take instrumental lessons were compared with a control group that had no instrumental training. It was demonstrated that the music group had significantly greater change scores in fine motor skills and auditory discrimination than the control group, whereas no significant between-group differences appeared in nonprimary domains such as verbal skills, visuo-spatial skills, and mathematical reasoning (Schlaug and Bangert, 2007).

In recent years, much interest has focused on the interaction of speech and song development. Since investigators of the music-language relationship have come up with a model of resource-sharing networks (RSN) for syntactic processing (Patel, 2007), it seems plausible to assume that early formal music training, which starts at age 3 at the earliest, may generate the same cognitive effect as early bilingual training. In bilingual studies, Bialystok and colleagues have shown that bilinguals reveal a cognitive advantage in processing speed, reaction time, and inhibition of spontaneous reflexes compared with mono-linguals when tested in a Simon task (a task of cognitive control) (Bialystok, Craik, Grady, et al., 2005; Bialystok, Craik, Klein, and Viswanathan, 2004; Bialystok, Craik, and Ryan, 2006; Bialystok and Martin, 2004). This advantage increases over time. Further research on the musical development of younger children should investigate more specific neural correlates of early music learning.

Conclusions

A main concern of parents, caregivers, teachers, and educational authorities is not to miss the right time when the learning window is open for the acquisition of specific skills. There are such sensitive phases in language and music when neural conditions are best prepared to support certain developments (e.g., of prosody or syntax in language or harmonic structures in music); however, one can never determine a limit for music learning and language acquisition in general. The most evident and efficient brain plasticity enables humans to learn something over the entire life span, although in different ways. It appears that it is easier to learn music—the intrinsic, genuine structure of music (i.e., its "grammar" and "syntax"), not the conceptual knowledge *about* music—at an age when the brain holds its highest degree of plasticity.

Parents are often worried about missing or neglecting something in terms of their children's intellectual and emotional growth. However, this concern can be minimized as long as children grow in a natural, rich environment that contains aural, visual, motor, and haptic stimuli within everyday life. The brain best knows what it needs for development, and it will take it from where it can get it. Of course, parental care and environmental support offer a wonderful opportunity to enhance and support the given potential to learn. Parents do not need to add extra stimuli to the natural environment where parents and siblings talk to the baby, move and touch it, and sing to the infant, where moving objects can be watched and sounds can be heard and differentiated regarding their pitch range, intensity, loudness, direction, and so forth. The child, then, will pick up from this varied acoustic and visual background what is needed for further development. However, since this cannot always be presumed, early childhood education programs are requested to compensate for the lack of environmental richness.

For educators of early childhood music, it is important to acquire and understand some basic knowledge about the developmental stages of a child, his or her cognitive growth, and vocal development. If one understands the mechanism of the phonological loop, which is fundamental in song and speech development, one can more adequately respond to the need to practice and internalize the motor integration of auditory stimuli during the singing and imitation of sound patterns. The increasing number of studies concerning early childhood music provide teachers, caregivers, and parents with, at times, contradicting information that makes it difficult to directly draw conclusions from research to practical applications. However, more solid knowledge of the brain mechanisms involved in music processing and music learning may help to avoid at least the omission of opportunities for young children to learn and experience music in an adequate way. Therefore, neuromusical and psychological research on music learning, perception, and cognition should be more strongly linked with music pedagogy (Gruhn and Rauscher, 2008) so that new understandings of learning and development will be able to affect and change educational thinking.

REFERENCES

Abrams, R. M. (1995). Some aspects of the fetal sound environment. In I. Deliège & J. A. Sloboda (Eds.), *Perception and cognition of music* (pp. 83–101). Hove, England: Psychology Press.

Abrams, R. M., Griffith, S. K., Huang, X., Sain, J., Langford, G., & Gerhardt, K. K. (1998). Fetal music perception: The role of sound transmission. *Music Perception, 15*(3), 307–317.

Al-Qahtani, N. H. (2005). Foetal responses to music and voice. *Australian and New Zealand Journal of Obstetrics and Gynecology, 45*(5), 414–417.

Bamberger, J. (1982). Revisiting children's drawings of simple rhythms: A function for reflection-in-action. In S. Strauss (Ed.), *U-shaped behavioral growth* (pp. 191–226). New York: Academic Press.

Bamberger, J. (1991). *The mind behind the musical ear.* Cambridge, MA: Harvard University Press.

Barrett, M. (1997). Invented notations: A view of young children's musical thinking. *Research Studies in Music Education, 8*(1), 2–14.

Barrett, M. (2002). Invented notations and mediated memory: A case study. *Bulletin of the Council for Research in Music Education, 153/154,* 55–62.

Barrett, M. (2004). Thinking about the representation of music: A case-study of invented notation. *Bulletin of the Council for Research in Music Education, 161/162,* 19–28.

Beyer, E. (1994). *Musikalische und sprachliche Entwicklung in der frühen Kindheit.* Hamburg, Germany: Kraemer.

Bialystok, E., Craik, F., Grady, C., Chau, W., Ishii, R., Gunji, A., et al. (2005). Effect of bilingualism on cognitive control in the Simon task: Evidence from MEG. *Neuroimage, 24*(1), 40–49.

Bialystok, E., Craik, F., Klein, R., & Viswanathan, M. (2004). Bilingualism, aging, and cognitive control: Evidence from the Simon task. *Psychology and Aging, 19*(2), 290–303.

Bialystok, E., Craik, F. I. M., & Ryan, J. (2006). Executive control in a modified antisaccade task: Effects of aging and bilingualism. *Journal of Experimental Psychology: Learning, Memory, and Cognition, 32*(6), 1341–1354.

Bialystok, E., & Martin, M. M. (2004). Attention and inhibition in bilingual children: Evidence from the dimensional change card sort task. *Developmental Science, 7*(3), 325–339.

Brown, S. (2000). The "musilanguage" model of music evolution. In N. L. Wallin, B. Merker, & S. Brown (Eds.), *The origins of music* (pp. 271–300). Cambridge, MA: MIT Press.

Brown, S. (2007). Contagious heterophony: A new theory about the origins of music. *Musicae Scientiae, 11*(1), 3–26.

Brown, S., Martinez, M. J., Hodges, D. A., Fox, P. T., & Parsons, L. M. (2004). The song system of the human brain. *Cognitive Brain Research, 20,* 363–375.

Chaudhury, S., Nag, T. C., & Wadhwa, S. (2006). Prenatal acoustic stimulation influences neuronal size and the expression of calcium-binding proteins in chick hippocampus. *Journal of Chemical Neuroanatomy, 32*(2–4), 117–126.

Chugani, H. T., Phelps, M. E., & Mazziota, J. C. (1987). Positron emission tomography study of human brain function development. *Annals of Neurology, 22*(4), 487–497.

Colwell, R., & Richardson, C. (Eds.). (2002). *The new handbook of research on music teaching and learning.* Oxford: Oxford University Press.

Costa-Giomi, E., Cohen, L. G., & Solan, D. (2008, July). *Infant music categorization.* Paper presented at the International Seminar on Research in Music Education, Porto, Portugal.

Costa-Giomi, E., Cohen, L. G., Solan, D., & Borck, A. (2008, August). *Categorization of melody during the first year of life.* Paper presented at the International Conference on Music Perception and Cognition 10, Sapporo, Japan.

Davidson, L., & Colley, B. (1987). Children's rhythmic development from age 5 to 7: Performance, notation, and reading of rhythm patterns. In I. Peery, W. Peery, & T. W. Draper (Eds.), Music and child development (pp. 107–136). New York: Springer-Verlag.

Davidson, L., & Scripp, L. (1988). Young children's musical representations: Windows on music cognition. In J. A. Sloboda (Ed.), *Generative processes in music* (pp. 195–230). Oxford: Clarendon.

Davidson, L., & Scripp, L. (1992). Surveying the coordinates of cognitive skills in music. In R. Colwell (Ed.), *Handbook of research on music teaching and learning* (pp. 392–413). New York: Schirmer.

DeCasper, A. J., & Fifer, W. (1980). Of human bonding: Newborns prefer their mothers' voices. *Science, 208*(4448), 1174–1176.

Dornes, M. (1993). *Der kompetente Säugling. Die präverbale Entwicklung des Menschen.* Frankfurt, Germany: Fischer.

Dowling, W. J. (1999). The development of music perception and cognition. In D. Deutsch (Ed.), *The psychology of music* (2nd ed., pp. 603–627). San Diego, CA: Academic Press.

Eliot, L. (1999). *What's going on in there? How the brain and mind develop in the first five years of life.* New York: Bantam.

Elschenbroich, D. (2001). *Weltwissen der Siebenjährigen.* München, Germany: Kunstmann.

Faller, W. (2001). *Von der Imitation zur Antizipation. Empirische Verhaltensbeobachtung zum musikalischen Lernen bei Kindern.* Unpublished diploma thesis, University of Music, Freiburg, Germany.

Faller, W., & Gruhn, W. (2002, July). *Music learning. From imitation to anticipation.* Proceedings of the 7th International Conference on Music Perception and Cognition, Sydney, Australia.

Fassbender, C. (1993). *Auditory grouping and segregation processes in infancy.* Hamburg, Germany: Kaste.

Feierabend, J. M., Saunders, T. C., Getnick, P. E., & Holohan, J. M. (1998). Song recognition among preschool-age children: An investigation of words and music. *Journal of Research in Music Education, 46*(3), 351–359.

Fernald, A. (1991). Prosody in speech to children: Prelinguistic and linguistic functions. *Annals of Child Development, 8,* 43–80.

Fitch, W. T. (2006). The biology and evolution of music: A comparative perspective. *Cognition, 100*(1), 173–215.

Flohr, J. W., & Trevarthen, C. (2008). Music learning in childhood. Early development of a musical brain and body. In W. Gruhn & F. H. Rauscher (Eds.), *Neurosciences in music pedagogy* (pp. 53–99). New York: Nova Science.

Flohr, J. W., Woodward, S., & Suthers, L. (1998). *Rhythm performance in early childhood.* Paper presented at the 8th International Society for Music Education Seminar of the Early Childhood Commission, Cape Town, South Africa.

Gagné, R. M. (1973). *The conditions of learning.* London: Holt, Rinehart & Winston.

Gembris, H. (2002). The development of musical abilities. In R. Colwell & C. Richardson (Eds.), *The new handbook of research on music teaching and learning* (pp. 487–508). New York: Oxford University Press.

Gembris, H. (2008). *Grundlagen musikalischer Begabung und Entwicklung* (3rd ed.), Vol. 20. Augsburg, Germany: Wißner.

Gerhardt, K. J., & Abrams, R. M. (2000). Fetal exposures to sound and vibroacoustic stimulation. *Journal of Perinatology, 20*(8), 21–30.

Gordon, E. E. (1979). *Primary Measures of Music Audiation (PMMA)*. Chicago: GIA Publ. Inc.

Gordon, E. E. (1997a). *Learning sequences in music (1980)*. Chicago: GIA.

Gordon, E. E. (1997b). *A music learning theory for newborn and young children (1990)*. Chicago: GIA.

Gordon, E. E. (2001). *Preparatory audiation, audiation, and music learning theory. A handbook of a comprehensive music learning sequence*. Chicago: GIA.

Gordon, E. E. (2003). *A music learning theory for newborn and young children*. Chicago: GIA.

Gordon, E. E. (2007). *Awakening newborns, children, and adults to the world of audiation. A sequential guide*. Chicago: GIA.

Gromko, J. E. (1994). Children's invented notations as measures of musical understanding. *Psychology of Music, 22*(2), 136–147.

Gruhn, W. (1997). Music learning—neurobiological foundations and educational implications. *Research Studies in Music Education, 9*, 36–47.

Gruhn, W. (1998). *Der Musikverstand. Neurobiologische Grundlagen des musikalischen Denkens, Hörens und Lernens* (2nd ed.). Hildesheim, Germany: Olms.

Gruhn, W. (1999). The development of mental representations in early childhood: A longitudinal study on music learning. In S. W. Yi (Ed.), *Music, mind, and science* (pp. 434–453). Seoul, South Korea: Seoul National University.

Gruhn, W. (2002). Phases and stages in early music learning. A longitudinal study on the development of young children's musical potential. *Music Education Research, 4*(1), 51–71.

Gruhn, W. (2006). The appearance of intelligence in music: Connections and distinctions between the concepts of musical and general intelligence. In L. V. Wesley (Ed.), *Intelligence: New research* (pp. 115–132). New York: Nova Science.

Gruhn, W., Kiesewalter, J., Joerger, C., & Borth, F. (2005, April). *What is "same" and "different" in pattern recognition by young children.* Paper presented at the Research in Music Education (RIME) IV, Exeter, England.

Gruhn, W., & Rauscher, F. H. (Eds.). (2008). *Neurosciences in music pedagogy.* New York: Nova Science.

Gruhn, W., Herb, U., Minkner, C., and Gollhofer, A. (in press). Motion analysis and musical abilities in pre-school children. *International Journal of Music Education.*

Hannon, E. E., & Trehub, S. E. (2005). Tuning in to musical rhythms: Infants learn more readily than adults. *Proceedings of the National Academy of Sciences of the United States of America, 102*(35), 12639–12643.

Hebb, D. (2002). *The organization of behavior (1949)*. Mahwah, NJ: Erlbaum.

Hepper, P. G. (1991). An examination of fetal learning before and after birth. *Irish Journal of Psychology, 12*, 95–107.

Hüther, G. (2006). *Die Macht der inneren Bilder*. Göttingen, Germany: Vandenhoeck & Ruprecht.

Huttenlocher, P. R. (1979). Synaptic density in human frontal cortex. *Brain Research, 163*(2), 195–205.

Huttenlocher, P. R. (1994). Synaptogenesis, synapse elimination, and neural plasticity in human cerebral cortex. In C. Nelson (Ed.), *Threats to optimal development. The Minnesota Symposia on child development: Vol. 27.* (pp. 35–54). Hillsdale, NJ: Erlbaum.

Jacoby, H. (1984). *Jenseits von "Musikalisch" und "Unmusikalisch."* Hamburg, Germany: Christians Verlag.

Jacoby, H. (2003). *Musik. Gespräche-Versuche 1953–1954. Dokumente eines Musikkurses* (erw. Neuausgabe mit Hörbeispielen von R. Weber ed.). Hamburg, Germany: Christians Verlag.

James, D. K., Spencer, C. J., & Stepsis, B. W. (2002). Fetal learning: A prospective randomized controlled study. *Ultrasound in Obstetrics and Gynecology, 20*(5), 431–438.

Jarvis, E. D. (2004). Learned birdsong and the neurobiology of human language. *Annals of the New York Academy of Science, 1016*, 749–777.

Jarvis, E. D. (2006). Evolution of brain structures for vocal learning in birds: A synopsis. *Acta Zoologica Sinica, 52*, 85–89.

Jusczyk, P. W., & Krumhansl, C. L. (1993). Pitch and rhythmic patterns affecting infants' sensitivity to musical phrase structure. *Journal of Experimental Psychology: Human Perception and Performance, 19*(3), 627–640.

Kemler Nelson, D., Jusczyk, P., Hirsh-Pasek, K., & Cassidy, K. (1989). How the prosodic cues in motherese might assist language learning. *Journal of Child Language, 16*(1), 55–68.

Kim, H., Lee, M. H., Chang, H. K., Lee, T. H., Lee, H. H., Shin, M. C., et al. (2006). Influence of prenatal noise and music on the spatial memory and neurogenesis in the hippocampus of developing rats. *Brain Development, 28*(2), 109–114.

Koelsch, S., Fritz, T., Schulze, K., Alsop, D., & Schlaug, G. (2005). Adults and children processing music: An fMRI study. *Neuroimage, 25*, 1068–1076.

Lecanuet, J.-P. (1996). Prenatal auditory experience. In I. Deliège & J. A. Sloboda (Eds.), *Musical beginnings* (pp. 3–34). Oxford: Oxford University Press.

Lehmann, A., Sloboda, J. A., & Woody, R. H. (2007). *Psychology for musicians. Understanding and acquiring the skills.* Oxford: Oxford University Press.

Leimbrink, K. (2010). Kommunikation von Anfang an. Die Entwicklung von Sprache in den ersten Lebensmonaten. Tübingen: Stauffenburg Verlag.

Leimbrink, K., Gruhn, W., & Hoffmann, L. (2007, September). *Preverbal interaction and the role of musical ements.* Paper presented at the Conference on the Evolution of Emotional Communication: From Sounds in Nonhuman Mammals to Speech and Music in Man, Hannover, Germany.

Levinowitz, L. M. (1989). An investigation of preschool children's comparative capability to sing songs with and without words. *Bulletin of the Council for Research in Music Education, 100*, 14–19.

Levinowitz, L. M., Barnes, P., Guerrini, S., Clement, M., D'April, P., & Morey, M. J. (1998). Measuring singing voice development in the elementary general music classroom. *Journal of Research in Music Education, 46*(1), 35–47.

Levitin, D. J. (2007). *This is your brain on music.* New York: Plume.

Liao, M.-Y. (2008). The effects of gesture use on young children's pitch accuracy for singing tonal patterns. *International Journal for Music Education, 26*(3), 197–211.

Liao, M.-Y., & Davidson, J. W. (2007). The use of gesture techniques in children's singing. *International Journal for Music Education, 25*(1), 82–94.

Malloch, S. (1999–2000). Mothers and infants and communicative musicality. *Musicae Scientiae, Special Issue,* 29–57.

Malloch, S., & Trevarthen, C. (Eds.). (2009). *Communicative musicality. Exploring the basis of human companionship.* Oxford: Oxford University Press.

Marler, P. (2000). Origins of music and speech. In N. L. Wallin, B. Merker, & S. Brown (Eds.), *The origins of music* (pp. 31–48). Cambridge, MA: MIT Press.

McDermott, J., & Hauser, M. (2005). The origins of music: Innateness, uniqueness, and evolution. *Music Perception, 23*(1), 29–59.

McMullen, E., & Saffran, J. R. (2004). Music and language. A developmental comparison. *Music Perception, 21*(3), 289–311.

McPherson, G. (Ed.). (2006). *The child as musician. A handbook of musical development.* New York: Oxford University Press.

Meltzoff, A. N., & Decety, J. (2003). What imitation tells us about social cognition: A rapprochement between developmental psychology and cognitive neuroscience. *Philosophical Transactions of the Royal Society of London, Series B, Biological Sciences, 358*(1431), 491–500.

Metzler, F. (1961). Die kindliche Melodieerfindung in ihrer Bedeutung für Theorie und Praxis der Musikerziehung. *Musik im Unterricht, 52,* 231–238.

Minkenberg, H. (1991). *Das Musikerleben von Kindern im Alter von 5 bis 10 Jahren* (vol. 4). Frankfurt, Germany: Lang.

Molino, J. (2000). Toward an evolutionary theory of music and language. In N. L. Wallin, B. Merker, & S. Brown (Eds.), *The origins of music* (pp. 165–176). Cambridge, MA: MIT Press.

Nakata, T., & Trebub, S. E. (2004). Infant's responsiveness to maternal speech and singing. *Infant Behavior and Development, 27*(4), 455–464.

Norton, A., Winner, E., Cronin, K., Overy, K., Lee, D. J., & Schlaug, G. (2005). Are there pre-existing neural, cognitive, or motoric markers for musical ability? *Brain and Cognition, 59*(2), 124–134.

Overy, K., Norton, A., Cronin, K., Gaab, N., Alsop, D., Winner, E., et al. (2004). Imaging melody and rhythm processing in young children. *NeuroReport, 15*(11), 1723–1726.

Overy, K., Norton, A., Cronin, K., Winner, E., & Schlaug, G. (2005). Examining rhythm and melody processing in young children using fMRI. In G. Avanzini, L. Lopez, S. Koelsch, & M. Majno (Eds.), *The neurosciences and music II: From perception to performance* (vol. 1060, pp. 210–218). New York: Annals of the New York Academy of Sciences.

Panicker, H., Wadhwa, S., & Roy, T. S. (2002). Effect of prenatal sound stimulation on medio-rostral neostriatum/hyperstriatum ventrale region of chick forebrain: A morphometric and immunohistochemical study. *Journal of Chemical Neuroanatomy, 24*(2), 127–135.

Panneton, R. K. (1985). *Prenatal auditory experience in human newborns.* Unpublished doctoral dissertation, University of North Carolina, Greensboro.

Papoušek, H., & Papoušek, M. (1992). Beyond emotional bonding: The role of preverbal communication in mental growth and health. *Infant Mental Health Journal, 13*(1), 43–53.

Papoušek, M. (1996). Intuitive parenting: A hidden source of musical stimulation in infancy. In I. Deliège & J. A. Sloboda (Eds.), *Musical beginnings: Origins and development of musical competence* (pp. 88–114). Oxford: Oxford University Press.

Parncutt, R. (2006). Prenatal development. In G. McPherson (Ed.), *The child as musician* (pp. 1–31). Oxford: Oxford University Press.

Patel, A. D. (2007, May). *Language, music, and the brain: A resource-sharing framework.* Paper presented at Language and Music as Cognitive Systems, Cambridge, England.

Patel, A. D. (2008). *Music, language, and the brain.* Oxford: Oxford University Press.

Phillips-Silver, J., & Trainor, L. J. (2005). Feeling the beat: Movement influences infant rhythm perception. *Science, 308*(5727), 1430.

Piaget, J. (1947). *La psychologie de l'intelligence.* Paris: Armand Colin.

Powers, N., & Trevarthen, C. (2009). Voices of shared emotion and meaning: Young infants and their mothers in Scotland and Japan. In S. Malloch & C. Trevarthen (Eds.), *Communicative musicality* (pp. 209–249). Oxford: Oxford University Press.

Rainbow, E. (1980). A final report on a three-year investigation of rhythmic abilities of preschool aged children. *Bulletin of the Council for Research in Music Education, 66/67*, 69–73.

Rauscher, F. H., Robinson, K. D., & Jens, J. J. (1998). Improved maze learning through early music exposure in rats. *Neurological Research, 20*(5), 427–432.

Révész, G. (1946). *Einführung in die Musikpsychologie.* Bern, Switzerland: Francke.

Rutkowski, J. (1990). The measurement and evaluation of children's singing voice development. *Quarterly Journal of Music Teaching and Learning, 1*, 81–95.

Rutkowski, J. (1997). The nature of children's singing voices: Characteristics and assessment. In B. A. Roberts (Ed.), *The phenomenon of singing* (pp. 201–209). St.John's, Newfoundland: Memorial University Press.

Rutkowski, J., & Miller, M. S. (2003). The effect of teacher feedback and modeling on first graders' use of singing voice and developmental music aptitude. *Bulletin of the Council for Research in Music Education, 156*, 1–10.

Saffran, J. R. (2003). Musical learning and language development. In C. F. G. Avanzini, D. Minciacchi, L. Lopez, & M. Majno (Eds.), *The neurosciences and music: Vol. 999* (pp. 397–401). New York: New York Academy of Sciences.

Saffran, J. R., & Griepentrog, G. J. (2001). Absolute pitch in infant auditory learning: Evidence for developmental reorganization. *Developmental Psychology, 37*(1), 74–85.

Saffran, J. R., Loman, M. M., & Robertson, R. R. M. (2000). Infant memory for musical experiences. *Cognition, 77*(1), 15–23.

Schlaug, G., & Bangert, M. (2007). Neural correlates of music learning and understanding. In W. Gruhn & F. H. Rauscher (Eds.), *Neurosciences in music pedagogy* (pp. 101–120). New York: Nova Science.

Schlaug, G., Norton, A., Overy, K., & Winner, E. (2005). Effects of music training on the child's brain and cognitive development. In G. Avanzini, S. Koelsch, L. Lopez, & M. Majno (Eds.), *Annals of the New York Academy of Sciences, 1060*, 219–230.

Schon, D., Boyer, M., Moreno, S., Besson, M., Peretz, I., & Kolinsky, R. (2008). Songs as an aid for language acquisition. *Cognition, 106*(2), 975–983.

Spitz, R. (1965). *The first year of life (ed. 2007)*. Boston: International Universities Press.

Spitz, R. (1983). *Dialogues from infancy. Selected papers*. New York: International Universities Press.

Stadler Elmer, S. (2000). *Spiel und Nachahmung. Über die Entwicklung der elementaren musikalischen Aktivitäten*. Aarau, Switzerland: Nepomuk.

Stadler Elmer, S., & Elmer, F.-J. (2000). A new method for analysing and representing singing. *Psychology of Music, 28*(1), 23–42.

Stone, J., Smith, H., & Murphy, L. (Eds.). (1973). *The competent infant*. New York: Basic Books.

Trainor, L. J. (2008, August). *The origins of rhythm in movement*. Paper presented at the International Conference on Music Perception and Cognition 10, Sapporo, Japan.

Trainor, L. J., & He, C. (2008, August). *Development of pitch processing in auditory cortex between 2 and 4 months of age*. Paper presented at the International Conference on Music Perception and Cognition 10, Sapporo, Japan.

Trainor, L. J., & Heinmiller, B. M. (1998). The development of evaluative responses to music: Infants prefer to listen to consonance over dissonance. *Infant Behavior and Development, 21*(1), 77–88.

Trainor, L. J., Tsang, C. D., & Cheung, V. H. W. (2002). Preference for sensory consonance in 2- and 4-month-old infants. *Music Perception, 20*(2), 187–194.

Trehub, S. E. (2003). Musical predispositions in infancy: An update. In I. Peretz & R. J. Zatorre (Eds.), *The cognitive neuroscience of music* (pp. 3–20). Oxford: Oxford University Press.

Trehub, S. E. (2006). Infants as musical connoisseurs. In G. McPherson (Ed.), *The child as musician* (pp. 33–49). Oxford: Oxford University Press.

Trehub, S. E., Schellenberg, E. G., & Kamenetsky, S. B. (1999). Infants' and adults' perception of scale structure. *Journal of Experimental Psychology: Human Perception and Performance, 25*(4), 965–975.

Trevarthen, C. (1999–2000). Musicality and the intrinsic motive pulse: Evidence from human psychobiology and infant communication. *Musicae Scientiae, special issue*, 155–215.

Upitis, R. (1987). Children's understanding of rhythm: The relationship between development and music training. *Psychomusicology, 7*(1), 41–60.

Valerio, W. H., Seaman, M. A., Yap, C. C., Santucci, P. M., & Tu, M. (2004, September). *Toddler music syntax acquisition in music play and general play environments: Cultural connections*. Paper presented at the Jahrestagung der Gesellschaft fuer Musikforschung, Weimar, Germany.

Valerio, W. H., Seaman, M. A., Yap, C. C., Santucci, P. M., & Tu, M. (2006). Vocal evidence of toddler music syntax acquisition: A case study. *Bulletin of the Council for Research in Music Education, 170*, 33–45.

Van den Bergh, B. R. H. (1992). Maternal emotions during pregnancy and fetal and neonatal behaviour. In J. G. Nijhuis (Ed.), *Fetal behaviour* (pp. 157–208). Oxford: Oxford University Press.

Wallin, N. L. (2000). *Biomusicology. Neurophysiological, neuropsychological and evolutionary perspectives on the origins and purposes of music*. New York: Pendragon.

Wallin, N. L., Merker, B., & Brown, S. (Eds.). (2000). *The origins of music.* Cambridge, MA: MIT Press.

Werner, H. (1917). Die melodische Erfindung im frühen Kindesalter. *Kaiserliche Akademie der Wissenschaften in Wien, Philosophisch-historische Klasse, Sitzungsberichte, 182*(4).

Wilkin, P. E. (1991). Prenatal and postnatal responses to music and sound stimuli—a clinical report. *Canadian Music Educator, 33,* 223–232.

Wilkin, P. E. (1996). A comparison of fetal and newborn responses to music and sound stimuli. *Bulletin of the Council for Research in Music Education, 127,* 163–169.

Winkler, I., Háden. G.P., Ladinig, O., Sziller, I., and Honing, H. (2009). Newborn infants detect the beat in music. *Proceedings of the National Academy of Sciences, 106,* 2468–2471.

Wirthner, M., & Zulauf, M. (Eds.). (2002). *A la recherche du développement musical.* Paris: L'Harmattan.

Young, L. P. (1982). *An investigation of young children's music concept development using nonverbal and manipulative techniques.* Unpublished doctoral dissertation, Ohio State University, Columbus.

Young, S. (2002). Young children's spontaneous vocalizations in free play: Observations of two- to three-year-olds in a day care setting. *Bulletin of the Council for Research in Music Education, 152,* 43–53.

Zenatti, A. (1993). Children's musical cognition and taste. In T. J. Tighe & W. J. Dowling (Eds.), *Psychology and music: The understanding of melody and rhythm* (pp. 177–196). Hillsdale, NJ: Erlbaum.

Zentner, M. & Eerola, T. (2010). Rhythmic engagement with music in infancy. *Proceedings of the National Academy of Sciences, 107,* 5768–5773.

Zimmer, R. and Volkamer, M. (1984). *Motoriktest für vier- bis sechsjährige Kinder, MOT 4-6.* Weinheim: Beltz.

Index

Page numbers followed by "*f*" or "*t*" refer to figures or tables, respectively.